L'Académie de droit international de La Haye

honorée du prix Wateler de la Paix (1936, 1950), du prix Félix Houphouët-Boigny pour la recherche de la paix (1992), de l'ordre du Rio Branco, Brésil (1999), et de la médaille de l'Institut royal d'études européennes, Espagne (2000)

The Hague Academy of International Law

awarded the Wateler Peace Prize (1936, 1950), the Félix Houphouët-Boigny Peace Prize (1992), the Order of Rio Branco, Brazil (1999), and the Medal of the Royal Institute of European Studies, Spain (2000)

ISBN 978-90-04-53865-8

Due Diligence in International Law

ACADEMIE DE DROIT INTERNATIONAL DE LA HAYE
THE HAGUE ACADEMY OF INTERNATIONAL LAW

Due Diligence in International Law

Samantha Besson

translated by
Sévrine Knuchel

BRILL | NIJHOFF

2023

Leiden/Boston

TABLE OF CONTENTS

BIOGRAPHICAL NOTE

Samantha Besson, born on 30 March 1973 in Beirut, Lebanon. Swiss and British national.

Bachelor and Master's degrees in Swiss and European Law (Universities of Fribourg and Vienna, lic.iur. 1996; *summa cum laude*); Magister Juris in European and Comparative Law (Balliol College, University of Oxford, M.Jur. 1998; *first class honours*); Doctorate in Swiss and European Law (University of Fribourg, Dr iur. 1999; *summa cum laude*); Habilitation in Legal Theory and in Swiss, Comparative, European and International Constitutional Law (University of Bern, 2004).

Associate Research Professor (SNSF professorship) for the project "Philosophy of European Law (PEOPEL)" at the University of Fribourg (2004-2008); Full Professor and Chair of Public International Law and European Law at the University of Fribourg (since 2005; part-time since 2019); Professor and Chair of International Law of Institutions at the Collège de France, Paris (since 2019). Vice-Dean of the Faculty of Law at the University of Fribourg for two mandates (2014-2020).

Lecturer and Senior Lecturer at the Universities of Oxford (2001-2004) and Geneva (2001-2005); Visiting Professor at the Universities of Zurich (2007-2010), Duke (2009), Lausanne (2010), Lisbon (2010-2019), Harvard (2014; Jeremiah Smith, Jr., Visiting Professor), at the Munich Advanced Course of International Law (2017) and Pennsylvania University (2019; Bok Visiting International Professor). Coordinator of the Advanced Course for Practitioners in Public and Private Law (2009-2013), Director of Studies (2013) and Special Course Lecturer (2020) at The Hague Academy of International Law. Member of the Editorial Board of *ESIL Reflections* (2016-2019) and *EJIL Reviews* (since 2017).

SNSF Post-doctoral Fellow (1999-2002: Visiting Scholar, Columbia Law School, 1999-2000, then University of Oxford, 2000-2002; Junior Research Fellow, The Queen's College, Oxford (2001-2004); Adam Smith Research Fellow, Glasgow Law School (2008); Research Fellow at the Wissenschaftskolleg zu Berlin (2011-2012) and at the Nantes Institute of Advanced Study (2017).

Member, then Vice-President of the Swiss Section of the International Commission of Jurists (2004-2015); Member of the Swiss Federal Commission against Racism (2008-2011); Member of the Scientific Board of the Swiss Institute of Comparative Law (2012-2020); Member of the Scientific Council of the Nantes Institute for Advanced Study (2013-2021); Human Rights Delegate for the Swiss Academies of Arts and Sciences (2013-2016); Member of the Board of the Swiss Academy of Humanities and Social Sciences (since 2017); Member of the Board of Directors of the Geneva Science and Diplomacy Anticipator Foundation (GESDA) (since 2019); Co-chair of the International Law Association Study Group "The International Law of Regional Organizations" (since 2021); Associate Member of the Institute of International Law (since 2021); Member of the Board of the Swiss Society of International Law (since 2022).

PRINCIPAL PUBLICATIONS

Monographs

Reconstruire l'ordre institutionnel international (Leçon inaugurale), Paris, Fayard / Collège de France, 2021.

Reconstructing the International Institutional Order [translated from French] (Inaugural Lectures of the Collège de France), Paris, Publications du Collège de France, 2021.

"La *due diligence* en droit international", *Recueil des cours*, Vol. 409 (2020), pp. 153-398.

"La *due diligence* en droit international", *Livres de poche de l'Académie de droit international de La Haye*, Leiden / Boston, Brill Nijhoff, 2021.

The Morality of Conflict: Reasonable Disagreement and the Law, Oxford, Hart, 2005.

L'égalité horizontale: l'égalité de traitement entre particuliers. Des fondements théoriques au droit privé suisse (Arbeiten aus dem Iuristischen Seminar der Universität Freiburg Schweiz No. 183), Fribourg, Editions Universitaires, 1999.

Textbooks

Droit international public: Précis de droit et résumés de jurisprudence, Bern, Stämpfli, 2019.

Droit constitutionnel européen: Précis de droit et résumés de jurisprudence, Bern, Stämpfli, 2019.

Droit international public: Abrégé de cours et résumés de jurisprudence, 3rd ed., Bern, Stämpfli, 2016 (1st ed. 2011, 2nd ed. 2013).

Droit constitutionnel européen: Abrégé de cours et résumés de jurisprudence, 3rd ed., Bern, Stämpfli, 2016 (1st ed. 2011, 2nd ed. 2013).

Völkerrecht/Droit international public – Aide-mémoire, with S. Breitenmoser, M. Sassolí, A. Petrig and A. R. Ziegler, 2nd ed., Zurich, Dike, 2013 (1st ed. 2010) (3rd ed. printed as an e-book, 2019, https://www.dike.ch/Besson-Voelkerrecht-Droit-international-public).

Traités internationaux. Recueil de textes de droit international public, with A. R. Ziegler, 4th ed., Bern, Stämpfli, 2020 (2nd ed. 2012, 3rd ed. 2016).

Internationale Verträge. Textsammlung in Völkerrecht, with A. R. Ziegler, 2nd ed., Bern, Stämpfli, 2012.

Edited volumes

Inventer l'Europe, Paris, Collège de France / Odile Jacob, 2022.

Theories of International Responsibility Law, with the assistance of M. Montaubin, Cambridge, Cambridge University Press, 2022.

Concerter les civilisations. Mélanges en l'honneur d'Alain Supiot, with S. Jubé, Paris, Seuil, 2020.

Le consentement en droit, with Y. Mausen and P. Pichonnaz, Zurich, Schulthess, 2018.

The Oxford Handbook on the Sources of International Law, with J. d'Aspremont, with the assistance of S. Knuchel, Oxford, Oxford University Press, 2017.

International Responsibility: Essays in Law, History and Philosophy, Zurich, Schulthess, 2017.

Comparing Comparative Law, with L. Heckendorn Urscheler and S. Jubé, Zurich, Schulthess, 2017.

L'Union européenne et le droit international / The European Union and International Law, with N. Levrat, Zurich, Schulthess, 2015.

Egalité et non-discrimination en droit international et européen / Equality and Non-Discrimination in International and European Law, with A. R. Ziegler, Zurich, Schulthess, 2014.

La Convention européenne des droits de l'homme et les cantons / Die Europäische Menschenrechtskonvention und die Kantone, with E. M. Belser, Zurich, Schulthess, 2014.
Le juge en droit international et européen / The Judge in International and European Law, with A. R. Ziegler, Zurich, Schulthess, 2013.
(Dés)ordres juridiques européens / European Legal (Dis)Orders, with N. Levrat, Zurich, Schulthess, 2012.
La Cour européenne des droits de l'homme après le Protocole 14 / Premier bilan et perspectives / The European Court of Human Rights after Protocol 14: First Assessment and Perspectives, Zurich, Schulthess, 2011.
Les principes en droit européen / Principles in European Law, with P. Pichonnaz, Zurich, Schulthess, 2011.
L'interprétation en droit européen / Interpretation in European Law, with E. Clerc and N. Levrat, Zurich, Schulthess, 2011.
The Philosophy of International Law, with J. Tasioulas, Oxford, Oxford University Press, 2010.
Legal Republicanism: National and International, with J. L. Martí, Oxford, Oxford University Press, 2009.
Des Valeurs pour l'Europe? Values for Europe?, with F. Cheneval and N. Levrat, Louvain-la-Neuve, Academia Bruylant, 2008.
Deliberative Democracy and Its Discontents / National and International Perspectives, with J. L. Martí, Aldershot, Ashgate, 2006.
Les droits de l'homme au centre / Human Rights at the Centre, with F. Werro and M. Hottelier, Zurich, Schulthess, 2006.

Special issues

"The Human Right to Science", special issue, *European Journal of Human Rights*, Vol. 4 (2015), pp. 403-518.
"The Relationship between European and International Law", special issue, *European Constitutional Law Review*, Vol. 5, No. 2 (2009), pp. 237-326.
"Future Challenges of European Citizenship", with A. Utzinger, special issue, *European Law Journal*, Vol. 13, No. 5 (2007), pp. 573-679.

Articles (of the last five years)

"Passeports européens à vendre? Le débat en droit européen et international de la citoyenneté et ses enjeux", *Annuaire suisse de droit européen / Schweizer Jahrbuch für Europarecht* (2021), pp. 375-401.
"The Public of International Law: A Farewell to Functions", *American Journal of International Law Unbound*, Vol. 115 (2021), pp. 307-311.
"Du droit de civilisation européen au droit international des civilisations: vers une institutionnalisation internationale des régions", *Swiss Review of International and European Law*, Vol. 31, No. 3 (2021), pp. 373-400.
"Reconstruire le droit international à partir des organisations régionales / Reconstructing International Law starting from Regional Organizations", *Revue européenne du droit*, Vol. 2 (2021), pp. 64-68.
"Sovereign States and their International Institutional Order: Carrying Forward Dworkin's Work on the Political Legitimacy of International Law", *Jus cogens*, Vol. 2, No. 2 (2020), pp. 111-138.
"COVID-19 and the WHO's Political Moment", *EJIL Talk!*, 25 June 2020, https://www.ejiltalk.org/covid-19-and-the-whos-political-moment/.
"Les droits de l'homme au service du marché ? Critique et réforme du droit international et européen des droits de l'homme en vue d'un renouveau démocratique", with M. Hauri, *Annuaire suisse de droit européen / Schweizer Jahrbuch für Europarecht* (2020), pp. 427-426.
"Due Diligence and Extraterritorial Human Rights Obligations: Mind the Gap!", *ESIL Reflections*, Vol. 9, No. 1 (2020), https://esil-sedi.eu/wp-content/uploads/2020/04/ESIL-Reflection-Besson-S.-3.pdf.
"Investment Citizenship and Democracy in a Global Age: Towards a Democratic

Interpretation of International Nationality Law", *Swiss Review of International and European Law*, Vol. 30, No. 1 (2020), pp. 525-547.

"International Courts and the Jurisprudence of Statehood", *Transnational Legal Theory*, Vol. 9, Nos. 3-4 (2019), pp. 30-64.

"International Human Rights Law and Mirrors", *ESIL Reflections*, Vol. 7, No. 2 (2018), https://esil-sedi.eu/fr/esil-reflection-international-human-rights-law-and-mirrors/.

"The Legitimate Actors of International Law-Making: Towards a Theory of International Democratic Representation", with J. L. Martí, *Jurisprudence*, Vol. 9, No. 3 (2018), pp. 504-540.

"Security and Human Rights: Mind the Balance! On Security in International Human Rights Law and the Dangers of the Normalization of Emergency", in "The Law in these Parts: International Law in the Occupied Palestinian Territories", special issue, *Quid? Fribourg Law Review* (2017), pp. 7-19.

"Individual and State Liability for an International Organization's Responsibility: The Challenge of Fairness Unveiled", in "Global Justice and International Law", special issue, *Italian Journal of Legal Philosophy*, Vol. 6, No. 1 (2017), pp. 51-78.

"Law Beyond the State: A Reply to Liam Murphy", *European Journal of International Law*, Vol. 28, No. 1 (2017), pp. 233-40.

"L'Etat, cet angle mort du droit international", *Quid? Fribourg Law Review* (2017), pp. 1-3.

"Subsidiarity in International Human Rights Law: What is Subsidiary about Human Rights?", *American Journal of Jurisprudence*, Vol. 61, No. 1 (2016), pp. 69-107.

"State Consent and Disagreement in International Law-Making: Dissolving the Paradox", *Leiden Journal of International Law*, Vol. 29, No. 2 (2016), pp. 289-316.

Reviews (of the last five years)

"Review of Francesco Lusa Bordin's *The Analogy between States and International Organizations*", *European Journal of International Law*, Vol. 32, No. 2 (2021), pp. 771-785.

"Review of José Alvarez's *The Impact of International Organizations on International Law*", *European Journal of International Law*, Vol. 30 (2019), pp. 344-349.

Chapters (of the last five years)

"Quand l'Europe invente, s'invente et se réinvente. Une introduction", in S. Besson (ed.), *Inventer l'Europe*, Paris, Collège de France / Odile Jacob, 2022, pp. 7-23.

"Theorizing International Responsibility Law, An Introduction", in S. Besson (ed.), *Theories of International Responsibility Law*, Cambridge, Cambridge University Press, 2022, pp. 1-24.

"L'égalité des Etats membres de l'Union européenne: un nouveau départ en droit international de l'organisation des États ?", in E. Dubout (ed.), *L'égalité des Etats membres de l'Union européenne*, Brussels, Bruylant, 2022, pp. 263-298.

"Justifications of Human Rights", in D. Moeckli, S. Shah and S. Sivakumaran (eds.), *International Human Rights Law*, 4th ed., Oxford, Oxford University Press, 2022, pp. 23-42.

"Le droit international des civilisations – Ou comment instituer la concertation des civilisations", in V. Pirenne-Delforge and L. Quintana Murci (eds.), *Civilisation(s). Questionner l'identité et la diversité. Actes du colloque de rentrée 2020 du Collège de France*, Paris, Odile Jacob, 2021, pp. 345-370.

"Cities as Democratic Representatives in International Law-Making", with J. L. Martí, in H. Aust and J. Nijman (eds.), *Research Handbook on International Law and Cities*, London, Edward Elgar, 2021, pp. 341-353.

"Article 5(4) Cst.: L'Etat régi par le droit international", in J. Dubey and V. Martenet (eds.), *Commentaire romand de la Constitution suisse*, Basel, Helbing, 2021, pp. 240-257.

"COVID-19 et le 'moment politique' de l'OMS", in S. Kuriyama, O. de Leonardis, C. Sonnenschein and I. Thioub (eds.), *Covid-19. Tour du monde*, Paris, Manucius, 2021, pp. 31-32.

"Que fait l'Europe ? Ce que le Coronavirus nous dit de l'état de l'Union", in Fondation du Collège de France (ed.), *Une boussole pour l'après*, Paris, Humensciences, 2020, pp. 101-110.

"The Holders of Human Rights: The Bright Side of Human Rights?", in T. Brooks (ed.), *The Oxford Handbook of Global Justice*, Oxford, Oxford University Press, 2020, pp. 99-121.

"L'autorité légitime du droit international comparé: Quelques réflexions autour du *monde* et du *droit des gens* de Vico", in S. Besson and S. Jubé (eds.), *Concerter les civilisations: Mélanges en l'honneur d'Alain Supiot*, Paris, Seuil, 2020, pp. 49-60.

"The Human Right to Democracy in International Law: Coming to Moral Terms with an Equivocal Legal Practice", in M. Susi, K. Odendahl and A. von Arnauld (eds.), *New Human Rights*, Cambridge, Cambridge University Press, 2019, pp. 481-489.

"Article 2: Non-Discrimination", with E. Kleber, in P. Alston and R. Tobin (eds.), *Commentary on the Convention on the Rights of the Child*, Oxford, Oxford University Press, 2019, pp. 41-72.

"In What Sense are Economic Rights Human Rights? Departing from their Naturalistic Reading in International Human Rights Law", in J. Queralt and B. van der Vossen (eds.), *Economic Liberties and Human Rights*, London, Routledge, 2019, pp. 45-68.

"Why and What (State) Jurisdiction: Legal Plurality, Individual Equality and Territorial Legitimacy", in J. Klabbers and L. Palombella (eds.), *The Challenge of Inter-Legality*, Cambridge, Cambridge University Press, 2019, pp. 91-132.

"Comparative Law and Human Rights", in M. Reimann and R. Zimmermann (eds.), *Oxford Handbook of Comparative Law*, 2nd ed., Oxford, Oxford University Press, 2019, pp. 1222-1249.

"Shared Responsibilities under the ECHR: Concurrent Jurisdictions, Duties and Responsibilities", in J. Motoc and A. van Aaken (eds.), *The ECHR and General International Law*, Oxford, Oxford University Press, 2018, pp. 155-177.

"La responsabilité solidaire des organisations internationales et des Etats – Une institution négligée", in A. Supiot (ed.), *La responsabilité solidaire*, Paris, Publications du Collège de France, 2018, pp. 121-159.

"The Influence of the Two Covenants on States Parties across Regions: Lessons for the Role of Comparative Law and Regions in International Human Rights Law", in D. Moeckli, H. Keller and C. Heri (eds.), *The Human Rights Covenants at 50: Their Past, Present and Future*, Oxford, Oxford University Press, 2018, pp. 243-276.

"Community Interests in International Law: Whose Interests Are They and How Does One Identify Them?", in E. Benvenisti and G. Nolte (eds.), *Community Interests across International Law*, Cambridge, Cambridge University Press, 2018, pp. 50-69.

"Community Interests in the Identification of International Law: With a Special Emphasis on Treaty Interpretation and Customary Law Identification", in E. Benvenisti and G. Nolte (eds.), *Community Interests across International Law*, Cambridge, Cambridge University Press, 2018, pp. 36-49.

"Human Rights and Justification: A Reply to Mattias Kumm", in A. D. Etinson (ed.), *Human Rights: Moral or Political?*, Oxford, Oxford University Press, 2018, pp. 262-268.

"Justifications of Human Rights", in D. Moeckli, S. Shah and S. Sivakumaran (eds.), *International Human Rights Law*, 3rd ed., Oxford, Oxford University Press, 2017, p. 22-40.

"Human Rights as Transnational Constitutional Law", in A. Lang and A. Wiener (eds.), *Handbook on Global Constitutionalism*, London, Edward Elgar, 2017, pp. 234-247.

"Introduction", with J. d'Aspremont, in S. Besson and J. d'Aspermont (eds.), *Oxford Handbook on the Sources of International Law*, Oxford, Oxford University Press, 2017, pp. 1-39.

"The Sources of International Human Rights Law: How General is General International Law?", in S. Besson and J. d'Aspremont (eds.), *Oxford Handbook on the Sources of International Law*, Oxford, Oxford University Press, 2017, pp. 837-870.

"International Responsibility: An Introduction", in S. Besson (ed.), *International Responsibility: Essays in Law, History and Philosophy* (Travaux de l'Ecole doctorale CUS 2016), Zurich, Schulthess, 2017, pp. 3-13.

"Human Rights in Relation", in S. Smet (ed.), *Human Rights Conflicts*, Oxford, Oxford University Press, 2017, pp. 23-37.
"EU General Principles *qua* EU Customary Law", in S. Vogenauer and S. Weatherill (eds.), *General Principles of EU Law*, Oxford, Hart, 2017, pp. 105-129.
"International Legal Theory *qua* Practice of International Law", in J. d'Aspremont, A. Nollkaemper and T. Gazzini (eds.), *International Law as a Profession*, Cambridge, Cambridge University Press, 2017, pp. 268-284.
"Introduction", in S. Besson, L. Heckendorn Urscheler and S. Jubé (eds.), *Comparing Comparative Law*, Zurich, Schulthess, 2017, pp. 9-16.
"L'évolution du contrôle européen: vers une subsidiarité toujours plus subsidiaire ?", in S. Touzé (ed.), *La Cour européenne des droits de l'homme: une confiance nécessaire pour une autorité renforcée*, Paris, Pedone, 2016, pp. 57-82.
"Legal Human Rights Theory", in K. Brownlee, K. Lippert-Ramussen and D. Coady (eds.), *Blackwell Companion to Applied Philosophy*, London, Wiley-Blackwell, 2016, pp. 328-341.
"Human Rights' Adjudication as Transnational Adjudication: Putting Domestic Courts as International Law Adjudicators in Perspective", in C. Binder, M. Footer and A. Reinisch (eds.), *International Law and ..., ESIL Proceedings of the 10th Anniversary Conference*, Oxford, Oxford University Press, 2016, pp. 43-65.
"Moral Philosophy and International Law", in F. Hoffmann and A. Orford (eds.), *Oxford Handbook of International Legal Theory*, Oxford, Oxford University Press, 2016, pp. 385-406.
"L'extra-territorialité des droits de l'homme internationaux: juridictions concurrentes, obligations conjointes et responsabilités partagées", in P. d'Argent (ed.), *Droit des frontières internationales. Actes des Journées franco-allemandes SFDI-DGIR 2014*, Paris, Pedone, 2016, pp. 245-259.
"Le droit de la famille sous l'angle des droits de l'homme – Quelques réflexions", in ASSH (ed.), *Le mariage et le partenariat entre norme et réalité. Actes du colloque du 23 juin 2015 à Berne*, Bern, ASSH, 2016, pp. 168-187.

LIST OF ABBREVIATIONS

ARIO	Articles on the Responsibility of International Organizations (ILC, Draft Articles on the Responsibility of International Organizations, 9 November 2011, adopted and submitted to the United Nations' General Assembly)
ARSIWA	Articles on the Responsibility of States for Internationally Wrongful Acts (ILC, Draft Articles on the Responsibility of States for Internationally Wrongful Acts, 12 December 2001, adopted in Resolution A/RES/56/83 by the United Nations' General Assembly)
CAT	Committee Against Torture
CCPR	Human Rights Committee
CESCR	Committee on Economic, Social and Cultural Rights
CITES	Convention on International Trade in Endangered Species of Wild Fauna and Flora of 3 March 1973
CJEU	Court of Justice of the European Union
CLN	Convention Relating to the Limitation of the Liability of Owners of Inland Navigation Vessels of 1 March 1973
ECHR	European Convention for the Protection of Human Rights and Fundamental Freedoms of 4 November 1950
ECtHR	European Court of Human Rights
EGC	General Court of the European Union
EU	European Union
HRC	Human Rights Council
IACtHR	Inter-American Court of Human Rights
ICJ	International Court of Justice
ICSID	International Centre for Settlement of Investment Disputes
IIL	Institute of International Law
ILA	International Law Association
ILC	International Law Commission
IO	International organisation
IPCC	Intergovernmental Panel on Climate Change
ITLOS	International Tribunal for the Law of the Sea
MARPOL	International Convention for the Prevention of Pollution from Ships of 2 November 1973, as modified by the Protocol of 17 February 1978
MNC	Multinational corporation
NGO	Non-governmental organisation
OECD	Organisation for Economic Co-operation and Development
OEIGWG	Open-Ended Intergovernmental Working Group
PCA	Permanent Court of Arbitration
PCIJ	Permanent Court of International Justice
SFDI	Société française du droit international / French Society for International Law
TFEU	Treaty on the Functioning of the European Union
UN	United Nations
UN Charter	Charter of the United Nations of 26 June 1945
VCDR	Vienna Convention on Diplomatic Relations of 18 April 1961

ACKNOWLEDGEMENTS

The present volume is a translation of the Special Course I gave in French at The Hague Academy of International Law in 2020 and that was published in the Collected Courses of The Hague Academy of International Law under the title "La *due diligence* en droit international" in 2021 (vol. 409). This translation would not have seen the light of day without the generous financial assistance of the Collège de France, and especially of the Fondation Hugot du Collège de France. I am grateful to Sévrine Knuchel for her precise and sensitive translation. I would also like to thank Manon Fabre for the careful editing, Tamara Grigoras for her meticulous proofreading and Simone Cartier and her team at The Hague Academy for their editorial support.

For their assistance with the researching, editing and/or proofreading of the French edition of this course between 2018 and 2020, I would like to thank Aurélie Galetto, Adrien Folly, Milène Hauri, Clémence Monnier, Leo Tiberghien and Manon Fabre, all of them former research assistants at the University of Fribourg. My appreciation also goes to The Hague Academy of International Law and its Curatorium for the invitation to give this course, and in particular Yves Daudet, Jean-Marc Thouvenin and Monique Legerman, as well as the students of the 2020 Winter Session for their questions and comments. Furthermore, I would like to thank my students at Penn Law School, where I gave a seminar on due diligence in international law in January 2019, as well as William Ewald and Stephen Perry for their kind invitation.

Finally, I wish to express my gratitude to Pierre d'Argent, Alexia de Vaucleroy, Giulio Bartolini, Alice Ollino, Hans van Loon and Rena Lee for our discussions on due diligence, and to Duncan Hollis and Roland Portmann for having, in different ways, included me in the work carried out by the group of government experts in the context of the UNGGE/OEWG on Developments in the Field of Information and Telecommunications in the Context of International Security in November 2019.

The English version of the course retains the lecture style of the original French edition. The research underlying the course was last updated in February 2022. However, the argument itself could not be revised and does not directly engage with scholarship published after

February 2020, including the numerous post-pandemic publications on due diligence in international health law.

Samantha Besson
Lausanne, 10 August 2022

INTRODUCTION

> "The decision of the Court does not, in this case, purport to establish a *general jurisprudence* applicable to all cases where a treaty instrument, or other binding legal norm, includes an obligation for States to prevent certain acts. Still less does the decision of the Court purport to find whether, apart from the texts applicable to specific fields, there is a *general obligation* on States to prevent the commission by other persons or entities of acts contrary to certain norms of general international law. The Court will therefore confine itself to determining the specific scope of the duty to prevent in the Genocide Convention, and to the extent that such a determination is necessary to the decision to be given on the dispute before it. This will, of course, not absolve it of the need to refer, if need be, to *the rules of law whose scope extends beyond the specific field covered by the Convention*."
>
> (ICJ, The case of *Application of the Convention on the Prevention and Punishment of the Crime of Genocide (Bosnia and Herzegovina* v. *Serbia and Montenegro)*, Judgment of 26 February 2007, *ICJ Reports 2007*, p. 43, para. 429)

"Due diligence" refers to *(i)* the diligence, vigilance or care *(ii)* which is owed, requested or expected.

The term "diligence" stems from the Latin *dis-ligentia*. It is composed of the prefix *dis* and the root *legere* (lit. "to gather"), referring together to the quality of those who demonstrate choice or care. Conversely, its violation amounts to *neg-ligentia*, negligence. This term is composed of the prefix *neg* and the root *legere*, referring together to the lack of choice or care.

The English expression "due diligence" was first coined in international arbitration at the end of the nineteenth century and during the first part of the twentieth century [1], when many Anglo-American practitioners of international law started drawing analogies with Roman private law [2]. Today, the notion has become pervasive, albeit in different wordings, in the decisions of the International Court of Justice (ICJ) and many other international judicial and quasi-judicial

1. See e.g. *Alabama Claims* Arbitration *(United States of America* v. *United Kingdom)*, Final Award of 15 September 1872, RAI Vol. II p. 713; *Frederick Wipperman* Arbitration *(United States of America* v. *Venezuela)*, Final Award of 2 September 1890, RAI Vol. III p. 3041; *William E. Chapman* Arbitration *(United States of America* v. *United Mexican States)*, Final Award of 24 October 1930, RIAA Vol. IV p. 632.

2. See H. Lauterpacht, *Private Law Sources and Analogies of International Law*, reprint, Clark, NJ, The Lawbook Exchange, 2013 (orig. 1927).

organs [3]. While "due diligence" may easily be translated into other languages, many references to the notion in international law actually resort to the English term that has over time become omnipresent [4]. And this, even if, until quite recently, most academic discussions on due diligence were conducted in languages other than English [5], notably in Romance languages such as French, Italian or Spanish [6].

3. See e.g. International Court of Justice (ICJ), The case of *Pulp Mills on the River Uruguay (Argentina* v. *Uruguay)*, Judgment of 20 April 2010, *ICJ Reports 2010*, p. 14, para. 101; ICJ, The case of *Certain Activities carried out by Nicaragua in the Border Area (Costa Rica* v. *Nicaragua)* and *Construction of a Road in Costa Rica along the San Juan River (Nicaragua* v. *Costa Rica)*, Judgment of 16 December 2015, *ICJ Reports 2015*, p. 665, para. 104; ICJ, The case of *Armed Activities on the Territory of the Congo (Democratic Republic of the Congo* v. *Uganda)*, Judgment of 19 December 2005, *ICJ Reports 2005*, p. 168, para. 247 ("duty of vigilance"). See also the United Nations' Committee on Economic, Social and Cultural Rights (CESCR), General Comment No. 24 on State obligations under the International Covenant on Economic, Social and Cultural Rights in the context of business activities, 10 August 2017, UN Doc. E/C.12/GC/24, paras. 15, 16, 17 and 31.

4. The recourse to the English term in other languages has actually obstructed the conceptual and normative clarification of due diligence. For an example of the kind of confusions hasty analogies between due diligence obligations under the ECHR and Anglo-American tort law may lead to, see V. Stoyanova, "Causation between State Omission and Harm within the Framework of Positive Obligations under the ECHR", *Human Rights Law Review*, Vol. 18 (2018), pp. 309-346; V. Stoyanova, "Common Law Tort of Negligence as a Tool for Deconstructing Positive Obligations under the European Convention on Human Rights", *International Journal of Human Rights*, Vol. 24, No. 5 (2019), pp. 632-655. For a critique, see D. Nolan, "Negligence and Human Rights Law: The Case for Separate Development", *Modern Law Review*, Vol. 76, No. 2 (2013), pp. 286-318; L. Lavrysen, "Causation and Positive Obligations under the European Convention on Human Rights: A Reply to Vladislava Stoyanova", *Human Rights Law Review*, Vol. 18 (2018), pp. 705-718.

5. General publications on due diligence in English have recently multiplied, however: see e.g. H. Blomeyer-Bartenstein, "Due Diligence", *Encyclopedia of Public International Law*, Vol. 10 (1987), pp. 138-143; R. Pisillo Mazzeschi, "The Due Diligence Rule and the Nature of the International Responsibility of States", *German Yearbook of International Law*, Vol. 35 (1992), pp. 9-51; T. Koivurova, "What is the Principle of Due Diligence", in J. Petman and J. Klabbers (eds.), *Nordic Cosmopolitanism: Essays in International Law for Martti Koskenniemi*, Leiden, Martinus Nijhoff, 2003, pp. 341-349; J. A. Hessbruegge, "The Historical Development of the Doctrines of Attribution and Due Diligence in International Law", *New York University Journal of International Law and Politics*, Vol. 26, No. 2 (2004), pp. 265-306; R. P. J. Barnidge, "The Due Diligence Principle under International Law", *International Community Law Review*, Vol. 8, No. 1 (2006), pp. 81-122; T. Koivurova, "Due Diligence", in R. Wolfrum (ed.), *Max Planck Encyclopedia of Public International Law*, Oxford, Oxford University Press, 2010 [online]; International Law Association (ILA), Study Group on Due Diligence in International Law, First and Second Rapports, Duncan French (Chair) and Tim Stephens (Rapporteur), 7 March 2014 and July 2016 [online]; J. Kulesza, *Due Diligence in International Law*, Leiden, Brill Nijhoff, 2016; A. Peters, H. Krieger and L. Kreuzer (eds.), *Due Diligence in International Law*, Oxford, Oxford University Press, 2020; A. Ollino, *Due Diligence Obligations under International Law*, Cambridge, Cambridge University Press, 2022.

6. A large proportion of the monographs on this theme are in French, Italian and Spanish. See e.g. P. A. Zannas, *La responsabilité internationale des États pour des*

In short, and for the purpose of the present analysis, the concept of due diligence and, conversely, of undue negligence in international law will be defined as

> "an (evaluative) standard of the conduct of States (and other public institutions of international law, such as international organisations [IOs]) (most often grafted onto an obligation of conduct [which is usually, but not always, a positive obligation to prevent, protect or remedy], but sometimes also considered, due to linguistic imprecision, as an obligation of conduct *per se*) which requires them to exercise care (also referred to as the "standard of care" or "duty of care") and thus also, conversely, to do no harm carelessly (also referred to as the "no harm rule" or "duty not to harm"), by adopting reasonable measures in order to protect the interests or rights of other States, IOs or national or foreign subjects against (risks of) (usually significant) harm caused by third parties (nationals or foreigners, other States or IOs, natural phenomena) situated on the territory, under the jurisdiction *stricto*

---

actes de négligence, Montreux, Ganguin & Laubscher, 1952; R. Pisillo Mazzeschi, *Due Diligence e responsabilità internazionale degli Stati*, Milan, Giuffrè, 1989; J. F. L. Contreras, *La noción de debida diligencia en derecho internacional público*, Barcelona, Atelier Libros Jurídicos, 2007; R. Pisillo Mazzeschi, "Responsabilité de l'État pour violation des obligations positives relatives aux droits de l'homme", *Recueil des cours*, Vol. 333 (2008), pp. 175-506; Société française du droit international (SFDI) (ed.), *Le standard de* due diligence *et la responsabilité internationale: Journée d'études franco-italienne du Mans*, Paris, Pedone, 2018; S. Besson, "La *due diligence* en droit international", *Recueil des cours*, Vol. 409 (2020), pp. 153-398; A. de Vaucleroy, *Le droit de la responsabilité internationale à l'épreuve des obligations de comportement*, 2023 (forthcoming). Several factors may account for this linguistic imbalance in the contemporary treatment of due diligence in international law. One explanation may lie in the fact that, in contrast to German and Swiss law, for instance, French, Italian and Spanish liability law (civil as well as public: see A. Antoine and T. Olson (eds.), *La responsabilité de la puissance publique en droit comparé*, Paris, Société de législation comparée, 2016) are based on *fault*, and the international lawyers trained or active within these legal regimes have thus demonstrated greater interest in this question under international law and looked to due diligence to understand it. On the other hand, Anglo-American civil (and by extension public) liability law and its theory are currently dominated by an economic interpretation, leading researchers in that tradition to address negligence primarily in terms of risk management and reduction. This renders due diligence under international law of lesser interest to them, from that perspective at least (see, however, J. Gardner, "Tort Law and its Theory", Oxford Legal Studies Research Paper No 2/2018; S. Perry, "The Role of the Duty of Care in a Rights-Based Theory of Tort Law", in A. Robertson and T. Hang Wu (eds.), *The Goals of Private Law*, Oxford, Hart, 2009, pp. 79-112; D. Nolan, "Deconstructing the Duty of Care", *Law Quarterly Review*, Vol. 129 (2013), pp. 559-588; J. Raz, "Responsibility and the Negligence Standard", *Oxford Journal of Legal Studies*, Vol. 30 (2010), pp. 1-18; S. Shiffrin, "The Moral Neglect of Negligence", in D. Sobel, P. Vallentyne and S. Wall (eds.), *Oxford Studies in Political Philosophy*, Vol. 3, Oxford, Oxford University Press, 2017, pp. 197-228; N. McDonald, "The Role of Due Diligence in International Law", *International and Comparative Law Quarterly*, Vol. 68, No. 4 (2019), pp. 1041-1054).

> *sensu* or, at least, under the control of the duty-bearing State (or other public institution), and provided that the latter had foreseen or ought to have (reasonably) foreseen the (risks of) harm and had the (reasonable) capacity to intervene, and whose violation amounts to undue or wrongful negligence". [7]

Due diligence is a well-established standard in international law, as confirmed by more than a century of abundant and constantly developing international jurisprudence [8]. It even appears in recent international treaties [9] and various international law codification

7. See J. Gardner, "Reasonable Person Standard", in H. LaFolette (ed.), *The International Encyclopedia of Ethics*, 2nd ed., Chichester, Wiley-Blackwell, 2019 [online], p. 6: "To be negligent, in the modern law, is to fail to take reasonable care in what one does to protect others whom one can reasonably foresee will be put at risk by what one does".

8. See e.g. *Alabama Claims* Arbitration, *op. cit. supra* note 1; *Frederick Wipperman* Arbitration, *op. cit. supra* note 1; *British Property in Spanish Morocco* Arbitration *(Spain* v. *United Kingdom)*, Final Award of 1 May 1925, RIAA Vol. II p. 615; *Island of Palmas* Arbitration *(The Netherlands* v. *United States of America)*, Final Award of 4 April 1928, RIAA Vol. II p. 829; *William E. Chapman* Arbitration, *op. cit. supra* note 1; *Trail Smelter* Arbitration *(United States of America* v. *Canada)*, Final Award of 11 March 1941, RIAA Vol. III p. 1938, para. 716; International Centre for Settlement of Investment Disputes (ICSID), *Asian Agricultural Products Ltd. (AAPL)* v. *Republic of Sri Lanka*, Case No. ARB/87/3, Final Award of 27 June 1990 (*AAPL* Arbitration), paras. 609-610; Permanent Court of Arbitration (PCA), *Indus Waters Kishenganga* Arbitration *(Pakistan* v. *India)*, Partial Award of 18 February 2013, PCA 2011-01, paras. 449-450; PCA, *South China Sea* Arbitration *(Philippines* v. *China)*, Final Award of 12 July 2016, PCA 2013-19, p. 296, para. 117. See also Dissenting Opinion of Judge Moore, in Permanent Court of International Justice (PCIJ), The case of the *S.S. Lotus (France* v. *Turkey)*, Judgment of 7 September 1927, *PCIJ Reports 1927*, Series A No. 10, p. 88; ICJ, The case of the *Corfu Channel (United Kingdom of Great Britain and Northern Ireland* v. *Albania)*, Judgment of 9 April 1949, *ICJ Reports 1949*, p. 4, p. 22; ICJ, The case of the *United States Diplomatic and Consular Staff in Tehran (United States of America* v. *Iran)*, Judgment of 24 May 1980, *ICJ Reports 1980*, p. 3, paras. 67-68; ICJ, The case of *Military and Paramilitary Activities in and against Nicaragua (Nicaragua* v. *United States of America)*, Judgment of 27 June 1986, *ICJ Reports 1986*, p. 14, paras. 157-158; ICJ, *Legality of the Threat or Use of Nuclear Weapons*, Advisory Opinion of 8 July 1996, *ICJ Reports 1996*, p. 226, paras. 241-242; ICJ, The case of *The Gabcikovo-Nagymaros Project (Hungary* v. *Slovakia)*, Judgment of 25 September 1997, *ICJ Reports 1997*, p. 7, para. 53; ICJ, The case of *Pulp Mills on the River Uruguay*, *op. cit. supra* note 3, para. 101; ICJ, The case of *Certain Activities carried out by Nicaragua in the Border Area*, *op. cit. supra* note 3, para. 104.

9. See e.g. Vienna Convention on Diplomatic Relations of 18 April 1961, UNTS, Vol. 500, p. 95 (VCDR), Art. 22 (2); United Nations Convention on the Law of the Sea of 10 December 1982, UNTS, Vol. 1834, p. 3, Arts. 58, 62, 94, 139, 192 and 194; Convention on Biological Diversity of 5 June 1992, UNTS, Vol. 1760, p. 79, Art. 3; Convention on the Law of the Non-Navigational Uses of International Watercourses of 21 May 1997, UNTS, Vol. 2999, Arts. 7 (1), 21 (2) and 22; International Health Regulations of 23 May 2005, UNTS, Vol. 2509, p. 79, Arts. 5, 13, 24, 32 and 34; Arms Trade Treaty of 2 April 2013, UNTS, Vol. 3013, Art. 6 (3); Council of Europe Convention on Preventing and Combatting Violence Against Women and Domestic Violence of 2 December 2016, CETS No. 210 (Istanbul Convention), Art. 5 (2).

projects [10], not to mention its multiple references in soft law instruments [11].

As a matter of fact, the notion is quite ancient. It dates back to antiquity, notably to Roman private law, and has since been found in multiple forms in numerous contemporary Western legal traditions. Its reception in international law was prompted by analogies to Roman private law, in particular in the writings of authors, such as Hugo Grotius, Alberico Gentili and Emer de Vattel. As mentioned before, due diligence's early positive legal traces were next to be found in the nineteenth and twentieth centuries. It occurred first in arbitral awards and then in the judicial decisions of international legal regimes relating to issues with transboundary dimensions, such as the international law of neutrality [12], the international law on the protection of aliens [13] and even international environmental law [14]. Back then, the issue of due

10. See e.g. Open-Ended Intergovernmental Working Group (OEIGWG), Human Rights Council (HRC), Revised Draft Legally Binding Instrument to Regulate, in International Human Rights Law, the Activities of Transnational Corporations and others Business Enterprises, Chairmanship Third Revised Draft, 17 August 2021 [online] (OEIGWG Draft), Art. 6.

11. See e.g. ILA, Committee on the Legal Principles relating to Climate Change, Declaration of Legal Principles Relating to Climate Change (Resolution 2/2014), 7-11 April 2014 [online], Arts. 7A and 7B; International Law Commission (ILC), Draft Articles on Prevention of Transboundary Harm from Hazardous Activities, with commentaries, *Yearbook of the International Law Commission*, Vol. II, Part 2 (2001), pp. 157-183, Arts. 1 and 3; ILC, Draft Articles on the Protection of Persons in the Event of Disasters, *Yearbook of the International Law Commission*, Vol. II, Part 2 (2016), pp. 12-16, Arts. 9 and 16; ILC, Draft Principles on the Protection of the Environment in Relation to Armed Conflict, *Yearbook of the International Law Commission*, Vol. II, Part 2 (2019), pp. 221-316, Principle 22.

12. See e.g. A. Ouedraogo, "La neutralité et l'émergence du concept de *due diligence* en droit international: l'affaire de l'Alabama revisitée", *Journal of the History of International Law*, Vol. 13, No. 2 (2011), pp. 307-346; A. Ouedraogo, "La *due diligence* en droit international: de la règle de la neutralité au principe général", *Revue générale de droit*, Vol. 42, No. 2 (2012), pp. 641-683.

13. See e.g. A. Verdross, "Règles internationales concernant le traitement des étrangers", *Recueil des cours*, Vol. 37 (1931), pp. 323-412; M. Hakimi, "State Bystander Responsibility", *European Journal of International Law*, Vol. 21, No. 2 (2010), pp. 341-385.

14. See e.g. E. Hey, "The Precautionary Concept in Environmental Policy and Law: Institutionalizing Caution", *Georgetown International Environmental Law Review*, Vol. 4 (1992), pp. 303-318; J. Brunnée, "Sic utere tuo ut alienum non laedas", in R. Wolfrum (ed.), *Max Planck Encyclopedia of Public International Law*, Oxford, Oxford University Press, 2010 [online]; I. Plakokefalos, "Prevention Obligations in International Environmental Law", *Yearbook of International Environmental Law*, Vol. 23, No. 1 (2012), pp. 3-43; H. Strydom, "The Due Diligence Principle in International Law and its Relevance for Climate Change Law", in V. Sancin (ed.), *International Environmental Law: Contemporary Concerns and Challenges*, Ljubljana, Založba, 2012, pp. 279-300; C. Jacquet, "Le recours à la notion de 'due diligence' par le juge international en droit de l'environnement", *L'Observateur des Nations Unies*, Vol. 34, No. 1 (2013), pp. 167-190; R. Yotova, "The Principles of Due Diligence and Prevention

diligence generally arose in relation to the responsibility of the State towards other States with respect to the conduct of private persons.

Over time, however, the scope of due diligence has extended to many other regimes of international law, including regimes applicable to non-transboundary situations and even sometimes to situations lacking any territorial dimension at all, such as international human rights law [15], international criminal law [16], international humanitarian law [17], the

in International Environmental Law", *Cambridge Law Journal*, Vol. 75, No. 3 (2016), pp. 445-448; B. Mayer, "The Relevance of the No-Harm Principle to Climate Change Law and Politics", *Asia-Pacific Journal of Environmental Law*, Vol. 19 (2016), pp. 79-104; S. Maljean-Dubois, "Les obligations de diligence dans la pratique: la protection de l'environnement", in SFDI (ed.), *Le standard de* due diligence *et la responsabilité internationale: Journée d'études franco-italienne du Mans*, Paris, Pedone, 2018, pp. 145-162; L. A. Duvic-Paoli, *The Prevention Principle in International Environmental Law*, Cambridge, Cambridge University Press, 2018; J. Brunnée, "Procedure and Substance in International Environmental Law", *Recueil des cours*, Vol. 405 (2020), pp. 75-240; J. E. Viñuales, "Due Diligence in International Environmental Law: A Fine-Grained Cartography", in A. Peters, H. Krieger and L. Kreuzer (eds.), *Due Diligence in International Law*, Oxford, Oxford University Press, 2020, pp. 111-128; L. Rajamani, "Due Diligence in International Climate Change Law", in A. Peters, H. Krieger and L. Kreuzer (eds.), *Due Diligence in International Law*, Oxford, Oxford University Press, 2020, pp. 163-182; C. Foster, *Global Regulatory Standards in Environmental and Health Disputes: Regulatory Coherence, Due Regard and Due Diligence*, Oxford, Oxford University Press, 2021.

15. See e.g. R. Pisillo Mazzeschi, 2008, *op. cit. supra* note 6; M. T. Kamminga, "Due Diligence Mania: The Misguided Introduction of an Extraneous Concept into Human Rights Discourse", in I. Westendorp (ed.), *The Women's Convention Turned 30*, Cambridge, Intersentia, 2012, pp. 407-413; O. De Schutter, A. Ramasastry, M. B. Taylor and R. C. Thompson, "Human Rights Due Diligence: The Role of States", December 2012 [online]; H. Tran, *Les obligations de vigilance des États parties à la Convention européenne des droits de l'homme: Essai sur la transposition en droit européen des droits de l'homme d'un concept de droit international général*, Brussels, Bruylant, 2013; K. Martin-Chenut, "Les mécanismes conventionnels de prévention des violations des droits de l'homme au niveau universel", in E. Decaux and S. Touzé (eds.), *La prévention des violations des droits de l'homme*, Paris, Pedone, 2015, pp. 61-89; H. Raspail, "Due diligence et droits de l'homme", in SFDI (ed.), *Le standard de* due diligence *et la responsabilité internationale: Journée d'études franco-italienne du Mans*, Paris, Pedone, 2018, pp. 107-134; M. Monnheimer, *Due Diligence Obligations in International Human Rights Law*, Cambridge, Cambridge University Press, 2021.

16. See e.g. L. van den Herik and E. Irving, "Due Diligence and the Obligation to Prevent Genocide and Crimes Against Humanity", in A. Peters, H. Krieger and L. Kreuzer (eds.), *Due Diligence in International Law*, Oxford, Oxford University Press, 2020, pp. 200-216. See also Y. Dinstein, "Command Responsibility", in R. Wolfrum (ed.), *Max Planck Encyclopedia of Public International Law*, Oxford, Oxford University Press, 2015 [online]; G. Mettraux, *The Law of Command Responsibility*, Oxford, Oxford University Press, 2009.

17. See e.g. G. Venturini, "Les obligations de diligence dans le droit international humanitaire", in SFDI (ed.), *Le standard de* due diligence *et la responsabilité internationale: Journée d'études franco-italienne du Mans*, Paris, Pedone, 2018, pp. 135-144; M. Longobardo, "The Relevance of the Concept of Due Diligence for International Humanitarian Law", *Wisconsin International Law Journal*, Vol. 37, No. 1 (2019), pp. 44-87; M. Longobardo, "Due Diligence in International Humanitarian

international law of the sea [18], the international law of water [19] and even international investment law [20] or international trade law [21]. Today, due diligence also applies to public institutions other than States, such as international organisations (IOs), and also benefits individuals and non-State actors. It even sometimes applies irrespective of a private person's conduct, especially to protect against harms caused by other States, IOs or natural disasters.

Nevertheless, the normative structure and the content of the concept of due diligence remain largely indeterminate. This level of indeterminacy with respect to such a well-established and widely used international legal principle may seem surprising at first, but it is probably the price to pay for its success. For instance, regarding the *nature* of due diligence, we have come to use this term to refer, interchangeably, to a "principle", a "standard", a "norm" or even an "obligation" or "duty" of conduct. The *sources* of due diligence also raise numerous questions. Beyond its inclusion in treaty provisions in special international legal regimes, it is unclear whether due diligence is also a general principle or maybe even

Law", in A. Peters, H. Krieger and L. Kreuzer (eds.), *Due Diligence in International Law*, Oxford, Oxford University Press, 2020, pp. 183-199.

18. See e.g. M. M. Mbengue, "The South China Sea Arbitration: Innovations in Marine Environmental Fact-Finding and Due Diligence Obligations", *American Journal of International Law*, Vol. 110 (2016), pp. 285-289; I. Caracciolo, "Due diligence et droit de la mer", in SFDI (ed.), *Le standard de* due diligence *et la responsabilité internationale: Journée d'études franco-italienne du Mans*, Paris, Pedone, 2018, pp. 163-187; E. Kelly, "The Precautionary Approach in the Advisory Opinion Concerning the Responsibilities and Obligations of States Sponsoring Persons and Entities with Respect to Activities in the Area", in International Tribunal for the Law of the Sea (ITLOS) (ed.), *The Contribution of the International Tribunal for the Law of the Sea to the Rule of Law: 1996-2016*, Leiden, Brill Nijhoff, 2018, pp. 45-57; D. König, "The Elaboration of Due Diligence Obligations as a Mechanism to Ensure Compliance with International Legal Obligations by Private Actors", in ITLOS (ed.), *The Contribution of the International Tribunal for the Law of the Sea to the Rule of Law: 1996-2016*, Leiden, Brill Nijhoff, 2018, pp. 83-95; I. Papanicolopulu, "Due Diligence in the Law of the Sea", in A. Peters, H. Krieger and L. Kreuzer (eds.), *Due Diligence in International Law*, Oxford, Oxford University Press, 2020, pp. 147-162.

19. See e.g. M. A. Fitzmaurice, "Due Diligence in the Use of International Watercourses", in A. Peters, H. Krieger and L. Kreuzer (eds.), *Due Diligence in International Law*, Oxford, Oxford University Press, 2020, pp. 129-146.

20. See e.g. E. de Brabandère, "Host States' Due Diligence Obligations in International Investment Law", *Syracuse Journal of International Law and Commerce*, Vol. 42, No. 2 (2015), pp. 319-362; A. de Nanteuil, "Due diligence et investissements étrangers", in SFDI (ed.), *Le standard de* due diligence *et la responsabilité internationale: Journée d'études franco-italienne du Mans*, Paris, Pedone, 2018, pp. 93-106; A. Rajput, "Due Diligence in International Investment Law: From the Law of Aliens to Responsible Investment", in A. Peters, H. Krieger and L. Kreuzer (eds.), *Due Diligence in International Law*, Oxford, Oxford University Press, 2020, pp. 273-287.

21. See e.g. M. Krajewski, "Due Diligence in International Trade Law", in A. Peters, H. Krieger and L. Kreuzer (eds.), *Due Diligence in International Law*, Oxford, Oxford University Press, 2020, pp. 312-328.

a customary principle. Finally, if its source lies in custom or the general principles of international law, one may wonder whether the *regime* of due diligence should not also be that of a standard or even an obligation of so-called general international law.

This threefold uncertainty regarding the nature, the sources and the regime of due diligence heavily weighs on international jurisprudence, as highlighted by the now-famous warning of the ICJ in the *Genocide* case cited above. In that judgment, the Court stressed that it did not purport to establish a "general jurisprudence" with regard to due diligence obligations, but, at the same time, did not exclude resorting to what it referred to as "the rules of law whose scope extends beyond the specific field" of the case [22].

Should one agree therefore with Riccardo Pisillo Mazzeschi when he claims that due diligence went from being a "mysterious" international legal concept to an "overrated" [23] or even an overused one?

To answer this question, the aim of this course is to critically assess the practice of due diligence in international law. This assessment should take place not only with regard to its equivalents in the comparative law of private and public liability [24], but also with respect to other related

22. See ICJ, The case of *Application of the Convention on the Prevention and Punishment of the Crime of Genocide (Bosnia and Herzegovina* v. *Serbia and Montenegro)*, Judgment of 26 February 2007, *ICJ Reports 2007*, p. 43, para. 429.

23. See R. Pisillo Mazzeschi, "Le chemin étrange de la due diligence: d'un concept mystérieux à un concept surévalué", in SFDI (ed.), *Le standard de* due diligence *et la responsabilité internationale: Journée d'études franco-italienne du Mans*, Paris, Pedone, 2018, pp. 323-338.

24. Translator's note: the French term *responsabilité* has been translated as "responsibility" in this course except where the term refers to contemporary domestic law, in which instances it is rendered as "liability". Author's note: In international responsibility law, "responsibility" is understood as a form of liability of States and, by extension, of IOs, i.e. as a set of secondary obligations that arise from the breach of primary obligations. See e.g. PCIJ, The case of the *Factory at Chorzów (Germany* v. *Poland)*, Judgment of 13 September 1928, *PCIJ Reports 1928*, Series A No. 17; *PCIJ Reports 1923*, The case of the *S.S. Wimbledon (United Kingdom* v. *Japan)*, Judgment of 17 August 1923, *PCIJ Reports 1923*, Series A No. 1; ICJ, The case of the *Corfu Channel*, *op. cit. supra* note 8; ICJ, The case of *Military and Paramilitary Activities in and against Nicaragua*, *op. cit. supra* note 8; ICJ, *Reparation for Injuries Suffered in the Service of the United Nations*, Advisory Opinion of 1 April 1949, *ICJ Reports 1949*, p. 174; ILC, Draft Articles on the Responsibility of International Organizations, 9 November 2011, adopted and submitted to the United Nations' General Assembly (ARIO); ILC, Draft Articles on the Responsibility of States for Internationally Wrongful Acts, 12 December 2001, adopted in Resolution A/RES/56/83 by the United Nations' General Assembly (ARSIWA). See also J. Crawford, *State Responsibility: The General Part*, Cambridge, Cambridge University Press, 2013, pp. 3-44; A. Pellet, "The Definition of Responsibility in International Law", in J. Crawford, A. Pellet and S. Olleson (eds.), *The Law of International Responsibility*, Oxford, Oxford University Press, 2010, pp. 3-16; J. Crawford and S. Olleson, "The Nature and Forms of International Responsibility", in M. Evans (ed.), *International*

notions of international law, such as the duty not to harm and the duty to prevent harm, as well as the precautionary principle or the principle of good neighbourliness. The aim is not only to determine whether such a principle, standard and/or obligation of due diligence does actually exist in general international law. The course also purports to outline its minimal general regime and examine its specificities in selected regimes of international law.

While it is difficult to pinpoint the exact role of the diligence standard in private and public liability law (both national and comparative) between a standard of qualification of the content of a primary obligation of conduct (notably an obligation not to harm), on the one hand, and an evaluative standard of compliance with those obligations within the responsibility regime [25], on the other, this difficulty is only heightened in international responsibility law. The authors of the codification of this law and in particular the last rapporteurs of the International Law Commission (ILC) carefully erased all traces of a subjective element by shifting the issue of fault back to the level of primary obligations. This course also aims at clarifying the status, largely informal and irritating, that due diligence currently occupies in international responsibility law [26]. This includes addressing the relationship of due diligence with the question of attribution of conduct and responsibility, the question of

---

Law, 5th ed., Oxford, Oxford University Press, 2018, pp. 415-449. On the relationship between "responsibility" in international law thus understood and *(i)* (primary) "obligations", *(ii)* "liability" to some negative response for wrongdoing (including for the breach of primary obligations, but not only), and *(iii)* "accountability" for one's (even non-wrongful) conduct, see A. Nollkaemper, "Responsibility", in J. d'Aspremont and S. Singh (eds.), *Concepts for International Law: Contributions to Disciplinary Thought*, Cheltenham, Edward Elgar, 2019, pp. 760-772; J. Crawford and J. Watkins, "International Responsibility", in S. Besson and J. Tasioulas (eds.), *The Philosophy of International Law*, Oxford, Oxford University Press, 2010, pp. 283-298, pp. 283-284. On the origins and critique of another, especially vexed distinction, specific to the ILC codification of international responsibility law, between "responsibility" *stricto sensu* (for internationally wrongful acts, identified as they are with unlawful acts) and so-called liability (for injurious consequences arising out of lawful acts), see P. d'Argent, "Responsibility or Liability: Is It That Simple?", in S. Besson (ed.), *Theories of International Responsibility Law*, Cambridge, Cambridge University Press, 2022, pp. 209-228.

25. See e.g. on the ambiguous relationship between duty of care (as a full-fledged obligation) and standard of care (as a standard of evaluation of compliance with this obligation and, thus, of responsibility) under Anglo-American law, D. Nolan, "Negligence", 2013, *op. cit. supra* note 4; S. Perry, 2009, *op. cit. supra* note 6.

26. See e.g. S. Heathcote, "State Omissions and Due Diligence: Aspects of Fault, Damage and Contribution to Injury in the Law of State Responsibility", in K. Bannelier, T. Christakis and S. Heathcote (eds.), *The ICJ and the Evolution of International Law: The Enduring Impact of the "Corfu Channel" Case*, London, Routledge, 2012, pp. 295-314, p. 304: "[D]ue diligence is a primary norm that *consists* of fault (negligence)."

causation and allocation of responsibility and the question of reparations in case of negligent conduct by States and/or IOs.

Generally, the present course presents itself as an international legal theory course at the service of international legal practice: it presents the practice of due diligence in international law while simultaneously interpreting, justifying, criticising and systematising it [27]. The increasing invocation of due diligence in the recent history of international law also provides a good opportunity to reflect on the state of this law and on the future of the international institutional order.

Following this introduction and preceding a general conclusion, the course is divided into four chapters. Chapter I is devoted to the history and "renaissance" of due diligence. Chapter II addresses the general regime of due diligence in international law: it examines its nature, its sources/regimes, its scope (personal, material, geographic and temporal), its conditions, its content, its variability and its limits. Chapter III engages with the obverse side of the coin by examining the role of due diligence in the law of international responsibility of States and IOs. Chapter IV is devoted to the specificities of due diligence in three special regimes of international law: international environmental law, international cybersecurity law and, finally, international human rights law.

Pedagogical reasons account for the course's structure, particularly for the analysis' separation between primary obligations and international legal responsibilities, but also for the distinction between the general and special regimes of due diligence in international law. Two comments should be made in that respect.

First, given due diligence's intermediary position between a qualification standard of the content of primary obligations and an evaluative standard of compliance with these obligations (and as such of the responsibility for the breach of these obligations), Chapters II and III should be read in relationship with each other. The tension but also, and more crucially, the complementarity which characterises the relationships between obligations and responsibilities in general and consequently between primary and secondary obligations in international law are even more heightened in the realm of due diligence. Second, given the relationship between the special regimes of due diligence and the consolidation of a minimal general regime, the

27. See S. Besson, "International Legal Theory *qua* Practice of International Law", in J. d'Aspremont, A. Nollkaemper and T. Gazzini (eds.), *International Law as a Profession*, Cambridge, Cambridge University Press, 2017, pp. 268-284.

former cannot be understood separately from the latter. It is essential to appreciate their mutual influences: the influence of each special regime on the general regime; the reverse influence of the general regime on each special regime; and, finally, the influence of each special regime on the others.

CHAPTER I

DUE DILIGENCE IN INTERNATIONAL LAW: HISTORY AND "RENAISSANCE"

"Territorial sovereignty, as has already been said, involves the exclusive right to display the activities of a State. This right has as corollary a duty: the obligation to protect within the territory the rights of other States, in particular their right to integrity and inviolability in peace and in war, together with the rights which each State may claim for its nationals in foreign territory."

(*Island of Palmas* Arbitration *[The Netherlands* v. *United States of America]*, Final Award of 4 April 1928, RIAA Vol. II p. 829, p. 839)

Introduction

The first chapter of this course is devoted, first, to (A) the origins of due diligence in international law and, second, to (B) the identification of the causes of its recent "renaissance" [28].

Solely by retracing the various steps of the evolution of due diligence in the history of international law can one fully grasp not only the hybrid nature of its contemporary regime, but also its potential for application to new regimes of international law (such as international cybersecurity law [29]) or even to new entities of international law (such

28. See J. Brunnée and T. Meshel, "Teaching an Old Law New Tricks: International Environmental Law Lessons for Cyberspace Governance", *German Yearbook of International Law*, Vol. 58 (2015), pp. 129-168, referring to international environmental law.

29. See e.g. D. Hollis and M. Finnemore, "Constructing Norms for Global Cybersecurity", *American Journal of International Law*, Vol. 110 (2016), pp. 425-479; E. Talbot Jensen and S. Watts, "A Cyber Duty of Due Diligence: Gentle Civilizer or Crude Destabilizer?", *Texas Law Review*, Vol. 95 (2017), pp. 1555-1577; M. N. Schmitt, "In Defense of Due Diligence in Cyberspace", *Yale Law Journal Forum*, Vol. 125 (2015), pp. 6881; M. Herdegen, "Possible Legal Framework and Regulatory Models for Cyberspace: Due Diligence Obligations and Institutional Models for Enhanced Inter-State Cooperation", *German Yearbook of International Law*, Vol. 58 (2015), pp. 169-188; M. Ney and A. Zimmermann, "Cyber-Security beyond the Military Perspective: International Law, Cyberspace, and the Concept of Due Diligence", *German Yearbook of International Law*, Vol. 58 (2015), pp. 51-66; S. J. Shackelford, S. Russell and A. Kuehn, "Unpacking the International Law on Cybersecurity Due Diligence: Lessons from the Public and Private Sectors", *Chicago Journal of International Law*, Vol. 17, No. 1 (2016), pp. 1-50; A. Benedek, "Due Diligence in Cyberspace, Guidelines for International and European Cyber Policy and Cybersecurity Policy", SWP Research Paper 7, Berlin, 2016 [online]; R. Kolb, "Reflections on Due Diligence Duties and Cyberspace", *German Yearbook of International Law*, Vol. 58 (2016), pp. 113-128;

as private collective entities, like multinational corporations [30] [MNCs] or non-governmental organisations [NGOs]).

A. The origins of due diligence in international law

As highlighted in the introduction, due diligence is an ancient notion which dates back to the law of antiquity. It was first and foremost present (under different forms) in Roman private law, but also in several other regimes of public responsibility. Given the reception of Roman law in the Western law tradition, followed by the wide influence of Western law since then, it is not surprising to find that this notion has spread to both Western and non-Western contemporary legal traditions.

In brief (and we will revert to this point in greater detail), the reception of due diligence in classical international law primarily arose from analogies to Roman private law initiated by authors such as Hugo Grotius or Alberico Gentili in the seventeenth century and later by Emer de Vattel in the eighteenth century. In modern international law, the first historical traces of these analogies – which by then were infused with references to national private law subsequent to the reception of Roman

D. Delibasis, "Cybersecurity and State Responsibility: Identifying a Due Diligence Standard for Prevention of Transboundary Threats", in J. Kulesza and R. Balleste (eds.), *Cybersecurity and Human Rights in the Age of Cybersurveillance*, Lanham, MD, Rowman & Littlefield, 2016, pp. 17-38; K. Bannelier-Christakis, "Obligations de diligence dans le cyberspace: qui a peur de la cyber-diligence ?", *Revue belge de droit international*, Vol. 50, No. 2 (2017), pp. 612-665; K. Bannelier-Christakis, "Le standard de due diligence et la cyber-sécurité", in SFDI (ed.), *Le standard de* due diligence *et la responsabilité internationale: Journée d'études franco-italienne du Mans*, Paris, Pedone, 2018, pp. 67-92; L. Chircop, "A Due Diligence Standard of Attribution in Cyberspace", *International and Comparative Law Quarterly*, Vol. 67, No. 3 (2018), pp. 643-668; H.-G. Dederer and T. Singer, "Adverse Cyber Operations: Causality, Attribution, Evidence, and Due Diligence", *International Law Studies*, Vol. 95 (2019), pp. 431-466; E. Talbot Jensen, "Due Diligence in Cyber Activities", in A. Peters, H. Krieger and L. Kreuzer (eds.), *Due Diligence in International Law*, Oxford, Oxford University Press, 2020, pp. 252-272.

30. See e.g. F. Marrella, "Protection internationale des droits de l'homme et activités des sociétés transnationales", *Recueil des cours*, Vol. 385 (2017), p. 33-435. See also J. Bonnitcha and R. McCorquodale, "The Concept of 'Due Diligence' in the UN Guiding Principles on Business and Human Rights", *European Journal of International Law*, Vol. 28, No. 3 (2017), pp. 899-919; J. Bonnitcha and R. McCorquodale, "The Concept of 'Due Diligence' in the UN Guiding Principles on Business and Human Rights: A Rejoinder to John Gerard Ruggie and John F. Sherman, III", *European Journal of International Law*, Vol. 28, No. 3 (2017), pp. 929-933; J. G. Ruggie and J. F. Sherman, "The Concept of 'Due Diligence' in the UN Guiding Principles on Business and Human Rights: A Reply to Jonathan Bonnitcha and Robert McCorquodale", *European Journal of International Law*, Vol. 28, No. 3 (2017), pp. 921-928; N. D. White, "Due Diligence Obligations of Conduct: Developing a Responsibility Regime for PMSCs", *Criminal Justice Ethics*, Vol. 31, No. 3 (2012), pp. 233-261.

law – could be found in arbitral, and then judicial, decisions of the end of the nineteenth century and the beginning of the twentieth century. At the time, these cases mainly related to international legal regimes with transboundary dimensions, such as the international law of neutrality, the international law on the protection of aliens (including foreign investors) and international environmental law. The question of due diligence generally arose in relation to the responsibility of the State, particularly State responsibility in relation to the conduct of private persons. By the second half of the twentieth century, the scope of due diligence had begun to extend to many other regimes of international law, including regimes applicable to situations lacking a transboundary dimension and even sometimes to situations without any territorial dimension at all, such as international human rights law, international criminal law, international humanitarian law and the international law of the sea. Currently, due diligence also applies to subjects other than States, in particular to certain IOs. Some scholars maintain that due diligence also binds private collective entities, like corporations, and sometimes even applies independently of the acts of other private persons, such as with respect to the acts of other States or IOs.

This section offers (1) a few historiographic remarks, followed by (2) a detailed genealogy of due diligence in contemporary international law.

1. The historiography of due diligence in international law

As a first methodological caveat, one should start by stating that a proper assessment of the history of due diligence would require a global comparative historical analysis.

Yet none of the historical studies consulted during the elaboration of this course presents such a global narrative about due diligence. The rare historical studies on the subject, which are few and far between [31], focus on the history of due diligence in the Western, mostly European, practice of international law. Admittedly, contemporary international law's history is embedded in the history of European and Western law, and it is especially true for due diligence. Broadening the scope of

31. See H. Lauterpacht, *op. cit. supra* note 2; J. A. Hessbruegge, *op. cit. supra* note 5; A. Ouedraogo, 2011, *op. cit. supra* note 12; J. Kulesza, *op. cit. supra* note 5; R. Kolb, 2016, *op. cit. supra* note 29; G. Bartolini, "The Historical Roots of the Due Diligence Standard", in A. Peters, H. Krieger and L. Kreuzer (eds.), *Due Diligence in International Law*, Oxford, Oxford University Press, 2020, pp. 23-41.

investigation of the recent history of that standard, which belongs to both national and international law and which was imported in other legal traditions as early as the nineteenth century, however, would allow for a more inclusive interpretation of the contemporary international legal regime on that matter. Such a historiography would also pave the way for the development of a comparative understanding of due diligence in international law and thus for a more universal understanding of that concept, which is essential to its legitimacy.

A second methodological warning relates to the risk of anachronism which is inherent to any historical narrative of a contemporary standard of international law.

Such a risk is especially high when the standard is as ancient as due diligence, which dates back to antiquity and which, in its modern tradition, is closely related to the emergence of the State, State sovereignty, States' exclusive personal and territorial jurisdiction and the public/private distinction. The same warning applies to the significance placed in the contemporary international regime of due diligence on the distinction between the State and private persons, particularly the State's relationship with private persons, nationality or even jurisdiction. The concept of States' international responsibility is also very recent and prone to give rise to anachronisms when transposed too swiftly onto circumstances prevailing before the nineteenth century.

Finally, one last methodological caveat relates to the "family resemblances" which unite various usages of the concept of due diligence, without being necessarily relevant to the elucidation of the contemporary concept of due diligence in international law.

This is the case in particular for the multiple and concurrent "due diligence" standards which are found in many legal traditions – even within the same national or regional legal tradition, depending on the legal field at issue. In international law, due diligence is a hybrid notion resulting from centuries of cross-evolution of various notions of due diligence in Roman private law and from the reception of these notions in national law for various purposes and in multiple languages [32]. As a result, those various standards or norms of conduct, which bear similar names in different legal traditions, have often very little in common. A corporation's fiduciary duty of diligence under Anglo-American business law, that is, the purely fiduciary duty of careful examination

32. On the historical vicissitudes of the formation of European law, see A. A. Wijffels, *Le droit européen a-t-il une histoire ? En a-t-il besoin ?* (Leçon inaugurale), Paris, Fayard / Collège de France, 2017.

and evaluation of a corporation by potential buyers, offers a good example thereof: the conceptual distance between that standard and the due diligence owed by States and IOs under international law is gaping. As we will see, moreover, the mere idea of the existence of a minimal general regime of due diligence common to the special regimes of international law is still disputed [33].

As a result, while the contemporary standard of due diligence under international law shares some commonalities with certain forms of due diligence under Roman private law [34], one should avoid any hasty conflations between the two. The same caution is required when considering analogies made to Western private law traditions, whether Anglo-American or otherwise, including when those traditions also derive from Roman private law [35]. As our analysis will show, due diligence in international law differs not only from most due diligence standards in Roman private law, but also from the various forms of the "diligence duty" in domestic private or public liability regimes (for example, the duty of care of the principal or owner in tort law or the duty of care of parent companies over their subsidiaries under commercial law), which are themselves hybrids of multiple receptions and reinterpretations of Roman private law figures.

A deeper examination of Roman private law reveals that it is first and foremost the figure of the *diligens pater familias* that is most akin to due diligence in contemporary international law. This objective standard is comparable to that of the reasonable man or woman currently applicable in certain traditions of private law. As we will see, the figure of the reasonable State, or even of the reasonable IO, can also be found in the contemporary practice of due diligence in international law, including in the standard of what can be reasonably expected from States or IOs in concrete circumstances [36]. Second, one should also mention the due diligence standard embedded in the duty not to harm in Roman private

33. Pro: ILA, Study Group on Due Diligence in International Law, First and Second Rapports, *op. cit. supra* note 5; A. Ouedraogo, 2011, *op. cit. supra* note 12; P. d'Argent and A. de Vaucleroy, "Le contenu de l'omission illicite: la non-utilisation de moyens raisonnables", in SFDI (ed.), *Le standard de* due diligence *et la responsabilité internationale: Journée d'études franco-italienne du Mans*, Paris, Pedone, 2018, pp. 255-279. Contra: R. Pisillo Mazzeschi, 2018, *op. cit. supra* note 23.

34. See R. Zimmermann, *The Law of Obligations: Roman Foundations of the Civilian Tradition*, Oxford, Clarendon Press, 1996; H. Lauterpacht, *op. cit. supra* note 2.

35. See also D. Hovell, "Due Process in the United Nations", *American Journal of International Law*, Vol. 110, No. 1 (2016), pp. 1-48.

36. See P. d'Argent and A. de Vaucleroy, *op. cit. supra* note 33.

law *(sic utere tuo at alienum non laedas)*. As will be further addressed, this duty not to harm the rights or interests of others by negligence in conducting one's own activities may be associated with the duty not to harm ("no harm rule") in contemporary international law and the way in which that duty integrates due diligence [37].

By contrast, however, one should reject any comparisons with the *diligentia quam in suis* or the *caveat emptor* principles which apply, respectively, to the depositary and to the buyer in Roman private law. These two forms of diligence are clearly distinct from due diligence in contemporary international law, the former because of its mainly subjective character [38] and the latter because of its self-referential dimension since the buyer is the sole beneficiary [39].

2. The genealogy of due diligence in international law

Schematically, there are six phases to the history of what we now call responsibility for negligence, that is, responsibility for a breach of due diligence by the public institutions of international law, that is, States and by extension IOs [40].

This six-part historical framework highlights the three potential scenarios for the international responsibility of States still at play

37. See J. Brunnée, 2010, *op. cit. supra* note 14.

38. It is important to emphasise that, under the international law on the protection of aliens and investors of the nineteenth and early twentieth century, due diligence tended to promote such a subjective *quam in suis* standard (see e.g. *British Property in Spanish Morocco* Arbitration, *op. cit. supra* note 8). This is no longer the standard of due diligence applicable under contemporary international human rights law: see M. Hakimi, *op. cit. supra* note 13.

39. One may draw parallels between this type of due diligence and the type applicable to the contribution to one's own injury, which is one of the circumstances affecting the way in which reparation is determined under international responsibility law (ARSIWA, *op. cit. supra* note 24, Art. 39; ARIO, *op. cit. supra* note 24, Art. 39. See e.g. D. J. Bederman, "Contributory Fault and State Responsibility", *Virginia Journal of International Law*, Vol. 30, No. 2 (1990), pp. 335-369) and perhaps is even an element determining whether *force majeure* or necessity can be invoked as circumstances precluding wrongfulness under international responsibility law (ARSIWA, *op. cit. supra* note 24, Arts. 23 (2) (b) and 25 (2) (b); ARIO, *op. cit. supra* note 24, Arts. 23 (2) (b) and 25 (2) (b)). One could also compare it to the fiduciary practice of due diligence under business law, which, as we will see, has gradually infiltrated international human rights law: many consider that it should be applied to private persons (especially MNCs) that may contribute to causing human rights violations negligently (see J. Bonnitcha and R. McCorquodale, "The Concept of 'Due Diligence' " and "A Rejoinder", *op. cit. supra* note 30; J. G. Ruggie and J. F. Sherman, *op. cit. supra* note 30).

40. See H. Lauterpacht, *op. cit. supra* note 2; J. A. Hessbruegge, *op. cit. supra* note 5; A. Ouedraogo, 2012, *op. cit. supra* note 12; J. Kulesza, *op. cit. supra* note 5; R. Kolb, 2016, *op. cit. supra* note 29; G. Bartolini, 2020, *op. cit. supra* note 31. It should be noted that this proposed genealogy of due diligence traces the history of both a legal idea and its practice.

today [41]. It sheds light on how they emerged progressively, in a non-linear, twisted and at times overlapping fashion: *(i)* strict responsibility (that is, independently of negligence) of the State (or, before the State, of the group) for any harm caused by its nationals (or, before nationality, by members of the group); *(ii)* responsibility of the State only by attribution of the conduct of an official organ which caused the harm (including *ultra vires*) (and thus independently of a negligent conduct of the State itself); and, in-between, *(iii)* responsibility of the State (or, before the emergence of the State, of the group) for breaches of its due diligence with respect to its nationals who caused the harm (and, before nationality, members of the group).

The first phase of due diligence's genealogy starts with *antiquity*. In antiquity, the Roman, as well as non-Roman (Assyrian and Egyptian, for example), practice of the responsibility of kings and other heads of empires and cities reveals the existence of a responsibility for negligent actions or omissions [42]. Even though this practice is only accessible via fragments, it indicates that the due diligence standard was applied regularly in case of harms caused on the territory of these kingdoms, empires or cities, in particular in their harbours or their coastal waters, by private persons (such as pirates) to private persons belonging to other kingdoms, empires or cities. The condition for this responsibility seems to have been, on the one hand, that these kingdoms, empires or cities and their rulers had some control over the persons who caused the harms (either because of their residing on the territory or their belonging to the community) and, on the other hand, that they acted negligently when attempting to prevent those harms.

This is true for the references to due diligence in Roman *jus gentium* [43]. However, and very interestingly, the *jus gentium* practice of

41. See ITLOS, *Responsibilities and Obligations of States Sponsoring Persons and Entities with Respect to Activities in the Area*, Advisory Opinion of 1 February 2011, *ITLOS Reports 2011*, p. 10, paras. 131 and 112:

"The expression 'to ensure' is often used in international legal instruments to refer to obligations in respect of which, while it is not considered reasonable to make a State liable for each and every violation committed by persons under its jurisdiction, it is equally not considered satisfactory to rely on mere application of the principle that the conduct of private persons or entities is not attributable to the State under international law (see ILC Articles on State Responsibility, Commentary to article 8, paragraph 1)."

42. See J. A. Hessbruegge, *op. cit. supra* note 5, pp. 265-266 and 276-279.

43. On the multiple, and at times contradictory, meanings of the term *jus gentium* (moral or social, and transnational or international) from the Roman era to the seventeenth century, see J. Waldron, *"Partly Laws Common to All Mankind": Foreign Law in American Courts*, New Haven, CT, Yale University Press, 2012; S. Besson, "L'autorité légitime du droit international comparé: Quelques réflexions autour du

due diligence was never openly paired with the forms of due diligence in Roman *jus civile*, even though a mutual influence between the two regimes is evident. As we will see, the connection between the due diligence standard in international law and the homonymic standards in domestic private law was only established in the seventeenth century at the time of the reception of certain principles of Roman private law in international law.

The second phase in due diligence's genealogy is to be situated in the *Middle Ages*. During the Middle Ages, a shift back to the Germanic traditions of collective responsibility of the group, tribe or clan for any harm caused by one of its members progressively takes root. Responsibility arose even when the group member did not act on behalf of the group and even without negligence on the part of the group's authorities. Some consider that this form of collective clan or tribal responsibility never fully disappeared during antiquity and coexisted with the practice of responsibility for due diligence violations even during the Roman period. Admittedly, even in Roman law, the separation between the group and its members was not yet complete, which entailed certain consequences for the responsibility of the group for the actions of its members [44].

No further changes occurred in legal practice until the late Middle Ages, when the automatic attribution of the actions of group members to the group and the resulting collective responsibility of the group on that sole basis began to be called into question. This occurred either because of the absence of negligence or, at least, of the lack of control of the group over its members.

The third phase in the genealogy of due diligence is to be situated *in the sixteenth and seventeenth centuries*. The pressure of what may be called "anthropomorphism" is indeed first perceptible among thinkers of the sixteenth and seventeenth centuries: they view the responsibility of the sovereign (who is progressively being separated from the group while the group is constituted as such, becomes legally distinct from its members and is eventually represented by that sovereign) as analogous to the responsibility of a private person (who is also being individualised at that time). Building upon individual responsibility for fault under Roman private law, the sovereign's responsibility is only justifiable on account of his or her own personal fault. The actions of the members of

---

monde et du *droit des gens* de Vico", in S. Besson and S. Jubé (eds.), *Concerter les civilisations: Mélanges en l'honneur d'Alain Supiot*, Paris, Seuil, 2020, pp. 49-60.

44. See J. A. Hessbruegge, *op. cit. supra* note 5, p. 279.

a group are no longer automatically attributed to the sovereign merely because they belong to that group [45].

At the same time, the due diligence of the Roman law regime of civil liability makes its way into international law through the reception of many Roman private law institutions and their transposition to the sovereign. This is primarily observable in the works of authors, such as Hugo Grotius [46] and Alberico Gentili [47]. The appearance of the *receptus* principle offers a good example thereof. According to this principle, sovereigns who receive an offender sought by another sovereign can be found responsible for a breach of due diligence if they do not surrender or otherwise punish him or her. The *patientia* principle is another example in point. According to this principle, sovereigns who permit harm to be done to the interests of other sovereigns or their subjects in a negligent fashion can be held responsible for such conduct [48].

However, it is important to emphasise that, at that time at least, the reception in international law of the due diligence of Roman private law was unfolding in complete ignorance of Roman *jus gentium* and even of the existence of a (fluctuating) distinction between *jus gentium* and *jus civile* on this question: reception renamed and reinvented a practice which amounted (without the name) to due diligence in *jus gentium* in light of a *jus civile* norm. It is precisely for that reason that trying to identify the exact original principle in Roman private law that corresponds to due diligence as it exists in international law in order to draw interpretative resources would be futile.

At first, it is, of course, the person of the sovereign who is found responsible (and only for his or her own fault, not for the fault of his or her organs, which had not yet been distinguished from the person of the sovereign, and even less for the fault of his or her subjects). Over time, and as early as the eighteenth century, the State will come to be separated from the person of the sovereign, and it is the sovereign State as such that will be found responsible.

The fourth phase of due diligence's genealogy is to be situated *between the eighteenth and the nineteenth centuries*. As sovereignty is detached from the person of the sovereign and increasingly assigned to the sovereign State, the distinct responsibility of the sovereign

45. See J. A. Hessbruegge, *op. cit. supra* note 5, pp. 281-287.

46. See H. Grotius, *On the Laws of War and Peace*, trans. F. W. Kelsey, New York, W. S. Hein & Co., 1995 (orig. *De jure belli ac pacis*, 1646), Vol. II, chap. XVII, XX, p. 437.

47. See A. Gentili, *Three Books on the Law of War*, trans. J. C. Rolfe, Oxford, Clarendon Press, 1933 (orig. *De Iure [Jure] Belli Libri Tres*, 1598), pp. 99-100.

48. See H. Grotius, *op. cit. supra* note 46, Vol. II, chap. XXI, II, p. 523.

State develops in lieu of the sovereign's. The sovereign State becomes responsible for the actions of its organs, but also for failing, by negligence, to prevent its subjects from harming others [49]. However, due diligence does not immediately extend to the harms caused by any person situated on the State's territory because of the lack of States' effective control over their territories at the time [50].

Christian Wolff's [51] and especially Emer de Vattel's [52] writings are clear on this point. They address both State responsibility for the conduct of its organs (even in the absence of fault) and responsibility for breach of the State's due diligence for the actions of its other subjects. It is precisely in the works of Emer de Vattel that the State's due diligence for the harms caused by its subjects is clearly articulated for the first time [53]. He distances himself from the anthropomorphism present in Hugo Grotius' work on State responsibility: the State is no longer equated with an individual whose responsibility would only be engaged by his or her own fault or, most crucially, by his or her own conduct [54].

Only in the nineteenth century is the medieval conception of a tribal or collective responsibility definitively replaced by that of a territorially sovereign State. In the wake of that development, the State's due diligence extends to the prevention of all harms, that is, not only those caused by its subjects, but also those emanating from its territory [55].

The fifth phase of due diligence's genealogy spans *from the nineteenth to the beginning of the twentieth century*. While private law analogies in international law have always been controverted and ardently discussed since the seventeenth century [56], the nineteenth century could have been fatal to them. Positivist lawyers of that era, including William Edward Hall [57], Lassa Oppenheim [58], Heinrich Triepel [59] and Dionisio

49. See J. A. Hessbruegge, *op. cit. supra* note 5, p. 287.
50. See *ibid*, pp. 284-285.
51. C. Wolff, *Principes du droit de la nature et des gens*, trans. J.-H.-S. Formey (1758), Caen, Presses Universitaires de Caen, 2012 (orig. *Jus naturae*, 1740-1748).
52. See E. de Vattel, *The Law of Nations*, trans. J. Chitty (1834), Cambridge, Cambridge University Press, 2011 (orig. *Le droit des gens*, 1758), Vol. II, chap. VI, paras. 72-74, p. 162.
53. See J. A. Hessbruegge, *op. cit. supra* note 5, pp. 288-292.
54. See E. de Vattel, *op. cit. supra* note 52, prelim. para. 6, p. lvi-lvii.
55. See J. A. Hessbruegge, *op. cit. supra* note 5, p. 292.
56. See H. Lauterpacht, *op. cit. supra* note 2.
57. W. E. Hall, *A Treatise on International Law*, Oxford, Clarendon Press, 1880.
58. L. Oppenheim, *International Law: A Treatise*, 1st ed., London, Longmans, 1905, Vol. I.
59. H. Triepel, "Les rapports entre le droit interne et le droit international", *Recueil des cours*, Vol. 1 (1923), pp. 73-121.

Anzilotti [60], strongly reject these analogies. Attempts to ascribe a "moral" dimension to State responsibility, in particular the idea of fault or negligence on the part of States, are also disfavoured. Among the justifications advanced for that resistance are the specificity and self-sufficiency of international law, as well as the specific features of States as collective and institutionalised subjects. If any principle of private Roman law subsists in these authors' argumentations, it is only on the basis of a scientific rationalisation [61] or, at least, of a generalisation and transformation of legal truths into general principles of justice.

More generally, utilitarianism takes root in the legal thinking of that era. This has several implications for the conceptualisation of the State, including the reconsideration of political fictions, such as that of the State's personality. From then on, the idea that States could incur responsibility on the ground of their own fault or negligence is entirely abandoned. At the time, the only State responsibility still retained under international law is the one resulting from the attribution to the State of the wrongful acts of its organs – including *ultra vires* – independently of any fault of the State itself [62].

As demonstrated by Hersch Lauterpacht [63], this evolution would likely have taken further hold if not for the resilience of State practice and especially the perpetuation of the resort to due diligence in that practice. In that respect, the pragmatism and strategic sense of the practitioners of international law of that time deserve emphasis. Anglo-American arbitrators played an important role because they were trained into the Anglo-American law of civil liability (tort law) and therefore were used to due diligence. It was these arbitrators who, as early as the end of the nineteenth century, embraced due diligence in their arbitral awards [64].

60. See D. Anzilotti, "Sugli effetti dell'inadempienza di obbligazioni internazionali aventi per oggetto una somma di danaro", *Rivista di Diritto Internazionale*, Vol. 7 (1913), pp. 53-67.

61. See A. A. Wijffels, *op. cit. supra* note 32, on the *jus commune* adopted *non ratione imperii*, but *imperio rationis*.

62. It was also near the end of the nineteenth century in Europe that national public or State liability law developed, following a model resembling that of civil liability (and therefore based on the fault of the State or not, depending on each national system). See A.-C. Favre, "Le droit de la responsabilité de l'État: les enjeux", in A.-C. Favre, V. Martenet and E. Poltier (eds.), *La responsabilité de l'État*, Geneva, Schulthess, 2012, pp. 9-21, pp. 11 *et seq*.

63. See H. Lauterpacht, *op. cit. supra* note 2. See also J. A. Hessbruegge, *op. cit. supra* note 5, pp. 300-302 on the issue of States' responsibility for the acts of insurrectional movements.

64. See e.g. *Alabama Claims* Arbitration, *op. cit. supra* note 1; *Frederick Wipperman* Arbitration, *op. cit. supra* note 1. As early as the end of the nineteenth century, the same praetorian dimension can be observed in national public (and civil, for that matter)

These awards eventually made their way into the jurisprudence of the first permanent international tribunals of the beginning of the twentieth century [65]. One of the most important characteristics of due diligence in international law to this day was already at work at the time: the "reasonableness" dimension of the conduct expected from States and, from then on, the inextricable relationship between due diligence's evaluation and judicial reasoning [66].

The sixth and final period of the genealogy of due diligence may be situated *between the twentieth century and today*. The regime of State responsibility as it emerges as early as the end of the nineteenth century strongly intensifies after World War II, as much in international as in national law [67]. This development results from the multiplication of States' international law obligations (especially human rights obligations) and, more generally, from the institutionalisation of the monitoring of compliance with international law obligations by IOs and international tribunals [68], particularly in the international law on reparations.

Concurrently, the enterprise of rationalisation of international law, which starts at the end of the nineteenth century and continues well into

liability law. It has maintained parallel to legislation in the field since the middle of the twentieth century. For a comparative study of national public liability law, see A. Antoine and T. Olson, *op. cit. supra* note 6.

65. See e.g. *British Property in Spanish Morocco* Arbitration, *op. cit. supra* note 8; *Island of Palmas* Arbitration, *op. cit. supra* note 8, p. 839; *William E. Chapman* Arbitration, *op. cit. supra* note 1; *Trail Smelter* Arbitration, *op. cit. supra* note 8, para. 716; Dissenting opinion of Judge Moore, in PCIJ, The case of the *S.S. Lotus*, *op. cit. supra* note 8, p. 88; ICJ, The case of the *Corfu Channel*, *op. cit. supra* note 8, p. 22.

66. See P. d'Argent and A. de Vaucleroy, *op. cit. supra* note 33; O. Corten, *L'utilisation du « raisonnable » par le juge international, discours juridique, raisons et contradictions*, Brussels, Bruylant, 1997.

67. For a comparison between national public liability law and international responsibility law, see A. Antoine and T. Olson, *op. cit. supra* note 6. One observes, at least within Western traditions of public liability law, an evolution very similar to that of the international law of State responsibility. On the one hand, civil and public liability regimes evolve closely to one another, as is the case in international law, and in symbiosis within each national legal order. On the other hand, even when the concept of State fault is rejected in the public liability regime (as it is the case under Swiss or German law), it is replaced, as it is also the case in international law, by an obligation of conduct with due diligence or, at least, by an obligation not to harm fundamental rights and interests by negligence.

68. See J. Crawford, *op. cit. supra* note 24; P. d'Argent, "Reparation, Cessation, Assurances and Guarantees of Non-Repetition in Situations of Shared Responsibility", in A. Nollkaemper and I. Plakokefalos (eds.), *Principles of Shared Responsibility in International Law: An Appraisal of the State of the Art*, Cambridge, Cambridge University Press, 2014, pp. 208-250; S. Besson, "International Responsibility: An Introduction", in S. Besson (ed.), *International Responsibility: Essays in Law, History and Philosophy* (Travaux de l'Ecole doctorale CUS 2016), Zurich, Schulthess, 2017, pp. 3-13.

the twentieth century, explains the increasingly clear rejection of any subjective or "moral" [69] dimension to State responsibility.

This persistence sheds light upon the relegation of the issue of fault and notably of negligence to the level of primary obligations [70] during the codification of the international law of State responsibility by the ILC (and in particular by its last Rapporteur on the topic, James Crawford [71]). The idea that States, as collective and instituted entities, could own the moral or mental qualities necessary to have intentions or be considered negligent is highly criticised then [72]. The first Rapporteur Roberto Ago, whose opinion on that point differs from that of Dionisio Anzilotti [73], insists on the importance of negligence for international responsibility. Ago tries to introduce a distinction between international obligations "requiring the adoption of a specific course of conduct" (i.e. due diligence obligations) and international obligations "requiring the achievement of a specific result" in his version of the Draft Articles on the Responsibility of States for Internationally Wrongful Acts, especially through the inclusion of a provision on international obligations "to prevent a given event" (Art. 23) [74]. His project is found to be too controversial, particularly from the point of view of the distinction between obligations of conduct and obligations of result in the civil law tradition [75], and eventually abandoned.

---

69. See H. Lauterpacht, *op. cit. supra* note 2.

70. See J. A. Hessbruegge, *op. cit. supra* note 5, p. 299; H. P. Aust and P. Feihle, "Due Diligence in the History of the Codification of the Law of State Responsibility", in A. Peters, H. Krieger and L. Kreuzer (eds.), *Due Diligence in International Law*, Oxford, Oxford University Press, 2020, pp. 42-58.

71. See ILC, Draft Articles on the Responsibility of States for Internationally Wrongful Acts, with commentaries, *Yearbook of the International Law Commission*, Vol. II, Part 2 (2001), pp. 35-37 (ARSIWA with commentaries). See also J. Crawford, *op. cit. supra* note 24.

72. See G. Palmisano, "Fault", in R. Wolfrum (ed.), *Max Planck Encyclopedia of Public International Law*, Oxford, Oxford University Press, 2007 [online]; S. Fleming, "Moral Agents and Legal Persons: The Ethics and the Law of State Responsibility", *International Theory*, Vol. 9, No. 3 (2017), pp. 466-489.

73. See D. Anzilotti, "La responsabilité internationale des États à raison des dommages soufferts par les étrangers", *Revue générale de droit international public* (1906), pp. 5-291.

74. See J. Crawford, *op. cit. supra* note 24, pp. 226-232.

75. See P. Reuter, *Institution internationales*, 4th ed., Paris, Presses universitaires de France, 1963; J. Combacau, "Obligations de résultat et obligations de comportement. Quelques questions et pas de réponse", in P. Reuter (ed.), *Mélanges offerts à Paul Reuter. Le droit international: unité et diversité*, Paris, Pedone, 1981, pp. 193-198; P.-M. Dupuy, "Reviewing the Difficulties of Codification: On Ago's Classification of Obligations of Means and Obligations of Result in Relation to State Responsibility", *European Journal of International Law*, Vol. 10 (1999), pp. 371-385.

As a result, the ILC's Articles on Responsibility of States for Internationally Wrongful Acts [76] (ARSIWA) adopted in 2001 and the Articles on the Responsibility of International Organizations [77] (ARIO) adopted in 2011 include no references to the nature of primary international law obligations, and the issue of due diligence has been relegated to the definition of these obligations [78]. Since then, the theory of international obligations has been flourishing, but outside the field of international responsibility [79]. As we will see, this focus on obligations of due diligence as being separate from responsibility for negligence has weighed upon the discussion of due diligence.

In the 1950s, however, judicial practice confirms, once again, the particular resilience of due diligence in the international law of State responsibility [80]. The role of that standard in the reasoning that undergirds the establishment of international responsibility accounts for its importance in the case law on that topic to this day. In turn, this resilience sheds light on the limitations of the attempts to confine the question of due diligence exclusively to the level of primary obligations.

The jurisprudential revival of due diligence in the twentieth century demonstrates that due diligence does not squarely fit the regime of either primary obligations or secondary obligations in the responsibility regime [81]. Since the nineteenth century, every attempt to confine them to one or the other side has fallen short. Among such attempts, the occasion which arose in 1949 to codify "certain basic rights and duties of States" [82] offers yet another example of that difficulty. The obligations regarded as primary obligations of due diligence could have been specified and included among those "basic rights and duties", but the ILC's project was discontinued [83].

---

76. ARSIWA, *op. cit. supra* note 24.

77. ARIO, *op. cit. supra* note 24.

78. On whether the ARIO, *op. cit. supra* note 24, reflect customary international law, see A. Pellet, "The ILC's Articles on State Responsibility for Internationally Wrongful Acts and Related Texts", in J. Crawford, A. Pellet and S. Olleson (eds.), *The Law of International Responsibility*, Oxford, Oxford University Press, 2010, pp. 75-94. Although the customary nature of these articles remains questionable, this course will rely upon them to discuss the responsibility of IOs for the breach of their due diligence obligations.

79. See e.g. R. Pisillo Mazzeschi, 2018, *op. cit. supra* note 23, pp. 326 *et seq.*; P. d'Argent and A. de Vaucleroy, *op. cit. supra* note 33.

80. See in particular ICJ, The case of the *Corfu Channel*, *op. cit. supra* note 8, pp. 22 and 35.

81. See H. Lauterpacht, *op. cit. supra* note 2.

82. See ILC, Draft Declaration on Rights and Duties of States, *Yearbook of the International Law Commission*, Vol. 1 (1949), pp. 286-290.

83. See S. Heathcote, *op. cit. supra* note 26.

Post-war jurisprudence on due diligence has persisted until today. Due diligence has even gained renewed appreciation since the 2000s [84]. In addition to this judicial and subsequently customary practice of due diligence since the 1960s, and especially in the 1990s, due diligence has also been recognised in multiple treaty provisions, particularly in international environmental law [85]. Subsequently, due diligence has also been recognised by certain unilateral acts adopted by IOs, such as the United Nations (UN) [86] or the European Union (EU) [87], but also more generally in the context of soft law norms, notably in international environmental law, international human rights law and international cybersecurity law [88].

84. See e.g. ICJ, The case of the *United States Diplomatic and Consular Staff in Tehran*, *op. cit. supra* note 8, paras. 67-68; ICJ, The case of *Military and Paramilitary Activities in and against Nicaragua*, *op. cit. supra* note 8, paras. 157-158; ICJ, *Legality of the Threat or Use of Nuclear Weapons*, *op. cit. supra* note 8, paras. 241-242; ICJ, The case of *The Gabcikovo-Nagymaros Project*, *op. cit. supra* note 8, para. 53; ICJ, The case of *Pulp Mills on the River Uruguay*, *op. cit. supra* note 3, para. 101; ICJ, The case of *Certain Activities carried out by Nicaragua in the Border Area*, *op. cit. supra* note 3, para. 104; PCA, *Indus Waters Kishenganga* Arbitration, *op. cit. supra* note 8, paras. 449-450; PCA, *South China Sea* Arbitration, *op. cit. supra* note 8, para. 117.

85. See VCDR, *op. cit. supra* note 9, Art. 22 (2); Convention on the Law of the Sea, *op. cit. supra* note 9, Arts. 58, 62, 94, 139, 192 and 194; Convention on Biological Diversity, *op. cit. supra* note 9, Art. 3; Convention on the Law of the Non-Navigational Uses of International Watercourses, *op. cit. supra* note 9, Arts. 7 (1), 21 (2) and 22; International Health Regulations (2005), *op. cit. supra* note 9, Arts. 5, 13, 24, 32 and 34; Arms Trade Treaty, *op. cit. supra* note 9, Art. 6 (3); Istanbul Convention, *op. cit. supra* note 9, Art. 5 (2).

86. See e.g. Secretary-General of the United Nations, Human Rights Due Diligence Policy on United Nations Support to non-United Nations Security Forces, Annex to the identical letters dated 25 February 2013 addressed to the President of the General Assembly and to the President of the Security Council, 5 March 2013, UN Doc. A/67/775-S/2013/110, Principle 2. See on this issue, N. D. White, "Due Diligence, the UN and Peacekeeping", in A. Peters, H. Krieger and L. Kreuzer (eds.), *Due Diligence in International Law*, Oxford, Oxford University Press, 2020, pp. 217-233.

87. See e.g. Directive 2004/35/CE of the European Parliament and of the Council of 21 April 2004 on Environmental Liability with regard to the Prevention and Remedying of Environmental Damage, OJ L 143 of 30 April 2004, pp. 56-75; Treaty on the Functioning of the European Union, OJ C 326 of 26 October 2012, pp. 1-390 (TFEU), Art. 191 (2).

88. See e.g. Human Rights Council (HRC), Guiding Principles on Business and Human Rights: Implementing the United Nations "Protect, Respect and Remedy" Framework, 16 June 2011, UN Doc. HR/PUB/11/04 [online], Principles 4 and 17; ILA, Declaration of Legal Principles Relating to Climate Change, *op. cit. supra* note 11, Arts. 7A and 7B; ILC, Draft Articles on Prevention of Transboundary Harm from Hazardous Activities, with commentaries, *op. cit. supra* note 11, Arts. 1 and 3; ILC, Draft Articles on the Protection of Persons in the Event of Disasters, *op. cit. supra* note 11, Arts. 9 and 16; M. N. Schmitt and L. Vihul (eds.), *Tallinn Manual 2.0 on the International Law Applicable to Cyber Operations, Prepared by the International Groups of Experts at the Invitation of the NATO Cooperative Cyber Defence Centre of Excellence*, 2nd ed., Cambridge, Cambridge University Press, 2017, Rules 6 and 7; Report of the Group of Governmental Experts on Developments in the Field of Information and Telecommunications in the Context of International Security, 22 July

The multiplication of special regimes providing for obligations known as due diligence obligations is one of the distinctive features of the evolution of due diligence in international law during the second half of the twentieth century. This development has two main causes which are also, subsequently, its two main consequences. The first is the extension of the personal scope of duty-bearers to other public institutions, that is, to IOs. The second is the extension of the material and geographic scope of due diligence to encompass (risks of) harms without a transboundary dimension, either because these harms occur entirely within the same territory, such as with international human rights law, or because these harms occur outside of national territories, on common spaces, such as with the international law of the sea or, more generally, international environmental law.

Having reached the contemporary stage of the genealogy of due diligence, we may legitimately wonder about the expansion of due diligence in the future. One possibility indeed is the extension of its personal scope to private persons and in particular to corporate or collective entities, such as MNCs or NGOs. This would imply that the two fields of due diligence in Roman law would finally come together: that of *jus civile* and that of *jus gentium*. But this convergence has not yet happened. It is due, among other reasons, to the absence of true obligations owed by private persons (physical or corporate) under private international law and consequently to the absence of international responsibility in case of breach of these obligations. This issue will be addressed in Chapter IV, in relation to the question of States' due diligence in case of human rights violations caused by MNCs and to what is known as "human rights due diligence" in the context of the self-regulation and soft law norms applicable to these same MNCs.

The only exception to the absence of due diligence obligations and/or responsibility for the negligent conduct of private persons in international law can be found in international criminal law, which provides that superiors can be held criminally responsible when their subordinates commit international crimes ("command responsibility"). The normative structure of command responsibility includes a due diligence standard with regard to the persons placed under the control

2015, UN Doc. A/70/173 (Cybersecurity Report), paras. 13 (c) and 28 (a) and (b); ILC, Draft Principles on the Protection of the Environment in Relation to Armed Conflict, *op. cit. supra* note 11, Principle 22.

of the superior [89]. This type of international criminal responsibility allows for commanders (military or military-equivalent) to be held responsible for the crimes committed by their subordinates provided that, on the one hand, the commander knew or should have known that his or her subordinate would commit a crime and, on the other, he or she did not take all necessary and reasonable measures in his or her power to prevent the crime's commission [90]. A full-fledged examination of command responsibility, however, would go beyond the scope of this course.

In conclusion, the genealogy of due diligence in international law draws attention to the remarkable continuity (despite some small variations at each period in time) of the question of what is owed by an instituted collective or "public" for the harm caused by its members even when they are not acting on its behalf. This observation calls for humility in front of our predecessors' ingenuity and for a reappraisal of the apparent novelty of the issue of due diligence in international law.

Another insight from this brief historical inquiry is that although due diligence has existed for a long time in international law, it never ceased to transform itself, be it with regard to the nature of the harm or the identity of the duty-bearers, authors or beneficiaries. This evolutionary dimension must be kept in mind during the analysis of the general regime of due diligence in international law, especially when considering its ability to adapt to new (risks of) harms in the future. In fact, and this is the third and final insight of our genealogy, the growing hybridity of solutions identified over time counsels for great caution when it comes to analogies or to the identification of "ready to use" due diligence regimes. Each transposition requires a fresh adaptation of the due diligence regime.

B. The "renaissance" of due diligence in international law

As indicated in the introduction, there is a perceptible resurgence in references to due diligence in the recent practice of international law.

This revival of due diligence may be attributed, to start with, to an increase in the risks of harms, to the diversification of both the sources of these harms and the entities causing them and to the addition of new

89. See G. Palmisano, *op. cit. supra* note 72; Y. Dinstein, *op. cit. supra* note 16.
90. See G. Mettraux, *op. cit. supra* note 16.

institutional duty-bearers capable of anticipating or preventing such harms.

It is therefore not surprising that the number of international legal regimes which provide for due diligence obligations has increased in recent years, as exemplified in international environmental law, international human rights law, international criminal law, international humanitarian law, the international law of the sea and international investment law. A renewal of the sources providing for due diligence obligations is also observable in all these regimes (particularly since the 1990s) and, after that (particularly since the 2000s), also in the international case law pertaining to these regimes [91]. In addition to the original source of due diligence in custom and general principles, one should mention the multiplication of conventional sources [92] and of the unilateral acts of IOs [93]. The increase in the number of references to due diligence within soft law [94] is also noticeable. The latter may be attributed not only to the need to somehow ground obligations of IOs and private entities, but also to the general crisis of multilateral treaties and the need to ground States' obligations differently [95].

This revival in the practice of due diligence since the 1990s has gone hand in hand with a renewal of academic interest in the topic [96]. It is

91. See ICJ, The case of *Pulp Mills on the River Uruguay*, *op. cit. supra* note 3, para. 101; ICJ, The case of *Certain Activities carried out by Nicaragua in the Border Area*, *op. cit. supra* note 3, para. 104; PCA, *Indus Waters Kishenganga* Arbitration, *op. cit. supra* note 8, paras. 449-450; PCA, *South China Sea* Arbitration, *op. cit. supra* note 8, para. 117.

92. See VCDR, *op. cit. supra* note 9, Art. 22 (2); Convention on the Law of the Sea, *op. cit. supra* note 9, Arts. 58, 62, 94, 139, 192 and 194; Convention on Biological Diversity, *op. cit. supra* note 9, Art. 3; Convention on the Law of the Non-Navigational Uses of International Watercourses, *op. cit. supra* note 9, Arts. 7 (1), 21 (2) and 22; International Health Regulations (2005), *op. cit. supra* note 9, Arts. 5, 13, 24, 32 and 34; Arms Trade Treaty, *op. cit. supra* note 9, Art. 6 (3); Istanbul Convention, *op. cit. supra* note 9, Art. 5 (2).

93. See e.g. Secretary-General of the United Nations, Human Rights Due Diligence Policy, *op. cit. supra* note 86, Principle 2; Directive 2004/35/CE, *op. cit. supra* note 87; TFEU, *op. cit. supra* note 87, Art. 191(2).

94. See e.g. HRC, Guiding Principles on Business and Human Rights, *op. cit. supra* note 88, Principles 4 and 17; ILA, Declaration of Legal Principles Relating to Climate Change, *op. cit. supra* note 11, Arts. 7A and 7B; ILC, Draft Articles on Prevention of Transboundary Harm from Hazardous Activities, with commentaries, *op. cit. supra* note 11, Arts. 1 and 3; ILC, Draft Articles on the Protection of Persons in the Event of Disasters, *op. cit. supra* note 11, Arts. 9 and 16; *Tallinn Manual 2.0*, *op. cit. supra* note 88, Rules 6 and 7; Cybersecurity Report, *op. cit. supra* note 88, paras. 13 (c) and 28 (a) and (b); ILC, Draft Principles on the Protection of the Environment in Relation to Armed Conflict, *op. cit. supra* note 11, Principle 22.

95. See J. Brunnée, 2020, *op. cit. supra* note 14.

96. See on the due diligence of international law in general: P. A. Zannas, *op. cit. supra* note 6; H. Blomeyer-Bartenstein, *op. cit. supra* note 5; R. Pisillo Mazzeschi,

the case as much for the issue of due diligence in specific regimes, like international environmental law or international human rights law, as for the standard of due diligence in general.

More than a mere reaction to the development of the practice of due diligence since the 1990s, this renewed interest can also be explained by the fact that earlier publications on due diligence tended to focus on its negative dimension, that is, negligence, and therefore on the issue of fault in the law of international responsibility [97]. As highlighted earlier, one of the consequences of the work of the ILC on the codification of the law of international responsibility has been to shift the issue of due diligence and its violation back to the realm of the so-called primary obligations of international law. By removing due diligence from the realm of international responsibility law, the ILC has not only sparked renewed doctrinal interest in the theory of obligations in international law [98], but has also initiated a process of redefinition of the positive norm of due diligence by international commentators [99].

As a matter of fact, a similar development is observable in national and comparative law, where the number of publications addressing the questions of the due diligence standard, the duty of care or the issue of negligence in the fields of civil [100] and public liability [101] is also on the rise.

1989, *op. cit. supra* note 6; R. Pisillo Mazzeschi, 1992, *op. cit. supra* note 5; T. Koivurova, 2003, *op. cit. supra* note 5; J. A. Hessbruegge, *op. cit. supra* note 5; R. P. J. Barnidge, 2006, *op. cit. supra* note 5; J. F. L. Contreras, *op. cit. supra* note 6; R. Pisillo Mazzeschi, 2008, *op. cit. supra* note 6; A. Ouedraogo, 2011, *op. cit. supra* note 12; A. Ouedraogo, 2012, *op. cit. supra* note 12; T. Koivurova, 2010, *op. cit. supra* note 5; ILA, Study Group on Due Diligence in International Law, First and Second Rapports, *op. cit. supra* note 5; J. Kulesza, *op. cit. supra* note 5; SFDI (ed.), 2018, *op. cit. supra* note 6; P. d'Argent and A. de Vaucleroy, *op. cit. supra* note 33; Y. Kerbrat, "Le standard de due diligence, catalyseur d'obligations conventionnelles et coutumières pour les États", in SFDI (ed.), *Le standard de* due diligence *et la responsabilité internationale: Journée d'études franco-italienne du Mans*, Paris, Pedone, 2018, pp. 27-38; R. Pisillo Mazzeschi, 2018, *op. cit. supra* note 23; A. Peters, H. Krieger and L. Kreuzer (eds.), *op. cit. supra* note 5; A. Ollino, *op. cit. supra* note 5.

97. See e.g. P. A. Zannas, *op. cit. supra* note 6. See R. Pisillo Mazzeschi, 2018, *op. cit. supra* note 23, pp. 323-324 and 326. The ICJ's case law, however, has always referred to "diligence" rather than to undue or wrongful "negligence".

98. See e.g. P. d'Argent, "Les obligations internationales", *Recueil des cours*, Vol. 417 (2021), pp. 27-210.

99. See R. Pisillo Mazzeschi, 2018, *op. cit. supra* note 23, p. 337.

100. See e.g. J. Raz, 2010, *op. cit. supra* note 6; S. Shiffrin, 2017, *op. cit. supra* note 6; S. Perry, 2009, *op. cit. supra* note 6; J. Gardner, 2018, *op. cit. supra* note 6; D. Nolan, "Negligence", 2013, *op. cit. supra* note 4.

101. See e.g. the different contributions in A. Antoine and T. Olson, *op. cit. supra* note 6.

This evolution calls for a reflection upon the reasons or the causes of what Jutta Brunnée and Tamar Meshel have called the "renaissance" [102] of due diligence in the practice and theory of contemporary international law. Such a reflection is necessary if only to provide a better answer to Riccardo Pisillo Mazzeschi's warning against the "overrating" of due diligence [103] or to meet Menno Kamminga's critique of the due diligence "mania" in international human rights law [104].

We have already mentioned the explanations underlying the crisis of certain sources of international law (in particular multilateral treaties) in areas where the customary standard of due diligence offers interesting resources, such as international environmental law or the developing international law on cybersecurity. One should also highlight the limitations inherent to international treaty law or custom as regards due diligence obligations. Their personal scope is often limited to States (for example, in the case of custom), while IOs are now said to owe a large number of due diligence obligations whose sources need to be clarified in international law.

It is possible to identify at least five other more specific reasons for this "renaissance" of due diligence in international law. These five reasons are largely interrelated because they concern different aspects of the same ongoing evolution which started in antiquity with the responsibility of the instituted collectivity or group for the harm caused by its members. That evolution pertains to the duty-bearers of due diligence, its beneficiaries and the sources of (risks of) harms.

First, and from the point of view of the duty-bearers of due diligence, the fragmentation of the international institutional order is an important reason for the "renaissance" of due diligence.

As we all know, States are no longer the only institutions in international law. Others have appeared over time: whether public, such as IOs, or private, such as MNCs or NGOs. As the international institutional landscape is being redesigned, it is sometimes difficult to clearly identify the obligations and responsibilities of each of these non-State, State-like or even inter-State institutions. Due diligence is the standard *par excellence* of good institutional organisation [105]. One of

102. See J. Brunnée and T. Meshel, *op. cit. supra* note 28, in international environmental law.

103. R. Pisillo Mazzeschi, 2018, *op. cit. supra* note 23.

104. M. T. Kamminga, *op. cit. supra* note 15.

105. See J. Klabbers, "Reflections on Role Responsibility: The Responsibility of International Organizations for Failing to Act", *European Journal of International Law*, Vol. 28, No. 4 (2017), pp. 1133-1161; R. Kolb, 2016, *op. cit. supra* note 29; D. Lévy,

the distinctive features of its historical evolution is to have accompanied the development of public institutions in the West. At each step of that institutional evolution, due diligence has made it possible to hold those institutions accountable for their negligence. In the current state of the international institutional order, invoking due diligence to derive normative consequences concerning the care which can reasonably be expected from new and still largely disorganised institutions on the basis, for instance, of the expectations set forth in their mandates is proving attractive.

Invoking due diligence absolves in particular the need to precisely qualify the nature of the institution and authority relationships at stake every time. Applying the due diligence standard indeed elides the need to choose between, on the one hand, fitting those authority relations within the framework of State sovereignty and the exclusive jurisdiction of a State on its territory [106] and, on the other hand, substituting or, at least, supplementing this framework, thereby sidestepping all the consequences either of these scenarios would have for the future of the State in international law. This issue will be further discussed in the examination of the duty-bearers of due diligence in Chapter II.

A second reason for the revival of due diligence that pertains as much to the duty-bearers of due diligence as to the sources of the relevant (risk of) harms is the erosion of the public/private distinction.

Since its origins in Roman law, this distinction has been the cornerstone of Western law, of the modern State and hence of international law itself. Yet it is becoming increasingly difficult to maintain in practice. One of the consequences of its erosion is the difficulty to distinguish the official or *de jure* organs of States (or IOs) from the private agents who increasingly act in their place or even, in some cases, without or against them. The fading of the distinction complicates the attribution of the conduct of private persons for the purpose of the international responsibility of States or IOs. To be operative, this attribution must indeed rely on the existence of a clear division in national law between the public (*de jure* or *de facto* State organs) and the private (persons who are not organs of the State). Such a clear-cut division is all the

"La responsabilité pour omission et la responsabilité pour risque en droit international public", *Revue générale de droit international public*, Vol. 65 (1961), pp. 752-753; M. G. Cohn, "La théorie de la responsabilité internationale", *Recueil des cours*, Vol. 68 (1939), pp. 209-324.

106. The ARIO's, *op. cit. supra* note 24, lack of success in practice confirms this point: the ARIO have the benefit of being modelled after the ARSIWA, *op. cit. supra* note 24, but pay a price for it in terms of their practical reception.

more important given that the notion of "prerogatives" or even that of public "functions" which can be delegated are themselves no longer very clear. Worse, instead of defining private persons and private prerogatives by reference to public persons and public prerogatives, it is the reverse approach that has now increasingly taken hold [107].

Invoking a due diligence violation in such cases evades the issue of attribution. It allows to hold the State (or IO) responsible for its failure to prevent a harm that was reasonably foreseeable, even though the State (or IO) may not directly be held, through attribution, responsible for the wrongful act which caused the harm.

This legal construct is even more useful now that private persons (including MNCs or NGOs) hold important powers and may be at the origin of harms which they have very few obligations under international law to prevent and even less to remedy. It is precisely for this reason that due diligence is frequently invoked in international environmental law, international human rights law and international humanitarian law, where the actions and omissions of private persons are often the cause of breaches of international law [108]. This issue will be further discussed in Chapter II, together with the examination of the duty-bearers of due diligence, as well as in Chapter IV, in the section (B) devoted to due diligence in international human rights law.

Third (and again from the point of view of the sources of [risks of] harms), harm prevention and, more generally, the advent of the security or so-called vigilance society [109] also account for the current revival of due diligence.

If interest in due diligence has increased since the 1990s, it is also because of the nature of the obligations which it qualifies, notably the obligations of prevention and precaution. Along with the growing importance of security in society and the increasing concerns for controlling or even managing risk, such obligations have seen an unprecedented rise in the recent practice of international law. It is especially the case in international environmental law, the international law of the sea, international health law [110] and international human rights law, but also now in an emerging field of international law which

107. See S. Besson, "International Courts and the Jurisprudence of Statehood", *Transnational Legal Theory*, Vol. 9, Nos. 3-4 (2019), pp. 30-64.

108. See D. König, *op. cit. supra* note 18, in the international law of the sea.

109. See M. Delmas-Marty, *Résister, responsabiliser, anticiper*, Paris, Editions du Seuil, 2013.

110. See International Health Regulations (2005), *op. cit. supra* note 9, Arts. 5, 13, 24, 32 and 34. See e.g. A. Coco and T. de Souza Dias, "Prevent, Respond,

integrates different principles and obligations from other regimes: international disaster law [111].

These are precisely the fields in which due diligence is often – falsely, as we will see – considered to be a full-fledged "obligation" and even the obligation or the original principle from which other preventive or precautionary obligations or principles can be derived [112]. Chapter II will return to this issue and will address the questions of the nature and material scope of due diligence in international law.

Fourth (and still from the point of view of the sources of the harms concerned by due diligence), the diffuse nature of the sources of (risks of) harms on the international level is also part of the reasons of due diligence's renewed success.

Because these new threats can be secret (such as cybersecurity threats), complex (such as climate change) or simply collective, they are difficult to address with the usual tools of international responsibility, especially through the individualised attribution of conduct to one particular institution. Due diligence compensates for this hurdle, and this explains its revival even if it also comes with its own share of difficulties.

In fact, it is the notion of diligent sovereignty which could itself foster the development of a conception of the sovereignty of States as equal members of the international institutional order [113] that is both more

---

Cooperate: States' Due Diligence Duties vis-à-vis the Covid-19 Pandemic", *Journal of International Humanitarian Legal Studies*, Vol. 11, No. 2 (2020), pp. 218-236.

111. See in particular ILC, Draft Articles on the Protection of Persons in the Event of Disasters, *op. cit. supra* note 11, Arts. 9 and 16. See e.g. V. Popovski, "State Negligence before and after Natural Disasters as Human Rights Violations", in C. Hobson, P. Bacon and R. Cameron (eds.), *Human Security and Natural Disasters*, London, Routledge, 2014, pp. 94-110; G. Bartolini, "Disaster Risk Reduction: An International Law Perspective", *Questions of International Law, Zoom-in*, Vol. 48 (2018), pp. 1-6; F. Zorzi Giustiniani, "Something Old, Something New: Disaster Risk Reduction in International Law", *Questions of International Law, Zoom-in*, Vol. 49 (2018), pp. 7-27; M. Aronsson-Storrier, "Beyond Early Warning Systems: Querying the Relationship between International Law and Disaster Risk (Reduction)", *Yearbook of International Disaster Law*, Vol. 1 (2018), pp. 51-69; K. L. H. Samuel, M. Aronsson-Storrier and K. Nakjavani Bookmiller (eds.), *The Cambridge Handbook of Disaster Risk Reduction and International Law*, Cambridge, Cambridge University Press, 2019; G. Bartolini, "A Universal Treaty for Disasters? Remarks on the International Law Commission's Draft Articles on the Protection of Persons in the Event of Disasters", *International Review of the Red Cross*, Vol. 99 (2019), pp. 1103-1137.

112. See ICJ, The case of *Pulp Mills on the River Uruguay*, *op. cit. supra* note 3, para. 101; ICJ, The case of *Certain Activities carried out by Nicaragua in the Border Area*, *op. cit. supra* note 3, paras. 104 and 204.

113. See also S. Shiffrin, 2017, *op. cit. supra* note 6, on the relationship between negligence and equal respect in public and private interpersonal relations.

solidary [114] and respectful. After all, in the international jurisprudence of the first part of the twentieth century, due diligence obligations were already considered as the "corollaries" of the rights constitutive of States' sovereign equality in a world in which they coexist as equals [115]. The standard of due diligence qualifies the type of obligations and responsibilities most likely to handle risks that transcend bilateral and transboundary relations between States [116], especially when those risks make multilateral and institutional cooperation urgent [117]. We will return to this point in Chapter II, in the analysis of the nature and the foundation of due diligence in international law.

Fifth, and finally, the transformation of the link between duty-bearers and beneficiaries of due diligence is another cause of its current "renaissance".

Due diligence initially benefited foreign persons who were officially residing on a State's territory (investors, for the most part), as exemplified by the international law on the protection of aliens. However, owing to

---

114. See Dissenting opinion of Judge Weeramantry, in ICJ, *Legality of the Threat or Use of Nuclear Weapons*, *op. cit. supra* note 8, para. 283:

> "Another approach to the applicability of environmental law to the matter before the Court is through the principle of good neighbourliness, which is both impliedly and expressly written into the United Nations Charter. This principle is one of the bases of modern international law, which has seen the demise of the principle that sovereign States could pursue their own interests in splendid isolation from each other. A world order in which every sovereign State depends on the same global environment generates a mutual interdependence which can only be implemented by co-operation and good neighbourliness."

See also M. Delmas-Marty, *Sortir du pot au noir: l'humanisme juridique comme boussole*, Paris, Buchet-Chastel, 2019, on the need to move from "solitary" sovereignty to "solidary" sovereignty.

115. See *Island of Palmas* Arbitration, *op. cit. supra* note 8; ICJ, The case of the *Corfu Channel, op. cit. supra* note 8. On this strong link between the coexistence of sovereign States and their due diligence obligations since the nineteenth century, see also S. Heathcote, *op. cit. supra* note 26.

116. See e.g. ICJ, *Legality of the Threat or Use of Nuclear Weapons*, *op. cit. supra* note 8, para. 29: "areas beyond national control". See also Convention on the Law of the Sea, *op. cit. supra* note 9, Art. 192; Convention relating to the Limitation of the Liability of Owners of Inland Navigation Vessels of 1 March 1973, UNTS (CLN), Art. 7; Convention on Biological Diversity, *op. cit. supra* note 9, Art. 3; Preamble of the United Nations Framework Convention on Climate Change, UNTS, Vol. 1771, p. 107; Declaration of the United Nations Conference on the Human Environment of 5 to 16 June 1972, UN Doc. A/CONF.48/14/Rev.1 (Stockholm Declaration), Principles 21 and 22; Rio Declaration on Environment and Development from the United Nations Conference on Environment and Development of 3 to 14 June 1992, UN Doc. A/CONF.151/26/Rev.1 (Vol. I) (Rio Declaration), Principle 2.

117. See also J. E. Viñuales, "A Human Rights Approach to Extraterritorial Environmental Protection: An Assessment", in N. Bhuta (ed.), *The Frontiers of Human Rights*, Oxford, Oxford University Press, 2016, pp. 177-222.

international human rights law and international criminal law, the scope of beneficiaries was progressively extended to any person under the jurisdiction or the control of a State [118]. In recent years, due diligence has been invoked outside of the modern framework of the territorial sovereignty of the State and even outside of the normative relationship which binds the State to the beneficiary of due diligence. The latter no longer necessarily holds a correlative right to the due diligence obligation. Due diligence has come to be invoked for the benefit of any private person, as long as the State has some control over the source of the harm which threatens that person. For example, it has been invoked in international environmental law [119], as much with respect to harm to the "commons", which concerns the interests of all, as with respect to harm to private persons outside of the jurisdiction and control of the duty-bearing State. Early signs of a similar evolution are also perceptible in international cybersecurity law [120].

However, as Chapter IV will demonstrate, it is crucial to undertake this reinvention of due diligence through new obligations rather than by continuing to allow it to accrue by means of international human rights law obligations. As will become clear in that chapter, indeed, the invocation of due diligence and its conditions as grounds of human rights obligations ultimately risks undermining the condition for the application of international human rights law in the first place, that is, "jurisdiction" or effective control of the State on the human right-holder [121].

We will revert to the different causes of the renewed interest in due diligence in the theory and practice of international law at the end of this course in the form of a critical assessment of due diligence in

118. See M. Hakimi, *op. cit. supra* note 13; C. Chinkin, "A Critique of the Public/Private Dimension", *European Journal of International Law*, Vol. 10, No. 2 (1999), pp. 387-395.

119. See J. E. Viñuales, 2016, *op. cit. supra* note 117; A. E. Boyle, "Human Rights and the Environment: Where Next?", *European Journal of International Law*, Vol. 23, No. 3 (2012), p. 613-642.

120. See K. Bannelier-Christakis, 2017, *op. cit. supra* note 29; J. Brunnée and T. Meshel, *op. cit. supra* note 28.

121. See also S. Besson, "Due Diligence and Extraterritorial Human Rights Obligations: Mind the Gap!", *ESIL Reflections*, Vol. 9, No. 1 (2020) [online]. Contra: A. Berkes, "Extraterritorial Responsibility of the Home States for MNCs' Violations of Human Rights", in Y. Radi (ed.), *Research Handbook on Human Rights and Investment*, London, Edward Elgar, 2018, pp. 304-344; V. Tzevelekos, "Reconstructing the Effective Control Criterion in Extraterritorial Human Rights Breaches: Direct Attribution of Wrongfulness, Due Diligence, and Concurrent Responsibility", *Michigan Journal of International Law*, Vol. 36, No. 1 (2014), pp. 129-178; J. E. Viñuales, 2016, *op. cit. supra* note 117; A. E. Boyle, 2012, *op. cit. supra* note 119.

international law. This chapter has endeavoured to show that some of the attractive features that account for due diligence's resurgence also contain, in germ, some of its greatest potential weaknesses, including the risk of exaggeration or distortion of its content. The general conclusion of this course will also offer suggestions and recommendations in that respect.

CHAPTER II

THE GENERAL REGIME OF DUE DILIGENCE IN INTERNATIONAL LAW

> "101. The Court points out that the principle of prevention, as a customary rule, has its origins in the due diligence that is required of a State in its territory. It is 'every State's obligation not to allow knowingly its territory to be used for acts contrary to the rights of other States' (*Corfu Channel (United Kingdom* v. *Albania), Merits, Judgment, ICJ Reports 1949*, p. 22). A State is thus obliged to use all the means at its disposal in order to avoid activities which take place in its territory, or in any area under its jurisdiction, causing significant damage to the environment of another State. This Court has established that this obligation 'is now part of the corpus of international law relating to the environment' (*Legality of the Threat or Use of Nuclear Weapons, Advisory Opinion, ICJ Reports 1996 (I)*, p. 242, para. 29)."
>
> (ICJ, The case of *Pulp Mills on the River Uruguay [Argentina* v. *Uruguay]*, Judgment of 20 April 2010, *ICJ Reports 2010*, p. 14, para. 101)

Introduction

This second chapter outlines the general or common, and thus minimal, regime of due diligence in contemporary international law.

To recall the working definition set out in the introduction, due diligence in international law refers to

> "an (evaluative) standard of the conduct of States (and other public institutions of international law, such as international organisations [IOs]) (most often grafted onto an obligation of conduct [which is usually, but not always, a positive obligation to prevent, protect or remedy], but sometimes also considered, due to linguistic imprecision, as an obligation of conduct *per se*) which requires them to exercise care (also referred to as the 'standard of care' or 'duty of care') and thus also, conversely, to do no harm carelessly (also referred to as the 'no harm rule' or 'duty not to harm'), by adopting reasonable measures in order to protect the interests or rights of other States, IOs or national or foreign subjects against (risks of) (usually significant) harm caused by third parties (nationals or foreigners, other States or IOs, natural phenomena) situated on the territory, under the jurisdiction *stricto*

sensu or, at least, under the control of the duty-bearing State (or other public institution), and provided that the latter had foreseen or ought to have (reasonably) foreseen the (risks of) harm and had the (reasonable) capacity to intervene, and whose violation amounts to undue or wrongful negligence".

This chapter examines each of these elements in turn and provides an outline of: (A) due diligence's nature and foundation; (B) its sources and regimes; (C) its scope (personal, material, geographic and temporal); (D) its conditions; (E) its content; (F) its variability; and (G) its limits.

The chapter's presentation of the general regime of due diligence in international law amounts both to the presentation of a minimal regime common to the special regimes and to the presentation of a common normative structure whose variable aspects may then be specified within each special regime. The regime of due diligence analysed and systematised below has grown out of a comparison of the practice of due diligence in several special regimes of international law and, through this framework, out of the identification of common features (or, conversely, variables) which together constitute a general, minimal regime of due diligence in international law [122]. The general and common regime of due diligence presented is only minimal. Chapter IV will turn to some of due diligence's variations in various special regimes, that is, international environmental law, international cybersecurity law and international human rights law.

As highlighted in Chapter I, because of the strong connection between due diligence and judicial reasoning, it is primarily through the study of international jurisprudence that the identification of the minimal general regime of due diligence can take place. Of course, the caveat issued by the ICJ in the *Genocide* case should be kept in mind. In that judgment, the Court refuses to establish a "general jurisprudence" relative to due diligence obligations of prevention or even to identify a general obligation in that field [123]. However, the Court admits to having recourse to "the rules of law whose scope extends beyond the specific

---

122. Pro: ILA, Study Group on Due Diligence in International Law, First and Second Rapports, *op. cit. supra* note 5; A. Ouedraogo, 2011, *op. cit. supra* note 12; P. d'Argent and A. de Vaucleroy, *op. cit. supra* note 33. Contra: R. Pisillo Mazzeschi, 2018, *op. cit. supra* note 23.

123. See ICJ, The case of *Application of the Convention on the Prevention and Punishment of the Crime of Genocide*, *op. cit. supra* note 22, para. 429. This was confirmed in ICJ, The case of *Armed Activities on the Territory of the Congo (Democratic Republic of the Congo* v. *Uganda)*, Judgment of 9 February 2022, *ICJ Reports 2022*, not yet published, para. 96.

field" at issue in the case and that such rules exist. To the extent that its jurisprudence also participates in the development of those rules, so does the present chapter's attempt at identifying a minimal general regime of due diligence.

A successful systematisation of due diligence's minimal general regime should build upon the identification of a truly common international law [124], that is, one which is sufficiently universal. For that we would need a full-fledged study of comparative international law on the topic of due diligence [125] that would examine the national practice of international law's due diligence in each State [126]. However, none of the studies consulted for this course's preparation provides such a comparison of due diligence (in national law [127] and/or international

124. On the importance of a common international law, see M. Delmas-Marty, *Pour un droit commun*, Paris, Editions du Seuil, 1994.

125. On the importance of comparative international law, see R. Urueña, "Law-Making Through Comparative International Law?", in R. Livoja and J. Petman (eds.), *International Law-Making: Essays in Honour of Jan Klabbers*, London, Routledge, 2014, pp. 149-68; S. Besson, "Comparative Law and Human Rights", in M. Reimann and R. Zimmermann, (eds.), *Oxford Handbook of Comparative Law*, 2nd ed., Oxford, Oxford University Press, 2019, pp. 1222-1249.

126. See also on the development of a customary international law of due diligence obligations, Separate opinion of Judge Donoghue, in ICJ, The case of *Certain Activities carried out by Nicaragua in the Border Area*, *op. cit. supra* note 3, para. 13.

127. For a first comparative project, see the "world tour" of the concept of public liability and responsibility in the edited volume by S. Besson (ed.), *Theories of International Responsibility Law*, Cambridge, Cambridge University Press, 2022. On this specific point, studies of private international law on due diligence are more advanced and already resort to comparative law on *private* liability, including due diligence therein: see e.g. M.-A. Renold, "The International Scope of Application of the Swiss Rules on the Due Diligence of Dealers in Cultural Property", in K. Boele-Woelki, T. Einhorn, D. Girsberger and S. Symeonides (eds.), *Convergence and Divergence in Private International Law: Liber Amicorum Kurt Siehr*, Zurich, Schulthess, 2010, pp. 847-856. It is also important to underline the projects of codification of a private law common to all EU Member States, including civil liability, and especially Art. VI: C-302 from C. von Bar, E. Clive and H. Schulte-Nölke (eds.), *Draft Common Frame of Reference, Prepared by the Study Group on a European Civil Code and the European Research Group on Existing EC Private Law (Acquis Group) Based in part on a revised version of the Principles of European Contract Law*, Munich, Sellier, 2009 [online], which incorporates the "reasonable standard of care" under the general heading "negligence". See also C. von Bar, *The Common European Law of Torts*, Vol. 2, Oxford, Oxford University Press, 2000; C. van Dam, *European Tort Law*, 2nd ed., Oxford, Oxford University Press, 2013; J. M. Smits, *The Good Samaritan in European Private Law: On the Perils of Principles Without a Programme and a Programme for the Future*, Deventer, Kluwer, 2000; J. Kortmann, *Altruism in Private Law: Liability for Nonfeasance and Negotiorum Gestio*, Oxford, Oxford University Press, 2005. The comparative law of domestic public liability (of States in particular) is also starting to develop: see e.g. D. Fairgrieve, M. Andenas and J. Bell (eds.), *Tort Liability of Public Authorities in Comparative Perspective*, London, British Institute of International and Comparative Law, 2002; D. Fairgrieve, *State Liability in Tort: A Comparative Law Study*, Oxford, Oxford University Press, 2003; K. Oliphant, "The Liability of Public Authorities in Comparative Perspective", in K. Oliphant (ed.), *The*

law) in its reception within different national legal orders, particularly outside of European or even Western [128] legal traditions. Such studies will have to be undertaken in the future, especially if due diligence is called to play an even more important role in international law: the universality of the general principles of international law is essential to their legitimate authority and as such to their respect.

A. The nature and foundation of due diligence

The nature or, more precisely, the normative structure of due diligence remains vague in the contemporary practice of international law, even in the context of its doctrinal systematisation. It is interchangeably addressed as *(i)* a principle; *(ii)* a standard (or a norm); or *(iii)* a duty (or an obligation) [129] of conduct.

With regard to the first categorisation, one should first underscore that the distinction between a "rule" [130] and a "principle", which is pivotal in legal theory, has not been fully received in international law. The two terms are not generally distinguished and rigorously used. In fact, nothing in the reference to due diligence as a "principle" [131] is incompatible with the two other types of categorisation. On the contrary, referring to due diligence as a "principle" adds to the other categorisations by highlighting different features related to its sources and its regime in international law.

Liability of Public Authorities in Comparative Perspective, Cambridge, Intersentia, 2016, pp. 847-887; A. Antoine and T. Olson, *op. cit. supra* note 6.

128. In that respect, and as I have argued elsewhere concerning human rights (S. Besson, "The Influence of the Two Covenants on States Parties across Regions: Lessons for the Role of Comparative Law and Regions in International Human Rights Law", in D. Moeckli, H. Keller and C. Heri (eds.), *The Human Rights Covenants at 50: Their Past, Present and Future*, Oxford, Oxford University Press, 2018, pp. 243-276), it is important to underline the intermediary role played by regional tribunals and quasi-judicial bodies in the identification of minimal transnational standards on a regional scale. These bodies are well-positioned to compare, and then consolidate, a potential transnational consensus, before comparing it again with what other regional tribunals have been able to identify. See S. Besson, "Comparative Law and Human Rights", 2019, *op. cit. supra* note 125.

129. The terms "duty" and "obligation" are used interchangeably in this course.

130. See, however, *British Property in Spanish Morocco* Arbitration, *op. cit. supra* note 8; ICJ, The case of *Pulp Mills on the River Uruguay*, *op. cit. supra* note 3, para. 101, referring to a "rule" of due diligence. See also ICJ, The case of *Pulp Mills on the River Uruguay, op. cit. supra* note 3, for an example of confusion between "rule" and "principle".

131. See e.g. *Trail Smelter* Arbitration, *op. cit. supra* note 8, para. 716; ICJ, The case of the *Corfu Channel*, *op. cit. supra* note 8, p. 22.

More precisely, the reference to due diligence as a "principle" of international law preserves the ambivalence [132] between a type of norm and its source [133]. On the one hand, *qua* type of norm, the term "principle" refers to a general norm or rule of international law [134]. This corresponds to the idea, which we will examine in the next section, of a general principle of due diligence: the existence of a minimal regime common to all special regimes of international law. The reference to the "principle" of due diligence *qua* source, on the other hand, will be addressed in the context of the study of the sources of due diligence in international law. At this stage, it suffices to refer to the historical study of due diligence in Chapter I. What the standard's jurisprudential history confirms indeed is that due diligence is both a general principle of law and a general principle of international law *stricto sensu*. However, maintaining a certain ambivalence about which category of general principles due diligence belongs to preserves international courts' leeway. They have indeed frequently used references to general principles as a way to avoid pronouncing on the customary nature of those principles and to sidestep a clear test of customary law [135]. As we will see, this results in a deliberate blurring of the line between a "principle" of due diligence and a customary "obligation" in that context [136].

As for the second and third normative categorisations of due diligence, the question which should be addressed is whether due diligence is a

132. See S. Besson, "General Principles in International Law: Whose Principles?", in S. Besson and P. Pichonnaz (eds.), *Les principes en droit européen / Principles in European Law* (Travaux de l'Ecole doctorale romande sur les fondements du droit européen 2010), Zurich, Schulthess, 2011, pp. 19-64.

133. Contra: R. Pisillo Mazzeschi, 2018, *op. cit. supra* note 23, pp. 334-335, who considers that a reference to "general principles" in this context necessarily implies a judgment on the sources of due diligence.

134. On these "general rules of international law", see ICJ, *Interpretation of the Agreement of the 25 March 1951 between the WHO and Egypt*, Advisory Opinion of 20 December 1980, *ICJ Reports 1980*, p. 73. On the three possible meanings of "general international law" (relating to *(i)* the source *(ii)* the personal scope or *(iii)* the content of this law), see S. Besson, "The Sources of International Human Rights Law: How General is General International Law?", in S. Besson and J. d'Aspremont (eds.), *Oxford Handbook on the Sources of International Law*, Oxford, Oxford University Press, 2017, pp. 837-870.

135. See P. d'Argent, "Les principes généraux à la Cour internationale de Justice", in S. Besson and P. Pichonnaz (eds.), *Les principes en droit européen / Principles in European Law*, Zurich, Schulthess, 2011, pp. 107-120.

136. See e.g. ICJ, The case of *Pulp Mills on the River Uruguay*, *op. cit. supra* note 3, para. 101. See also Judge Dugard's critique, in ICJ, The case of *Certain Activities carried out by Nicaragua in the Border Area*, *op. cit. supra* note 3, para. 7, especially with regard to the "principles" of prevention, precaution and cooperation.

"standard" [137] of conduct (of prevention, protection or reparation) which qualifies, is grafted onto [138] or embedded in [139] an obligation [140] or, on the contrary, whether due diligence should be considered as an "obligation" [141] of conduct in itself.

As others have convincingly explained, the reference to an "obligation" or "duty" [142] of due diligence is a linguistic shorthand or even a linguistic misnomer [143]. Due diligence is a standard or a norm of conduct grafted onto an obligation which it qualifies and with which it may of course be associated, but it should not be conflated with that obligation.

The same ambivalence between a standard and an obligation of due diligence is actually observable in Anglo-American tort law. In that context, the due diligence standard is often misnamed "duty of care" or "duty not to harm carelessly". However, here again, due diligence does not amount to a true obligation, but to a standard ("standard of care" or even "standard of negligence" [144]) which qualifies an obligation of protection or, at least, the protection of interests worthy of protection [145]. How otherwise are we to restrict the scope of such an obligation? It certainly cannot be understood as a general obligation not to harm anyone at any time. It must be possible to identify the rights and interests which are to be protected and whose identification may then give rise to an obligation not to harm by negligence [146].

137. See e.g. *British Property in Spanish Morocco* Arbitration, *op. cit. supra* note 8; ICSID, *AAPL* Arbitration, *op. cit. supra* note 8, paras. 609-610; ICJ, The case of *The Gabcikovo-Nagymaros Project*, *op. cit. supra* note 8, para. 140; ITLOS, *Responsibilities and Obligations of States Sponsoring Persons and Entities with Respect to Activities in the Area*, *op. cit. supra* note 41, para. 117; PCA, *South China Sea* Arbitration, *op. cit. supra* note 8, para. 117.

138. For the term "grafted", see R. Kolb, 2016, *op. cit. supra* note 29.

139. For the term "embedded", see S. Perry, 2009, *op. cit. supra* note 6.

140. See e.g. Separate opinion of Judge Dugard, in ICJ, The case of *Certain Activities carried out by Nicaragua in the Border Area*, *op. cit. supra* note 3, paras. 7-9.

141. See e.g. ICJ, The case of *Pulp Mills on the River Uruguay*, *op. cit. supra* note 3, para. 101; ICJ, The case of *Certain Activities carried out by Nicaragua in the Border Area*, *op. cit. supra* note 3, paras. 104 and 204.

142. See e.g. Separate opinion of Judge Dugard, in ICJ, The case of *Certain Activities carried out by Nicaragua in the Border Area*, *op. cit. supra* note 3, paras. 6-7; Separate opinion of Judge Donoghue, in ICJ, The case of *Certain Activities carried out by Nicaragua in the Border Area*, *op. cit. supra* note 3, para. 9. See also ILC, Draft Principles on the Protection of the Environment in Relation to Armed Conflict, *op. cit. supra* note 11, Principle 22. See still ICJ, The case of *Armed Activities on the Territory of the Congo*, 2005, *op. cit. supra* note 3, para. 247 ("duty of vigilance").

143. See P. d'Argent and A. de Vaucleroy, *op. cit. supra* note 33; R. Pisillo Mazzeschi, 2018, *op. cit. supra* note 23.

144. On this term, see J. Raz, 2010, *op. cit. supra* note 6.

145. See e.g. S. Perry, 2009, *op. cit. supra* note 6; D. Nolan, "Negligence", 2013, *op. cit. supra* note 4.

146. See e.g. D. Nolan, "Negligence", 2013, *op. cit. supra* note 4.

When one reads the phrases "obligation of due diligence" or "duty of diligence" in international law, one should therefore understand them to be expressing "obligation of (x with) due diligence" and not just "obligation of due diligence" independently of the rights and interests protected that ground that obligation. Without a specific obligation of x on which the due diligence standard may be grafted, the due diligence obligation is not yet a true obligation and is only named as such. For our analytical purposes, it is important to keep the distinction in mind when the term "due diligence obligation" is used [147]. Given that the normative consequences of the due diligence standard can only be apprehended through the obligation which it qualifies, however, it is easy to understand why it is most commonly referred to in terms of that obligation.

International jurisprudence suffers from that same terminological ambivalence [148]. This actually explains why the earliest international decisions on the matter refer to due diligence as an "obligation not to harm (by negligence)" the rights and interests of other States (including their people) as identified by international law [149]. As the ICJ explained in the *Corfu Channel* case [150], that obligation is even constitutive of State sovereignty: it is the normative counterpart or "corollary" [151] of the sovereign rights of the State.

What the distinction between the standard and the obligation of due diligence implies then is that international law (both general and

147. While, in some special regimes of international law, obligations of x with due diligence are simply referred to as due diligence obligations (see e.g. international investment law or international environmental law), other regimes directly refer solely to the obligations of conduct or obligations of means and hint separately (or not at all) at the due diligence standard (e.g. in international human rights law, where positive obligations do not necessarily mention due diligence).

148. See e.g. Separate opinion of Judge Dugard, in ICJ, The case of *Certain Activities carried out by Nicaragua in the Border Area, op. cit. supra* note 3, para. 9; Separate opinion of Judge Donoghue, in ICJ, The case of *Certain Activities carried out by Nicaragua in the Border Area, op. cit. supra* note 3, para. 10; ITLOS, *Responsibilities and Obligations of States Sponsoring Persons and Entities with Respect to Activities in the Area, op. cit. supra* note 41, para. 131; ITLOS, *Request for an Advisory Opinion submitted by the Sub-Regional Fisheries Commission*, Advisory Opinion of 2 April 2015, *ITLOS Reports 2015*, p. 4, para. 129. See for the same opinion, P. d'Argent and A. de Vaucleroy, *op. cit. supra* note 33, p. 258.

149. See e.g. *Trail Smelter* Arbitration, *op. cit. supra* note 8, para. 716; ICJ, The case of the *Corfu Channel, op. cit. supra* note 8, p. 22; ICJ, *Legality of the Threat or Use of Nuclear Weapons, op. cit. supra* note 8, paras. 241-242.

150. See ICJ, The case of the *Corfu Channel, op. cit. supra* note 8, p. 22. See also Separate opinion of Judge Donoghue, in ICJ, The case of *Certain Activities carried out by Nicaragua in the Border Area, op. cit. supra* note 3, para. 8.

151. See *Island of Palmas* Arbitration, *op. cit. supra* note 8, p. 839.

special) should, in each case, first specify the rights and interests of other States and consequently what must be diligently protected so as not to result in undue or wrongful negligence [152].

According to the international case law, those rights include the right to territorial integrity [153] or the right to protect its nationals [154], which are constitutive of State sovereignty in general international law [155]. More recently, the right to the preservation of marine fauna and flora and, more generally, human rights have joined that list. As a result, it is now possible to consider that a general obligation not to harm (by negligence; also referred to as the "no harm rule" or "duty not to harm") also exists in international human rights law and in international environmental law, including an obligation to prevent harm to the environment in a diligent fashion [156].

In addition to rights, mere "interests" can also be identified and protected by international law, without (yet) necessarily constituting proper "rights" of States [157] or individuals [158] or even (conventional or customary) "obligations" under international law [159]. Indeed, negligence

152. See P. d'Argent and A. de Vaucleroy, *op. cit. supra* note 33, p. 255.

153. See e.g. *Island of Palmas* Arbitration, *op. cit. supra* note 8, p. 839; *Trail Smelter* Arbitration, *op. cit. supra* note 8, para. 716.

154. See e.g. *British Property in Spanish Morocco* Arbitration, *op. cit. supra* note 8; *Island of Palmas* Arbitration, *op. cit. supra* note 8, p. 839.

155. It is not because sovereignty is both a source of rights protected by due diligence and a source of due diligence obligations that due diligence is a standard based on reciprocity (of sovereignty). Nor can it be inferred that this standard solely applies between (sovereign) States.

156. See J. Brunnée, 2010, *op. cit. supra* note 14; J. Brunnée, 2020, *op. cit. supra* note 14.

157. An interest protected by international law may ground an obligation, but that obligation may not necessarily correspond to a right of the holder of the interest and beneficiary of the protection afforded by the obligation. This does not, of course, preclude the State's responsibility for the breach of this obligation from becoming a source of individual rights: see J. Gardner, "Relations of Responsibility", in R. Cruft, M. H. Kramer and M. R. Reiff (eds.), *Crime, Punishment, and Responsibility: The Jurisprudence of Antony Duff*, Oxford, Oxford University Press, 2011, pp. 87-102; S. Perry, "Torts, Rights, and Risk", in J. Oberdiek (ed.), *Philosophical Foundations of the Law of Torts*, Oxford, Oxford University Press, 2014, pp. 38-64 (Contra: J. Oberdiek, "The Moral Significance of Risking", *Legal Theory*, Vol. 18 (2012), pp. 339-356).

158. On the contribution of international human rights law and, more broadly, of individual rights to the development of State liability in comparative domestic law, see A. Antoine and T. Olson, *op. cit. supra* note 6, p. 17; H. Belrhali, "La responsabilité de la puissance publique en droit comparé. Conclusion", in A. Antoine and T. Olson (eds.), *La responsabilité de la puissance publique en droit comparé*, Paris, Société de législation comparée, 2016, p. 545. This development has had drawbacks in both domestic and international responsibility law, such as identifying State responsibility, including for negligence, too closely with the violation of individual rights.

159. See ICJ, The case of the *Corfu Channel*, *op. cit. supra* note 8, p. 22; Dissenting opinion of Judge Weeramantry, in ICJ, *Legality of the Threat or Use of Nuclear Weapons op. cit. supra* note 8, p. 496. See also D. Lévy, *op. cit. supra* note 105, pp. 752-753.

is not simply the negative articulation of positive obligations of conduct [160]: as we will see, not only are obligations of (x with) due diligence not always positive obligations, but they do not necessarily pre-exist as "obligations" whose content should be identified as such before their violation [161]. As we observed in Chapter I, it is precisely in that respect that due diligence obligations do not entirely fit within the category of primary obligations of international law [162]. Chapter III, dedicated to due diligence in international responsibility law, will re-examine this thorny question.

Another point worthy of emphasis is that qualifying due diligence as a "standard" as opposed to a full-fledged "obligation" is without prejudice to the quality of its legal normativity. It does not imply, in particular, that it is a legal norm of lesser quality, let alone a non-legal norm or soft law. Standards exist in (hard) law as well, and their degree of normativity may be completely ordinary or sometimes even very high. To quote Jean Salmon, a legal standard is a "[n]orm of a high level of abstraction and generality, whose content must be concretised for its application, but whose legality is not contested" [163]. The distinctiveness of "standards" by comparison with other legal norms is their flexibility. They are norms or measures of average or literally "normal" conduct

160. See J. Klabbers, 2017, *op. cit. supra* note 105. This is what P. d'Argent and A. de Vaucleroy, *op. cit. supra* note 33, p. 260, underestimate by hastily associating the content of an obligation of due diligence with that of a wrongful omission (see p. 264) (see also R. Kolb, 2016, *op. cit. supra* note 29; T. Koivurova, 2010, *op. cit. supra* note 5, for a similar position). At times, indeed, it is the determination of a wrongful omission's content by the international judge that enables us to recover the content of a due diligence obligation *ex post*, while establishing the international responsibility of the duty-bearer.

161. For a similar discussion on the determination *a posteriori* of the content of positive obligations in international human rights law, see e.g. R. Pisillo Mazzeschi, 2008, *op. cit. supra* note 6.

162. The same is true in Anglo-American tort law: see S. Shiffrin, 2017, *op. cit. supra* note 6; J. Raz, 2010, *op. cit. supra* note 6. In fact, the same distinction can be found within civil liability regimes that are more continental, in particular in Switzerland or Germany, where the element of fault (as well as negligence) has partly been replaced by an element of unlawfulness. This structure is clearly apparent in the public liability regimes of those two legal orders: the State's fault (and negligence) is replaced either *(i)* by an "objective" duty of diligence in the form of rules of conduct (referred to as "unlawfulness by conduct"); or *(ii)* by reference to fundamental rights and interests protected by the legal order to which it is forbidden to cause harm intentionally or negligently (curiously referred to as "unlawfulness by result") (see e.g. A.-C. Favre, "La responsabilité des autorités lors de la prévention des dangers naturels", *ASPAN, Territoire et environnement*, Vol. 6 (2007), pp. 1-19; A.-C. Favre, 2012, *op. cit. supra* note 62).

163. J. Salmon, *Dictionnaire de droit international public*, Brussels, Bruylant, 2001, p. 1049.

which should be followed and against which a given conduct should be assessed [164].

That being said, there is a trend of "hard law softening" currently discernible in the practice of international law. It consists in softening hard international law into soft law and does not, unfortunately, spare the due diligence standard [165]. It is particularly visible in the new international legal regime of cybersecurity: according to some States, due diligence in that field necessarily belongs to soft law because of its "standard" quality. These States emphasise, for example, that due diligence was defined as a "voluntary, non-binding nor[m] of responsible behaviour of States" in the 2015 UN report on cybersecurity [166]. We will return to this issue in Chapter IV.

Now, having described the nature of due diligence *qua* standard of conduct under international law, it remains necessary to reflect further upon the foundation or justification of such a standard of conduct. What is it that provides the foundation for such a standard of care for the rights or interests identified by international law as worthy of protection (or, conversely, the foundation for a "no harm" standard of those rights or interests)?

According to the ICJ [167], due diligence is constitutive of the sovereign equality of States. More precisely, it must be considered as the normative counterpart or "corollary" of the equality of the sovereign rights of States [168]. This justification has two prongs.

The first prong of the foundation of due diligence in international law is the equality, particularly the equal autonomy, of peoples and their States.

On the level of interpersonal morality, the obligation not to harm (by negligence) the rights and interests of others is justified by the respect for their equal autonomy [169]. Similarly, the foundation of the inter-State obligation not to harm (by negligence) also resides in equality, namely

164. On "standards" in international law, see e.g. Y. Radi, *La standardisation internationale. Contours d'une théorie dialectique de la formation du droit*, Brussels, Larcier, 2013, pp. 44 *et seq.*; P. Reuter, *op. cit. supra* note 75; P. d'Argent and A. de Vaucleroy, *op. cit. supra* note 33; R. Kolb, *La bonne foi en droit international*, Paris, Presses universitaires de France, 2001, pp. 115 *et seq.*

165. See R. Pisillo Mazzeschi, 2018, *op. cit. supra* note 23, pp. 329-330.

166. See Cybersecurity Report, *op. cit. supra* note 88, para. 13. See also generally K. Bannelier-Christakis, 2017, *op. cit. supra* note 29.

167. See ICJ, The case of the *Corfu Channel*, *op. cit. supra* note 8, p. 22. See also Separate opinion of Judge Donoghue, in ICJ, The case of *Certain Activities carried out by Nicaragua in the Border Area*, *op. cit. supra* note 3, para. 8.

168. See *Island of Palmas* Arbitration, *op. cit. supra* note 8, p. 839.

169. See S. Shiffrin, 2017, *op. cit. supra* note 6; J. Raz, 2010, *op. cit. supra* note 6.

sovereign equality [170]. Given that peoples and their States are not alone in the world [171], but, on the contrary, and to paraphrase Hannah Arendt [172], build a world together that rests upon their sovereign equality, they should respect the rights and interests of others with due diligence.

This is precisely the meaning of the related principle of good neighbourliness in international law (Art. 74 of the Charter of the United Nations [UN Charter]) [173]. Over time, this obligation to do no harm expanded to encompass the rights and interests *common* to peoples and their States, both in each State's territory and in the spaces common to States [174]. This obligation broke free therefore from the bilateral relationship of neighbourliness and, in particular, from the reciprocity of sovereignty [175]. We will return to this point in the examination of the personal scope and content of due diligence.

The second prong of the justification or foundation of due diligence (and, conversely, of responsibility for negligence) lies in the relation between responsibility and control. To quote Joseph Raz [176], being unable to control what lies within our "domain of secure competence" would be an incomplete form of "being in the world".

What characterises due diligence in international law is the collective, and then institutional, dimension of law or sovereign competence and by extension of the duty-bearer of the due diligence obligation. The State's institutional nature and ability to have organs and dedicated resources come with a higher level of competence, but also imply a higher level of necessary control over (external) sources of harm, resulting in an obligation to prevent, protect against or remedy that harm with due diligence. Control can be personal, of course, but also, by extension in the modern era, territorial – even if it is no longer always necessary, as we will see. This form of equal institutional organisation and thus of

170. See J. Klabbers, 2017, *op. cit. supra* note 105; D. Lévy, *op. cit. supra* note 105, pp. 752-753; M. G. Cohn, *op. cit. supra* note 105.

171. See J. Raz, 2010, *op. cit. supra* note 6; J. Raz, *From Normativity to Responsibility*, Oxford, Oxford University Press, 2011 ("being in the world").

172. See H. Arendt, *On Revolution*, New York, Viking Press, 1963, p. 175.

173. Charter of the United Nations of 26 June 1945, UNTS, Vol. 1, p. XVI (UN Charter). See Dissenting opinion of Judge Weeramantry, in ICJ, *Legality of the Threat or Use of Nuclear Weapons*, *op. cit. supra* note 8, para. 283.

174. See ICJ, *Legality of the Threat or Use of Nuclear Weapons*, *op. cit. supra* note 8, paras. 241-242; ICJ, The case of *The Gabcikovo-Nagymaros Project*, *op. cit. supra* note 8, para. 53; ICJ, The case of *Pulp Mills on the River Uruguay*, *op. cit. supra* note 3, para. 101; ICJ, The case of *Certain Activities carried out by Nicaragua in the Border Area*, *op. cit. supra* note 3, para. 104.

175. Contra: S. Maljean-Dubois, *op. cit. supra* note 14.

176. See J. Raz, 2010, *op. cit. supra* note 6.

equal competence of control that the sovereign State exercises grounds due diligence in international law.

In sum, it is the individuals' equality of competence and control and, in international law, the equality of States' sovereignty which found or justify due diligence. In our social circumstances, equal respect requires that we bear responsibility for the harm which we cause to others when we do not ensure a reasonable control of what belongs to our respective sphere of competence. This accounts for the "corollarity" between the rights and competences of sovereign States and their due diligence obligations first identified in the *Palmas Island* case [177].

B. The sources and regimes of due diligence

The question of due diligence's sources in international law is closely related to the question of its regime. The present section will therefore address both issues together while distinguishing between: (1) the due diligence standard in general international law and (2) due diligence obligations in the special regimes of international law.

1. The due diligence standard in general international law

As previously highlighted, international jurisprudence often refers to due diligence either as a "principle" (general or otherwise) [178] or as a "general obligation" [179].

This twofold reference preserves a certain ambivalence between a type of norm and its (general) "regime", on the one hand, and the (general) "source" of that norm, on the other. One may therefore consider that due diligence belongs to general international law on two grounds: first, on the ground of its regime and from the point of view of its general content and, second, on the ground of its sources and their general personal scope [180].

177. See *Island of Palmas* Arbitration, *op. cit. supra* note 8; ICJ, The case of the *Corfu Channel, op. cit. supra* note 8, p. 22. See also Separate opinion of Judge Donoghue, in ICJ, The case of *Certain Activities carried out by Nicaragua in the Border Area, op. cit. supra* note 3, para. 8.

178. See e.g. *Trail Smelter* Arbitration, *op. cit. supra* note 8, para. 716; ICJ, The case of the *Corfu Channel, op. cit. supra* note 8, p. 22; ICJ, *Legality of the Threat or Use of Nuclear Weapons, op. cit. supra* note 8, paras. 241-242.

179. See e.g. ICJ, *Legality of the Threat or Use of Nuclear Weapons, op. cit. supra* note 8, pp. 241-242 ("general obligation"). See also ICJ, The case of *The Gabcikovo-Nagymaros Project, op. cit. supra* note 8, para. 53; ITLOS, *Responsibilities and Obligations of States Sponsoring Persons and Entities with Respect to Activities in the Area, op. cit. supra* note 41, para. 131 ("general obligation of due diligence").

180. On the three possible, and partially interdependent, conceptions of "general international law" (relating to *(i)* the source, *(ii)* the personal scope or *(iii)* the content

On the one hand, characterising due diligence as a "principle" makes it possible to treat it, *qua* type of norm, as a "general rule of international law" [181]. This corresponds to the idea that there would be a general regime of due diligence, that is, a minimal regime of the due diligence standard common to all international legal regimes. The international case law on due diligence has emphasised that qualification on several occasions since its inception [182].

The reference to the "principle" of due diligence *qua* source, on the other hand, places due diligence among the general principles of law envisioned by Article 38 (1) (c) of the Statute of the ICJ, as well as among the general principles of international law *stricto sensu* [183]. As highlighted in Chapter I, such a qualification is clearly appropriate because, ever since the end of the nineteenth century and through the middle of the twentieth century, due diligence has originated as much from the national judicial practice of States pertaining to responsibility as from international judicial practice [184].

Nevertheless, the qualification of "general principle" by the international judge preserves a certain ambiguity with regard to the customary nature of that principle – especially in the absence of all the validating conditions for the existence of a customary norm [185]. This

---

of this law), see S. Besson, "The Sources of International Human Rights Law", *op. cit. supra* note 134.

181. See ICJ, *Interpretation of the Agreement of the 25 March 1951 between the WHO and Egypt*, *op. cit. supra* note 134.

182. See e.g. *Trail Smelter* Arbitration, *op. cit. supra* note 8, para. 716; ICJ, The case of the *Corfu Channel*, *op. cit. supra* note 8, p. 22.

183. Statute of the International Court of Justice of 18 April 1946, UNTS, Vol. 33, p. 993. See S. Besson, 2011, *op. cit. supra* note 132.

184. See *Alabama Claims* Arbitration, *op. cit. supra* note 1; *Frederick Wipperman* Arbitration, *op. cit. supra* note 1; *British Property in Spanish Morocco* Arbitration, *op. cit. supra* note 8; *Island of Palmas* Arbitration, *op. cit. supra* note 8, p. 839; *William E. Chapman* Arbitration, *op. cit. supra* note 1; *Trail Smelter* Arbitration, *op. cit. supra* note 8, para. 716; ICSID, *AAPL* Arbitration, *op. cit. supra* note 8, paras. 609-610; PCA, *Indus Waters Kishenganga* Arbitration, *op. cit. supra* note 8, paras. 449-450; PCA, *South China Sea* Arbitration, *op. cit. supra* note 8, para. 117. See also Dissenting opinion of Judge Moore, in PCIJ, The case of the *S.S. Lotus*, *op. cit. supra* note 8, p. 88; ICJ, The case of the *Corfu Channel*, *op. cit. supra* note 8, p. 22; ICJ, The case of the *United States Diplomatic and Consular Staff in Tehran*, *op. cit. supra* note 8, paras. 67-68; ICJ, The case of *Military and Paramilitary Activities in and against Nicaragua*, *op. cit. supra* note 8, paras. 157-158; ICJ, *Legality of the Threat or Use of Nuclear Weapons*, *op. cit. supra* note 8, paras. 241-242; ICJ, The case of *The Gabcikovo-Nagymaros Project*, *op. cit. supra* note 8, para. 53; ICJ, The case of *Pulp Mills on the River Uruguay*, *op. cit. supra* note 3, para. 101; ICJ, The case of *Certain Activities carried out by Nicaragua in the Border Area*, *op. cit. supra* note 3, para. 104.

185. See e.g. ICJ, The case of *Pulp Mills on the River Uruguay*, *op. cit. supra* note 3, para. 101. More generally, see P. d'Argent, 2011, *op. cit. supra* note 135; C. J. Tams, "The Development of International Law by the International Court of

ambiguity is likely at the root of the vagueness which appears to be deliberately maintained between a general "principle" of due diligence (with reference to its source) and a general "obligation" of due diligence (which as such would be customary) in the international jurisprudence relating to international environmental law [186]. As highlighted in the previous section, the ICJ has in that context succeeded in turning the due diligence "standard" into a due diligence "obligation" [187]. After a second move through which it requalified due diligence as a customary "obligation", the Court was able, in a last reversal, to use this ambiguity to derive other obligations which it considers to be equally customary, including an obligation of diligent prevention [188] in international environmental law.

Once again, it is important to take note of the strong link that binds together general principles *qua* source of international law and judicial reasoning. This confirms the intimate relation between the due diligence standard and the international judge [189]. Unsurprisingly, it is in the most "judiciarised" regimes of international law, such as international environmental law and international human rights law, that due diligence is most prevalent: the best assessment of what is "reasonably" owed or expected of a duty-bearer is indeed provided by judicial reasoning. This issue will be addressed again later in this chapter, in the discussion of the content, variability and limits of due diligence.

Independently of its source in the general principles of law or the general principles of international law *stricto sensu* and regardless of the ambiguous relation between principles and custom in international jurisprudence, the due diligence standard which qualifies the general

Justice", in *Decisions of the ICJ as Sources of International Law?*, Rome, International and European Papers, 2018, pp. 63-106 [online].

186. See e.g. ICJ, The case of *Pulp Mills on the River Uruguay*, *op. cit. supra* note 3.

187. See e.g. ICJ, The case of *Pulp Mills on the River Uruguay*, *op. cit. supra* note 3, para. 101; ICJ, The case of *Certain Activities carried out by Nicaragua in the Border Area*, *op. cit. supra* note 3, paras. 104 and 204. More precisely, the argument of the ICJ, The case of *Pulp Mills on the River Uruguay*, *op. cit. supra* note 3, undergoes three shifts: *(i)* the standard of due diligence becomes a full-fledged obligation; *(ii)* it qualifies as a customary obligation; and *(iii)* the principle or obligation of prevention is derived from it, rather than the other way round.

188. See ICJ, The case of *Pulp Mills on the River Uruguay*, *op. cit. supra* note 3, para. 101. See also Separate opinion of Judge Dugard, in ICJ, The case of *Certain Activities carried out by Nicaragua in the Border Area*, *op. cit. supra* note 3, para. 7. For a critique of the "catalystic" role for customary obligations taken on by international jurisprudence with regard to due diligence in international environmental law, see Y. Kerbrat, 2018, *op. cit. supra* note 96; S. Maljean-Dubois, *op. cit. supra* note 14.

189. See S. Besson, 2011, *op. cit. supra* note 132.

obligation not to harm (carelessly; also known as the "no harm rule" or "duty not to harm") the rights and interests protected by international law also finds its source in customary international law. This results from the early international case law [190] and its validating [191] role of the customary nature of due diligence. Since at least the end of the nineteenth century, this has been verified by the now general and regular practice and *opinio juris* of States. The genealogy of the responsibility for negligence outlined in Chapter I confirms this point.

2. Due diligence obligations in the special regimes of international law

The existence and customary source under international law of a general standard of due diligence and of a corresponding general "obligation" to do no harm carelessly does not imply the generality of all obligations of (x with) due diligence [192].

Quite the opposite: as explained earlier, special obligations of (x with) due diligence require the specification of the protected rights and interests, namely, the specification of a particular obligation not to harm with due diligence. Each special regime must identify these obligations or, at the very least, specific rights and interests when specific due diligence obligations on the matter do not yet exist. Of course, some of those rights and interests are also protected by general international law, both with respect to their content (and as such their regime) and their sources [193]. In fact, in accordance with the principle of *lex specialis*, special regimes may entail a specific due diligence standard.

190. See e.g. *Trail Smelter* Arbitration, *op. cit. supra* note 8, para. 716; ICJ, The case of the *Corfu Channel, op. cit. supra* note 8, p. 22; ICJ, *Legality of the Threat or Use of Nuclear Weapons, op. cit. supra* note 8, paras. 241-242. See also Dissenting opinion of Judge Weeramantry, in ICJ, *Legality of the Threat or Use of Nuclear Weapons, op. cit. supra* note 8, p. 496.

191. On the validation of customary international law by the international judge, see D. Regan, "International Adjudication: A Response to Paulus – Courts, Custom, Treaties, Regimes, and the WTO", in S. Besson and J. Tasioulas (eds.), *The Philosophy of International Law*, Oxford, Oxford University Press, 2010, pp. 225-244; S. Besson, "De quelques considérations philosophiques sur la justice internationale – Ou comment dépasser l'amour impossible entre droit international et justice internationale", in S. Besson and A. R. Ziegler (eds.), *Le juge en droit international et européen / The Judge in International and European Law* (Travaux de l'Ecole doctorale romande sur les fondements du droit européen 2012), Zurich, Schulthess, 2013, pp. 15-41.

192. See ICJ, The case of *Application of the Convention on the Prevention and Punishment of the Crime of Genocide, op. cit. supra* note 22, para. 429. See also Separate opinion of Judge Donoghue, in ICJ, The case of *Certain Activities carried out by Nicaragua in the Border Area, op. cit. supra* note 3, paras. 13-15.

193. See e.g. *Trail Smelter* Arbitration, *op. cit. supra* note 8, para. 716; ICJ, The case of the *Corfu Channel, op. cit. supra* note 8, p. 22; ICJ, *Legality of the Threat or Use of Nuclear Weapons, op. cit. supra* note 8, paras. 241-242.

It is for this reason that a detailed study of due diligence in three special regimes of international law is provided in Chapter IV.

Of course, what is constitutive of a special regime of due diligence may also be extended to another regime by analogy or may generalise until becoming an integral part of the minimal and common regime of due diligence in international law. However, in the absence of sufficient conclusive elements, especially as to the generality of an obligation of (x with) due diligence, it is important to be cautious about generalising the characteristics of a special regime of due diligence (due diligence in the international law of the sea or in international human rights law, for example) and applying them to another special regime (international cybersecurity law, for example) [194]. Differences will often derive from the nature of the specific obligation of x (or of the protected rights and interests) on which due diligence is grafted and whose conduct it qualifies.

For example, the progressive replacement of due diligence obligations in the international law on the protection of aliens with due diligence obligations from international human rights law [195] does not mean that the history of due diligence ends there. As indicated in the first chapter, the history of due diligence does not necessarily have to proceed solely by means of the continual extension of due diligence obligations under international human rights law – an extension which has now gone as far as undermining the normative structure of that regime. We will return to this issue in the section dedicated to due diligence in international human rights law (Chap. IV.B).

The international law on neutrality, the international law on the protection of aliens and international environmental law are all examples of special regimes of due diligence obligations in international law. More recent additions to that list include international human rights law, international criminal law, international humanitarian law, the international law of the sea and international investment law. The evolution is fast-paced: as Chapter IV will highlight, obligations of due diligence would also exist in international cybersecurity law, even though the grounds for these obligations, namely, the protected rights and interests, still have to be specified.

It is important to emphasise that the sources of the general regime of the due diligence standard in international law are not necessarily

194. See J. Brunnée and T. Meshel, *op. cit. supra* note 28; A. Takano, "Due Diligence Obligations and Transboundary Environmental Harm: Cybersecurity Applications", *Laws*, Vol. 7, No. 4 (2018), pp. 1-12.

195. See C. Chinkin, *op. cit. supra* note 118; M. Hakimi, *op. cit. supra* note 13.

reflected in the sources of due diligence in the special regimes of international law and vice versa. For example, while the due diligence obligation of harm prevention under international environmental law has been deemed customary by international jurisprudence [196], that determination does not imply that such a general obligation exists in every international legal regime. This is actually the point of the ICJ's warning in the *Genocide* case [197].

In the special regimes of due diligence in international law, the sources of the due diligence standard and of the obligations which integrate that standard range from general principles and custom to multilateral [198] or bilateral [199] treaties.

As previously indicated, the first conventional obligations of due diligence date back to the 1960s, but they have multiplied since the 1990s, especially in international environmental law [200]. Conventional obligations of due diligence are therefore quite recent and not very numerous. International tribunals have both validated and interpreted all these sources. The stream of international decisions (both arbitral [201] and judicial [202]) on the matter has continued to flow since the nineteenth

196. See ICJ, *Legality of the Threat or Use of Nuclear Weapons, op. cit. supra* note 8, paras. 241-242; ICJ, The case of *The Gabcikovo-Nagymaros Project, op. cit. supra* note 8, para. 53; ICJ, The case of *Pulp Mills on the River Uruguay, op. cit. supra* note 3, para. 101; ICJ, The case of *Certain Activities carried out by Nicaragua in the Border Area, op. cit. supra* note 3, para. 104.

197. See ICJ, The case of *Application of the Convention on the Prevention and Punishment of the Crime of Genocide, op. cit. supra* note 22, para. 429.

198. See e.g. VCDR, *op. cit. supra* note 9, Art. 22 (2); Convention on the Law of the Sea, *op. cit. supra* note 9, Arts. 58, 62, 94, 139, 192 and 194; Convention on Biological Diversity, *op. cit. supra* note 9, Art. 3; Convention on the Law of the Non-Navigational Uses of International Watercourses, *op. cit. supra* note 9, Arts. 7 (1), 21 (2) and 22; Arms Trade Treaty, *op. cit. supra* note 9, Art. 6 (3); Istanbul Convention, *op. cit. supra* note 9, Art. 5 (2). See also OEIGWG Draft, *op. cit. supra* note 10, Art. 6.

199. See also ICSID, *AAPL* Arbitration, *op. cit. supra* note 8, paras. 609-610, which mentions the customary and treaty sources of the due diligence standard.

200. See e.g. Convention on the Law of the Sea, *op. cit. supra* note 9, Arts. 94 and 194; Convention on Biological Diversity, *op. cit. supra* note 9, Art. 3; Convention on the Law of the Non-Navigational Uses of International Watercourses, *op. cit. supra* note 9, Arts. 7 (1), 21 (2) and 22; Preamble of the United Nations Framework Convention on Climate Change, *op. cit. supra* note 116, p. 107.

201. See e.g. *Alabama Claims* Arbitration, *op. cit. supra* note 1; *Frederick Wipperman* Arbitration, *op. cit. supra* note 1; *British Property in Spanish Morocco* Arbitration, *op. cit. supra* note 8; *Island of Palmas* Arbitration, *op. cit. supra* note 8, p. 839; *William E. Chapman* Arbitration, *op. cit. supra* note 1; *Trail Smelter* Arbitration, *op. cit. supra* note 8, para. 716. As well as more recently: ICSID, *AAPL* Arbitration, *op. cit. supra* note 8, paras. 609-610; PCA, *Indus Waters Kishenganga* Arbitration, *op. cit. supra* note 8, paras. 449-450; PCA, *South China Sea* Arbitration, *op. cit. supra* note 8, para. 117.

202. See e.g. Dissenting opinion of Judge Moore, in PCIJ, The case of the *S.S. Lotus, op. cit. supra* note 8, p. 88; ICJ, The case of the *Corfu Channel, op. cit. supra* note 8,

century and even intensified since the 2000s. This is especially the case for decisions in international environmental law [203], particularly in the international law of the sea [204], and in international human rights law [205].

In addition, in as early as the 1990s, due diligence was recognised in the various unilateral acts of IOs [206] (UN or EU, for example), but also more generally in soft law. It is the case in particular in international environmental law [207], international human rights law [208] and international cybersecurity law [209]. The works of professional organisations of international law, such as the Institute of International

p. 22; ICJ, The case of the *United States Diplomatic and Consular Staff in Tehran*, *op. cit. supra* note 8, paras. 67-68; ICJ, The case of *Military and Paramilitary Activities in and against Nicaragua*, *op. cit. supra* note 8, paras. 157-158.

203. See e.g. ICJ, *Legality of the Threat or Use of Nuclear Weapons*, *op. cit. supra* note 8, paras. 241-242; ICJ, The case of *The Gabcikovo-Nagymaros Project*, *op. cit. supra* note 8, para. 53; ICJ, The case of *Pulp Mills on the River Uruguay*, *op. cit. supra* note 3, para. 101; ICJ, The case of *Certain Activities carried out by Nicaragua in the Border Area*, *op. cit. supra* note 3, para. 104.

204. See e.g. ITLOS, *Responsibilities and Obligations of States Sponsoring Persons and Entities with Respect to Activities in the Area*, *op. cit. supra* note 41, paras. 110-112; ITLOS, *Request for an Advisory Opinion submitted by the Sub-Regional Fisheries Commission*, *op. cit. supra* note 148, para. 129.

205. See e.g. ICJ, The case of *Armed Activities on the Territory of the Congo*, 2005, *op. cit. supra* note 3, paras. 247-248; ICJ, The case of *Application of the Convention on the Prevention and Punishment of the Crime of Genocide*, *op. cit. supra* note 22, para. 431; Inter-American Court of Human Rights (IACtHR), Case of *Velasquez-Rodriguez* v. *Honduras*, Judgment of 29 July 1988, Series C No. 4, para. 172; European Court of Human Rights (ECtHR), Case of *Opuz* v. *Turkey*, No. 33401/02, Judgment of 9 June 2009, paras. 129-130; ECtHR, Case of *Talpis* v. *Italy*, No. 41237/14, Judgment of 2 March 2017, paras. 29 and 98-99; IACtHR, *The Environment and Human Rights*, Advisory Opinion OC-23/17 of 15 November 2017, Series C No. 23. Mention should also be made of the UN's human rights treaty bodies' observations and findings, especially: CESCR, General Comment No. 24, *op. cit. supra* note 3, paras. 15-16 and 30 *et seq.*; Committee Against Torture (CAT), General Comment No. 4 on the implementation of Article 3 of the Convention in the context of Article 22, 4 September 2018, UN Doc. CAT/C/GC/4, para. 30; Human Rights Committee (CCPR), *Basem Ahmed Issa Yassin and others* v. *Canada*, Communication No. 2285/2013, 7 December 2017, UN Doc. CCPR/C/120/D/2285/2013, paras. 6.5. *et seq.*; CCPR, General Comment No. 36 on Article 6 of the International Covenant on Civil and Political Rights, on the right to life, 3 September 2019, UN Doc. CCPR/C/GC/36, paras. 21-22.

206. See e.g. Secretary-General of the United Nations, Human Rights Due Diligence Policy, *op. cit. supra* note 86, Principle 2; Directive 2004/35/CE, *op. cit. supra* note 87; TFEU, *op. cit. supra* note 87, Art. 191 (2).

207. See e.g. Stockholm Declaration, *op. cit. supra* note 116, Principles 21 and 22; Rio Declaration, *op. cit. supra* note 116, Principles 2, 14 and 15.

208. See e.g. HRC, Guiding Principles on Business and Human Rights, *op. cit. supra* note 88, Principles 4 and 17; Secretary-General of the United Nations, Human Rights Due Diligence Policy, *op. cit. supra* note 86, Principle 2.

209. See e.g. *Tallinn Manual 2.0*, *op. cit. supra* note 88, Rules 6 and 7; Cybersecurity Report, *op. cit. supra* note 88, paras. 13 (c) and 28 (a) and (b).

Law (IIL)[210], the International Law Association (ILA)[211] or the ILC[212], also refer regularly to due diligence.

As Chapter I indicated, several factors account for the important place of due diligence obligations within soft law. One of them is the emergence of potential new duty-bearers whose due diligence obligations cannot be specified by international law's sources, that is, treaties, custom or general principles. Another is the expansion of the competences of IOs and yet another the crisis of multilateral treaties.

One of the difficulties raised by soft law in that context, and one which is a frequent object of criticism, is the lack of rigour which characterises the treatment of due diligence[213]. For example, the due diligence of private persons is often conflated with the due diligence of public institutions (the due diligence expected from corporations under corporate law is simply applied to IOs or, conversely, that of States is merely transposed onto MNCs, for instance); categories get easily distorted (for example, complicity as a ground of attribution of responsibility is regularly mixed up with responsibility for negligence); and, finally, technoscientific standards mingle with normative considerations in the specification of due diligence's content. These issues will be addressed in the sections of this course dedicated to due diligence in international human rights law (Chap. IV.B), international environmental law and international cybersecurity law (Chap. IV.A).

C. The scope of due diligence

One may distinguish between the (1) personal; (2) material; (3) geographic; and (4) temporal dimensions of the scope of due diligence obligations.

---

210. See e.g. Institute of International Law (IIL), Resolution "International Responsibility of States for Injuries on their Territory to the Person or Property of Foreigners", Leo Strisower (Rapporteur) 1 September 1927 (IIL Resolution of 1927), Art. 3.

211. See e.g. ILA, Committee on the Accountability of International Organisations, Final Report, Berlin Conference (2004); ILA, Declaration of Legal Principles Relating to Climate Change, *op. cit. supra* note 11, Arts. 7A and 7B.

212. See e.g. ILC, Draft Articles on Prevention of Transboundary Harm from Hazardous Activities, with commentaries, *op. cit. supra* note 11, Arts. 1 and 3; ILC, Draft Articles on the Protection of Persons in the Event of Disasters, *op. cit. supra* note 11, Arts. 9 and 16; ILC, Draft Principles on the Protection of the Environment in Relation to Armed Conflict, *op. cit. supra* note 11, Principle 22.

213. See e.g. S. Michalowski, "Due Diligence and Complicity: A Relationship in Need of Clarification", in S. Deva and D. Bilchitz (eds.), *Human Rights Obligations of Business: Beyond the Corporate Responsibility to Respect?*, Cambridge, Cambridge University Press, 2013, pp. 218-242. See also the exchange of views between J. Bonnitcha and R. McCorquodale, "The Concept of 'Due Diligence' " and "A Rejoinder", *op. cit. supra* note 30, as well as J. G. Ruggie and J. F. Sherman, *op. cit. supra* note 30.

1. *The personal scope of due diligence*

The specificity of due diligence obligations lies in their triangular dimension: they (a) bind a legal subject (the duty-bearers of due diligence); (b) for the benefit of another legal subject (the beneficiaries of due diligence); and (c) in relation to a third party that is the source of harm (the third parties of due diligence).

(a) *The duty-bearers of due diligence*

The duty-bearer of due diligence is the duty-bearer of the obligation of (x with) due diligence on which the eponymous standard is grafted.

Depending on the obligation on which due diligence is grafted, there can be one or several duty-bearers of due diligence. It is the case, for example, when the obligation of (x with) due diligence is an obligation *omnium* because of the types of rights and interests protected by international law [214]. Each special regime of international law determines the duty-bearers of due diligence by recognising a number of rights or interests which must be protected by these various international institutions and which may in turn give rise to due diligence obligations.

The duty-bearers of due diligence can be States, of course, as has been the case in international law since the seventeenth century. However, given the historical origins and the institutional background of States, as well as the egalitarian and institutional justifications of due diligence, any organised and institutionalised form of social and

214. On the concurrent due diligence obligations (in international human rights law) of an IO and a host State, see L. Gasbarri, "Overlapping Responsibility: The Legal Relationship between the International Organization and the Host State", in A. de Guttry, M. Frulli, E. Greppi and C. Macchi (eds.), *The Duty of Care of International Organizations Towards their Civilian Personnel: Legal Obligations and Implementation Challenges*, The Hague, T.M.C. Asser Press, 2018, pp. 103-125. More generally, on the plurality of "jurisdiction", obligations and responsibilities among different States and/or IOs, in case of breach of these obligations in international human rights law and on their different articulations, see S. Besson, "L'extra-territorialité des droits de l'homme internationaux: juridictions concurrentes, obligations conjointes et responsabilités partagées", in P. d'Argent (ed.), *Droit des frontières internationales. Actes des Journées franco-allemandes SFDI-DGIR 2014*, Paris, Pedone, 2016, pp. 245-259; S. Besson, "Shared Responsibilities under the ECHR: Concurrent Jurisdictions, Duties and Responsibilities", in J. Motoc and A. van Aaken (eds.), *The ECHR and General International Law*, Oxford, Oxford University Press, 2018, pp. 155-177. As we will see, the due diligence standard and the obligations which it qualifies depend on the control over the source of the (risk of) harm and vary according to the degree of that control. This is also the key to their mutual articulation in case of multiple duty-bearers of due diligence, and the same applies to allocating responsibilities and possibly reparations in case of concurrent responsibilities.

political group could be the duty-bearer of a due diligence obligation. Cities and regions (at the infranational level), inter-State organisations or even supranational political communities, such as the EU or the UN, may also be duty-bearers of obligations of (x with) due diligence under international law.

Turning to IOs as institutional duty-bearers of due diligence obligations [215], one observes important variations. The EU is clearly considered to owe due diligence obligations under EU law [216], but also under some international legal regimes applicable to the EU [217]. The same is true for the UN, at least in some areas of UN law [218],

215. See e.g. A. O'Donoghue, "The Exercise of Governance Authority by International Organisations: The Role of Due Diligence Obligations after Conflict", in M. Saul and J. A. Sweeney (eds.), *International Law and Post-Conflict Reconstruction Policy*, London, Routledge, 2015, pp. 45-65; J. Klabbers, 2017, *op. cit. supra* note 105; E. Lagrange, "La responsabilité des organisations internationales pour violation d'une obligation de diligence", in SFDI (ed.), *Le standard de* due diligence *et la responsabilité internationale: Journée d'études franco-italienne du Mans*, Paris, Pedone, 2018, pp. 189-230; E. Campbell, E. Dominic, S. Stadnik and Y. Wu, "Due Diligence Obligations of International Organizations under International Law", *New York University Journal of International Law and Politics*, Vol. 50, No. 2 (2018), pp. 541-604.

216. See e.g. Directive 2004/35/CE, *op. cit. supra* note 87; TFEU, *op. cit. supra* note 87, Art. 191 (2). See also European General Court (EGC), Case of *Front Polisario* v. *Council of the European Union*, T-512/12, Judgment of 10 December 2015; Court of Justice of the European Union (CJEU), Opinion of Advocate General M. Melchior Wathelet, in the Case *Western Sahara Campaign UK, The Queen* v. *Commissioners for Her Majesty's Revenue and Customs, Secretary of State for Environment, Food and Rural Affairs*, C266/16, Conclusions of 10 January 2018. See also A. Berkes, "The Extraterritorial Human Rights Obligations of the EU in its External Trade and Investment Policies", *Europe and the World: A Law Review*, Vol. 2, No. 5 (2018), pp. 1-21; C. M. J. Ryngaert and R. Fransen, "EU Extraterritorial Obligations with Respect to Trade with Occupied Territories: Reflections after the Case of Front Polisario before EU Courts", *Europe in the World: A Law Review*, Vol. 2, No. 1 (2018), pp. 1-20; E. Kassoti, "The *Front Polisario v Council* Case: The General Court, *Völkerrechtsfreundlichkeit* and the External Aspect of European Integration", *Insight: European Papers*, Vol. 2, No. 1 (2017), pp. 339-356.

217. See e.g. in the international law of the sea: Convention on the Law of the Sea, *op. cit. supra* note 9, Arts. 2, 4 and 6 Annex IX; ITLOS, *Request for an Advisory Opinion submitted by the Sub-Regional Fisheries Commission*, *op. cit. supra* note 148, paras. 164-173. See e.g. in international human rights law: Istanbul Convention, *op. cit. supra* note 9, Art. 5 (2); Convention on the Rights of Persons with Disabilities of 13 December 2006, UNTS, Vol. 2515, p. 3, Art. 14. See also P. Palchetti, "La violation par l'Union européenne d'une obligation de *due diligence*", in SFDI (ed.), *Le standard de* due diligence *et la responsabilité internationale: Journée d'études franco-italienne du Mans*, Paris, Pedone, 2018, pp. 231-242; L. Gasbarri, "Responsabilità di un'organizzane internazionale in materie di competenza esclusiva: imputazione e obbligo di risultato secondo il Tribunale internazionale per il diritto del mare", *Rivista di diritto internazionale*, Vol. 98, No. 3 (2015), pp. 911-917.

218. See e.g. Agreement between the United Nations and the Government of Haiti concerning the status of the United Nations Operation in Haiti of 9 July 2004, UNTS, Vol. 2271, p. 235, Art. IV. See e.g. H. P. Aust, "The UN Human Rights Due Diligence Policy: An Effective Mechanism Against Complicity of Peacekeeping Forces", *Journal of Conflict and Security Law*, Vol. 20, No. 1 (2015), pp. 61-73;

even if, for now, most of these obligations stem from soft law [219].

One should address three principled objections or, at least, three hurdles before the personal scope of due diligence obligations can be extended to IOs in general.

First, the special obligations under international law of most IOs (with the exception of the EU) are not yet very developed. This is particularly evident in international human rights law, for example, and has stymied the emergence of due diligence obligations and responsibilities for negligence of IOs. Yet the intensification of the criticism of functionalism and the growing identification of the need to constrain the activities of IOs by imposing more international legal obligations upon them accommodates some optimism [220]. It is important to note that these remarks concern the applicability of international law's due diligence standard to IOs and not the applicability of the due diligence standard of the private law of the State before whose tribunals an IO would have to answer for civil liability [221].

Second, the institutional and organisational diversity of IOs can be problematic to the extent that it makes it difficult to determine what can be reasonably expected from them with respect to due diligence outside of a specific case. In the absence of a minimal content of the due diligence standard of an IO, variability would become the rule rather than a qualification of the rule, as we will see it is. The specialty of the competences attributed to IOs would therefore threaten the very possibility of a minimal standard of "good government" applicable to IOs. Of course, this minimal content might grow along with the development of the obligations and responsibilities of IOs over time and, with it, a better articulation of the institutional and political

---

J. Klabbers, 2017, *op. cit. supra* note 105; A. Creta, "Implementation of the Duty of Care by the United Nations", in A. de Guttry, M. Frulli, E. Greppi and C. Macchi (eds.), *The Duty of Care of International Organizations Towards Their Civilian Personnel: Legal Obligations and Implementation Challenges*, The Hague, T.M.C. Asser Press, 2018, pp. 167-208; N. D. White, 2020, *op. cit. supra* note 86.

219. See e.g. Secretary-General of the United Nations, Human Rights Due Diligence Policy, *op. cit. supra* note 86. See also H. P. Aust, 2015, *op. cit. supra* note 218; A. O'Donoghue, *op. cit. supra* note 215; J. Klabbers, 2017, *op. cit. supra* note 105; E. Lagrange, *op. cit. supra* note 215; E. Campbell, E. Dominic, S. Stadnik and Y. Wu, *op. cit. supra* note 215; A. Creta, *op. cit. supra* note 218.

220. See in particular J. Klabbers, "The EJIL Foreword: The Transformation of International Organizations Law", *European Journal of International Law*, Vol. 26, No. 1 (2015), pp. 9-82.

221. On this issue, see e.g. K. Boon, "The United States as Good Samaritan: Immunity and Responsibility", *Chicago Journal of International Law*, Vol. 16 (2016), pp. 341-385; D. Hovell, *op. cit. supra* note 35.

continuity between these organisations and States [222]. After all, it did happen for States whose institutional features were progressively refined and unified by international law from the end of the Middle Ages to the modern era, allowing for the development of the minimal content of States' "good government" standard [223]. As the next section will highlight, that standard eventually consolidated into the due diligence standard of States.

Finally, the third difficulty lies in the justification of the due diligence standard of an IO which cannot be the same as the justification of the due diligence of States. As we recall, the due diligence of States in international law is grounded partly in their sovereign equality and partly in their competence and ability to exercise institutional control. Admittedly, IOs share with States an organised and institutionalised structure, but they are neither sovereign nor equal, nor are they considered to have the kind of competences and jurisdiction that States have under international law.

As for the first dimension of due diligence's justification, IOs are neither sovereign nor equal among themselves; most crucially, they are not equal to States and vice versa [224]. Admittedly, it is possible to justify the due diligence obligations of IOs that find themselves in State-like situations, as with UN peacebuilding missions after armed conflicts or other forms of territorial or spatial administration exercised by IOs (border zones or refugee camps, for example) [225]. For other organisations, the egalitarian dimension of the due diligence of IOs has yet to be identified in our ever-evolving international institutional order.

Yet the existence of IOs as well as States' interactions within and with these IOs have already substantially influenced inter-State relations. In those circumstances, these relations have acquired a complex quality rising above mere relations of good neighbourliness between sovereign equals. It would therefore not be far-fetched to let the due

---

222. On this project of institutional continuity between States and IOs, see S. Besson, *Reconstruire l'ordre institutionnel international* (Leçon inaugurale), Paris, Fayard / Collège de France, 2021; S. Besson, "Review of Francesco Lusa Bordin's *The Analogy between States and International Organizations*", *European Journal of International Law*, Vol. 32, No. 2 (2021), pp. 771-785.

223. On the good government standard in the history of European law, see A. A. Wijffels, *op. cit. supra* note 32.

224. Contra e.g. J. L. Dunoff, "Is Sovereign Equality Obsolete? Understanding Twenty-First Century International Organizations", *Netherlands Yearbook of International Law*, Vol. 43 (2012), pp. 99-127.

225. See e.g. H. P. Aust, 2015, *op. cit. supra* note 218; A. O'Donoghue, *op. cit. supra* note 215, mentioning "quasi-States" and "institutional governance authority"; L. Gasbarri, 2018, *op. cit. supra* note 214.

diligence standard, which went from an interindividual application to an inter-State one, continue its evolution, but this time on a supra-State level. In fact, the egalitarian and as such relational dimension of due diligence should be used to reorganise relations between States and IOs and between IOs themselves. These relations clearly need to be "reordered" in order to better safeguard individual and State equality at the international level. For instance, the legitimate authority of IOs should be better tied to that of their Member States and thereby to their peoples, which would resituate individual and State political equality at the core of the mandate of IOs. Such an egalitarian political mandate, as well as the kind of control powers that IOs receive from their Member States (and therefore from their peoples), would make it possible in turn to ground a general obligation not to harm (carelessly) these people's rights and interests [226].

The second dimension of the justification of States' due diligence obligations, that is, the institutional or organisational dimension of the control exercised by States, does not raise as many difficulties with regard to IOs. The "institutional" nature of IOs, like the institutional nature of States, as well as the fact that they have their own organs and resources, implies that they have the necessary degree of competence and control over the sources of the (risks of) harm and therefore an obligation to prevent, protect against or remedy that harm with due diligence. As previously highlighted, States' due diligence is grounded in their control powers and in similar portions of institutional autonomy, following the link made in interpersonal morality between the competence of individuals and the justification of their due diligence.

Of course, the nature of IOs' competences and control, in contrast to that of States, is not (yet) personal – as there are neither individual subjects of an IO nor nationality holders thereof – and even less territorial – as there are neither IO territories nor IO territorial competences (yet). But the same was true for pre-State institutional collectivities and even for States before the modern era and the development of States' territorial and personal jurisdiction. As the first chapter highlighted, these pre-modern and pre-State instituted collectivities were nonetheless deemed to be duty-bearers of due diligence. Public institutions can exercise

226. By analogy to the invocation of the UN mandate proposed by J. Klabbers, 2017, *op. cit. supra* note 105, as the foundation of the due diligence obligation of the UN (for its mission to protect peace and security) in relation to the failure to prevent the cholera pandemic in Haiti or to intervene in Rwanda. See also E. Lagrange, *op. cit. supra* note 215.

power and control over sources of (risks of) harm through "links" that need to be related neither to nationality nor to territory. It is in fact already the case for States in some regimes of international law, such as environmental law. We will return to this point in the examination of the geographic scope of due diligence.

The international responsibility system based on the competences of the EU offers an excellent illustration of this potential. The EU is a duty-bearer of due diligence obligations within its areas of competence. This is so even if Member States are implementing these obligations within the framework of their own (personal and territorial) competences of implementation of EU law – and without direct attribution of their actions to the EU as organs (according to Art. 7 ARIO) [227]. This has consequences for the nature of the control necessary for the emergence of due diligence obligations for the EU. These due diligence obligations are deemed breached even when Member States – rather than EU organs – exercise personal or territorial control over the source of harm (in the hypothesis where the source of harm is a ship flying the flag of a Member State, for instance) [228], including when there is no attribution of the conduct of these States [229] to the EU.

While the IOs' ability to be duty-bearers of due diligence gives rise to many questions, the quality of private persons, such as MNCs, is even more controversial. One of the most pressing issues regarding duty-bearers of due diligence in international law is currently whether MNCs can also be duty-bearers of due diligence obligations under

227. See P. J. Kuijper, "Attribution — Responsibility — Remedy: Some Comments on the EU in Different International Regimes", *Revue belge de droit international*, Vol. 47, No. 1 (2013), pp. 57-77.

228. See e.g. Convention on the Law of the Sea, *op. cit. supra* note 9, Arts. 2, 4 and 6 Annex IX; ITLOS, *Request for an Advisory Opinion submitted by the Sub-Regional Fisheries Commission*, *op. cit. supra* note 148, paras. 164-173.

229. Contra: P. Palchetti, *op. cit. supra* note 217. Nor is it the point to hold the EU responsible for the breach of its due diligence obligation with respect to the actions of its Member States, even though this can happen (in fact, the opposite is more likely to occur when Member States of an IO, such as the EU or the UN, have due diligence obligations in relation to the actions of that IO: see e.g. ECtHR, Case of *Bosphorus Hava Yolları Turizm ve Ticaret Anonim Şirketi* v. *Ireland*, No. 45036/98, Judgment of 30 June 2005, paras. 152-153; ECtHR, Case of *Michaud* v. *France*, No. 12323/11, Judgment of 6 December 2012, para. 103; ECtHR, Case of *Al-Dulimi* v. *Switzerland*, No. 5809/08, Judgment of 26 November 2013 (Chamber of the Second Section), paras. 114 *et seq*.; Dissenting Opinion of Judge Keller, in ECtHR, Case of *Al-Dulimi* v. *Switzerland*, No. 5809/08, Judgment of 21 June 2016 (Grand Chamber), paras. 11 *et seq*.; CCPR, General Comment No. 36, *op. cit. supra* note 205, paras. 21-22). Rather, the EU's due diligence obligations apply, for example, with respect to the actions of ships flying the national flag of one of its Member States (without attribution of these ships' conduct to a Member State or to the EU itself).

international law for the actions of other persons (a subsidiary company, for example).

After all, like IOs, these institutions can be subjected to international law. Admittedly, while the former are constituted of States and may therefore be said to be of a public nature, the latter are constituted of private persons and are of a private nature. From the point of view of the history of due diligence and of the standard's origin in Roman private law, however, the argument of the private nature of MNCs should not be considered decisive.

Under many regimes of domestic private law, MNCs must abide by different standards known as "human rights due diligence" or "corporate due diligence" [230]. They must also abide by such standards under certain soft law instruments in international human rights law [231] even if those due diligence standards are, once again, analogous to those established under domestic private law [232]. Binding international legal instruments on the matter are currently being negotiated [233]. Some of them echo the obligations and responsibilities of States under international human rights law (including due diligence obligations *stricto sensu*) by reminding them that these obligations and responsibilities require the creation of due diligence obligations for MNCs under national law [234]. The latter are, once more, diligence duties under domestic private law, and they may someday become duties under private international law if States succeed in harmonising their minimal content.

230. See French Commercial Code (Ccom/FR), introduced by the French law No. 2017-399 on the "vigilance duty" of parent companies of 27 March 2017 [online], Arts. L225-102-4 and L225-102-5; Modern Slavery Act 2015 of the United Kingdom of 26 March 2015 [online]; Swiss federal popular initiative "Entreprises responsables – pour protéger l'être humain et l'environnement", Feuille fédérale 2017 6043-6044 [online] and the counter-proposals to this Swiss federal popular initiative "Entreprises responsables – pour protéger l'être humain et l'environnement" [online].

231. See e.g. HRC, Guiding Principles on Business and Human Rights, *op. cit. supra* note 88. See also CESCR, General Comment No. 24, *op. cit. supra* note 3, para. 30; IACtHR, *The Environment and Human Rights*, *op. cit. supra* note 205; CCPR, *Basem Ahmed Issa Yassin and others* v. *Canada*, *op. cit. supra* note 205, paras. 6.5-6.7.

232. See F. Marrella, *op. cit. supra* note 30.

233. See e.g. OEIGWG Draft, *op. cit. supra* note 10. More generally on the different options of international law in this field, see O. de Schutter, "Towards a New Treaty on Business and Human Rights", *Business and Human Rights Journal*, Vol. 1, No. 1 (2015), pp. 41-67.

234. See N. D. White, 2012, *op. cit. supra* note 30; V. Chetail, "The Legal Personality of Multinational Corporations, State Responsibility and Due Diligence: The Way Forward", in D. Alland, V. Chetail, O. de Frouville and J. E. Viñuales (eds.), *Unité et diversité du droit international: écrits en l'honneur du Professeur Pierre-Marie Dupuy*, Leiden, Martinus Nijhoff, 2014, pp. 105-130.

Currently, however, their content remains entirely open [235]: it depends on the national legal order of each State as does the corresponding civil liability regime in case of violation of these diligence duties. In short, the content of diligence duties under domestic private law (or maybe, someday, under private international law) should clearly be distinguished from the due diligence obligations of States and IOs analysed in this course.

In any event, as with IOs, three principled objections or, at least, three hurdles would have to be overcome before the personal scope of international law's due diligence can be extended to MNCs.

As mentioned in Chapter I, the primary difficulty is the lack of obligations owed by MNCs under international law upon which the due diligence standard can be grafted and therefore the absence of responsibilities for negligence of these private subjects under international law (outside of international criminal law). Yet nothing fundamentally precludes the creation of such special obligations of due diligence.

Second, just like with IOs, the most important obstacle to the establishment of a minimal standard of due diligence for MNCs remains the diversity of their legal and institutional structures. How is it possible to define, in the absence of a common understanding of what MNCs are, what should be the normal behaviour of a good or reasonable MNC? As for IOs, the need to clarify the legal and institutional nature of MNCs under international law is becoming pressing [236]. If it has been possible to unify the minimal institutional criteria constitutive of States, it should be possible to do the same for other corporative institutions which come next in the history of legal personalities and institutional fictions [237]. The identification of the minimal content of the due diligence of MNCs could actually instil an international law of corporations. This is, after all, what occurred with States through the development of the

235. For a project that catalogues and compares these different national traditions of due diligence in order to identify a common regime, and in relation to HRC, Guiding Principles on Business and Human Rights, *op. cit. supra* note 88, see O. De Schutter, A. Ramasastry, M. B. Taylor and R. C. Thompson, *op. cit. supra* note 15, pp. 55-57.

236. On the lack of a definition of corporations in international law, see J. G. Ruggie, "Multinationals as Global Institution: Power, Authority and Relative Autonomy", *Regulation & Governance*, Vol. 12 (2018), pp. 317-333; F. Johns, "Theorizing the Corporation in International Law", in A. Orford and F. Hoffmann (eds.), *The Oxford Handbook of the Theory of International Law*, Oxford, Oxford University Press, 2016, pp. 635-654.

237. On the history of the relationship between corporations and States, see A. Supiot, "État, Entreprise et Démocratie", in P. Musso (ed.), *L'entreprise contre l'Etat?*, Paris, Manucius / IEA de Nantes, 2017, pp. 13-31.

international law of statehood at the end of the nineteenth century and what may soon be the case for IOs.

The third and final difficulty is the foundation of MNCs' due diligence. Clarifying that foundation makes it necessary to confront not only the thorny question of the institutional relations between MNCs and States and the role of the public/private distinction in international law, but also the issue of their precise relationship to the sovereign equality of States and their peoples.

In conclusion, the corporate due diligence and, more precisely, the human rights due diligence of MNCs under soft law remain, to this day, entirely distinct from the due diligence of States and IOs under international law. On the one hand, there is the regime of the domestic private law standard applicable to corporations violating human rights by way of self-regulation, under soft law or maybe, someday, under private international law. That regime should be distinguished, on the other hand, from the due diligence regime applicable to States and IOs under international law. The coexistence of distinct regimes of due diligence is obviously problematic [238]. We will return to this concern in Section B of Chapter IV, which is devoted to due diligence in international human rights law, including in the context of business.

(b) The beneficiaries of due diligence

The beneficiary of due diligence refers to the person(s) or entity(ies) whose rights and interests are protected by the specific obligation of (x with) due diligence and therefore, more generally, by international law [239].

It can be one subject alone or several subjects collectively, notably, if the obligation of due diligence is an obligation *erga omnes*. It is the case in international environmental law and international human rights law, where due diligence obligations are owed to several States and peoples together [240].

238. See the exchange of views between J. Bonnitcha and R. McCorquodale, "The Concept of 'Due Diligence' " and "A Rejoinder", *op. cit. supra* note 30, as well as J. G. Ruggie and J. F. Sherman, *op. cit. supra* note 30; N. D. White, 2012, *op. cit. supra* note 30.

239. See also P. d'Argent and A. de Vaucleroy, *op. cit. supra* note 33, mentioning "persons protected" by due diligence.

240. On the invocation of responsibility in those cases, see ARSIWA, *op. cit. supra* note 24, Arts. 40-41 and 42 *et seq.*; ARIO, *op. cit. supra* note 24, Arts. 41-42 and 43 *et*

As previously indicated, the interests of the beneficiaries of due diligence can be recognised by international law as obligations *stricto sensu* and even as corresponding rights. However, it does not have to be the case: it is sufficient that the interests protected by international law are recognised as such and therefore are able to ground due diligence obligations [241] even without corresponding rights of the beneficiaries.

Because due diligence is by nature grafted upon an obligation not to harm which is specific to the protection of certain rights or interests, it is the own nature of these interests and then of that specific obligation which determines on a case-by-case basis whether the beneficiary holds a corresponding "right" *stricto sensu*. This implies that a due diligence obligation is not necessarily a "perfect" obligation, in that a correlative right to the due diligence obligation does not always exist [242]. Each special regime of international law must determine whether the obligation is "directed" to a beneficiary who thereby becomes a right-holder of the obligation not to cause harm by negligence. It is the case under international human rights law, for example, but not necessarily under international humanitarian law or international environmental law.

Moreover, even if a special obligation of due diligence is directed and corresponds to a right of the beneficiary, these rights and obligations are not necessarily mutual or reciprocal: the beneficiary may not be able to become duty-bearer of a due diligence obligation. It is not because sovereignty is the source of both rights protected by due diligence and due diligence obligations that due diligence is always founded upon reciprocity and by extension exclusively applicable between States.

This difference between the quality of beneficiary of due diligence and the quality of holder of a corresponding right reveals an important difference among due diligence obligations depending on the regimes of international law at stake. While these obligations all share the same due diligence standard, they are not necessarily similar in every aspect, including in the rights of their beneficiaries. Thus, even if international

seq. See G. Gaja, "Do States Have a Duty to Ensure Compliance with Obligations *Erga Omnes* by Other States?", in M. Ragazzi (ed.), *International Responsibility Today: Essays in Memory of Oscar Schachter*, Leiden, Martinus Nijhoff, 2005, pp. 31-36.

241. See ICJ, The case of the *Corfu Channel*, *op. cit. supra* note 8, p. 22; Dissenting opinion of Judge Weeramantry, in ICJ, *Legality of the Threat or Use of Nuclear Weapons, op. cit. supra* note 8, p. 496. See also D. Lévy, *op. cit. supra* note 105, pp. 752-753; J. Klabbers, 2017, *op. cit. supra* note 105.

242. Contra: J. E. Viñuales, 2016, *op. cit. supra* note 117.

environmental law and international human rights law have come to include due diligence obligations of a similar content (like participation rights), those obligations are not interchangeable to the point of exempting the emergence of human rights and their corresponding obligations (including of due diligence) from the "jurisdiction" condition imposed by international human rights law (i.e. effective control of the State over the alleged right-holders) [243].

The absence of a right of the beneficiary of a due diligence obligation towards the duty-bearer implies that the beneficiary's normative relation with the duty-bearer is not necessarily strong. As previously noted, the normative relation that grounds a due diligence obligation is the relation of the duty-bearer to the source of the (risk of) harm because the duty-bearer must exercise some control over that source. Of course, a breach of the due diligence obligation will give rise to responsibility and therefore to new rights for the beneficiary (see Arts. 42 *et seq.* ARSIWA; Arts. 43 *et seq.* ARIO). However, these rights are of a different type and arise from a new normative relation (of responsibility) created by the injury which was caused and by the obligation to remedy it [244].

Since the sixteenth century, the beneficiaries of due diligence can be either States or private persons depending upon the rights or interests protected by international law. Persons or entities are identified as beneficiaries of due diligence through the rights and interests protected by international law and have therefore evolved along with those rights and interests. At first, these were mostly aliens, in accordance with the international law on the protection of aliens; then any person residing on the national territory; and, finally, any person, in accordance with international human rights law [245]. Foreign nationality or territorial residency are no longer required in order to be the beneficiary of a due diligence obligation under contemporary international law. Today, other subjects of international law (IOs, for instance) have progressively been added to the list of beneficiaries provided that their rights or interests are protected under international law.

Even when harm affects a material or tangible object, it is the persons' rights and interests with regard to this object that are protected

243. See also S. Besson, 2020, *op. cit. supra* note 121. Contra: J. E. Viñuales, 2016, *op. cit. supra* note 117; A. E. Boyle, 2012, *op. cit. supra* note 119.

244. See D. Nolan, "Negligence", 2013, *op. cit. supra* note 4; S. Perry, 2009, *op. cit. supra* note 6; J. Gardner, 2011, *op. cit. supra* note 157.

245. On this evolution, see M. Hakimi, *op. cit. supra* note 13.

by international law (and not the object itself). It is notably the case of harms affecting common interests known as interests "of humanity", which are interests shared by the peoples of the different States of the world [246]. Examples include interests related to the marine environment or to the air [247].

One might further wonder about the inclusion of the rights or interests of future generations in the personal scope of due diligence (given the principle of intergenerational equity [248]). It is difficult to provide a general answer to this question outside the field of international environmental law [249] or the right to protection of the world cultural and natural heritage [250], where the answer is clearly positive. Not every international legal regime protects the interests (and especially the rights) of future generations. For example, under international human rights law, due diligence obligations are correlative to the rights of human right-holders, and holding such rights depends on a certain capacity to claim them. In that field, there are no due diligence obligations owed to those who have not yet been born [251].

246. On the notion of common interests and the false opposition between these interests and State interests (incorrectly regarded as necessarily self-interested), see S. Besson, "Community Interests in International Law: Whose Interests Are They and How Does One Identify Them?", in E. Benvenisti and G. Nolte (eds.), *Community Interests across International Law*, Cambridge, Cambridge University Press, 2018, pp. 50-69; G. Gaja, "The Protection of General Interests in the International Community", *Recueil des cours*, Vol. 364 (2013), pp. 9-185.

247. See e.g. ICJ, *Legality of the Threat or Use of Nuclear Weapons*, *op. cit. supra* note 8, para. 29 ("areas beyond national control"). See also Convention on the Law of the Sea, *op. cit. supra* note 9, Art. 192; CLN, *op. cit. supra* note 116, Art. 7; Convention on Biological Diversity, *op. cit. supra* note 9, Art. 3; Preamble of the United Nations Framework Convention on Climate Change, *op. cit. supra* note 116; Stockholm Declaration, *op. cit. supra* note 116, Principles 21 and 22; Rio Declaration, *op. cit. supra* note 116, Principle 2.

248. See E. B. Weiss, "Intergenerational Equity", in R. Wolfrum (ed.), *Max Planck Encyclopedia of Public International Law*, Oxford, Oxford University Press, 2013 [online].

249. See ICJ, The case of *The Gabcikovo-Nagymaros Project*, *op. cit. supra* note 8, paras. 53 and 141.

250. See Convention Concerning the Protection of the World Cultural and Natural Heritage of 16 November 1972, UNTS, Vol. 1037, p. 151, Art. 4. See e.g. G. Bartolini, "Disaster Risk Reduction and Cultural Heritage", in K. Samuel and K. Bookmiller (eds.), *Cambridge Handbook of Disaster Risk Reduction and International Law*, Cambridge, Cambridge University Press, 2019, pp. 421-442.

251. See e.g. with regard to the human right to a healthy environment, Supreme Court of the Netherlands, Case of *De Staat de Nederland (Ministerie van Infrastructuur en Milieu)* v. *Stichting Urgenda*, 19/00135, 20 December 2019, para. 5.6.2. See more generally: J. H. Knox, "Constructing the Human Right to a Healthy Environment", *Annual Review of Law and Social Science*, Vol. 16 (2020), pp. 79-95.

(c) *The third parties of due diligence*

The duty-bearer of due diligence obligations in international law is required to take a number of diligent measures to prevent, protect against or remedy a (risk of) harm caused to the beneficiary not by its own conduct (i.e. most often, the conduct of its organs/agents which is then attributed to the duty-bearer), but by what one may refer to as the third party of due diligence.

This third party is the source of the (risk of) harm and makes up the third angle of due diligence's triangular relationship. It is the person or entity with whom the duty-bearer of due diligence must be in relation and especially exercise control over for the due diligence obligation to arise: the due diligence duty arises from its ability to exercise control over that party. This is actually why due diligence obligations under international law differ from obligations known as "bystander responsibility". The latter indeed are justified independently from any relation between the duty-bearer and the beneficiary or between the duty-bearer and the third party that causes the harm [252].

Two remarks are in order with respect to the duty-bearer's "control" over the third party at the origin of the (risk of) harm: the first relates to its type and the other to its degree.

First, it is essential not to confuse the "control" which the duty-bearer exercises over a third party with the duty-bearer's "competence" or "jurisdiction" [253] to exercise this control under international law (territorial, personal, protective or universal jurisdiction) [254].

---

252. On the latter, see M. Hakimi, *op. cit. supra* note 13; J. M. Smits, *op. cit. supra* note 127.

253. See e.g. for "jurisdiction and/or control", Convention on the Law of the Sea, *op. cit. supra* note 9, Art. 194; Convention on Biological Diversity, *op. cit. supra* note 9, Art. 3; Preamble of the United Nations Framework Convention on Climate Change, *op. cit. supra* note 116; Stockholm Declaration, *op. cit. supra* note 116, Principles 21 and 22; Rio Declaration, *op. cit. supra* note 116, Principle 2; ILA, Declaration of Legal Principles Relating to Climate Change, *op. cit. supra* note 11, Arts. 7A and 7B; ICJ, *Legality of the Threat or Use of Nuclear Weapons*, *op. cit. supra* note 8, paras. 241-242; ICJ, The case of *The Gabcikovo-Nagymaros Project*, *op. cit. supra* note 8, para. 53. See, however, for "jurisdiction" only, ICJ, The case of *Pulp Mills on the River Uruguay*, *op. cit. supra* note 3, para. 101; OEIGWG Draft, *op. cit. supra* note 10, Art. 6. For a discussion, see F. Violi, "The Function of the Triad 'Territory', 'Jurisdiction' and 'Control', in Due Diligence Obligations", in A. Peters, H. Krieger and L. Kreuzer (eds.), *Due Diligence in International Law*, Oxford, Oxford University Press, 2020, pp. 75-91.

254. See S. Besson, "Why and What (State) Jurisdiction: Legal Plurality, Individual Equality and Territorial Legitimacy", in J. Klabbers and L. Palombella (eds.), *The Challenge of Inter-Legality*, Cambridge, Cambridge University Press, 2019, pp. 91-132.

As emphasised in international jurisprudence, this control may derive from any type of "link" (political or not) between the duty-bearer and that third party [255]. It may correspond to the (personal or territorial) jurisdiction of a State over the third party at the origin of the (risk of) harm if that third party is a national [256] of that State or if it is acting from that State's territory [257]. But it can also exist independently from the third party's nationality (in the case of an occupying State, for example) or even independently from any territorial or extraterritorial control over that party. Because of a growing disjunction between the competence to control and the actual capacity to control in practice [258] and the resulting weakening of the competence-control-responsibility nexus that grounds due diligence, a due diligence obligation may also imply an obligation to exercise or even acquire jurisdiction pursuant to international law. Chapter IV will show that it can be the case in international human rights law [259].

Second, control over the third party that is the source of the (risk of) harm can be very loose. It does not need to be "effective" control as required under international responsibility law for the purpose of attribution of a private person's conduct to the State (Art. 8 ARSIWA). The ICJ defines "effective control" over a private person or a group of private persons as the capacity to influence or initiate the constitutive elements of an operation and the ability to discontinue them if they are still ongoing [260]. As will be explained in Chapter III, in case of

255. See ICJ, The case of *Application of the Convention on the Prevention and Punishment of the Crime of Genocide*, *op. cit. supra* note 22, para. 430 ("political links, as well as links of all other kinds"). See also ICJ, The case of *Armed Activities on the Territory of the Congo*, 2022, *op. cit. supra* note 123, paras. 75 and 98.

256. See ICJ, The case of *Armed Activities on the Territory of the Congo*, 2005, *op. cit. supra* note 3.

257. See ICJ, The case of *Application of the Convention on the Prevention and Punishment of the Crime of Genocide*, *op. cit. supra* note 22; ICJ, The case of *Armed Activities on the Territory of the Congo*, 2022, *op. cit. supra* note 123, para. 95.

258. On this development and for a discussion of its potential normative consequences, see S. Besson, "Why and What (State) Jurisdiction", 2019, *op. cit. supra* note 254; C. M. J. Ryngaert, *Jurisdiction in International Law*, 2nd ed., Oxford, Oxford University Press, 2015.

259. On the relationship between jurisdiction under general international law and jurisdiction under international human rights law and, more generally, on the relationship between the competences and obligations of States, see S. Besson, "The Extra-territoriality of the European Convention on Human Rights: Why Human Rights Depend on Jurisdiction and What Jurisdiction Amounts to", *Leiden Journal of International Law*, Vol. 25, No. 4 (2012), pp. 857-884; S. Besson, 2020, *op. cit. supra* note 121.

260. See ICJ, The case of *Military and Paramilitary Activities in and against Nicaragua*, *op. cit. supra* note 8; ICJ, The case of *Application of the Convention on*

breach of a due diligence obligation, a State will be responsible for its own negligent conduct; the conduct of the private person is not attributed to the State. As a result, control can, but does not need to, be as effective in the context of due diligence as for the purpose of conduct attribution. Most crucially, control does not need to be active or necessarily intentional [261]. We will return to this point in the discussion of the variability of due diligence depending on the degree of control exercised by the duty-bearer over the source of the (risk of) harm.

In light of the above, it is essential to distinguish this type of control over the third party which is the source of the (risk of) harm from yet another type of "control" and "jurisdiction" in international law: "jurisdiction" in the sense of (effective and regular) control over a right-holder under international human rights law [262]. Such control is one of the conditions governing the emergence of human rights and the grounding of their corresponding duties [263].

Unlike the control that grounds due diligence and which pertains to the third party as the source of the (risk of) harm, effective control in international human rights law must be exercised over the human right-holder and therefore over the beneficiary of the due diligence obligation when that obligation corresponds to a human right. Unlike a simple due diligence obligation which arises from the control relationship between the duty-bearer and the third party that is the source of the (risk of) harm, therefore, a due diligence obligation relating to a human right also rests upon a second normative relation of (effective) control, this time between the duty-bearer and the right-holder who is the beneficiary of due diligence.

This is an important distinction between international human rights law and other international legal regimes, such as international

---

the Prevention and Punishment of the Crime of Genocide, *op. cit. supra* note 22; ICJ, The case of *Armed Activities on the Territory of the Congo*, 2005, *op. cit. supra* note 3.

261. See A. Seibert-Fohr, "From Complicity to Due Diligence: When Do States Incur Responsibility for their Involvement in Serious International Wrongdoing?", *German Yearbook of International Law*, Vol. 60 (2018), pp. 667-707, on the relations between responsibility by attribution of conduct, responsibility for complicity and responsibility for negligence in ICJ, The case of *Application of the Convention on the Prevention and Punishment of the Crime of Genocide*, *op. cit. supra* note 22.

262. On these different types of "jurisdiction" and control, see S. Besson, 2012, *op. cit. supra* note 259. More generally on "jurisdiction" in the context of international human rights law, see M. Milanovic, *Extraterritorial Application of Human Rights Treaties: Law, Principles, and Policy*, Oxford, Oxford University Press, 2011.

263. See ECtHR, Case of *Al-Skeini and others* v. *The United Kingdom*, No. 55721/07, Judgment of 7 July 2011; ICJ, *Legal Consequences of the Construction of a Wall in the Occupied Palestinian Territory*, Advisory Opinion of 9 July 2004, *ICJ Reports 2004*, p. 136.

environmental law, which feature due diligence obligations that do not entail a control relationship over the beneficiaries. While these two regimes include many due diligence obligations that address the same content (corresponding, for example, to participation rights), this distinction explains why these obligations are not interchangeable. Most crucially, human rights and their corresponding duties (including due diligence obligations) cannot emerge without satisfying the condition of "jurisdiction" and thus the condition of the effective control by the State over the alleged right-holders [264].

There is a trend among a number of authors in international human rights law [265] and even among some non-judicial international human rights bodies [266] that makes it important to stress this point. In appealing to the kind of control over third parties required by due diligence, indeed, they seek to progressively reduce the conditions of "jurisdiction" and effective control over human right-holders to a mere control of the duty-bearer over the sources of (risks of) human rights restriction or even to a mere causal connection between the duty-bearer and the restriction [267]. Such an interpretation does not only turn the conditions of the emergence of human rights and obligations upside down. It also calls into question the normative relation between human right-holders

264. Contra: J. E. Viñuales, 2016, *op. cit. supra* note 117; A. E. Boyle, 2012, *op. cit. supra* note 119.

265. See e.g. V. Tzevelekos, *op. cit. supra* note 121; A. Berkes, "Extraterritorial Responsibility of the Home States", 2018, *op. cit. supra* note 121; S. Grosbon, "L'Observation générale n°24 du Comité des droits économiques, sociaux et culturels sur les obligations des États dans le contexte des activités des entreprises: vigilance raisonnable et extraterritorialité", *Journal européen des droits de l'homme*, Vol. 19, No. 4 (2018), pp. 355-371; O. de Frouville, "La responsabilité des Etats pour les activités extraterritoriales des entreprises et l'interprétation de la notion de 'juridiction' par le Comité des droits de l'homme", in *Justice et Droits de l'homme. Mélanges en hommage à Christine Chanet*, Paris, Pedone, 2019, pp. 67-86.

266. See on the extraterritoriality of due diligence obligations relating the human right to a healthy environment: IACtHR, *The Environment and Human Rights*, *op. cit. supra* note 205. Contra: Supreme Court of the Netherlands, *De Staat de Nederland (Ministerie van Infrastructuur en Milieu)* v. *Stichting Urgenda*, *op. cit. supra* note 251, para. 5.6.2. See on the extraterritoriality of States' positive obligations to ensure that the MNCs under their jurisdiction (pursuant to international law) do not cause human rights violations abroad: CCPR, General Comment No. 36, *op. cit. supra* note 205; CCPR, *Basem Ahmed Issa Yassin and others* v. *Canada*, *op. cit. supra* note 205, paras. 6.5-6.7 (see also Concurring opinion of Olivier de Frouville and Yadh Ben Achour, in CCPR, *Basem Ahmed Issa Yassin and others* v. *Canada*, *ibid.*, paras. 8-11); CESCR, General Comment No. 24, *op. cit. supra* note 3, para. 30.

267. See e.g. CESCR, General Comment No. 24, *op. cit. supra* note 3, para. 30; IACtHR, *The Environment and Human Rights*, *op. cit. supra* note 205, para. 104.h; CCPR, General Comment No. 36, *op. cit. supra* note 205, paras. 21-22; Concurring opinion of de Frouville and Ben Achour, in CCPR, *Basem Ahmed Issa Yassin and others* v. *Canada*, *op. cit. supra* note 205, paras. 8 *et seq.*

and duty-bearers and the fundamental status which they establish. That interpretation also lays bare the sheer misunderstanding of the nature and foundation of due diligence obligations which, as explained earlier, must be attached to rights or interests to arise in the first place. The due diligence standard cannot, by itself, ground a human rights obligation, nor can it ground a due diligence obligation solely on the basis of a relation of control and causation without consideration for the interests to be protected and for the nature of these interests. Section B of Chapter IV, which is devoted to due diligence in international human rights law, will provide a fuller examination of these distinctions and their importance [268].

The third party of due diligence may be any legal subject [269] over which the duty-bearer exercises control. Not only can it be a private person, irrespective of nationality, but also a State [270] or even an IO [271]. It can also be a natural phenomenon or a technical installation over which the duty-bearer has control.

If the link between the third party and the duty-bearer of due diligence is a link of nationality, complex considerations may arise when the third party is a legal person [272], like an MNC. To this day, the

268. See also S. Besson, 2020, *op. cit. supra* note 121.

269. See ICJ, The case of *Application of the Convention on the Prevention and Punishment of the Crime of Genocide*, *op. cit. supra* note 22, para. 429 ("other persons or entities").

270. On the due diligence of a State with regard to the actions of another State over which it exercises "control", see e.g. ECtHR, Case of *El-Masri* v. *The Former Yugoslav Republic of Macedonia*, No. 39630/09, Judgment of 13 December 2012.

271. On the due diligence of a Member State with regard to the actions of an IO over which it exercises "control" (with or without "presumption of equivalence"), see e.g. ECtHR, *Bosphorus* v. *Ireland*, *op. cit. supra* note 229, paras. 152-153; ECtHR, *Michaud* v. *France*, *op. cit. supra* note 229, para. 103; ECtHR, Case of *Avotiņš* v. *Latvia*, No. 17502/07, Judgment of 23 May 2016 (for the EU); ECtHR, *Al-Dulimi* v. *Switzerland*, *op. cit. supra* note 229, paras. 114 *et seq.* (for the UN); Dissenting opinion of Judge Keller, in ECtHR, *Al-Dulimi* v. *Switzerland* (Grand Chamber), *op. cit. supra* note 229, paras. 11 *et seq.* See, however, on the lack of automatic territorial control of the host State over the IO in the absence of "jurisdiction", ECtHR, Case of *Djokaba Lambi Longa* v. *The Netherlands*, No. 33917/12, Judgment of 9 October 2012; in contrast with CCPR, General Comment No. 36, *op. cit. supra* note 205, paras. 21-22, which recognises the State's obligation of territorial control. See also ILA, Committee on the Accountability of International Organisations, Final Report, Berlin Conference (2004), *op. cit. supra* note 211. See K. Daugirdas, "Member States' Due Diligence Obligations to Supervise International Organizations", in A. Peters, H. Krieger and L. Kreuzer (eds.), *Due Diligence in International Law*, Oxford, Oxford University Press, 2020, pp. 59-74. It should be noted that the opposite can also occur and, although there is not yet a practice in that respect, it is possible to conceive a due diligence obligation owed by an IO for the actions of its Member State over which it has "control".

272. On this question, see A. Berkes, "Extraterritorial Responsibility of the Home States", 2018, *op. cit. supra* note 121.

international legal criteria governing the nationality of legal persons and its opposability on the international plane vary (ranging from the law of the State where the corporation has its statutory seat, the law of the State in which the corporation is incorporated, to the law of the State which exercises control over the corporation). Fortunately, the control exercised over a legal person that is the source of harm does not need to rest upon nationality. As mentioned above, it can also be territorial, jurisdictional or even derive from other kinds of "links" [273].

Some have raised the question of the applicability of due diligence to the duty-bearer itself (notably for the actions of its *de jure* or *de facto* organs or of any private person whose conduct can be attributed to it), that is to say, whether its own conduct endangering the beneficiary can engage its responsibility for negligence. After all, this is how negligence, as opposed to intentional tort, is conceived of under Anglo-American civil liability law. It was also one of the applications of due diligence under Roman private law, as explained in Chapter I. Several examples thereof can actually be found among existing obligations of conduct under international law, such as the obligation to judge with diligence in international human rights law [274].

Yet such obligations do not correspond to the paradigm of due diligence obligations in international law. As highlighted in Chapter I, due diligence obligations in international law are owed by international law institutions (such as States or IOs) and as such by institutions whose nature is precisely to mediate or channel responsibility for contingencies whose source is external. It is important to keep in mind that responsibility for negligence is neither a form of collective responsibility for private contingencies nor a form of responsibility of institutions aimed exclusively at their own contingencies or at contingencies attributable to them.

In any event, the difficulty is that the international responsibility of States or IOs is not based on fault (either intentional or negligent), but on the attribution of an objective breach of international law. Of course, a primary obligation of international law may have its breach conditioned upon a subjective element of fault and have a due diligence requirement in that respect, which may in turn give rise to responsibility for wrongful negligence. Likewise, it is also possible to take into account the intentional or negligent character of the breach in

273. See e.g. CESCR, General Comment No. 24, *op. cit. supra* note 3, paras. 30 *et seq.*
274. See H. Raspail, *op. cit. supra* note 15.

the evaluation of responsibility (aggravated, for instance) and to adjust the reparation on that basis. This issue will be addressed in Chapter III, which is devoted to due diligence in international responsibility law.

2. The material scope of due diligence

Due diligence obligations require their duty-bearers not to harm by negligence a right or an interest protected by international law. The material scope of due diligence is open: it depends on the scope of the obligation of (general or special) international law upon which it is grafted. This is true both for the nature of the relevant harm and for the context in which this (risk of) harm occurs. The harm can be physical, moral or even purely legal.

Nonetheless, the observation of the different international legal regimes reveals two further requirements: *(i)* a minimal level of risk of harm and *(ii)* a minimal level of gravity of harm.

First, the risk is often described as needing to be "real" and "immediate" and not merely virtual or remote [275]. Yet the question remains open and each regime seems to modulate these two different criteria to increase the degree of required diligence. The earlier discussion of due diligence with regard to risks of harms to which future generations may be exposed can therefore arise again in this context.

Second, the potential harm is often described as needing to be "serious" [276], "important" [277] or "severe" [278]. Again, this question remains open. Each regime seems able to modulate these different criteria so as to increase the degree of required diligence by lowering the minimal threshold for its application. Above that minimal threshold, the degree of the risk of harm, the gravity of the harm or the vulnerability to the harm are as many "parameters" of variability of what is expected from

275. This seems to be the case in international human rights law, including at the European level: see e.g. ECtHR, *Opuz* v. *Turkey*, *op. cit. supra* note 205, paras. 129-130.

276. See e.g. *Trail Smelter* Arbitration, *op. cit. supra* note 8, para. 716; Convention on the Law of the Sea, *op. cit. supra* note 9, Part XII; *Tallinn Manual 2.0*, *op. cit. supra* note 88, Rules 6 and 7.

277. See e.g. ILC, Draft Articles on Prevention of Transboundary Harm from Hazardous Activities, with commentaries, *op. cit. supra* note 11, Art. 3; Convention on the Law of the Non-Navigational Uses of International Watercourses, *op. cit. supra* note 9, Art. 7 (1); VCDR, *op. cit. supra* note 9, Art. 22 (2). See also ICJ, The case of *Certain Activities carried out by Nicaragua in the Border Area*, *op. cit. supra* note 3; ICJ, The case of *Pulp Mills on the River Uruguay*, *op. cit. supra* note 3, para. 101.

278. See e.g. Rio Declaration, *op. cit. supra* note 116, Principles 14 and 15.

the duty-bearer of due diligence in the specific circumstances of each case. We will return to this issue later in this chapter.

The issue of the reality and immediacy of harm may eventually raise the question of whether a mere risk of such a harm without any realisation thereof is sufficient to amount to a breach of the due diligence obligation.

Again, the answer depends on each special regime of international law and on the nature of the obligation to which due diligence is attached. As we will see, certain due diligence obligations (of prevention, notably) require the occurrence of the harm for the obligation to be considered violated (necessary condition). And this is so even if the obligation is not an obligation of result and if, as a result, the mere occurrence of the harm does not suffice to breach the obligation of prevention (insufficient condition) [279]. However, not all due diligence obligations function in that manner [280]. In the other cases, one may consider that exposure to a risk can constitute a (legal) harm: the latter is a derivative harm precisely because an actual harm (that to which the risk pertains) might occur [281].

In any event, international responsibility law requires, at least for obligations of reparation to arise, the occurrence of the harm and of an injury, by opposition to the mere violation of the due diligence obligation. In some special regimes of international law, the existence of an injury does not amount to a condition of international responsibility: a breach of an international law obligation is considered sufficient to trigger responsibility and may even be deemed a "legal" injury, while obligations of reparation remain dependent on the harm's occurrence and an injury. As we will see, under the general regime of international responsibility law as well, the occurrence of a harm and an injury are

279. See e.g. Convention on the Prevention and Punishment of the Crime of Genocide of 9 December 1948, UNTS, Vol. 78, p. 277, Arts. I and V. See also ICJ, The case of *Application of the Convention on the Prevention and Punishment of the Crime of Genocide*, *op. cit. supra* note 22, paras. 221-222 and 430-431. See more generally J. Crawford, *op. cit. supra* note 24, pp. 227-228, on Art. 14 (3) ARSIWA, *op. cit. supra* note 24.

280. See e.g. VCDR, *op. cit. supra* note 9, Art. 22 (2). See also *Trail Smelter* Arbitration, *op. cit. supra* note 8; ICJ, The case of *Pulp Mills on the River Uruguay*, *op. cit. supra* note 3, para. 101; ICJ, The case of *Certain Activities carried out by Nicaragua in the Border Area*, *op. cit. supra* note 3, para. 104. See more generally J. Crawford, *op. cit. supra* note 24, pp. 227-228.

281. On this debate in Anglo-American tort law theory, see C. Finkelstein, "Is Risk a Harm?", *University of Pennsylvania Law Review*, Vol. 151 (2003), pp. 963-1001; J. Oberdiek, *op. cit. supra* note 157; S. Perry, 2014, *op. cit. supra* note 157.

not among the conditions of responsibility [282]. The issue is left to the content of the primary due diligence obligation.

3. *The geographic scope of due diligence*

Due diligence obligations do not have a particular geographic scope. Each international legal regime determines that scope by reference to the rights and interests protected by the due diligence obligations and to the duty-bearers controlling the sources of (risks of) harm to these rights and interests.

As previously indicated, the duty-bearer's "control" over the third party at the origin of the (risk of) harm is personal even if it does not need to be grounded in the nationality of that third party and as such in personal competence or "jurisdiction". As a result, control does not need to correspond to a territorial competence or "jurisdiction" or even to any territorial form of control [283] for due diligence to arise. While control may be territorial (either *stricto sensu* over an official territory [284] or extraterritorially over a foreign territory [285]), a territorial or spatial dimension is not necessary to its existence [286]. The harm or its source may be located outside of the duty-bearing State's territory, as long as

282. See A. E. Boyle, "State Responsibility and International Liability for Injurious Consequences of Acts Not Prohibited by International Law: A Necessary Distinction?", *International and Comparative Law Quarterly*, Vol. 39 (1990), pp. 1-26, arguing that "liability for risks" should be the title of the ILC's 2001 Draft Articles on Prevention of Transboundary Harm from Hazardous Activities, *op. cit. supra* note 11.

283. See e.g. for "jurisdiction and/or control", Convention on the Law of the Sea, *op. cit. supra* note 9, Art. 194; Convention on Biological Diversity, *op. cit. supra* note 9, Art. 3; Preamble of the United Nations Framework Convention on Climate Change, *op. cit. supra* note 116; Stockholm Declaration, *op. cit. supra* note 116, Principles 21 and 22; Rio Declaration, *op. cit. supra* note 116, Principle 2; ILA, Declaration of Legal Principles Relating to Climate Change, *op. cit. supra* note 11, Arts. 7A and 7B; ICJ, *Legality of the Threat or Use of Nuclear Weapons, op. cit. supra* note 8, paras. 241-242; ICJ, The case of *The Gabcikovo-Nagymaros Project, op. cit. supra* note 8, para. 53. See, however, for "jurisdiction" only, ICJ, The case of *Pulp Mills on the River Uruguay, op. cit. supra* note 3, para. 101. For a discussion, see F. Violi, *op. cit. supra* note 253.

284. See e.g. *Trail Smelter* Arbitration, *op. cit. supra* note 8; *Island of Palmas* Arbitration, *op. cit. supra* note 8.

285. See e.g. ICJ, The case of *Armed Activities on the Territory of the Congo*, 2005, *op. cit. supra* note 3, para. 246; ICJ, *Legal Consequences for States of the Continued Presence of South Africa in Namibia (South West Africa) notwithstanding Security Council Resolution 276 (1970) du Conseil de sécurité*, Advisory Opinion of 21 June 1971, *ICJ Reports 1971*, p. 16, para. 118. See also ILC, Draft Principles on the Protection of the Environment in Relation to Armed Conflict, *op. cit. supra* note 11, Principle 22.

286. See ICJ, The case of *Application of the Convention on the Prevention and Punishment of the Crime of Genocide, op. cit. supra* note 22, para. 425.

the latter exercises the necessary control over the harm's source. They can even be situated in common spaces outside of any State's territory.

Historically, due diligence obligations were independent from territorial control since, as explained in the previous chapter, they pre-existed the consolidation of the modern State. Later, they were, at least for a while, associated with State sovereignty and as such with States' territorial control and integrity. It should therefore not come as a surprise that, in the international case law of the end of the nineteenth and of the beginning of the twentieth century, the first conventional and customary obligations of due diligence were recognised in relation to a transboundary harm. The principle of good neighbourliness and due diligence precisely met in that context. Since the second half of the twentieth century, however, due diligence has progressively come to be applied to (risks of) purely internal harm linked to the territory of a single State (i.e. without extraterritorial element), such as in international human rights law, or, conversely, to (risks of) harms occurring in spaces common to States and situated outside of their respective territories, such as in the international law of the sea or international environmental law [287].

The open geographic scope of due diligence has consequences for the nascent international legal field of international cybersecurity law. Information and communication technologies have a territorial anchorage, which implies that States are considered to have territorial jurisdiction over them with all the resulting international legal obligations [288], including due diligence obligations related to territorial sovereignty. Nonetheless, the (risks of) harm that such technologies can cause cannot easily be traced back to the control over one particular territory. Hence the temptation to devise a new space called "cyberspace" [289] and develop corresponding non-territorial obligations of due diligence. Notwithstanding the question of whether that space legally exists, it should not be invoked in order to evade due diligence's scope of application, territorial or not. This issue will be addressed in detail in Chapter IV.

---

287. See ICJ, *Legality of the Threat or Use of Nuclear Weapons*, *op. cit. supra* note 8, paras. 241-242.

288. See e.g. Cybersecurity Report, *op. cit. supra* note 88, paras. 13 (c) and 28 (a) and (b); Ministère français des Armées, Droit international appliqué aux opérations dans le cyberespace, 2019 [online].

289. On this question, see K. Bannelier-Christakis, 2017, *op. cit. supra* note 29; K. Bannelier-Christakis, 2018, *op. cit. supra* note 29; R. Kolb, 2016, *op. cit. supra* note 29; J. Brunnée and T. Meshel, *op. cit. supra* note 28.

4. *The temporal scope of due diligence*

Due diligence obligations do not have a particular temporal scope. Each international legal regime determines that scope by reference to the rights and interests to protect and to the duty-bearers controlling the sources of (risks of) harm to these rights and interests.

As previously highlighted, a number of special regimes set the minimal threshold for the application of due diligence as a "real" and "immediate" risk of harm [290]. However, this is not always the case, and some regimes include future and therefore non-immediate risks provided that such risks are certain.

In that respect, it is necessary to examine the relationship between due diligence and the principle of precaution in international environmental law [291]. As a reminder, the principle of precaution [292] requires that measures of "anticipation" [293] be taken against very serious or irreversible forthcoming risks which, in the current state of scientific knowledge, remain uncertain but probable. The detailed requirements of the principle of precaution and its progressive relationship on a temporal plane with the prevention principle [294], as well the role

290. This seems to be the case in international human rights law, including at the European level: see e.g. ECtHR, Case of *Opuz* v. *Turkey*, *op. cit. supra* note 205, paras. 129-130.

291. See ITLOS, *Responsibilities and Obligations of States Sponsoring Persons and Entities with Respect to Activities in the Area*, *op. cit. supra* note 41, para. 131. See also L. Chen, "Realizing the Precautionary Principle in Due Diligence", *Dalhousie Journal of Legal Studies*, Vol. 25 (2016), pp. 1-24.

292. Some prefer to use the term "approach" because the binding nature and the general source of that principle are not yet established under international law. The jurisprudence of the ICJ on this question is not clear: see ICJ, The case of *Pulp Mills on the River Uruguay*, *op. cit. supra* note 3, although the ITLOS's is more so: see ITLOS, *Responsibilities and Obligations of States Sponsoring Persons and Entities with Respect to Activities in the Area*, *op. cit. supra* note 41. For a situational analysis, see L. d'Ambrosio, G. Giudicelli-Delage and S. Manacorda (eds.), *Principe de précaution et métamorphoses de la responsabilité*, Paris, Mare et Martin, 2018; A. Alemanno, "The Precautionary Principle", in C. Baudenbacher (ed.), *The Handbook of EEA Law*, Cham, Springer, 2016, pp. 839-852; M. Schröder, "Precautionary Approach/Principle", in R. Wolfrum (ed.), *Max Planck Encyclopedia of Public International Law*, Oxford, Oxford University Press, 2014 [online]; M. Pyhälä, A. C. Brusendorff and H. Paulomäki, "The Precautionary Principle", in M. Fitzmaurice, D. M. Ong and P. Merkouris (eds.), *Research Handbook on International Environmental Law*, Cheltenham, Edward Elgar, 2010, pp. 203-226; M. M. Mbengue, *Essai sur une théorie du risque en droit international public: L'anticipation du risque environnemental et sanitaire*, Paris, Pedone, 2009; J. Cazala, *Le principe de précaution en droit international*, Louvain-la-Neuve, Anthemis, 2006; E. Hey, 1992, *op. cit. supra* note 14.

293. See M. Delmas-Marty, 2013, *op. cit. supra* note 109; M. M. Mbengue, 2009, *op. cit. supra* note 292.

294. It is a continuum according to the ILA, Declaration of Legal Principles Relating to Climate Change, *op. cit. supra* note 11, Arts. 7A and 7B, because, along with the

of scientific knowledge in that area of international law, are beyond the scope of this course. We will return to this issue in Chapter IV, however, in relation to due diligence in international environmental law.

Due diligence obligations are obligations of conduct and as such continuing obligations (pursuant to Art. 14 (2) and (3) ARSIWA). They arise as soon as the risk of a reasonably foreseeable harm manifests itself and endure over time because they bind their duty-bearer until the risk disappears or the harm occurs [295]. Most obligations imply not only prevention and protection against the harm, but also reparation afterwards, and are therefore both retrospective and prospective. Due diligence obligations can also be deemed progressive to the extent that they are "best efforts" obligations [296] or obligations to "ensure" to the utmost of the available resources [297]. Their realisation is progressive, and the duty-bearer must adopt the measures most suited to protect the rights and interests at risk, making due diligence obligations also evolutive and adaptive over time.

It is important not to confuse the moment of the emergence of a due diligence obligation with that of its breach under international responsibility law. Certain due diligence obligations (such as preventive obligations [298], although there are some exceptions) are deemed breached only once the harm occurs (Art. 14 (3) ARSIWA), whereas others are deemed breached over the entire period during which the (risk of) harm persists (Art. 14 (2) ARSIWA). Chapter III, which is devoted to due diligence in international responsibility law, will examine these issues in greater detail.

evolution of scientific knowledge and certainty, the obligation of precaution may turn into an obligation of prevention. See also A. Trouwborst, "Prevention, Precaution, Logic and Law: The Relationship between the Precautionary Principle and the Preventive Principle in International Law and Associated Questions", *Erasmus Law Review*, Vol. 2, No. 2 (2009), pp. 105-127; G. Hafner and I. Buffard, "Obligations of Prevention and the Precautionary Principle", in J. Crawford, A. Pellet and S. Olleson (eds.), *The Law of International Responsibility*, Oxford, Oxford University Press, 2010, pp. 521-534.

295. See ICJ, The case of *The Gabcikovo-Nagymaros Project*, *op. cit. supra* note 8, para. 140.

296. See R. Pisillo Mazzeschi, 2018, *op. cit. supra* note 23.

297. See Convention Concerning the Protection of the World Cultural and Natural Heritage, *op. cit. supra* note 250, Art. 4. See e.g. G. Bartolini, 2019, *op. cit. supra* note 250, pp. 429-430.

298. See ICJ, The case of *Application of the Convention on the Prevention and Punishment of the Crime of Genocide*, *op. cit. supra* note 22, paras. 221-222 and 430-431. See also J. Crawford, *op. cit. supra* note 24, pp. 226-232.

D. The conditions of due diligence

For a due diligence obligation to arise, in addition to the conditions of the obligation itself (effective control of the duty-bearer over the human right-holder in international human rights law, for instance), a number of conditions specific to the due diligence standard must be fulfilled.

Two of these conditions are related to the circumstances or capacities of the duty-bearer, seeking to ensure that it is reasonable to expect diligence, vigilance or care from it, following in this respect the principle of "ought implies can".

The first condition is knowledge of the (risk of) harm. It is necessary to verify that the potential duty-bearer of due diligence knows the (risk of) harm against which it should protect the rights and interests to which the specific due diligence obligation is attached. Depending on the circumstances, knowledge of the (risk of) harm can be both "actual" or "constructive" [299]: it is necessary to establish what the potential duty-bearer either *(i)* "knew" or *(ii)* "should have known".

This criterion is the first condition of application of due diligence obligations in international human rights law [300], in particular in the regime of the European Convention for the Protection of Human Rights (ECHR) [301], where it is referred to as "reasonable foreseeability". The same criterion appears in other international legal regimes, such as international diplomatic law [302].

Evaluating reasonable foreseeability, that is, the actual or constructive knowledge of the risk by the duty-bearer, proves difficult in practice. It is important to establish a causal link or nexus, however tenuous, between the measures taken (or not) by the duty-bearer and the

299. On the latter, see ICJ, The case of the *Corfu Channel, op. cit. supra* note 8, p. 22; ICJ, The case of *Application of the Convention on the Prevention and Punishment of the Crime of Genocide, op. cit. supra* note 22, para. 431. The ICJ does not always assess the presence of this second form of knowledge: see ICJ, The case of *Military and Paramilitary Activities in and against Nicaragua, op. cit. supra* note 8, para. 157.

300. See e.g. CESCR, General Comment No. 24, *op. cit. supra* note 3, para. 32.

301. Convention for the Protection of Human Rights and Fundamental Freedoms of 4 November 1950, ETS No. 5. See e.g. ECtHR, Case of *Osman* v. *The United Kingdom*, No. 23452/94, Judgment of 28 October 1998, para. 116; ECtHR, Case of *Opuz* v. *Turkey, op. cit. supra* note 205, para. 129; ECtHR, Case of *O'Keeffe* v. *Ireland,* No. 35810/09, Judgment of 28 January 2014, paras. 144-149; ECtHR, Case of *Talpis* v. *Italy, op. cit. supra* note 205, paras. 98-99 and 129.

302. See e.g. ICJ, The case of the *United States Diplomatic and Consular Staff in Tehran, op. cit. supra* note 8, para. 68.

increase in risk [303], as well as the duty-bearer's knowledge of that causal nexus [304]. This point will be further developed in the examination of the reasonable content and the variability parameters of due diligence, as well as in the analysis of causation in the context of responsibility for the breach of a due diligence obligation.

The second condition is the duty-bearer's ability to take measures. This condition seeks to verify that the potential duty-bearer is able to be diligent and may therefore be required to be such.

This criterion is also the second condition for the application of due diligence obligations in international human rights law, notably in the regime of the ECHR [305], where it is referred to as "reasonable ability" (or reasonable capacity). The same criterion appears in other international legal regimes, such as international diplomatic law [306].

Because these two conditions relate to what can be reasonably expected from or owed by the potential duty-bearer of due diligence, they will be further examined in the next section (E) devoted to due diligence's content, notably in relation to the standard of the reasonable State or IO in international law. Moreover, these two conditions become variability parameters since due diligence's content may vary depending on the degree of actual or constructive knowledge and on the degree of ability of the duty-bearer. We will therefore also return to the issue in the section (F) devoted to due diligence's variability.

E. The content of due diligence

An obligation of (x with) due diligence framed in the negative is an obligation not to carelessly harm the rights and interests protected by international law. The content of the due diligence standard strongly depends therefore on the content of the obligation upon which it is grafted. The due diligence standard merely qualifies that content by requiring the duty-bearer to exercise reasonable care in performing its conduct in compliance with its obligation.

303. See e.g. ECtHR, Case of *Luginbuhl* v. *Switzerland*, No. 42756/02, Judgment of 17 January 2006.

304. On the "real prospect of altering the outcome or mitigating the harm" test, see e.g. ECtHR, Case of *O'Keeffe* v. *Ireland*, *op. cit. supra* note 301, para. 149.

305. See e.g. ECtHR, Case of *Osman* v. *The United Kingdom*, *op. cit. supra* note 301, para. 116; ECtHR, Case of *Opuz* v. *Turkey*, *op. cit. supra* note 205, para. 129; ECtHR, Case of *O'Keeffe* v. *Ireland*, *op. cit. supra* note 301, paras. 144-149; ECtHR, Case of *Talpis* v. *Italy*, *op. cit. supra* note 205, paras. 98-99 and 129.

306. See e.g. ICJ, The case of the *United States Diplomatic and Consular Staff in Tehran*, *op. cit. supra* note 8, para. 68.

In order to better discern the specific content of the due diligence standard, it is necessary to distinguish between (1) the types of specific obligations upon which the due diligence standard is grafted (*obligation* of due diligence); (2) the measures of care or the absence of nuisance by negligence qualifying the content of this specific obligation (obligation of due *diligence*); and (3) the reasonable character of the measures required to comply with that obligation (obligation of *due* diligence).

1. Obligations of x with due diligence

As previously highlighted, due diligence is a standard of conduct that is attached to and qualifies an obligation of (x with) due diligence, which is why it is often simply referred to as a due diligence obligation.

Most of these specific obligations are obligations of conduct. It is also possible, however, to subject the behavioural component of an obligation of result to the due diligence standard [307]. In any case, international tribunals primarily identify due diligence obligations with obligations of conduct, often by contrasting them with obligations of result [308].

These obligations of diligent conduct can be obligations of prevention [309], protection or reparation [310]. Depending on their content, they can be substantive (disarming private military groups, for example) or procedural (initiating an environmental impact assessment, for example). This distinction between substantive and procedural

307. The obligation to issue a judgment in international human rights law may be considered as an obligation of result, which includes a conduct component qualified by the due diligence standard. In this case, however, diligence is owed with regard to the actions of the duty-bearer of the obligation, and not with regard to the actions of a third party, as previously envisioned.

308. See ICJ, *Legality of the Threat or Use of Nuclear Weapons, op. cit. supra* note 8, paras. 99-100; ICJ, The case of *Application of the Convention on the Prevention and Punishment of the Crime of Genocide op. cit. supra* note 22, para. 430; ICJ, The case of *Pulp Mills on the River Uruguay, op. cit. supra* note 3, para. 186; ITLOS, *Responsibilities and Obligations of States Sponsoring Persons and Entities with Respect to Activities in the Area, op. cit. supra* note 41, paras. 109-110; ITLOS, *Request for an Advisory Opinion submitted by the Sub-Regional Fisheries Commission, op. cit. supra* note 148, paras. 125 and 129. See also P. d'Argent and A. de Vaucleroy, *op. cit. supra* note 33, pp. 256-259. Contra: R. Pisillo Mazzeschi, 1992, *op. cit. supra* note 5; R. Pisillo Mazzeschi, 2018, *op. cit. supra* note 23 (on the terms).

309. See e.g. Convention on the Law of the Non-Navigational Uses of International Watercourses, *op. cit. supra* note 9, Arts. 7 (1), 21 (2) and 22; Istanbul Convention, *op. cit. supra* note 9, Art. 5 (2); Arms Trade Treaty, *op. cit. supra* note 9, Art. 6 (3).

310. See e.g. Convention on the Law of the Sea, *op. cit. supra* note 9, Arts. 63 and 192. On the diversity of specific due diligence obligations, see also R. Pisillo Mazzeschi, 2018, *op. cit. supra* note 23, p. 329; J. Crawford, *op. cit. supra* note 24, p. 230.

obligations of due diligence was introduced by case law, notably in international environmental law, and has proven less than clear or even useful in practice [311]. We will return to this issue several times in the remainder of this course.

Most of the time, obligations of (x with) due diligence are positive obligations and require an active conduct (enacting criminal law, signalling the presence of a bomb, conducting an environmental impact assessment, by way of examples). They can also be negative obligations, such as obligations to refrain from harming (not providing military assistance to an armed group, for example) [312]. In that respect, it is important to emphasise that, in the same way that the normative quality of due diligence is not inferior merely because it is a standard, so too is its normative quality not inferior merely because the specific obligation which it qualifies is deemed either positive or negative. However, while an obligation can be positive or negative, the due diligence standard itself is always positive and is breached by omission (negligence) [313].

Distinguishing between these different types of due diligence obligations is crucial: while certain obligations of conduct cannot be conceived of without an integrated standard of due diligence (obligations of prevention, for instance), this standard can also be integrated into obligations that are not preventive [314]. This was one of the critiques raised by James Crawford and other jurists from the civil law tradition [315] against Roberto Ago's draft Article 23 ARSIWA [316]. Today, due diligence's complete identification with preventive, precautionary or cooperative obligations in the jurisprudence on international environmental law is particularly problematic in that respect [317]. As

311. See J. Brunnée, 2020, *op. cit. supra* note 14.

312. See e.g. Convention on the Law of the Sea, *op. cit. supra* note 9, Art. 192; PCA, *South China Sea* Arbitration, *op. cit. supra* note 8, para. 941. See also P. d'Argent and A. de Vaucleroy, *op. cit. supra* note 33, p. 267; A. Seibert-Fohr, *op. cit. supra* note 261.

313. See also S. Shiffrin, 2017, *op. cit. supra* note 6, writing that: "Negligence may involve a failure to take due care, where due care requires an omission or an action, and the failure may itself involve an omission or an action."

314. See also J. Crawford, *op. cit. supra* note 24, pp. 226-232; P. d'Argent and A. de Vaucleroy, *op. cit. supra* note 33, p. 259.

315. See P.-M. Dupuy, 1992, *op. cit. supra* note 75; J. Combacau, *op. cit. supra* note 75; P. Reuter, *op. cit. supra* note 75.

316. See J. Crawford, *op. cit. supra* note 24, pp. 226-232.

317. See e.g. ITLOS, *Responsibilities and Obligations of States Sponsoring Persons and Entities with Respect to Activities in the Area*, *op. cit. supra* note 41, para. 117, referring, in the same paragraph, to the "obligation" and the "standard" of due diligence. See also Separate opinion of Judge Dugard, in ICJ, The case of *Certain Activities carried out by Nicaragua in the Border Area*, *op. cit. supra* note 3, para. 7,

discussed earlier, it is guided by considerations pertaining to the sources and regime of due diligence: the ICJ recognised the customary nature of these specific obligations by deriving them from the due diligence standard, which the Court deemed, for that purpose, to be a customary obligation of general international law [318].

Distinguishing the types of due diligence obligations is particularly important when it comes to differentiating between a breach of due diligence (i.e. when due diligence is integrated into other types of obligations) and a breach of an obligation of diligent prevention, particularly with regard to the role of the occurrence of harm for that breach. While the generality of this characteristic is not beyond doubt [319], most preventive obligations can only be considered breached once the harm which they sought to prevent has occurred. This would apply even if the harm's occurrence does not necessarily mean that the obligation has been breached (contrary to what would be the case with an obligation of result) provided, of course, all reasonable preventive measures have been taken [320]. We will re-examine this issue in the presentation of different aspects of due diligence in international responsibility law in the next chapter.

Distinguishing between types of due diligence obligations is also illuminating when addressing the nettlesome (and regrettable) distinction now made in international environmental law [321] and

---

who, in the same sentence, refers to due diligence as an "obligation" and a "standard" of conduct.

318. See e.g. ICJ, The case of *Pulp Mills on the River Uruguay*, *op. cit. supra* note 3, paras. 101 and 204; ICJ, The case of *Certain Activities carried out by Nicaragua in the Border Area*, *op. cit. supra* note 3, para. 104. By way of a reminder, the argument in ICJ, The case of *Pulp Mills on the River Uruguay*, *op. cit. supra* note 3, undergoes three shifts: *(i)* the standard of due diligence becomes a full-fledged obligation; *(ii)* it is then qualified as a customary obligation; and *(iii)* the principle or obligation of prevention is derived from that customary obligation, rather than the other way round.

319. It is precisely this doubt that compels the ICJ to specify that it is not developing a "general jurisprudence" applicable to all the obligations of prevention in international law: see ICJ, The case of *Application of the Convention on the Prevention and Punishment of the Crime of Genocide*, *op. cit. supra* note 22, para. 429.

320. See ICJ, The case of *Application of the Convention on the Prevention and Punishment of the Crime of Genocide*, *op. cit. supra* note 22, paras. 221-222 and 430-431. In this regard, one must distinguish between the obligation of prevention under Arts. I and V of the Convention on the Prevention and Punishment of the Crime of Genocide, *op. cit. supra* note 279, and the obligation under VCDR, *op. cit. supra* note 9, Art. 22 (2). See also on this issue, J. Crawford, *op. cit. supra* note 24, pp. 226-232; P. d'Argent and A. de Vaucleroy, *op. cit. supra* note 33.

321. See in particular ICJ, The case of *Pulp Mills on the River Uruguay*, *op. cit. supra* note 3; ICJ, The case of *Certain Activities carried out by Nicaragua in the Border Area*, *op. cit. supra* note 3; Separate opinions of Judges Dugard, paras. 6 *et seq.* and Donoghue, paras. 9 *et seq.*, in the latter case.

international human rights law [322] between procedural and substantive obligations of prevention [323].

The role given to the harm's occurrence in the breach of obligations of diligent prevention in international environmental law has indeed led to the identification of due diligence obligations which could be breached even without the occurrence of such a harm. Such obligations were named, for want of a better alternative, procedural preventive obligations (an obligation to assess the risk related to a building's construction, for example) as opposed to substantive preventive obligations (a prohibition on constructing a building that poses a certain risk, in that example) [324]. This distinction is criticised on the ground that it makes little sense, but also because it rests upon an erroneous generalisation of the condition of the occurrence of the harm for the breach of all obligations of diligent prevention [325]. This problem is further discussed below, as well as in Chapter IV on due diligence in international environmental law.

2. *Due diligence measures or the absence of nuisance by negligence*

The due diligence standard and by extension the obligations upon which it is grafted require the adoption of (measures of) "diligence", "vigilance" or "care" [326] with regard to the rights or interests that these obligations protect.

---

322. See H. Raspail, *op. cit. supra* note 15.

323. See the masterful discussion on this issue in J. Brunnée, 2020, *op. cit. supra* note 14; J. Brunnée, "International Environmental Law and Community Interests: Procedural Aspects", in E. Benvenisti and G. Nolte (eds.), *Community Obligations in International Law*, Oxford, Oxford University Press, 2018, pp. 151-175. See also Y. Kerbrat, "Obligations procédurales et obligations de fond en droit international des dommages transfrontières", in I. Prezas (ed.), *Substance et procédure en droit international public: dialectique et influences croisées*, Paris, Pedone, 2016, pp. 7-18.

324. See e.g. ICJ, The case of *Certain Activities carried out by Nicaragua in the Border Area*, *op. cit. supra* note 3, para. 104. See also ICJ, The case of *Application of the Convention on the Prevention and Punishment of the Crime of Genocide*, *op. cit. supra* note 22, paras. 221-222 and 430-431.

325. For a critique, see J. Brunnée, 2020, *op. cit. supra* note 14, for whom the obligations of diligent prevention in international environmental law may be breached without the occurrence of the harm to be prevented. She therefore considers that the separate identification of procedural obligations of prevention is not only impossible, but superfluous. See also S. Maljean-Dubois, *op. cit. supra* note 14.

326. On these different terms and their interchangeability in practice, see ICJ, The case of *Pulp Mills on the River Uruguay*, *op. cit. supra* note 3, para. 101; ICJ, The case of *Armed Activities on the Territory of the Congo*, 2005, *op. cit. supra* note 3, paras. 246-248; PCA, *Indus Waters Kishenganga* Arbitration, *op. cit. supra* note 8, para. 450.

As previously highlighted, an obligation of due diligence is often framed negatively as an obligation not to harm carelessly the rights and interests protected by international law [327]. The due diligence measures which must be adopted in accordance with due diligence obligations can also be addressed in the negative as the absence of nuisance by negligence.

Due diligence obligations are best efforts obligations [328] which demand the adoption of measures that are the most apt to protect the rights and interests involved in the context of the conduct required by the obligation qualified by the due diligence standard. The notion of good faith is contained in this observation of the required diligence [329].

The precise content of the diligent measures which must be taken or, alternatively, of the measures constituting nuisance by negligence which must be avoided depends upon the circumstances and in particular on the following: *(i)* the minimal threshold of what can reasonably be expected from duty-bearers *in general* in those circumstances; and *(ii)* different parameters specific to the duty-bearer that may change what can be reasonably expected from that *specific* duty-bearer. The following analysis of the "reasonable" content of due diligence will address the issue of the minimal threshold, while the next section (F) will focus on variability parameters. A third issue, *(iii)* the maximal threshold or ceiling of what can be expected as due diligence, will be addressed at the end of this chapter in the discussion of the limits of due diligence (G).

3. *The reasonable character of diligence*

The due diligence standard is a standard of conduct requiring the duty-bearer of the due diligence obligation to demonstrate diligence, vigilance or care, which is "due" [330], "requested" or "reasonable" [331].

327. See e.g. *Trail Smelter* Arbitration, *op. cit. supra* note 8, para. 716; ICJ, The case of the *Corfu Channel*, *op. cit. supra* note 8, p. 22; ICJ, *Legality of the Threat or Use of Nuclear Weapons*, *op. cit. supra* note 8, paras. 241-242.

328. See R. Pisillo Mazzeschi, 2018, *op. cit. supra* note 23.

329. See R. Kolb, 2001, *op. cit. supra* note 164.

330. See e.g. ICJ, The case of *Application of the Convention on the Prevention and Punishment of the Crime of Genocide*, *op. cit. supra* note 22, para. 430.

331. There is also sometimes reference to diligence *voulue* (see e.g. Secretary-General of the United Nations, Human Rights Due Diligence Policy, *op. cit. supra* note 86, Principle 2), but this French translation of the English term "due" is the least normative as it reduces due diligence to a mechanical reflex of the circumstances.

One should therefore determine what is a "reasonable" State or IO under international law in order to identify what can objectively be expected from the duty-bearer as the minimal threshold of due diligence. The reasonableness test is two-pronged: it includes a first test of "impersonal" reasonableness and a second test of reasonableness "tailored" to the circumstances of the case [332]. The present section is devoted to the first prong, while the second prong, which relates to the variability of due diligence, will be examined in the next section (F).

What should guide us in this first prong of the test is what a reasonable State or IO would have done (or not) in the circumstances and therefore the minimum that could be expected from the duty-bearer of the due diligence obligation. "Normality" [333] is a term that is sometimes used to refer to a norm or the average behaviour constitutive of a legal standard such as due diligence [334]. This kind of minimal normality results, for instance, and as we will see in the context of due diligence's variability parameters, from drawing the distinction between the duty-bearer's "actual" knowledge and its "constructive" knowledge [335]: the duty-bearer must be diligent not only with regard to the risk of harm which it "knew" of, but also with regard to the risk which it "should have known" of if it were a reasonable State or IO.

It is notoriously difficult to determine what is a "reasonable" man or woman in domestic private law, particularly in the context of civil liability [336]. This difficulty explains why the "reasonable" is a standard or extrajudicial figure that often becomes the object of a legalisation process in national legal regimes [337]. Such a "legalisation", and even "proceduralisation" in some cases, of a normative standard that is not

332. See also J. Gardner, "The Many Faces of the Reasonable Person", *Law Quarterly Review*, Vol. 131 (2015), pp. 563-584; J. Gardner, 2019, *op. cit. supra* note 7.

333. See IIL Resolution of 1927, *op. cit. supra* note 210, Art. 3 ("The State is not responsible for injurious acts committed by individuals except when the injury results from the fact that it has omitted to take the measures to which, under the circumstances, it was proper *normally* to resort in order to prevent or check such actions"). See also A. Verdross, *op. cit. supra* note 13, p. 388.

334. On "standards" in international law, see e.g. Y. Radi, *op. cit. supra* note 163, p. 44 *et seq.*; P. Reuter, *op. cit. supra* note 75; P. d'Argent and A. de Vaucleroy, *op. cit. supra* note 33; R. Kolb, 2001, *op. cit. supra* note 164, p. 115 *et seq.*; J. Salmon, *op. cit. supra* note 163, p. 1049.

335. On the latter, see ICJ, The case of the *Corfu Channel*, *op. cit. supra* note 8; ICJ, The case of *Application of the Convention on the Prevention and Punishment of the Crime of Genocide*, *op. cit. supra* note 22, para. 431. This second form of knowledge is not always considered by the ICJ: ICJ, The case of *Military and Paramilitary Activities in and against Nicaragua*, *op. cit. supra* note 8, para. 157.

336. See J. Gardner, 2015, *op. cit. supra* note 332; J. Gardner, 2019, *op. cit. supra* note 7.

337. See *ibid.*

strictly legal is a way to constrain judges' normative appreciation or evaluation. In domestic environmental law, for instance, the various impact assessments and other procedures that are now part of the content of obligations of due diligence in the field of risk prevention have come to crowd out the appreciation previously afforded to domestic judges.

Yet, as well explained by John Gardner [338], the specificity of law's normativity lies precisely in its ability to include/exclude or, at least, modulate the role of morality in law. John Gardner aptly explains that the reasonable man or woman standard in Anglo-American civil liability law does not therefore amount to a legal standard entirely defined by law (even if, as we just said, lawyers have a tendency to legalise it), but to a standard allowing for "legal deregulation" from inside and within the legal order itself. The same may be argued about the role of the notion of the reasonable State or IO in international law.

The notion of "reasonable" is even more difficult to apprehend in international law because of its transposition to a collective and institutionalised subject. The same trend towards legalising the reasonableness test may therefore be observed in international law. It is actually further exacerbated by international law's specific characteristics. The distrust of the international judge is greater for reasons related to the absence of compulsory international jurisdiction and, for a while at least, to the proliferation of international tribunals [339]. As a result, States tend to specify, for instance in international treaties, what due diligence requires from them. It is one of the reasons which might explain the increasing number of conventional guarantees of that standard since the 1990s. The crisis of multilateral treaties, however, has rendered that process more difficult. This is probably why, as explained earlier, the legal specification of the content of due diligence has recently continued outside of treaties and by means of soft law.

There is an interesting connection one may make here between that process of "legalisation" in international law of the non-legal figure of the reasonable State and of the due diligence standard and the vexed position of due diligence between primary obligations of international law and the secondary rules of international responsibility law. As we will see in Chapter III, the irritating role of due diligence between a standard qualifying the content of a primary obligation and an evaluative standard of compliance with those obligations within the responsibility

338. See *ibid.*
339. See S. Besson, 2013, *op. cit. supra* note 191.

regime confirms that the legalisation of the reasonableness test cannot be complete and that there is room for legal deregulation through due diligence in international law as well.

This trend toward legalising the content of due diligence in contemporary international law has had two main consequences: its technicisation and its proceduralisation.

First of all, professional and technoscientific standards of prevention, especially of environmental harm, have multiplied [340]. These standards make for a faster identification of what the due diligence obligations of States and IOs require and reduce the need of a normative assessment. Such standards' virtue is therefore said to lie in the objectivisation [341] and even universalisation of the content of obligations of due diligence.

This is a development that was first observed in domestic law (especially in environmental law), where technoscientific standards have become omnipresent: normative appreciations (of what is just or reasonable) in law are replaced by epistemic determinations (of what is true) in science. The technicisation or technoscientific standardisation [342] of due diligence is also especially prevalent with regard to the principles of precaution and prevention in international environmental law [343]. Those principles and the related due diligence obligations make technoscientific certainty a parameter of what can

340. See e.g. ICJ, The case of *Pulp Mills on the River Uruguay*, *op. cit. supra* note 3, paras. 223-224 (by reference to the European Commission's December 2001 Reference Document on the Best Available Techniques for Integrated Pollution Prevention and Control in the Pulp and Paper Industry, which the Parties have identified as the reference text for this sector [IPPC-BAT 2001 standards]); ITLOS, *Responsibilities and Obligations of States Sponsoring Persons and Entities with Respect to Activities in the Area*, *op. cit. supra* note 41, para. 117; PCA, *South China Sea* Arbitration, *op. cit. supra* note 8, para. 117. See Judge Donoghue's resistance to a purely domestic reference to soft law in her Separate opinion, in ICJ, The case of *Certain Activities carried out by Nicaragua in the Border Area*, *op. cit. supra* note 3, para. 13 (in the absence of sufficient State practice to establish an international custom). See also on the development of technoscientific standards in international environmental law, M. M. Mbengue, 2016, *op. cit. supra* note 18.

341. See P. d'Argent and A. de Vaucleroy, *op. cit. supra* note 33, pp. 268 *et seq*.

342. The term "standardisation" used here is not the same as the term "standard" *qua* norm used to describe due diligence in this course (see also R. Kolb, 2016, *op. cit. supra* note 29). Here, "standardisation" refers to an effort of normalisation or "regulation" of an international legal norm and therefore more fundamentally to its legal "de-normativisation" so to speak. See also Y. Radi, *op. cit. supra* note 163, on this meaning of standardisation.

343. See ILA, Declaration of Legal Principles Relating to Climate Change, *op. cit. supra* note 11, Arts. 7A and 7B. See also ICJ, The case of *Pulp Mills on the River Uruguay*, *op. cit. supra* note 3; ITLOS, *Responsibilities and Obligations of States Sponsoring Persons and Entities with Respect to Activities in the Area*, *op. cit. supra* note 41.

reasonably be expected from the duty-bearer. The same phenomenon of technicisation may also be observed in international human rights law [344]. In those regimes, the "reasonable" State or IO has therefore become a "scientific" State or IO [345]. Unfortunately, the introduction of these standards often feeds into a more general process evoked earlier in this course: the progressive transformation of hard standards of international law into soft ones (the so-called softening of hard law) [346].

The introduction of these soft law technoscientific standards into the specification of the content of due diligence can occur either with a reference thereto inserted in hard law (so-called *renvoi*) or independently. This happens most often in international environmental law, but international human rights law is not far behind [347]. When treaties themselves refer to these soft law norms, such references give them legal validity (by *renvoi*) and international tribunals can legitimately apply them in interpreting these treaties [348]. Yet judicial practice has also been using such norms to interpret some treaties even without a *renvoi*. This practice is often justified on the ground of the high degree of diffusion of these soft law norms or standards [349]. While this second trend is rarer, it nonetheless exists and is concerning [350].

344. See e.g. Supreme Court of the Netherlands, *De Staat de Nederland (Ministerie van Infrastructuur en Milieu)* v. *Stichting Urgenda*, *op. cit. supra* note 251, para. 7.5.2. For a critique, see A. Berkes, "Extraterritorial Responsibility of the Home States", 2018, *op. cit. supra* note 121. See also Separate opinion of Judge Ranjeva, in ICJ, The case of *Application of the Convention on the Prevention and Punishment of the Crime of Genocide*, *op. cit. supra* note 22.

345. See J. Gardner, 2015, *op. cit. supra* note 332, on the same development in Anglo-American tort law, where the scientist has become the paradigm of the reasonable man or woman.

346. See P. d'Argent and A. de Vaucleroy, *op. cit. supra* note 33.

347. See e.g. the reference to HRC, Guiding Principles on Business and Human Rights, *op. cit. supra* note 88, in CESCR, General Comment No. 24, *op. cit. supra* note 3; IACtHR, *The Environment and Human Rights*, *op. cit. supra* note 205.

348. See e.g. Convention on the Law of the Sea, *op. cit. supra* note 9, Art. 210 (6); Statute of the River Uruguay of 26 February 1975, UNTS, Vol. 1295, p. 331, Art. 41. See ICJ, The case of *Pulp Mills on the River Uruguay*, *op. cit. supra* note 3, para. 197. See P. d'Argent and A. de Vaucleroy, *op. cit. supra* note 33, pp. 270-271.

349. See e.g. the security standards of the International Atomic Energy Agency or also the standards in the Annexes to the International Convention for the Prevention of Pollution from Ships of 2 November 1973, UNTS, Vol. 1340, p. 61 (MARPOL). See ICJ, The case of *Pulp Mills on the River Uruguay*, *op. cit. supra* note 3, paras. 200 and 196, which (very obliquely) refers to them through the Administrative Commission of the River Uruguay. See also PCA, *South China Sea* Arbitration, *op. cit. supra* note 8, para. 956, which (squarely) refers to them through the Convention on International Trade in Endangered Species of Wild Fauna and Flora of 3 March 1973, UNTS, Vol. 993, p. 243 (CITES). See P. d'Argent and A. de Vaucleroy, *op. cit. supra* note 33, pp. 271 *et seq*.

350. See ICJ, The case of *Whaling in the Antarctic (Australia* v. *Japan: New Zealand intervening)*, Judgment of 31 March 2014, *ICJ Reports 2014*, p. 226.

Additionally, some States invoke *renvois* to soft law in their domestic law in the context of international law's interpretation [351]. The latter approach carries with it all the controversies that the opposability of domestic law can raise in international law [352].

Second, proceduralisation is another consequence of the trend towards legalising due diligence in contemporary international law.

Mistrust of the reasonableness test and the corresponding impulse to control the related judicial discretion are also at the root of the distinction between so-called substantive and procedural preventive obligations in international environmental law [353] and of the latter's multiplication. Most of the time, indeed, procedural preventive obligations require the duty-bearers of due diligence to follow a long "checklist" and to abide by different procedural steps, such as initiating an environmental impact assessment [354]. Complying with such obligations is straightforward. As a result, international tribunals are less likely to be accused of activism in ensuring compliance with them than if they evaluate what would have been "reasonable" for States or IOs to do in these circumstances [355].

The proceduralisation of international environmental law unfolds, however, at the expense of the evaluation of the reasonable content of due diligence and, more generally, of due diligence itself. It operates in at least two ways [356]. On the one hand, binding obligations set forth in multilateral treaties on environmental protection are reduced to procedural preventive obligations [357]. This creates an artificial

---

351. See e.g. the discussion in PCA, *South China Sea* Arbitration, *op. cit. supra* note 8; ITLOS, *Responsibilities and Obligations of States Sponsoring Persons and Entities with Respect to Activities in the Area*, *op. cit. supra* note 41.

352. See Judge Donoghue's resistance to endorse a purely domestic reference to soft law in her Separate opinion, in ICJ, The case of *Certain Activities carried out by Nicaragua in the Border Area*, *op. cit. supra* note 3, para. 13 (in the absence of a State practice sufficient to establish an international custom).

353. See J. Brunnée, 2020, *op. cit. supra* note 14.

354. *Ibid.*

355. It was the case in the very controversial PCA, *South China Sea* Arbitration, *op. cit. supra* note 8. See M. M. Mbengue, 2016, *op. cit. supra* note 18. The same remark can be made with regard to the *Urgenda* case in The Netherlands (Supreme Court of the Netherlands, *De Staat de Nederland (Ministerie van Infrastructuur en Milieu)* v. *Stichting Urgenda*, *op. cit. supra* note 251, para. 5.4.3) and compliance with due diligence obligations related to the right to a healthy environment being reduced to a certain percentage of emissions based on soft law's technoscientific standards, especially those from the Intergovernmental Panel on Climate Change (IPCC), *Climate Change 2007: Mitigation. Contribution of Working Group III to the Fourth Assessment Report of the Inter-governmental Panel on Climate Change*, Cambridge / New York, Cambridge University Press, 2007 [online].

356. See J. Brunnée, 2020, *op. cit. supra* note 14.

357. See e.g. Paris Agreement of 12 December 2015, UNTS, Vol. 54113.

intensification of the distinction between procedural and substantive obligations. Moreover, a disproportionate emphasis is placed on compliance with preventive procedures to the detriment of compliance with substantive measures of prevention. On the other hand, these same treaties transform substantive preventive obligations into obligations of result [358]. This causes a progressive reduction in the number of obligations (including substantive obligations) of conduct and as such of due diligence obligations in general.

International environmental law is by no means the only international legal regime to have "proceduralised" the normative evaluation specific to the examination of compliance with due diligence [359]. It is also occurring in international human rights law, for instance in relation to the content of ECHR obligations or inside the judicial review by the European Court of Human Rights (ECtHR). When the time comes to assess compliance with positive obligations of prevention or protection with diligence, indeed, the ECtHR increasingly satisfies itself with verifying that different procedural steps have been taken domestically (organising a parliamentary debate or exercising judicial review, for example) without further examining the content of the reasoning of national authorities [360].

In order to better understand the standard of the "reasonable" State outside of such conventional or soft law specifications, the place to look into is the international case law on the topic [361]. Over time, international judges have indeed consolidated a minimal institutional or organisational standard of "good government" [362] or "well-organised

358. See e.g. Kyoto Protocol of the United Nations Framework Convention on Climate Change of 11 December 1997, UNTS, Vol. 2303, p. 162.

359. See the general critique of contemporary international law by M. Koskenniemi, "International Law's Futures: Yesterday, Today, Tomorrow", in R. Hoffmann and S. Kadelbach (eds.), *Law Beyond the State: Pasts and Futures*, Frankfurt, Campus Verlag, 2016, pp. 71-92.

360. See O. M. Arnardóttir, "The 'Procedural Turn' under the European Convention on Human Rights and Presumptions of Convention Compliance", *International Journal of Constitutional Law*, Vol. 15, No. 1 (2017), pp. 9-35; E. Dubout, "Procéduralisation et subsidiarité du contrôle de la Cour européenne des droits de l'homme", in F. Sudre (ed.), *Le principe de subsidiarité au sens de la Convention européenne des droits de l'homme*, Brussels, Nemesis, 2014, pp. 265-300.

361. See e.g. *Island of Palmas* Arbitration, *op. cit. supra* note 8, pp. 854-855 ("display therein the activities of a State"). See also ICSID, *AAPL* Arbitration, *op. cit. supra* note 8, para. 77.

362. See J. Klabbers, 2017, *op. cit. supra* note 105; D. Lévy, *op. cit. supra* note 105, pp. 752-753; M. G. Cohn, *op. cit. supra* note 105 ("*bona res publica*"). On the standard of good government in the history of European law, see A. A. Wijffels, *op. cit. supra* note 32. This notion is to be preferred to that of good governance, which is now widespread even in international law (see e.g. Supreme Court of the Netherlands,

State" [363] from the practice of States. That standard is dynamic and evolves over time, but it sets, at a given moment, a minimal general threshold of due diligence [364].

This good government standard is both internal to the State and external and applicable to States' international relations. Examples of the first type of standards include principles relating to the good organisation of States [365]. Some can be found among States' general positive obligations in international human rights law, such as a minimal democratic regime, the separation of powers or judicial review [366]. The second type of standard comprises all those principles pertaining to multilateral cooperation between States. Many such standards can be found in international environmental law, such as the duties of evaluation, information, consultation, negotiation or cooperation [367].

To come back to a point left open earlier in this chapter, one may wonder about what these international minimal standards of good government precisely include when it comes to determining the minimal content of the due diligence of IOs rather than States.

To start with, it is possible, as is often the case in the international law on IOs [368], to reason by analogy and *mutatis mutandis*. Yet such an approach quickly reaches its limits and here even more so given that due diligence's original justification is grounded in States' sovereign equality. How could such minimal standards of diligence be transposed to IOs which are not only diverse but whose institutional dimension

---

De Staat de Nederland (Ministerie van Infrastructuur en Milieu) v. *Stichting Urgenda*, *op. cit. supra* note 251, para. 6.5). Indeed, the notion of good governance, and that is the point, no longer allows one to distinguish between political and legal government and other forms of management and control (especially economic and scientific). On the distinction between "government" and "governance", see A. Supiot, *La gouvernance par les nombres, cours au Collège du France (2012-2014)*, Paris, Fayard, 2018.

363. See e.g. R. Kolb, 2016, *op. cit. supra* note 29; S. Heathcote, *op. cit. supra* note 26.

364. See P. d'Argent and A. de Vaucleroy, *op. cit. supra* note 33, p. 267.

365. See e.g. ILC, Draft Articles on Prevention of Transboundary Harm from Hazardous Activities, with commentaries, *op. cit. supra* note 11, Commentary of Art. 3, para. 17 ("the degree of care in question is that expected of a good Government. It should possess a legal system and sufficient resources to maintain an adequate administrative apparatus to control and monitor the activities"). See R. Kolb, 2016, *op. cit. supra* note 29; J. Klabbers, 2017, *op. cit. supra* note 105.

366. See S. Besson, "International Courts", 2019, *op. cit. supra* note 107.

367. See e.g. ILC, Draft Articles on Prevention of Transboundary Harm from Hazardous Activities, with commentaries, *op. cit. supra* note 11, Commentary of Art. 3, p. 164, paras. 10-11, but also Art. 4, pp. 167-168 and Art. 7, pp. 169-171. See also J. E. Viñuales, 2016, *op. cit. supra* note 117; J. Brunnée and T. Meshel, *op. cit. supra* note 28.

368. See F. L. Bordin, *The Analogy between States and International Organizations*, Cambridge, Cambridge University Press, 2018; S. Besson, 2021, *op. cit. supra* note 222.

does not include territories or peoples and whose political relationship with their Member States' territories and peoples is therefore indirect to say the least?

As mentioned before, it is nonetheless possible to refer to the egalitarian and as such relational dimension of due diligence to justify the reorganisation of the relations between States and IOs, on the one hand, and among IOs, on the other. These relations are now clearly in need of "reordering". This can and should be done without necessarily falling into the trap of analogies to sovereignty and equality among States. The legitimate authority of IOs should be rearticulated with that of their Member States and therefore of their peoples, situating sovereign equality at the core of the mandate of IOs. It would then be possible to derive the content of their due diligence from that mandate [369] and from the minimal competences that IOs receive from their Member States and peoples. In turn, one could hope to identify minimal standards of good institutional organisation by drawing on this new articulation between the competences of IOs and the sovereignty of their (States)peoples.

In order to be deemed constitutive of a minimal threshold of reasonable diligence in international law, the good government standard applicable to States and maybe, as just argued, to IOs should be sufficiently common and therefore universal [370]. This issue is admittedly difficult, especially because the notions of "reason" and "reasonable" are predominantly Western. The criteria of the reasonable State that were mentioned earlier relate to the Western notion of State as it was universalised by international law upon the other States of the world as early as the nineteenth century, in particular by the ICJ [371] and then in the practice of IOs [372].

369. For the UN, see J. Klabbers, 2017, *op. cit. supra* note 105.

370. This is in fact an old critique: see M. Hakimi, *op. cit. supra* note 13. It is interesting to note that, at the time, there was a dispute on this issue between European States advocating for a universal minimal treatment of foreign nationals in international investment law and Latin American States insisting on national treatment to counter the Western imperialism of due diligence and its "civilizational" minima (the so-called Calvo Doctrine): see A. Ouedraogo, 2011, *op. cit. supra* note 12; A. Ouedraogo, 2012, *op. cit. supra* note 12. On the standard of civilisation in general international law and its critique, see M. Koskenniemi, *The Gentle Civilizer of Nations*, Cambridge, Cambridge University Press, 2001, pp. 134-135.

371. See S. Besson, "International Courts", 2019, *op. cit. supra* note 107.

372. See G. F. Sinclair, *To Reform the World: The Legal Powers of International Organizations and the Making of Modern States*, Oxford, Oxford University Press, 2017. See also S. Besson, "International Courts", 2019, *op. cit. supra* note 107, on the influence of the Western, and especially functionalist, conception of the State of

For a universal justification and to found its claim to universality, it is important to make the standard of due diligence more inclusive of other forms of governmentality and non-Western equivalents of due diligence developed in other legal cultures. As the first chapter highlighted, this can be done by resorting more intensely to comparative international law, for example in international jurisprudence [373]. One could consider different forms of political relations with a territory or legal forms of the political relations between members of a political community other than nationality. In any event, it would be detrimental to leave the monopoly of the alleged "universalisation" of the content of due diligence to proceduralisation and technoscientific standardisation, which operate by mere uniformisation and impose the conception of the strongest top down.

There is one dimension of the standard of due diligence that has been criticised for its lack of universality, and that is its reliance on the public/private distinction. As acknowledged at several points during this course, the standard of due diligence in international law rests, both in its historical origins and in its foundations, upon the Roman, then Western and eventually international distinction between public and private [374]. Yet this distinction is not necessarily shared by all legal cultures which are nonetheless ruled by international law.

As indicated in Chapter I, however, while the erosion of this distinction (and the growing difficulty to distinguish the organs of States/IOs from their private agents or from private persons whose actions cannot be attributed to them) partly explains the recent success of due diligence in international law, maintaining this distinction between the State's (or the IO's) public institutions and private persons is also one the conditions of the success of the due diligence standard.

As a matter of fact, due diligence's reliance on the public/private distinction protects against "all things public" excesses of which totalitarianism in the 1940s was an illustration, as well as against "all things private" excesses to which contemporary "corporatism" could lead. At each stage of its history, indeed, due diligence made it possible

---

the nineteenth and twentieth centuries on the organisation of IOs and, in return, on the influence of the latter organisation of IOs on that of their Member States.

373. See S. Besson, "International Courts", 2019, *op. cit. supra* note 107.

374. See A. Supiot, "The Public–Private Relation in the Context of Today's Refeudalization", *International Journal of Constitutional Law*, Vol. 11, No. 1 (2013), pp. 129-145; L. Casini, "'Down the Rabbit-Hole': The Projection of the Public/Private Distinction Beyond the State", *International Journal of Constitutional Law*, Vol. 12, No. 2 (2014), pp. 402-428.

to hold the instituted public, collectivity, group, tribe or clan responsible for the actions of its members. What is remarkable, however, is that it succeeded in doing so by opening a third way. Due diligence does not identify the responsibility of the group (clan or tribe) with that of its individual members in a collective responsibility mode, holding the group responsible every time a member misbehaves. So doing, it avoids fostering the "all things public" inclination. At the same time, however, the international law standard of due diligence does not sever the group's responsibility entirely from that of its individual members. It does not limit that responsibility to cases where an attribution of conduct and/or responsibility may take place under contemporary international responsibility law. So doing, it avoids favouring the "all things private" inclination. Quite the opposite in fact: responsibility for negligence identifies the conditions under which an instituted collective or public must bear responsibility for its own negligence with regard to conduct which its institutions have not been able to control. In so doing, due diligence strikes a careful balance between the public and the private.

As a result, even if anti-imperialist critiques of the public/private distinction should, of course, be taken into account (feminist critiques [375], in particular), it is important to understand what it takes to have a State and protect the "good government" that contemporary international law guarantees. Reforms should be approached with caution even when they are necessary to bring about more inclusion. As highlighted in the introduction, the due diligence standard has recently become an indispensable resource to navigate the troubled waters of the international institutional order. One should not too hastily question its underlying distinction because of its historical origins, but, on the contrary, strive to justify it in the most universal way possible, for instance by resorting to comparative international law and by exploring new ways of instituting the public.

F. The variability of due diligence

Due diligence is a variable standard, but (1) this variability is a disputed notion which must first be clarified, and (2) the different

375. See e.g. C. Chinkin, *op. cit. supra* note 118; L. Grans, "The Concept of Due Diligence and the Positive Obligation to Prevent Honour-Related Violence: Beyond Deterrence", *The International Journal of Human Rights*, Vol. 22, No. 5 (2018), pp. 733-755.

parameters upon which due diligence's variability depends must also be analysed.

1. The principle of variability of due diligence

The standard of due diligence is a standard of conduct requiring the duty-bearer of the due diligence obligation to demonstrate vigilance or reasonable care [376]. As mentioned earlier, the reasonableness test comprises two prongs: a first test of impersonal reasonableness discussed in the previous section (E.3) and a second test of personalised reasonableness in the specific circumstances of the case which this section addresses [377]. Beyond this minimal and impersonal threshold of reasonably required diligence, indeed, the reasonability of due diligence still has to be personalised or contextualised.

Due diligence is a "variable" [378] standard of conduct and hence a "best efforts" standard. As mentioned before, it should be adjusted to the concrete abilities of its duty-bearer following the principle of "ought implies can". There is nothing atypical in that: any norm, even universal, should be specified and contextualised in a given social setting before giving rise to concrete obligations [379]. This contextualisation of the due diligence standard is all the more essential in a world characterised by marked differences between States and between IOs. It allows to vouch for international law's claim to universality while respecting the diversity of the political, social and economic circumstances [380] of each people and then of each State or IO. This is also the meaning of the idea of "common but differentiated responsibilities", notably in international environmental law [381].

To that extent, it is correct to say that the variable character of due diligence leaves some discretion or even some flexibility for States and

376. See ICJ, The case of *Application of the Convention on the Prevention and Punishment of the Crime of Genocide*, *op. cit. supra* note 22, para. 430.

377. See also J. Gardner, 2015, *op. cit. supra* note 332; J. Gardner, 2019, *op. cit. supra* note 7.

378. See e.g. ITLOS, *Responsibilities and Obligations of States Sponsoring Persons and Entities with Respect to Activities in the Area*, *op. cit. supra* note 41, para. 117; PCA, *South China Sea* Arbitration, *op. cit. supra* note 8, para. 117.

379. See J. Raz, *The Practice of Value*, Oxford, Clarendon Press, 2003. On the necessary concretisation of due diligence obligations in the context of human rights, see e.g. ECtHR, Case of *Opuz* v. *Turkey*, *op. cit. supra* note 205, para. 130.

380. See e.g. in international investment law, ICSID, *Pantechniki S.A.* v. *Albania*, Case No. ARB/07/21, Final Award of 30 July 2009. See also E. de Brabandère, *op. cit. supra* note 20.

381. See E. Hey, "Common but Differentiated Responsibilities", in R. Wolfrum (ed.), *Max Planck Encyclopedia of Public International Law*, Oxford, Oxford University Press, 2010 [online].

IOs [382]. Nonetheless, this discretion is not complete, and due diligence does not amount to an entirely relative standard. In that respect, two observations are in order.

First, the variable character of due diligence does not make it a "subjective" standard, unlike, for example, certain due diligence standards under Roman private law, such as *diligentia quam in suis*. The latter requires the duty-bearer to demonstrate the same level of care with regard to others as for itself. It actually used to be applied in the international law on the protection of aliens [383]. As highlighted earlier, however, the due diligence standard endorsed in contemporary international law is different: it is both objective in its minimal content and subjective with regard to its adaptability to the duty-bearer's specific circumstances [384]. Of course, the terms "objective" and "subjective" have very different meanings in this context [385] and must be used with caution.

Second, due diligence's variable character does not make it a profoundly "indeterminate" standard [386]. The personalised reasonableness test calls for a new reasoning each time, but that process enables and even guarantees a determined conclusion. This is precisely what judicial reasoning is about. Once again, this confirms the intimate connection between due diligence and international judicial reasoning. In that respect, the standard's development in special regimes of international law where international judicial review remains rare, such as international humanitarian law, warrants further examination. Conversely, the importance that due diligence has taken in highly judiciarised regimes, such as international human rights law, international investment law and the international law of the sea [387], is easily understandable.

382. See also P. d'Argent and A. de Vaucleroy, *op. cit. supra* note 33, pp. 262 *et seq.*; O. Corten, 1997, *op. cit. supra* note 66, p. 151.

383. See e.g. *British Property in Spanish Morocco* Arbitration, *op. cit. supra* note 8. See more generally, M. Hakimi, *op. cit. supra* note 13. See also A. Ouedraogo, 2011, *op. cit. supra* note 12; A. Ouedraogo, 2012, *op. cit. supra* note 12.

384. On the notion of "common, but differentiated responsibilities" in international environmental law, see J. Brunnée, 2018, *op. cit. supra* note 323.

385. They are also used to refer to subjective (for fault) or objective (without fault) responsibility. See also P. d'Argent and A. de Vaucleroy, *op. cit. supra* note 33, p. 265-259.

386. See also P. d'Argent and A. de Vaucleroy, *op. cit. supra* note 33, pp. 262 *et seq.*; O. Corten, 1997, *op. cit. supra* note 66, p. 151.

387. On the judicial identification of a minimal threshold of due diligence in this context, see ITLOS, *Responsibilities and Obligations of States Sponsoring Persons and Entities with Respect to Activities in the Area*, *op. cit. supra* note 41, para. 159.

Beyond the minimal threshold of reasonably required diligence discussed in the previous section, the objective test of reasonable due diligence still has to be personalised or contextualised and adapted to the specific circumstances of the duty-bearer in order to determine what could reasonably have been expected from it in the given circumstances. Several "factors" or "parameters" of due diligence's variability [388] determine the duty-bearer's capacity for action. These different parameters of variability are applicable not only beyond the reasonably required minimum [389] examined in the previous section, but also under the reasonably required maximum, which will be addressed in the next section in the context of the limits of due diligence.

2. The parameters of variability of due diligence

Among the "factors" or "parameters" of due diligence's variability, the following six will be discussed below: (a) the knowledge of the (risk of) harm; (b) the capacity of the duty-bearer to take measures; (c) the degree of control over the source of harm; (d) the degree of the risk of harm; (e) the severity of the potential harm; and (f) the vulnerability or special quality of the duty-bearer. These different criteria correspond to various elements already inventoried and discussed in the analysis of the material or personal scope of due diligence or of its conditions.

Providing evidence of the existence of these different parameters and as a result of the content and possible violation of the expected diligence often proves challenging in specific cases [390]. We have already examined the issue of the proof of causation [391] and of the knowledge thereof, but other parameters are even harder to prove. Each special regime determines whether States have a margin of appreciation in the evaluation of these variability parameters, especially in the context of the review exercised by an international tribunal [392]. International

388. See ICJ, The case of *Application of the Convention on the Prevention and Punishment of the Crime of Genocide*, *op. cit. supra* note 22, para. 430.

389. See e.g. ITLOS, *Responsibilities and Obligations of States Sponsoring Persons and Entities with Respect to Activities in the Area*, *op. cit. supra* note 41, para. 159.

390. See R. Pisillo Mazzeschi, 2018, *op. cit. supra* note 23.

391. See I. Plakokefalos, "Causation in the Law of State Responsibility and the Problem of Overdetermination: In Search of Clarity", *European Journal of International Law*, Vol. 26, No. 2 (2015), pp. 471-492. For a presumption of causality and reversal of the burden of proof of the causal nexus in case of breach of due diligence in a context of territorial occupation, see ICJ, The case of *Armed Activities on the Territory of the Congo*, 2022, *op. cit. supra* note 123, para. 95.

392. On this question, see ICJ, The case of *Certain Activities carried out by Nicaragua in the Border Area*, *op. cit. supra* note 3, para. 153. See also P. d'Argent and A. de Vaucleroy, *op. cit. supra* note 33, p. 277.

human rights law, for example, has devised its own regime of States' margin of appreciation depending on the rights concerned and on the existence of a transnational consensus on the matter.

(a) Knowledge of the (risk of) harm

Depending on the circumstances, knowledge of the (risk of) harm refers to both "actual" or "constructive" knowledge [393]: it is necessary to verify what the duty-bearer *(i)* "knew" or *(ii)* "should have known".

As indicated earlier, the "reasonable foreseeability" criterion is the first condition of application of the due diligence obligation in international human rights law [394], notably in the ECHR regime [395]. Other international legal regimes, such as international diplomatic law, include the same criterion [396].

The more the duty-bearer knew or should have known that there was a risk of harm, the higher its vigilance should have been. Depending on the circumstances, this knowledge may be difficult to distinguish from a (potential) intention to harm *(dolus)*. Some special regimes of international law differentiate between intention to harm and negligence, but that is not always the case. Knowledge encompasses harm and the risk of harm and calls for a detailed and nuanced examination of the known or implied causation between a given conduct and the (risk of) harm [397]. We will return to the issue of causation in the chapter on due diligence in international responsibility law.

(b) Capacity to adopt measures

As mentioned earlier, the capacity of the duty-bearer to adopt measures, that is, what the duty-bearer *can* do, has a bearing on the diligence that he *ought* to demonstrate in a specific case.

---

393. On the latter, see ICJ, The case of the *Corfu Channel*, *op. cit. supra* note 8, p. 22; ICJ, The case of *Application of the Convention on the Prevention and Punishment of the Crime of Genocide*, *op. cit. supra* note 22, para. 431. The ICJ does not always consider this second form of knowledge: ICJ, The case of *Military and Paramilitary Activities in and against Nicaragua*, *op. cit. supra* note 8, para. 157.

394. See e.g. CESCR, General Comment No. 24, *op. cit. supra* note 3, para. 32.

395. See e.g. ECtHR, Case of *Osman* v. *The United Kingdom*, *op. cit. supra* note 301, para. 116; ECtHR, Case of *Opuz* v. *Turkey*, *op. cit. supra* note 205, para. 129; ECtHR, Case of *O'Keeffe* v. *Ireland*, *op. cit. supra* note 301, paras. 144-149; ECtHR, Case of *Talpis* v. *Italy*, *op. cit. supra* note 205, para. 99.

396. See e.g. ICJ, The case of the *United States Diplomatic and Consular Staff in Tehran*, *op. cit. supra* note 8, para. 68.

397. See also V. Stoyanova, 2018, *op. cit. supra* note 4.

This criterion of "reasonable ability" is the second condition of application of the due diligence obligation in international human rights law, notably in the ECHR regime [398]. It can also be found in other international legal regimes, such as international diplomatic law [399].

The diligence reasonably owed by the duty-bearer will vary depending on the means at its disposal and their relation with the means that would have been necessary to prevent or protect against the (risk of) harm, as well as with the means which are reasonably at the disposal of a State or an IO in such circumstances [400]. Depending on the case, such means and capacities can be technical, financial, human or even logistical.

(c) Control over the source of the (risk of) harm

The diligence expected from the duty-bearer will vary depending on the degree of control over the third party that is the source of the (risk of) harm [401].

As previously indicated, the nature of this control may also vary: it can be physical, economic, technical or judicial. The control may rest upon jurisdictional links in accordance with international law (for instance, personal competence and control over nationals or territorial competence and control over any person or source of harm on a given territory), but also upon other "links" allowing to control persons, a territory or any other source of harm [402].

The type of control exercised over the source of (risk of) harm will in turn affect its degree. Thus, if the control is jurisdictional due to the nationality of a corporation or the flag of the ship at the origin of the harm, for example, the degree of control will not be the same as if the control were territorial. In international human rights law, the degree of

398. See e.g. ECtHR, Case of *Osman* v. *The United Kingdom*, *op. cit. supra* note 301, para. 116; ECtHR, Case of *Opuz* v. *Turkey*, *op. cit. supra* note 205, para. 129; ECtHR, Case of *O'Keeffe* v. *Ireland*, *op. cit. supra* note 301; ECtHR, Case of *Talpis* v. *Italy*, *op. cit. supra* note 205.

399. See e.g. ICJ, The case of the *United States Diplomatic and Consular Staff in Tehran*, *op. cit. supra* note 8, para. 68.

400. See e.g. *Alabama Claims* Arbitration, *op. cit. supra* note 1; ICJ, The case of *Military and Paramilitary Activities in and against Nicaragua*, *op. cit. supra* note 8, paras. 157-158; ICJ, The case of *Pulp Mills on the River Uruguay*, *op. cit. supra* note 3, para. 101; PCA, *South China Sea* Arbitration, *op. cit. supra* note 8, para. 755.

401. See e.g. ICJ, The case of the *United States Diplomatic and Consular Staff in Tehran*, *op. cit. supra* note 8, para. 68.

402. See ICJ, The case of *Application of the Convention on the Prevention and Punishment of the Crime of Genocide*, *op. cit. supra* note 22, para. 430 ("political links, as well as links of all other kinds").

control as well as the degree of due diligence are lower when the control over the source of the (risk of) harm is exercised extraterritorially [403].

(d) Degree of the risk of harm

The degree of due diligence may vary depending on whether the objective degree of risk of harm is high [404] and on the extent of the actual or constructive knowledge of that risk and its assessment by the duty-bearer. The same is true for the requirement of "real and immediate" character of the risk of harm under international human rights law [405].

(e) Severity of the potential harm

Due diligence may also vary depending on the severity of the potential harm [406]. This is particularly so in international human rights law, where the degree of expected diligence is higher if the right at issue is more fundamental than others [407] (right to life or prohibition of torture, for instance).

(f) Vulnerability or special quality of the beneficiary

The degree of expected diligence will be higher if the victim, that is, the beneficiary of due diligence, is vulnerable. This includes persons highly exposed to risk, such as residents of polluted areas [408], children [409] or women [410]. The special quality of the beneficiary or of the person

403. See e.g. ICJ, The case of *Application of the Convention on the Prevention and Punishment of the Crime of Genocide, op. cit. supra* note 22; ICJ, The case of *Armed Activities on the Territory of the Congo*, 2005, *op. cit. supra* note 3. See also R. Kolb, 2016, *op. cit. supra* note 29.

404. See e.g. ITLOS, *Responsibilities and Obligations of States Sponsoring Persons and Entities with Respect to Activities in the Area, op. cit. supra* note 41, para. 117; PCA, *South China Sea* Arbitration, *op. cit. supra* note 8, para. 117.

405. See e.g. ECtHR, Case of *Opuz* v. *Turkey*, *op. cit. supra* note 205, paras. 129-130.

406. See e.g. ITLOS, *Responsibilities and Obligations of States Sponsoring Persons and Entities with Respect to Activities in the Area, op. cit. supra* note 41, para. 117; PCA, *South China Sea* Arbitration, *op. cit. supra* note 8, para. 117.

407. See e.g. ECtHR, Case of *Opuz* v. *Turkey*, *op. cit. supra* note 205, para. 130.

408. See e.g. ILA, Declaration of Legal Principles Relating to Climate Change, *op. cit. supra* note 11, Arts. 7A and 7B.

409. See e.g. ECtHR, Case of *O'Keeffe* v. *Ireland*, *op. cit. supra* note 301, para. 144.

410. See e.g. ECtHR, Case of *Opuz* v. *Turkey*, *op. cit. supra* note 205, paras. 129-130 and 159; ECtHR, Case of *Talpis* v. *Italy*, *op. cit. supra* note 205, paras. 29 and 98-99. See also L. Grans, *op. cit. supra* note 375; C. Benninger-Budel (ed.), *Due Diligence and its Application to Protect Women from Violence*, Leiden, Martinus Nijhoff, 2008.

to protect is another criterion of variability, notably in international diplomatic law [411].

It is in international human rights law that the parameter of vulnerability has been most used to heighten the degree of due diligence [412]. This criterion has also been used to loosen the conditions of due diligence in this regime, especially the condition of risk immediacy [413].

G. *The limits of due diligence*

One of the specificities of due diligence obligations is that they are obligations of conduct or more particularly obligations to "ensure" or to use "best efforts" [414] rather than "guarantee" a certain result. Due diligence obligations do not trigger strict or absolute responsibility for any harm caused to the protected rights and interests and are therefore not unlimited [415].

Even though due diligence is a variable standard which must adjust to the circumstances of each case, it cannot place a disproportionate burden upon its duty-bearer, which raises the question of its ultimate limits. These are its superior or upper limits; the issue of its inferior or lower limits (and in particular the immediacy and gravity of the [risk of] harm) was already addressed in relation to the material scope and reasonable content of due diligence.

Among limits within each special regime, one can mention material or resource limits [416], including the financial or economic cost [417] of due diligence. Limits can also be of a legal character [418], such as

---

411. See e.g. *William E. Chapman* Arbitration, *op. cit. supra* note 1. See P. d'Argent and A. de Vaucleroy, *op. cit. supra* note 33, p. 274.

412. See e.g. ECtHR, Case of *O'Keeffe* v. *Ireland*, *op. cit. supra* note 301, paras. 144-149; ECtHR, Case of *Talpis* v. *Italy*, *op. cit. supra* note 205, paras. 29 and 98-99.

413. See ECtHR, Case of *Talpis* v. *Italy*, *op. cit. supra* note 205, paras. 29 and 98-99. See, however, the recent evolution in the case law: ECtHR, Case of *Valiuliene* v. *Lithuania*, No. 33234/07, Judgment of 26 March 2013, a decision, which marks a return to the test developed in ECtHR, Case of *Osman* v. *The United Kingdom*, *op. cit. supra* note 301, para. 116. In this respect, see also the Dissenting opinion of Judge Pinto, in ECtHR, Case of *Valiuliene* v. *Lithuania*, *ibid.*

414. See ECtHR, Case of *Talpis* v. *Italy*, *op. cit. supra* note 205, paras. 29 and 98-99.

415. See *Frederick Wipperman* Arbitration, *op. cit. supra* note 1 ("the State is no insurer of lives").

416. See e.g. ECtHR, Case of *Opuz* v. *Turkey*, *op. cit. supra* note 205, para. 129; ECtHR, Case of *Osman* v. *The United Kingdom*, *op. cit. supra* note 301, para. 116.

417. See e.g. ICJ, The case of *The Gabcikovo-Nagymaros Project*, *op. cit. supra* note 8, para. 140; PCA, *Indus Waters Kishenganga* Arbitration, *op. cit. supra* note 8, para. 449.

418. See e.g. ICJ, The case of *Application of the Convention on the Prevention and Punishment of the Crime of Genocide*, *op. cit. supra* note 22, para. 430; *Alabama*

potential conflicts with concurring international law obligations [419]. In international human rights law, for instance, obligations to respect the human rights of others and even concurring rights of the same due diligence beneficiaries should be taken into consideration, as well as, more generally, respect for procedural guarantees [420].

The best way to balance due diligence obligations and justified restrictions or limits remains open. Both old and recent jurisprudence refer to "proportionality" [421]. The reasonable measures to be taken by the diligent duty-bearer should be tailored to the obligation's objective, but also to the capacities at stake, which is evocative of the "aptitude test" applied in the evaluation of a measure's proportionality [422].

Yet, as is well-known, there is nothing more indeterminate than proportionality in international law. Many different principles and tests bear that name without having much in common [423]. In addition, in view of the contemporary critique of certain proportionality practices in international law (among which proportionality *stricto sensu*), it is important to remain cautious with regard to the proportionality test which should be applied in the context of due diligence.

In short, these critiques are especially concerned about the prevalent understanding of proportionality as an instrumental rationality test and to the latter's reduction to a cost-benefit economic analysis. As a matter of fact, many theorists of domestic civil liability law have advanced the same objection against this kind of *Law & Economics*-

---

Claims Arbitration, *op. cit. supra* note 1 ("the insufficiency of legal means of action").

419. See e.g. the notion of "due regard" in the Convention on the Law of the Sea, *op. cit. supra* note 9, Arts. 56 (2) and 58 (3); ICJ, The case of *Pulp Mills on the River Uruguay*, *op. cit. supra* note 3. See also M. Forteau, "The Legal Nature and Content of 'Due Regard' Obligations in Recent International Case Law", *International Journal of Marine and Coastal Law*, Vol. 34, No. 1 (2019), pp. 25-42.

420. See e.g. ECtHR, Case of *Opuz* v. *Turkey*, *op. cit. supra* note 205, para. 129; ECtHR, Case of *Osman* v. *The United Kingdom*, *op. cit. supra* note 301, para. 116. On this issue and the importance of not overextending the content of due diligence obligations, see the Dissenting opinion of Judge Spano, in ECtHR, Case of *Talpis* v. *Italy*, *op. cit. supra* note 205, paras. 15-16. See also ICJ, The case of *Application of the Convention on the Prevention and Punishment of the Crime of Genocide*, *op. cit. supra* note 22.

421. See *Alabama Claims* Arbitration, *op. cit. supra* note 1. See, however, also ECtHR, Case of *Opuz* v. *Turkey*, *op. cit. supra* note 205, paras. 129-130; CCPR, General Comment No. 36, *op. cit. supra* note 205, para. 21. See also indirectly P. d'Argent and A. de Vaucleroy, *op. cit. supra* note 33, p. 263.

422. See P. d'Argent and A. de Vaucleroy, *op. cit. supra* note 33.

423. See G. Letsas, "Rescuing Proportionality", in R. Cruft, S. M. Liao and M. Renzo (eds.), *Philosophical Foundations of Human Rights*, Oxford, Oxford University Press, pp. 316-340.

inspired consequentialist reading of tort law. They especially criticise the application of the utility maximisation and risk minimisation principle that accompanies such a proportionality test in the evaluation of negligence [424]. This critique matters to the present argument. In international environmental law, indeed, a test of maximisation of harm prevention is already used as a proportionality test to evaluate whether the due diligence standard has been respected [425].

Given the diversity of the regimes in which due diligence obligations arise, it would be especially unwise to reduce the balancing of due diligence obligations with possible contrary obligations to pure quantitative balancing. As a matter of fact, this issue has been hotly debated among human rights theorists for many years in the context of the resolution of human rights conflicts, in particular with regard to the quantitative balancing between human rights and (military, health, etc.) security considerations [426]. In that context, the necessity test that has been proposed instead rests upon an egalitarian and relational reading of proportionality [427]. Such an egalitarian interpretation of proportionality would be well-suited to qualitative balancing in the context of due diligence. The justification of that standard lies indeed in the equality (of sovereignty) of States and peoples. Its content and its limits should therefore also be interpreted in light of that equal relation.

As observed in previous sections, one of due diligence's strengths is to bring the reasonableness test back to the heart of international judicial reasoning. One should therefore strive to bring judges to resort to judicial reasoning also when fixing the maximal threshold of due diligence [428]. It would be regrettable to deprive international legal reasoning of this unique normative resource and to hastily reduce the evaluation of what can be reasonably expected of a public institution in a concrete case and given all applicable limits to a mere economic rationality test. The issue of the upper limits of due diligence – like

424. See e.g. J. Gardner, "What is Tort Law For? Part 1: The Place of Corrective Justice", *Law and Philosophy*, Vol. 30 (2011), pp. 1-50; S. Perry, 2009, *op. cit. supra* note 6; D. Nolan, "Negligence", 2013, *op. cit. supra* note 4. Contra: H. Hurd, "Finding No Fault with Negligence", in J. Oberdiek (ed.), *Philosophical Foundations of the Law of Torts*, Oxford, Oxford University Press, 2013, pp. 387-405.

425. See e.g. ILA, Declaration of Legal Principles Relating to Climate Change, *op. cit. supra* note 11, Art. 7A (3).

426. On this critique, see S. Besson, "Human Rights in Relation", in S. Smet (ed.), *Human Rights Conflicts*, Oxford, Oxford University Press, 2017, pp. 23-37.

427. See G. Letsas, *op. cit. supra* note 423.

428. See P. d'Argent and A. de Vaucleroy, *op. cit. supra* note 33, pp. 263 and 277-278, by reference in particular to O. Corten, 1997, *op. cit. supra* note 66, pp. 151-158 and 165.

the issue of its lower limits in relation to the objective standard of the reasonable State or IO – should be at the centre of the evaluation of what can reasonably be expected from a State or an IO in light of all the circumstances of the case.

Far from being a source of complete discretion for States, and as such a source of indeterminacy which should be contained as much as possible, the determination of what is reasonable to do or not to do in given circumstances offers enough room for its contextualisation in concrete situations and hence for more justice in international law. In exchange, reasonable diligence requires that the institutions that govern us justify their actions and omissions. In other words, they should provide reasons [429] for and account for their actions and omissions. Yet they cease to do so when deliberation about what is reasonable is replaced by an exclusively economic calculation of costs or by a purely scientific verification of a process. Worse, these forms of control and verification are often delegated to professional associations or to scientific experts whom international judges are now compelled to follow instead of deliberating together about the reasons advanced and exchanged by our States and IOs.

429. See J. Gardner, 2015, *op. cit. supra* note 332; J. Gardner, 2019, *op. cit. supra* note 7, on the reasonable man or woman as a "justified" man or woman, i.e. as a man or woman who "justifies" himself or herself. Even if they are not always right, at least they provide reasons for their actions or positions.

CHAPTER III

DUE DILIGENCE IN INTERNATIONAL RESPONSIBILITY LAW

> "462. The Court cannot however leave it at that. Since it now has to rule on the claim for reparation, it must ascertain whether, and to what extent, the injury asserted by the Applicant is the consequence of wrongful conduct by the Respondent with the consequence that the Respondent should be required to make reparation for it, in accordance with the principle of customary international law stated above. In this context, the question just mentioned, whether the genocide at Srebrenica would have taken place even if the Respondent had attempted to prevent it by employing all means in its possession, becomes directly relevant, for the definition of the extent of the obligation of reparation borne by the Respondent as a result of its wrongful conduct. The question is whether there is a sufficiently direct and certain causal nexus between the wrongful act, the Respondent's breach of the obligation to prevent genocide, and the injury suffered by the Applicant, consisting of all damage of any type, material or moral, caused by the acts of genocide. Such a nexus could be considered established only if the Court were able to conclude from the case as a whole and with a sufficient degree of certainty that the genocide at Srebrenica would in fact have been averted if the Respondent had acted in compliance with its legal obligations. However, the Court clearly cannot do so. As noted above, the Respondent did have significant means of influencing the Bosnian Serb military and political authorities which it could, and therefore should, have employed in an attempt to prevent the atrocities, but it has not been shown that, in the specific context of these events, those means would have sufficed to achieve the result which the Respondent should have sought. Since the Court cannot therefore regard as proven a causal nexus between the Respondent's violation of its obligation of prevention and the damage resulting from the genocide at Srebrenica, financial compensation is not the appropriate form of reparation for the breach of the obligation to prevent genocide."
>
> (ICJ, The case of *Application of the Convention on the Prevention and Punishment of the Crime of Genocide [Bosnia and Herzegovina* v. *Serbia and Montenegro]*, Judgment of 26 February 2007, *ICJ Reports 2007*, p. 43, para. 462)

Introduction

The third chapter of this course examines the obverse side of the due diligence coin in international law: its role in international responsibility law.

Due diligence is indeed both a standard grafted upon a primary obligation of international law which it qualifies and a dimension of international responsibility for the violation of that obligation [430]. Due diligence has a dual nature, therefore. It cannot be restricted to the field of "primary" rules (obligations) nor to the field of "secondary" rules (responsibilities) of international law. This generates important conceptual difficulties when defining the regime of a notion that is both a standard qualifying an obligation of conduct and a type of responsibility.

On this point, due diligence in international law does not fundamentally differ from its equivalent in domestic civil or public liability law [431]. It is international responsibility law itself that makes it more difficult to apprehend in that context. As explained in Chapter I, the ARSIWA and the ARIO fully removed the "subjective" element (i.e. fault and negligence) from the regime of international responsibility of States and IOs. As a result, even in the context of international responsibility law, the assessment of due diligence for the purpose of establishing the responsibility of a State or an IO should in principle be made exclusively through the examination of the content of the primary obligation and its breach.

The due diligence standard was intentionally excluded from the "secondary" rules of international responsibility law and shifted back to the field of international law's "primary" rules. And yet, as observed in the first two chapters of this course, it does not squarely fit there. The relationship between the due diligence standard and the special obligation which it qualifies is not easy to grasp, especially because the primary obligation qualified by due diligence does not always necessarily pre-exist its violation. This course will further show that due diligence has in fact persisted within international responsibility law. It permeates many steps of the international judicial reasoning establishing responsibility for the breach of a due diligence obligation, that is, responsibility for negligence, even if it should no longer play a role therein. Due diligence has persisted as an irritant in international responsibility law since the nineteenth century, owing to the international judge and to its special place in international judicial reasoning.

Due to scope constraints and with a view to remaining coherent with the course's focus on due diligence obligations in international law,

430. See e.g. S. Heathcote, *op. cit. supra* note 26, p. 304, on the "artificiality" of the construction of due diligence as a primary obligation ("[D]ue diligence is a primary norm that *consists* of fault [negligence]").

431. Compare e.g. S. Heathcote, *op. cit. supra* note 26, to D. Nolan, "Negligence", 2013, *op. cit. supra* note 4.

which for now are obligations of States and IOs, the present chapter's analysis concentrates on the responsibility for negligence of States and IOs. This has two consequences for the personal scope of the proposed argument.

First, the chapter will not address international responsibility law governing the negligence of private natural persons, that is, individuals.

After all, one of the characteristics of the due diligence standard in international law is to qualify obligations of conduct of public international institutions, which today are mainly States and IOs. As highlighted in Chapter I, notwithstanding its origins, the due diligence standard clearly departs from the standards of Roman private law and from the various national traditions of civil liability in that respect.

Presently, international law includes only very few primary obligations owed by individuals that could be qualified by the due diligence standard and engage the international responsibility of the individuals concerned. These questions primarily fall under domestic private law, private international law or even under transnational self-regulation. While Article 58 ARSIWA and Article 66 ARIO expressly reserve the possibility of concurrence between individual responsibility and State and/or IO responsibility, such cases remain rare except for scenarios of attribution of conduct [432].

The only regime of contemporary international law providing for international individual responsibility is international criminal law. As a matter of fact, international criminal law includes a figure of international responsibility resembling [433] that of the negligence of States or IOs: "command responsibility". Command responsibility can be either intentional or negligent [434]. The latter's normative structure is akin to responsibility for the breach of States' or IOs' due diligence. An extensive comparison would certainly be interesting [435], including

432. On the issue of the lack of modalities of plural responsibility between States/IOs and private persons in international responsibility law, see in particular J. d'Aspremont, A. Nollkaemper, I. Plakokefalos and C. Ryngaert, "Sharing Responsibility Between Non-State Actors and States in International Law: Introduction", *Netherlands International Law Review*, Vol. 62 (2015), pp. 49-67.

433. See e.g. L. van den Herik and E. Irving, *op. cit. supra* note 16. For a critique of criminal analogies in international responsibility law, see O. Corten, "La 'complicité' dans le droit de la responsabilité internationale: un concept inutile ?", *Annuaire français de droit international*, Vol. 57 (2011), pp. 57-84.

434. In this regard, see Y. Dinstein, *op. cit. supra* note 16; G. Mettraux, *op. cit. supra* note 16.

435. On the commonalities between State negligence in international responsibility law and responsibility of the superior in international criminal law, see G. Palmisano, *op. cit. supra* note 72; J. Klabbers, 2017, *op. cit. supra* note 105.

of the need to ensure coherence between the regimes of individual and institutional international responsibility when the obligation can be breached by an individual as well as by an institution, as is the case with the obligation to prevent genocide [436]. The issue of the appreciation of the knowledge of the risk of harm of a person who is both a commander and an organ of a State or IO is also significant, but lies outside of the scope of the present chapter.

Second, this chapter will also leave aside the question of the international responsibility of corporate or collective private persons (such as MNCs) for due diligence violations. We will return to this issue in Chapter IV.

As indicated in Chapter II, indeed, these entities do not yet owe due diligence obligations under international law. Consequently, they do not incur actual international responsibility for their breach. However, it is true that such due diligence obligations are now the subject of several soft law instruments under international human rights law [437] and may eventually be included in a legally binding instrument [438]. These instruments mostly refer to States' positive obligations and responsibilities (including obligations and responsibilities of due diligence *stricto sensu*), but also require, as part of States' due diligence obligations and responsibilities, the prescription of due diligence obligations to MNCs under domestic law ("human rights due diligence" [439], for instance). MNCs' due diligence duties are essentially domestic private law duties. They may someday become private international law duties if States succeed in harmonising their minimal content. For now, this content remains entirely open: it depends on the domestic legal order of each State as does their corresponding civil liability regime in case of breach. In any event, such duties should not

436. See B. I. Bonafè, *The Relationship between State and Individual Responsibility for International Crimes*, Leiden, Martinus Nijhoff, 2009; P. Webb, "Binocular Vision: State Responsibility and Individual Criminal Responsibility for Genocide", in L. van den Herik and C. Stahn (eds.), *The Diversification and Fragmentation of International Criminal Law*, Leiden, Martinus Nijhoff, 2012, pp. 117-148; J. Heieck, *A Duty to Prevent Genocide: Due Diligence Obligations Among the P5*, Cheltenham, Edward Elgar, 2018; R. Leme, "Individual Criminal Liability and State Responsibility for Genocide: Boundaries and Intersections", *American University International Law Review*, Vol. 34, No. 1 (2018), pp. 89-142.

437. See e.g. HRC, Guiding Principles on Business and Human Rights, *op. cit. supra* note 88. See also CESCR, General Comment No. 24, *op. cit. supra* note 3, para. 30; IACtHR, *The Environment and Human Rights*, *op. cit. supra* note 205; CCPR, *Basem Ahmed Issa Yassin and others* v. *Canada*, *op. cit. supra* note 205, paras. 6.5-6.7.

438. See e.g. OEIGWG Draft, *op. cit. supra* note 10.

439. See N. D. White, 2012, *op. cit. supra* note 30.

be confused with the primary due diligence obligations of States and IOs under international law nor with the international responsibility regime applicable to their breach by States and IOs, which is the subject of the present chapter [440].

Finally, a few methodological warnings are in order before beginning our reflection.

The dual nature of due diligence straddles primary obligations and secondary rules of responsibility. As a result, the judicial practice analysed in Chapter II concerns both the place of due diligence among primary obligations of conduct which it qualifies and its role in establishing the responsibility of States and IOs for their breach. Because judicial decisions are adopted after a breach, they address subsequent responsibility. While this chapter might refer to cases cited earlier in this course, it will strive to avoid reiterations as much as possible.

Moreover, and this will be the second caveat, to this day judicial practice essentially pertains to State responsibility for negligence. There is very little practice related to the responsibility of IOs, including with respect to the ARIO. Regardless, because it is important to examine the specificities of breaches of due diligence obligations by IOs, each step of our analysis will endeavour to determine what could and should be the responsibility for negligence of an IO. The ARSIWA and ARIO regimes will be examined upfront and, unless otherwise indicated, the interpretations of the former also apply to the latter *mutatis mutandis*. The regime of responsibility for negligence of the EU, under both EU and international law, provides valuable insight in this respect. Judicial practice on this responsibility regime has actually already developed both under international human rights law [441] and the international law of the sea [442].

440. See the debate between J. Bonnitcha and R. McCorquodale, "The Concept of 'Due Diligence'" and "A Rejoinder", *op. cit. supra* note 30, and J. G. Ruggie and J. F. Sherman, *op. cit. supra* note 30.

441. See e.g. EGC, Case of *Front Polisario* v. *Council of the European Union*, *op. cit. supra* note 216; CJEU, Opinion of the Advocate General Wathelet, in the case *Western Sahara Campaign*, *op. cit. supra* note 216. See also A. Berkes, "The Extraterritorial Human Rights Obligations of the EU", 2018, *op. cit. supra* note 216; C. M. J. Ryngaert and R. Fransen, *op. cit. supra* note 216; E. Kassoti, *op. cit. supra* note 216.

442. See e.g. Convention on the Law of the Sea, *op. cit. supra* note 9, Arts. 2, 4 and 6 and Annex IX; ITLOS, *Request for an Advisory Opinion submitted by the Sub-Regional Fisheries Commission*, *op. cit. supra* note 148, paras. 164-173. See also P. Palchetti, *op. cit. supra* note 217; L. Gasbarri, 2015, *op. cit. supra* note 217.

The present chapter starts by addressing (A) the place of negligence in international responsibility law. For the rest, it is divided into three sections corresponding to the three parts of the regime of international responsibility law and, accordingly, of the ARSIWA and ARIO: (B) due diligence and the conditions of responsibility; (C) due diligence and the content of responsibility; and (D) due diligence and the implementation of responsibility. Each of these sections will highlight the persisting role of due diligence in international responsibility law.

A. Negligence in international responsibility law

The first element to emphasise with regard to international responsibility law as it has been codified by the ARSIWA and the ARIO [443] since 2001 and 2011 is the absence of fault (either intentional *[dolus]* or negligent *[culpa]*) among the conditions of the international responsibility of States and IOs. By way of a reminder, international responsibility results from *(i)* an action or omission which constitutes a breach of a (primary) international obligation; *(ii)* attributable to a State or IO; and *(iii)* provided that no circumstances preclude wrongfulness.

Even though (1) international responsibility is a responsibility without fault, and as such without negligence, (2) fault and negligence nevertheless play a role in international responsibility law.

1. International responsibility without fault

One of the consequences of excluding fault from the general regime of the international responsibility of States and IOs is that this regime (unlike many domestic regimes of civil and even public liability) [444] cannot be divided between responsibility for (a harm caused by) fault and responsibility (for a harm caused) without fault (i.e. "strict" or "absolute" responsibility). The international responsibility of States and IOs is by definition "without fault": it ensues from the (attributable) violation of a legal obligation. Of course, this primary obligation may include a subjective element and provide that it can only be violated

443. See ARISWA with commentaries, *op. cit. supra* note 71, pp. 26-154; ILC, Draft Articles on the Responsibility of International Organizations, with commentaries, *Yearbook of the International Law Commission*, Vol. II, Part 2 (2011), pp. 46-105 (ARIO with commentaries).

444. For a comparative study, see A. Antoine and T. Olson, *op. cit. supra* note 6, pp. 23-28.

intentionally, by negligence, or both. If that is the case, the assessment of fault will be made exclusively in the examination of the content of the alleged primary obligation and of its alleged violation.

This explains why a conceptual equivalent to strict responsibility (i.e. without fault) cannot, by definition, exist under international law, unlike what is the case under domestic law. It is difficult indeed to devise a concurrent special regime of international responsibility that would apply when a person or an institution exposes others to high risk and should be held responsible even without intentional fault or negligence [445] when that is already what the general regime of international responsibility seems to provide.

Yet the ILC envisioned creating just such a responsibility regime in the wake of the codification of the primary regime of international responsibility. At the time, it was to be called international responsibility "for lawful acts" (strictly speaking "non-wrongful acts") since ordinary international responsibility, including responsibility for fault, is "for unlawful acts" (strictly speaking "wrongful acts") [446]. The 2001 Draft Articles on Prevention of Transboundary Harm from Hazardous Activities and the 2006 Draft Principles on the Allocation of Loss in the Case of Transboundary Harm out of Hazardous Activities proceeded from that vision [447].

Neither project was adopted in a General Assembly resolution in the end. The difficulty lies indeed in drawing a distinction between the responsibility set forth in these draft articles from the ordinary responsibility for internationally wrongful acts arising from the breach of a preventive due diligence obligation, such as under international environmental law. The 2001 Draft Articles on Prevention of Transboundary Harm provide for due diligence obligations [448] and give

---

445. Regimes of liability without fault are usually divided between "simple" regimes (where an "objective" duty of vigilance must be breached) and "aggravated" regimes (where there is no vigilance duty to be breached, and the harm's occurrence is enough to trigger liability).

446. See D. Lévy, *op. cit. supra* note 105; A. E. Boyle, 1990, *op. cit. supra* note 282; J. Barboza, "International Liability for the Injurious Consequences of Acts Not Prohibited by International Law and Protection of the Environment", *Recueil des cours*, Vol. 247 (1994), pp. 293-405.

447. See ILC, Draft Articles on Prevention of Transboundary Harm from Hazardous Activities, with commentaries, *op. cit. supra* note 11; ILC, Draft Principles on the Allocation of Loss in the Case of Transboundary Harm out of Hazardous Activities, *Yearbook of the International Law Commission*, Vol. II, Part 2 (2006), pp. 59-95.

448. See first P.-M. Dupuy, "Due Diligence in the International Law of Liability", in Organisation for Economic Co-operation and Development (OECD) (ed.), *Legal Aspects of Transfrontier Pollution*, Paris, OECD, 1977, pp. 369-379.

rise, in the case of a breach, to a responsibility which it is difficult not to consider as a responsibility "for internationally wrongful acts" *qua* "unlawful" acts [449]. To avoid this difficulty, the last version of these Draft Articles sets forth a "negligence standard" instead of a primary obligation of due diligence [450]. Yet, in view of what has been indicated in Chapter II, such a distinction between the due diligence standard and the obligation which it qualifies is artificial, as much under the international law of primary obligations as under international responsibility law.

This fundamental conceptual and logical issue explains why the 2001 and 2006 Principles departed from the original vision and no longer aimed at building a distinct "responsibility" regime [451]. They are now conceived as a "prevention" system joined with a reparation and insurance system specific to responsibility for negligence in dangerous activities [452].

Nothing, however, would prevent resuming the project of a regime of international responsibility "for lawful acts" by removing the due diligence duty materialised as an obligation of conduct. Doing so would evade the criticism that this project is a disguised form of responsibility for unlawful acts. The newly created responsibility would truly be strict responsibility, that is, responsibility without fault, and even aggravated responsibility, that is, without unlawful act. It would be grounded in the "non-causal" quality of certain dangerous State conducts, that is, conducts which do not hinge upon an independent decision or an act controlled by either of the parties involved and which, because of the circumstances, elude all standards of reasonable conduct, such as due diligence [453].

449. The 2001 Draft Articles, *op. cit. supra* note 24, follow a model of "simple" responsibility – strict or without fault – and are based upon the breach of a diligence duty "objectivised" in the form of a rule of conduct. They cannot, by definition, give rise to responsibility for lawful acts.

450. See A. E. Boyle, 1990, *op. cit. supra* note 282; M. Seršić, "Due Diligence: Fault-Based Responsibility or Autonomous Standard?", in R. Wolfrum, M. Seršić and T. M. Sošić (eds.), *Contemporary Developments in International Law: Essays in Honour of Budislav Vukas*, Leiden, Brill Nijhoff, 2016, pp. 151-172.

451. See A. E. Boyle, 1990, *op. cit. supra* note 282; M. Seršić, 2016, *op. cit. supra* note 450.

452. See *ibid.*

453. On the justification of strict liability (including without a diligence duty objectivised as a rule of conduct), see S. Perry, "The Impossibility of General Strict Liability", *Canadian Journal of Law & Jurisprudence*, Vol. 1, No. 2 (1988), pp. 147-171. See also S. Shiffrin, "Enhancing Moral Relationships Through Strict Liability", *University of Toronto Law Journal*, Vol. 66, No. 3 (2016), pp. 353-379; J. Gardner, "The Negligence Standard: Political, Not Metaphysical", *Modern Law Review*, Vol. 80 (2017), pp. 1-21.

Such a responsibility (one with a system of insurance fund, for instance) already exists in international law, for example with regard to States' unilateral spatial activities [454], marine pollution [455] and nuclear incidents [456]. This type of responsibility could be a source of inspiration for other areas of international law regulating dangerous activities for humankind and its environment [457].

2. *Fault in international responsibility*

Returning to the main regime of international responsibility for wrongful acts, fault and by extension negligence (i.e. the violation of due diligence) are not meant to appear in the ARSIWA and the ARIO since they qualify the primary obligations. Nor should they be part therefore of the examination of the breach of these obligations and its attribution [458].

As mentioned in Chapter I, responsibility for negligence was included in preliminary versions of the Articles, at least in Roberto Ago's draft [459], in particular under draft Article 23 on preventive obligations [460]. Both jurists from the civil law tradition [461] and the last Rapporteur, James

454. See Convention on the International Liability for Damage Caused by Space Objects of 29 March 1972, UNTS, Vol. 961, p. 187, Art. II, which distinguishes between States' "absolute" responsibility in certain cases from their responsibility "for fault" in others. See J. A. Dennerley, "State Liability for Space Object Collisions: The Proper Interpretation of 'Fault' for the Purposes of International Space Law", *European Journal of International Law*, Vol. 29, No. 1 (2018), pp. 281-301.

455. See Protocol of 2010 to the International Convention on the Liability and Compensation of Damage in Connection with the Carriage of Hazardous and Noxious Substances by Sea of 30 April 2010; International Convention on Civil Liability for Oil Pollution Damage of 29 November 1969, UNTS, Vol. 973, p. 3; International Convention on the Establishment of an International Fund for Compensation for Oil Pollution Damage of 18 December 1971, UNTS, Vol. 1110, p. 57.

456. See Vienna Convention on Civil Liability for Nuclear Damage of 21 May 1963, UNTS, Vol. 1063, p. 265.

457. Comparative domestic law of public liability confirms the progression of a public liability "without fault": see A. Antoine and T. Olson, *op. cit. supra* note 6, pp. 26-28.

458. On the distinction between responsibility for the breach of a primary due diligence obligation and responsibility for fault, see in particular D. Anzilotti, 1906, *op. cit. supra* note 73.

459. See A. Gattini, "La notion de faute à la lumière du projet de convention de la Commission du Droit International sur la responsabilité internationale", *European Journal of International Law*, Vol. 3, No. 2 (1992), pp. 253-284; A. Gattini, "Smoking/No Smoking: Some Remarks on the Current Place of Fault in the ILC Draft Articles on State Responsibility", *European Journal of International Law*, Vol. 10, No. 2 (1999), pp. 397-404. See also H. P. Aust and P. Feihle, *op. cit. supra* note 70.

460. See J. Crawford, *op. cit. supra* note 24, pp. 226-232.

461. See P.-M. Dupuy, 1992, *op. cit. supra* note 75; J. Combacau, *op. cit. supra* note 75; P. Reuter, *op. cit. supra* note 75.

Crawford, found the proposed distinction between obligations of prevention and obligations of result too controversial [462]. It was therefore abandoned and sent back to the different regimes of primary obligations of international law.

Nevertheless, due diligence, even if it should in principle be absent from the Articles, still occupies a central place in the reasoning about State and IO responsibility. It is the case (a) explicitly in a series of ARSIWA and ARIO provisions and (b) in other tacit forms which will be highlighted in the remainder of this chapter.

(a) Explicit traces of negligence in international responsibility law

There are mainly three residual explicit references to due diligence in the ARSIWA and the ARIO.

The first reference, which has already been mentioned in this course (Chap. II.C.4), is the extension in time of the breach of international obligations, especially obligations of diligent prevention (Art. 14 (3) ARSIWA; Art. 12 (3) ARIO) [463].

This provision does not concern all due diligence obligations because some of them are not preventive obligations [464]. It is nonetheless relevant for our purpose because all obligations of prevention are due diligence obligations. Article 14 (2) ARSIWA (and by extension Art. 12 (2) ARIO), which provides that the breach of continuing obligations extends in time, is also pertinent since most due diligence obligations are continuing obligations.

This provision underscores one of international responsibility's reinforcing roles with respect to continuing obligations. Their breach further extends their progressive nature (Art. 29 ARSIWA; Art. 29 ARIO) [465]. This has consequences in practice for the prolongation of the

462. See J. Crawford, *op. cit. supra* note 24; ILC, Second Report on State Responsibility, by Mr James Crawford, Special Rapporteur, 17 March 1999, UN Doc. A/CN.4/498, paras. 52 *et seq*. See also C. Economides, "Content of the Obligation: Obligation of Means and Obligations of Result", in J. Crawford, A. Pellet and S. Olleson (eds.), *The Law of International Responsibility*, Oxford, Oxford University Press, 2010, pp. 371-382.

463. See also ICJ, The case of *Application of the Convention on the Prevention and Punishment of the Crime of Genocide*, *op. cit. supra* note 22, paras. 221-222 and 430-431.

464. See e.g. VCDR, *op. cit. supra* note 9, Art. 22 (2).

465. See e.g. ICJ, The case of *The Gabcikovo-Nagymaros Project*, *op. cit. supra* note 8.

temporal scope of due diligence obligations [466]. Obviously, this provision does not imply that due diligence obligations, including preventive due diligence obligations, do not arise prior to the occurrence of the harm or even prior to their breach [467]. On the contrary, the ICJ confirmed in the *Genocide* case that these obligations take effect as soon as the conditions of due diligence are fulfilled and as soon as reasonable measures could have been taken [468].

The second explicit trace of due diligence in the ARSIWA and the ARIO is contributory fault. In short, it is the negligence by which a State or IO contributes to one of the elements of the responsibility regime set forth under the ARSIWA or the ARIO. Interestingly, contributory fault may concern both the responsible States or IOs and the States or IOs harmed by these responsible States or IOs.

On the one hand, a State or IO may contribute to one of the circumstances affecting the wrongfulness of an action or omission violating international law. This is the case, for instance, when the negligence of a State or IO contributes to the situation of necessity (Art. 25 (2) (b) ARSIWA; Art. 25 (2) (b) ARIO) [469] or to *force majeure* (Art 23 (2) (b) ARSIWA; Art. 23 (2) (b) ARIO) [470]. If it can be established that the responsible State or IO has contributed by negligence to the situation of necessity or to the situation of *force majeure*, it will not be able to invoke it to preclude the wrongfulness of its acts and will be held responsible for them. On the other hand, a State or IO may contribute to its own injury (Art. 39 ARSIWA;

466. See P. Jacob, "Le contenu de la responsabilité de l'État négligent", in SFDI (ed.), *Le standard de* due diligence *et la responsabilité internationale: Journée d'études franco-italienne du Mans*, Paris, Pedone, 2018, pp. 281-296. See in particular ICJ, The case of *Military and Paramilitary Activities in and against Nicaragua, op. cit. supra* note 8; ICJ, The case of *Pulp Mills on the River Uruguay, op. cit. supra* note 3; ICJ, The case of *LaGrand (Germany* v. *United States of America)*, Judgment of 27 June 2001, *ICJ Reports 2001*, p. 466; ICJ, The case of *Armed Activities on the Territory of the Congo*, 2005, *op. cit. supra* note 3.

467. See also ICJ, The case of *Application of the Convention on the Prevention and Punishment of the Crime of Genocide, op. cit. supra* note 22, paras. 221-222 and 430-431; Separate opinion of Judge Donoghue, in ICJ, The case of *Certain Activities carried out by Nicaragua in the Border Area, op. cit. supra* note 3.

468. See ICJ, The case of *Application of the Convention on the Prevention and Punishment of the Crime of Genocide, op. cit. supra* note 22, para. 431.

469. See ARSIWA with commentaries, *op. cit. supra* note 71, pp. 85-90; ARIO with commentaries, *op. cit. supra* note 443, pp. 74-75. In this regard, see also S. Heathcote, *op. cit. supra* note 26 for a discussion on ICJ, The case of the *Corfu Channel, op. cit. supra* note 8.

470. See ARSIWA with commentaries, *op. cit. supra* note 71, pp. 80-83; ARIO with commentaries, *op. cit. supra* note 443, pp. 72-73.

Art. 39 ARIO) [471]. This intentional or negligent contribution to injury has a bearing upon the reparation which may be sought by the injured State or IO even if it does not exonerate the responsible State or IO from responsibility.

Many grey areas still surround this notion of contribution to injury [472]. For instance, it is necessary to clarify the role that contributory fault plays in the causal nexus which connects the wrongful act or omission to the injury [473]. As indicated earlier (and we will return to this point in greater detail later on), causation was neglected in the ARSIWA and the ARIO as was the injury to which it is linked [474]. The breach of a due diligence obligation can raise issues of causation as to both the breach (the occurrence of the event which had to be prevented, for instance) and to the reparation [475]. Moreover, because this breach is often only one of the (complementary or cumulative) causes [476] of the injury, it must be articulated with the other wrongful acts at the origin of the same injury. However, as we will see, this articulation has not yet been achieved by international jurisprudence [477].

The third residual trace of negligence in the ARSIWA and the ARIO is the seriousness of the breach of obligations arising under peremptory norms of international law (Art. 40 ARSIWA; Art. 41 ARIO) [478]. Article 40 (2) ARSIWA (and by extension Art. 41 (2) ARIO) specifies that the failure to fulfil the obligation must be "gross and systematic" [479]. This wording suggests that an intentional or negligent failure to meet the obligation should amount to an "aggravated" breach [480] of peremptory

471. See ARSIWA with commentaries, *op. cit. supra* note 71, pp. 117-120; ARIO with commentaries, *op. cit. supra* note 443, pp. 81-82. For a detailed discussion, see also D. J. Bederman, *op. cit. supra* note 39.

472. See D. J. Bederman, *op. cit. supra* note 39.

473. See *ibid.*

474. See I. Plakokefalos, 2015, *op. cit. supra* note 391; V. Stoyanova, 2018, *op. cit. supra* note 4.

475. See I. Plakokefalos, 2015, *op. cit. supra* note 391; P. Jacob, *op. cit. supra* note 466.

476. See B. Stern, "The Obligation to Make Reparation", in J. Crawford, S. Olleson and A. Pellet (eds.), *The Law of International Responsibility*, Oxford, Oxford University Press, 2010, pp. 563-571; P. d'Argent, 2014, *op. cit. supra* note 68.

477. See e.g. ICJ, The case of *Application of the Convention on the Prevention and Punishment of the Crime of Genocide*, *op. cit. supra* note 22, para. 462.

478. See E. Wyler, "From State Crime to Responsibility for Serious Breaches of Obligations under Peremptory Norms of General International Law", *European Journal of International Law*, Vol. 13, No. 5 (2002), pp. 1147-1160.

479. See ARSIWA with commentaries, *op. cit. supra* note 71, pp. 120-121; ARIO with commentaries, *op. cit. supra* note 443, p. 83.

480. See also M. Pacholska, *Complicity and the Law of International Organizations*, London, Edward Elgar, 2020, pp. 168-208.

law. If that were the case, negligence could trigger the special obligations of Article 41 ARSIWA (Art. 42 ARIO), in particular the obligation to cooperate to bring the serious breaches of peremptory norms to an end and the obligation of non-recognition of the acts in breach of peremptory norms.

(b) Tacit traces of negligence in international responsibility law

Although due diligence is not formally a "secondary" rule of the international responsibility law set forth under the ARSIWA and the ARIO, it remains present in a tacit and diffuse way at each step of the reasoning underlying international responsibility.

The remainder of this chapter provides a detailed analysis of these residual traces. As regards the conditions of responsibility (discussed in Section B), such traces are present not only in relation to attribution, but also in the assessment of the breach of a due diligence obligation. With regard to the content of responsibility (discussed in Section C), the determination of reparation in accordance with the causal nexus between the negligent act and the injury also shows such traces. As regards the implementation of responsibility (discussed in Section D), a breach of due diligence may potentially contribute to multiplying the number of responsible States or IOs and complexifying the allocation and invocation of responsibilities.

Generally, one can easily dismiss the objection according to which the very idea of a responsibility for "fault" and as such for negligence is incompatible with the collective and institutionalised nature of the State or IO [481].

The fault of a State or IO should indeed be distinguished from criminal law's *mens rea* which requires that a State or IO have a state of mind and capacities analogous to those of a natural person. As explained in the last two chapters, the due diligence and wrongful negligence of States and IOs are assessed differently. One may therefore endorse the applicability of that standard even to collective and institutionalised

481. As for the argument (see S. Fleming, *op. cit. supra* note 72) that the responsibility of States is a responsibility by attribution rather than a responsibility for fault, it falsely opposes "attribution" and "negligence" as grounds of responsibility. As we will see, all responsibilities, including responsibility for negligence, are attributive, at least according to ARSIWA, *op. cit. supra* note 24, Art. 4. Furthermore, responsibility for negligence allows the State to be held accountable for its own negligent actions (i.e. the actions of its organs that are attributed to it) with regard to the actions of private actors precisely when attributing the conduct of these private persons to the State is not possible.

entities like States [482] or IOs. The ARSIWA and the ARIO actually also include references to the "knowledge" of States or IOs (Arts. 16, 17 and 18 ARSIWA; Arts. 14, 15 and 16 ARIO and Arts. 58, 59 and 60 ARIO). Moreover, the commentaries [483] and jurisprudence [484] mention "intention" to assist or circumvent as grounds of indirect responsibility of States or IOs.

Notwithstanding that and despite assertions to the contrary [485], making due diligence a standard of conduct grafted upon a primary obligation changes neither its content nor its applicability to a State or IO. If responsibility for negligence is not applicable to States or IOs, how would it then be possible to subject them to a standard of diligent conduct in the first place?

B. Due diligence and the conditions of international responsibility

The first step of our inquiry into the residual traces of due diligence in the contemporary regime of the international responsibility of States and IOs begins with the conditions of that responsibility and the place of due diligence in that context.

As indicated in the previous section, there are three conditions to the international responsibility of States and IOs: *(i)* an action or omission which amounts to the breach of a (primary) obligation of international law; *(ii)* that is attributable to a State or IO; and *(iii)* provided no circumstances preclude wrongfulness. Fault and by extension negligence are not one of these conditions. One must therefore treat due diligence as a standard potentially grafted upon a specific primary obligation whose content must be established before proving its breach and attributing it to the responsible State or IO.

Viewed through that prism, none of these three conditions of responsibility for the violation of a due diligence obligation, that is, for negligence, should be seen as particularly problematic at this stage of the course. Indeed, Chapter II already explained how to establish

482. See G. Palmisano, *op. cit. supra* note 72; P. d'Argent and A. de Vaucleroy, *op. cit. supra* note 33.

483. See ARSIWA with commentaries, *op. cit. supra* note 71, pp. 69-74; ARIO with commentaries, *op. cit. supra* note 443, pp. 65-67 and 98-100.

484. See ICJ, The case of the *Corfu Channel, op. cit. supra* note 8; ICJ, The case of the *United States Diplomatic and Consular Staff in Tehran, op. cit. supra* note 8; ICJ, The case of *Application of the Convention on the Prevention and Punishment of the Crime of Genocide, op. cit. supra* note 22.

485. See D. Anzilotti, 1906, *op. cit. supra* note 73.

the content of a special obligation of due diligence and studied each element of its normative regime.

Due diligence's content, first of all, includes its shares of complexities, of course, especially the test of reasonableness and its variability. Proving negligence is therefore likely to be difficult. Moreover, the content of due diligence may not be fully defined in advance of the reasoning underlying responsibility [486]. The previous chapters have shown indeed that the due diligence standard is not always able to guide the conduct of States or IOs entirely *ex ante* [487].

On the issue of breach, secondly, the previous section already highlighted the rules of Article 14 ARSIWA (Art. 12 ARIO) on the time of the breach of due diligence obligations, which are continuing and sometimes also preventive obligations. The second chapter further discussed the specificities of some obligations of prevention (with due diligence) whose violation requires the occurrence of the harm even if – unlike what is the case for obligations of result – that occurrence does not necessarily imply that these obligations have been breached [488]. Difficulties in terms of proof will likely arise in relation to this element as well.

Finally, attributing the breach of a due diligence obligation does not (usually) [489] give rise to major difficulties. Most of the time, it is a wrongful omission, that is, a breach of a positive obligation whose subject (State or IO) is identified by the obligation [490]. The usual rules on attribution to States or IOs are applicable: their negligence is, first and foremost, that of their *de jure* or *de facto* organs in accordance with Article 4 ARSIWA or Article 6 ARIO, and the conduct of these organs is attributable to these States or IOs [491].

---

486. See J. Klabbers, 2017, *op. cit. supra* note 105. Sometimes, it is the determination of the content of the wrongful omission by the international judge when establishing the international responsibility of the duty-bearer that makes it possible to reconstitute the content of a due diligence obligation *ex post* and for the future.

487. See ICJ, The case of the *Corfu Channel*, *op. cit. supra* note 8, p. 22. See also D. Lévy, *op. cit. supra* note 105, pp. 752-753.

488. See ICJ, The case of *Application of the Convention on the Prevention and Punishment of the Crime of Genocide*, *op. cit. supra* note 22, paras. 221-222 and 430-431, by opposition to ICJ, The case of *Certain Activities carried out by Nicaragua in the Border Area*, *op. cit. supra* note 3. See also J. Brunnée, 2020, *op. cit. supra* note 14.

489. P. d'Argent and A. de Vaucleroy, *op. cit. supra* note 33, p. 260, who underestimate this point when they associate the content of a due diligence obligation with that of a wrongful omission (see also p. 264) (see also R. Kolb, 2016, *op. cit. supra* note 29; T. Koivurova, 2010, *op. cit. supra* note 5).

490. See P. d'Argent and A. de Vaucleroy, *op. cit. supra* note 33, p. 260.

491. This becomes clear when one compares the two phases of ICJ, The case of the *United States Diplomatic and Consular Staff in Tehran*, *op. cit. supra* note 8.

Additional complexities may nonetheless emerge in determining whether the conditions of responsibility for negligence are met. First, it can be difficult (1) to distinguish responsibility for negligence from other types of responsibilities by attribution of conduct or by attribution of responsibility for the harm caused by private persons. Besides, the exact role of causation in establishing the breach of a due diligence obligation may also (2) become a source of complexity when the injury was caused by other States or IOs.

1. *Responsibility for negligence and the condition of attribution*

In principle, responsibility for negligence should not give rise to major attribution issues. Most of the time, indeed, responsibility for negligence flows from a wrongful omission, that is, from the violation of a positive obligation of due diligence whose duty-bearer is identified by the obligation [492]. The attribution of the breach of a due diligence obligation unfolds in accordance with the usual rules on attribution of conduct of a *de jure* or *de facto* organ of the State or IO to the State or IO involved.

It may be difficult, however, to distinguish the responsibility of a State or IO for negligence (of its *de jure* or *de facto* organs) with regard to (a risk of) harm caused by a private person from two other forms of responsibility under international responsibility law: responsibility by (direct) attribution of the conduct of the private person, on the one hand, and responsibility by (indirect) attribution of the responsibility of another State or IO (because of complicity, for instance), on the other.

Chapter I presented the genealogy of due diligence in the history of public responsibility in international law. That history reveals how the three scenarios of the international responsibility of States with regard to the harm caused by private persons have progressively emerged. These three scenarios are still at work in international law today, and they are [493]: *(i)* strict responsibility (i.e. independently of negligence)

492. See P. d'Argent and A. de Vaucleroy, *op. cit. supra* note 33, p. 260.

493. See ITLOS, *Responsibilities and Obligations of States Sponsoring Persons and Entities with Respect to Activities in the Area*, *op. cit. supra* note 41, para. 112: "The expression 'to ensure' is often used in international legal instruments to refer to obligations in respect of which, while it is not considered reasonable to make a State liable for each and every violation committed by persons under its jurisdiction, it is equally not considered satisfactory to rely on mere application of the principle that the conduct of private persons or entities is not attributable to the State under international law (see ILC Articles on State Responsibility, Commentary to article 8, paragraph 1)." See also D. König, *op. cit. supra* note 18.

of the State (or, before the State, of the group) for any harm caused by its nationals (or, in pre-nationality times, by a member of the group); *(ii)* responsibility of the State only by attribution of the conduct of the official organ which caused the harm (including *ultra vires*) (and thus independently of any negligence of the State itself); and, in-between, *(iii)* responsibility of the State (or, before the State, of the group) for breaches of its due diligence with respect to its national who caused the harm (and, before nationality, to the member of the group).

Keeping these three scenarios in mind helps us understand how responsibility for negligence may be useful in case of lack of attribution of the *conduct* of a private person to a State or IO and why it is discussed in the context of the international responsibility of States or IOs. It is also useful to appreciate how difficult it is to distinguish the responsibility for negligence of a State or IO with regard to the dangerous activities of a private person from its responsibility for *complicity* with other States and IOs, that is, by attribution of their responsibility.

The following subsections will carefully examine these two scenarios of responsibility by attribution by opposition to responsibility for negligence: (a) responsibility by attribution of the conduct of private persons; and (b) responsibility by attribution of the responsibility of other States or IOs. The analysis will highlight how they differ from responsibility for negligence and expose the latter's comparative advantages [494].

(a) Responsibility for negligence and responsibility by attribution of the conduct of private persons

Articles 4 to 11 ARSIWA (Arts. 6 to 9 ARIO) set forth several grounds for attributing conducts to a State or IO depending on whether: the conduct is that of a *de jure* or *de facto* State organ or of a person exercising public powers (Arts. 4 to 7 ARSIWA; Arts. 6 to 9 ARIO); or the conduct is that of a private person or a group of private persons

494. See also O. Corten, 2011, *op. cit. supra* note 433; O. Corten and P. Klein, "The Limits of Complicity as a Ground of Responsibility: Lessons Learned from the *Corfu Channel* Case", in K. Bannelier, T. Christakis and S. Heathcote (eds.), *The ICJ and the Evolution of International Law: The Enduring Impact of the "Corfu Channel" Case*, London, Routledge, 2012, pp. 315-334; A. Seibert-Fohr, *op. cit. supra* note 261; M. Starita, "Négligence illicite et responsabilités multiples: partage ou cumul de responsabilités ?", in SFDI (ed.), *Le standard de* due diligence *et la responsabilité internationale: Journée d'études franco-italienne du Mans*, Paris, Pedone, 2018, pp. 297-321.

associated with or controlled in different ways by the State (Arts. 8 to 11 ARSIWA).

The conditions for attributing the conduct of private persons to States are very rigorous to the extent that such attribution leads to holding the States directly responsible for that conduct. One example is when the private person is under the State's effective control according to Article 8 ARSIWA. The ICJ defines the notion of "effective control" over a person or a group of private persons quite strictly as the capacity to influence or even initiate the constitutive elements of an operation and to discontinue them if they are still ongoing [495].

By contrast, the responsibility for negligence of States and IOs allows for the State or IO to be held responsible not for the harm caused by the private person, as that person's action or omission cannot be imputed to that State or IO [496], but for its own negligent action or omission (that of its *de jure* or *de facto* organs according to Art. 4 ARSIWA or Art. 6 ARIO) with respect to the actions or omissions of that private person. Responsibility for negligence partly compensates for the absence of (direct) responsibility of the State or IO by attribution of the conduct of that private person.

This possibility is very useful when attribution under one of the grounds of Articles 4 to 11 ARSIWA (Arts. 6 to 9 ARIO) is not possible for a variety of reasons. It could be because the private person's activities are secret or diffuse, making it difficult to examine the existence of a delegation of public powers or any form of effective control (according to Arts. 5 and 8 ARSIWA), as is often the case with cybersecurity threats [497]. Moreover, the erosion of the public/private distinction and the increasing privatisation of public functions complicate the determination, under domestic law, of what falls under State or IO prerogatives, as well as the distinction between State and IO organs and their private agents.

In these circumstances, and even if applying the due diligence standard comes with its own share of difficulties, the responsibility of the State or of the IO for its own negligence is often easier to establish than its direct responsibility by attribution of the conduct of private persons.

495. See ICJ, The case of *Military and Paramilitary Activities in and against Nicaragua*, *op. cit. supra* note 8; ICJ, The case of *Application of the Convention on the Prevention and Punishment of the Crime of Genocide*, *op. cit. supra* note 22; ICJ, The case of *Armed Activities on the Territory of the Congo*, 2005, *op. cit. supra* note 3.

496. The terms "attribution" and "imputation" of conduct and responsibility are used interchangeably in this course.

497. See also K. Bannelier-Christakis, 2017, *op. cit. supra* note 29.

This explains the difference between the "effective control" required for the application of Article 8 ARSIWA and the simple "control" over the source of the (risk of) harm required for the application of due diligence, as explained above in Chapter II.

However, the comparatively greater ease with which it is possible to engage the responsibility for negligence of a State or IO comes with an important drawback: the negligent State or IO is held responsible for its own negligence and not for the action or omission which caused the (risk of) harm. While the injury is the same, the wrongful act at stake is not. This has, of course, consequences for the content of its responsibility, including its obligation to make reparation. It also has a bearing upon the measures implementing responsibility, especially the type of countermeasures (self-defence, for instance) [498]. We will return to this question later in the chapter.

(b) Responsibility for negligence and responsibility by attribution of the responsibility of another State or IO

Attribution of responsibility to a State or IO because of assistance, control or coercion exercised over another State or IO (Arts. 16, 17 and 18 ARSIWA; Arts. 14, 15 and 16 ARIO and Arts. 58, 59 and 60 ARIO) covers cases where a direct attribution of the conduct of a State or IO (and as such of its organs) to another State or IO is otherwise not possible (pursuant to Art. 6 ARSIWA or Art. 7 ARIO).

It does not, however, cover the case of assistance, control or coercion exercised by a State over a private person who caused the (risk of) harm. In those circumstances, the State or IO can only incur responsibility by direct attribution of that person's conduct. A State or IO to which the acts of that private person are attributed in accordance with Articles 4 to 11 ARSIWA (Arts. 6 to 9 ARIO) may further be attributed the responsibility of another State or IO which it aided or assisted, over which it exercised some control or which it coerced with the help of that private person. However, aid or assistance provided by a State or IO to the private persons who caused the harm cannot give rise to an attribution of the responsibility of these persons, except if these persons' conduct is attributable to that State or IO. In such cases, the only remaining

498. See *ibid.*

option is the State's or IO's independent responsibility for negligence [499].

The difference between responsibility for negligence and responsibility by attribution on the ground of complicity (or even control [500] or coercion, although the former ground of attribution is closer to negligence) principally arises in State (or IO) to State (or IO) relations: a State or IO which aids or assists another State or IO may do so in breach of a due diligence obligation and could as a result incur responsibility for negligence. However, unlike responsibility for complicity, control or coercion, responsibility for negligence does not lead to attributing the responsibility of the third party that is the source of harm. The negligent State or IO bears responsibility for its own negligence and is not attributed, even indirectly, the responsibility for the action or omission by which the (risk of) harm occurred. While the injury is the same, the wrongful act at issue is not. This has consequences for the content of responsibility, including the obligation to make reparation. It also has a bearing upon the measures implementing responsibility, especially the type of countermeasures (self-defence, for instance) [501]. We will revert to this question later in the chapter.

This fundamental difference between the consequences of responsibility for complicity and responsibility for negligence explains why the conditions governing responsibility by attribution of responsibility, including on the ground of complicity, are so strict. It also explains why some States or authors are increasingly interested in adjusting the conditions of responsibility for complicity so as to make it easier to apply to situations which would otherwise fall solely under the conditions of responsibility for negligence.

Distinguishing direct responsibility for negligence from indirect responsibility (i.e. by attribution of responsibility) for complicity [502] has

499. See especially ICJ, The case of *Application of the Convention on the Prevention and Punishment of the Crime of Genocide*, *op. cit. supra* note 22, para. 462. For an analysis in favour of a responsibility for negligence in this case, see A. Seibert-Fohr, *op. cit. supra* note 261.

500. On the notion of control and the role of the intention to control to ground such an attribution of responsibility, see ARSIWA with commentaries, *op. cit. supra* note 71, pp. 71-73; ARIO with commentaries, *op. cit. supra* note 443, pp. 66-67 and 99.

501. See also K. Bannelier-Christakis, 2017, *op. cit. supra* note 29.

502. On complicity in international responsibility law in general, see M. Jackson, *Complicity in International Law*, Oxford, Oxford University Press, 2015; H. P. Aust, *Complicity and the Law of State Responsibility*, Cambridge, Cambridge University Press, 2011; V. Lanovoy, "Complicity in an Internationally Wrongful Act", in A. Nollkaemper and I. Plakokefalos (eds.), *Principles of Shared Responsibility in International Law: An Appraisal of the State of the Art*, Cambridge, Cambridge

not always been easy [503]. Quite the opposite, for a long time, the two constructions overlapped in State practice. The distinction only became clearer with the judgment of the ICJ in the *Corfu Channel* case [504]. The ICJ has confirmed its jurisprudence several times since then [505].

Today, the separation between the two types of responsibility is complete: responsibility for complicity is set forth under Article 16 ARSIWA (Art. 14 ARIO), while the ARSIWA and the ARIO remain silent with regard to responsibility for negligence. A consequence of this separation has been to strengthen the conditions governing responsibility for complicity. In that respect, a number of authors, like Olivier Corten, lament the codification of responsibility for complicity rather than negligence [506]. They consider that responsibility for complicity is useless, impossible to apply and most of all not grounded in custom unless interpreted as a responsibility for negligence, which it should never have ceased to be in the first place.

In brief, the five elements distinguishing responsibility for negligence from responsibility for complicity in accordance with the ARSIWA and the ARIO and their interpretation in practice are the following [507].

First, the responsibility for negligence of a State or IO is not a responsibility by attribution of either the conduct or the responsibility of another person regardless of whether that person is private or public, such as a State or IO. What matters is the negligent act of the State or IO itself. Responsibility for negligence can be triggered by the (risk of) harm caused by a private person, whereas current international responsibility law does not provide for complicity with a private person and attribution of that private person's responsibility to the assisting State or IO [508].

University Press, 2014, pp. 134-168; V. Lanovoy, *Complicity and its Limits in the Law of International Responsibility*, Oxford, Hart, 2016; I. Plakokefalos, "The Use of Force by Non-State Actors and the Limits of Attribution of Conduct: A Reply to Vladyslav Lanovoy", *European Journal of International Law*, Vol. 28, No. 2 (2017), pp. 587-593; Pacholska, *op. cit. supra* note 480.

503. See O. Corten, 2011, *op. cit. supra* note 433; O. Corten and P. Klein, *op. cit. supra* note 494.

504. See ICJ, The case of the *Corfu Channel*, *op. cit. supra* note 8, pp. 22-23.

505. See ICJ, The case of the *United States Diplomatic and Consular Staff in Tehran*, *op. cit. supra* note 8, paras. 67-68; ICJ, The case of *Application of the Convention on the Prevention and Punishment of the Crime of Genocide*, *op. cit. supra* note 22, para. 462.

506. See especially O. Corten, 2011, *op. cit. supra* note 433; O. Corten and P. Klein, *op. cit. supra* note 494, p. 331.

507. See O. Corten and P. Klein, *op. cit. supra* note 494, p. 332.

508. See ARSIWA with commentaries, *op. cit. supra* note 71, pp. 69-71.

Second, responsibility for negligence may flow from both actions and omissions, whereas complicity is necessarily active. Responsibility for complicity requires active aid or assistance and cannot accordingly result from a mere omission [509].

Third, a breach of due diligence (i.e. negligence) does not require that the aid or assistance be undertaken with an intent to breach international law, unlike what is required for the assisting State or IO [510]. It suffices that the negligent State or IO knew or should have known that a (risk of) harm would occur and did not act diligently in that respect. The negligent State or IO may have intended to aid or assist the private person at the origin of the harm, but that is not required [511].

Fourth, the knowledge of the assisting State or IO must be effective or actual [512], whereas the negligent State or IO may be held responsible even if it did not know that the (risk of) harm would occur: it is sufficient that it should have known. Constructive knowledge suffices, in other words [513].

Finally, responsibility for complicity requires that the assisting State or IO be bound by the same obligation as the principally responsible State or IO whose responsibility is attributed to that State or IO because of the aid or assistance provided [514]. In case of responsibility for negligence, the private person at the origin of the harm does not have to be bound by a given international law obligation, even less by

509. See *ibid.*

510. See *ibid.* See also H. Moynihan, "Aiding and Assisting: The Mental Element under Article 16 of the International Law Commission's Articles on State Responsibility", *International and Comparative Law Quarterly*, Vol. 67 (2018), pp. 455-471; O. Corten, 2011, *op. cit. supra* note 433. Contra: H. P. Aust, 2011, *op. cit. supra* note 502; Pacholska, *op. cit. supra* note 480.

511. See ICJ, The case of *Application of the Convention on the Prevention and Punishment of the Crime of Genocide*, *op. cit. supra* note 22, para. 420.

512. See ARSIWA with commentaries, *op. cit. supra* note 71, pp. 69-71. Contra: Pacholska, *op. cit. supra* note 480, pp. 168-208, who distinguishes simple complicity from aggravated complicity precisely by reference to the breach of the due diligence standard.

513. In that respect, one must mention the *Guiding Principles on Shared Responsibility in International Law* (A. Nollkaemper, J. d'Aspremont, C. Ahlborn, B. Boutin, N. Nedeski and I. Plakokefalos, "Guiding Principles on Shared Responsibility in International Law", *European Journal of International Law*, Vol. 31, No. 1 (2020), pp. 15-72), especially Principle 6 on complicity. It provides, on the one hand, for a loosening of the conditions of current ARSIWA, *op. cit. supra* note 24, Art. 16 precisely to include constructive and not only actual knowledge, and, on the other, abandons the requirement of intent. This project aims to develop principles of international responsibility that can apply to circumstances in which a plurality of States are responsible at the same time and for the same injury. There is no mention of due diligence, however, even though the proposed responsibility is akin to responsibility for negligence.

514. See ARSIWA with commentaries, *op. cit. supra* note 71, pp. 69-71.

the same obligation as the negligent State or IO: what matters is the due diligence obligation of the negligent State or IO. Because private persons' obligations under international law are not yet very developed outside of international criminal law, this last point is often decisive, especially in international human rights law.

In practice, however, these differences tend to fade again in practice. This should come as no surprise given the important limits constraining the complicity regime set forth under Article 16 ARSIWA (Art. 14 ARIO).

Thus certain ambiguities have been observed in international human rights law lately, particularly in ECtHR litigation on State responsibility for the acts of the organs of another State [515]. However, it is unclear whether this ambivalence is artificially maintained to give rise to a new (and larger) conception of responsibility for complicity or if it simply results from mistaken reasoning or a lack of rigour [516]. Without going as far as suggesting a new ground of responsibility by attribution of the conduct of another State [517], the ECtHR clearly appears to be exceeding the contours of responsibility for negligence. The intention of the State involved seems to matter more in these cases than in the context of responsibility for the breach of a due diligence obligation [518]. And yet, the ECtHR does not seem to strictly abide by the conditions of responsibility for complicity [519]. The Court does not respect the

515. See e.g. ECtHR, Case of *El-Masri* v. *The Former Yugoslav Republic of Macedonia*, *op. cit. supra* note 270, para. 206. See also S. Michalovski, *op. cit. supra* note 213.

516. See J. Crawford and A. Keene, "The Structure of State Responsibility under the European Convention on Human Rights", in J. Motoc and A. van Aaken (eds.), *The ECHR and General International Law*, Oxford, Oxford University Press, 2018, pp. 178-198, for the first interpretation. See, however, H. Keller and R. Walther, "Evasion of the International Law of State Responsibility? The ECtHR's Jurisprudence on Positive and Preventive Obligations under Article 3", *The International Journal of Human Rights*, Vol. 24, No. 7 (2019), pp. 957-978; V. Stoyanova, 2018, *op. cit. supra* note 4, for the second.

517. See M. Milanovic, "State Acquiescence or Connivance in the Wrongful Conduct of Third Parties in the Jurisprudence of the European Court of Human Rights", 2019 [online].

518. See e.g. ECtHR, Case of *El-Masri* v. *The Former Yugoslav Republic of Macedonia*, *op. cit. supra* note 270, para. 206. Contra, however: ECtHR, Case of *Al Nashiri* v. *Romania*, No. 33234/12, Judgment of 31 May 2018; Case of *Abu Zubaydah* v. *Lithuania*, No. 46454/11, Judgment of 31 May 2018. See M. Milanovic, 2019, *op. cit. supra* note 517; J. Crawford and A. Keene, *op. cit. supra* note 516, p. 189. Contra: H. Keller and R. Walther, *op. cit. supra* note 516; V. Stoyanova, 2018, *op. cit. supra* note 4, who considers that creating very extensive positive due diligence obligations as well as a responsibility for negligence outside the ARSIWA model of behaviour and responsibility attribution is a hallmark of international human rights law.

519. See M. Milanovic, 2019, *op. cit. supra* note 517.

condition of intention and confines itself to establishing acquiescence or connivance of one State by another [520], suggesting therefore that the ECtHR is outlining a lighter form of responsibility for complicity.

In fact, it is mostly in the wake of the development of threats of private origin, particularly in the context of terrorism [521] or cyberattacks [522], that the difference between responsibility for complicity and responsibility for negligence is now called into question [523].

In that context, certain scholars have been inclined to smooth over the distinctions between responsibility for negligence and responsibility for complicity [524]. The aim seems to be to establish a responsibility by attribution of responsibility not only for the injury itself, but for the facts which caused the injury, which is not provided by responsibility for negligence. According to those authors, the scope of States' or IOs' responsibility for complicity should be broadened to include complicity to the actions of private persons and therefore to their responsibilities [525]. Such proposals are open to many critiques. Some relate to the absence of corresponding obligations of the private persons involved [526] and thus to the impossibility of holding a State or IO responsible by attribution of a responsibility which cannot exist. Others simply bemoan the erosion of the due diligence standard of the State or IO and the dilution of the responsibility for negligence of public institutions which this new conception of responsibility for complicity would elicit, should it ever

520. ECtHR, Case of *El-Masri* v. *The Former Yugoslav Republic of Macedonia*, *op. cit. supra* note 270, para. 206. See also M. Milanovic, 2019, *op. cit. supra* note 517; A. Nollkaemper, "The ECtHR Finds Macedonia Responsible in Connection with Torture by the CIA, but on What Basis?", *EJIL Talk!*, 24 December 2012 [online].

521. See F. Dubuisson, "Vers un renforcement des obligations de diligence en matière de lutte contre le terrorisme ?", in K. Bannelier, T. Christakis, O. Corten and B. Delcourt (eds.), *Le droit international face au terrorisme*, Paris, Pedone, 2002, pp. 141-157; R. P. J. Barnidge, *Non-State Actors and Terrorism: Applying the Law of State Responsibility and the Due Diligence Principle*, The Hague, T.M.C. Asser Press, 2008.

522. See K. Bannelier-Christakis, 2017, *op. cit. supra* note 29.

523. On the issue of the lack of modalities of plural responsibility of States/IOs and private persons in international responsibility law, see especially J. d'Aspremont, A. Nollkaemper, I. Plakokefalos and C. Ryngaert, *op. cit. supra* note 432.

524. See e.g. A. Seibert-Fohr, *op. cit. supra* note 261.

525. See e.g. L. Chircop, *op. cit. supra* note 29; V. Lanovoy, "The Use of Force by Non-State Actors and the Limits of Attribution of Conduct", *European Journal of International Law*, Vol. 28, No. 2 (2017), pp. 563-585; V. Lanovoy, "The Use of Force by Non-State Actors and the Limits of Attribution of Conduct: A Rejoinder to Ilias Plakokefalos", *European Journal of International Law*, Vol. 28, No. 2 (2017), pp. 595-599; R. P. J. Barnidge, 2008, *op. cit. supra* note 521. For a critique, see I. Plakokefalos, 2017, *op. cit. supra* note 502.

526. In the context of cybersecurity, see e.g. K. Bannelier-Christakis, 2017, *op. cit. supra* note 29.

be applied in practice [527]. This new type of responsibility for complicity would come dangerously close to a form of collective responsibility, especially State responsibility, for the wrongful acts of their nationals or residents without attribution of conduct.

To end these considerations on the difference between responsibility for negligence and responsibility by attribution (including for complicity), it is necessary to examine that same relationship in greater detail, this time in the context of State responsibility for IOs and, conversely, IO responsibility for States.

Under the international law on IO responsibility, there is a fourth ground of (indirect) attribution of the responsibility of an IO to a State or IO or of a State to an IO: the circumvention of one's international obligations on the authorisation or command of the other (Arts. 17 and 61 ARIO). This ground of responsibility by attribution is specific to the distinct but composite legal personality of IOs and to their relationships with Member States. As with responsibility for complicity, IOs' and States' responsibility for circumvention may easily be conflated with responsibility for negligence: by authorising or enjoining a Member State or IO to commit a wrongful act, the IO or the Member State may be circumventing a due diligence obligation. It is therefore important to carefully distinguish these two types of responsibility [528].

Among the conditions of responsibility (by attribution) for circumvention differing from those of responsibility for negligence, the following one deserves to be mentioned. Responsibility for negligence does not require an intention to circumvent one's international obligations, unlike what is required from the State or IO which circumvents its obligations. However, unlike responsibility for complicity, control or coercion, responsibility for circumvention does not require that the State or IO whose responsibility is attributed be bound by the same obligations as the State or IO circumventing its obligations (Arts. 17 (3) and 61 (2) ARIO). These two types of responsibility are so similar that one could almost conclude that it does not really amount to responsibility by attribution, but rather to responsibility for negligence.

Unfortunately no practice has yet developed with regard to these two ARIO provisions. The nearest instances differ with respect to the

527. See especially O. Corten, 2011, *op. cit. supra* note 433; O. Corten and P. Klein, *op. cit. supra* note 494, p. 331.
528. See e.g. M. Starita, *op. cit. supra* note 494. See also K. Daugirdas, *op. cit. supra* note 271.

intention criterion and therefore tend to further assimilate responsibility for circumvention with responsibility for negligence.

This is observable in the ECtHR's jurisprudence according to which the Member States of an IO cannot invoke that status to defend themselves against an allegation of a breach of the ECHR. Each Member State incurs a due diligence obligation to ensure that its IO protects human rights in a manner which can be considered at least equivalent to that of the ECHR [529]. There is as a result no need to circumvent ECHR obligations to give rise to responsibility for the breach of the equivalence obligation [530]. Obviously, in the ECtHR system, only States are bound by human rights obligations and might incur responsibility for their breaches. As a result, there would be no interest for the ECtHR to attribute the responsibility of the IO to the State: the Member State is directly responsible before the Court for its own negligence [531].

2. *Responsibility for negligence and the condition of the breach of international law*

The second difficulty with respect to the general conditions of international responsibility in the context of responsibility for negligence is the exact role of causation in establishing the breach of a due diligence obligation, especially when the harm was also caused by other responsible States or IOs.

In principle, causation is not a part of the conditions of international responsibility set forth under the ARSIWA and the ARIO. Moreover, unlike what is the case under domestic law on civil and public liability [532], injury is no condition of international responsibility (even

529. On a Member State's responsibility for breaches of due diligence obligations with regard to the actions of an IO over which it exercises control (with or without presumption of equivalence), see e.g. ECtHR, *Bosphorus* v. *Ireland*, *op. cit. supra* note 229, paras. 152-153; ECtHR, *Case of Michaud* v. *France*, *op. cit. supra* note 229, para. 103; ECtHR, Case of *Al-Dulimi* v. *Switzerland*, *op. cit. supra* note 229, paras. 114 *et seq*. (for the UN). See also the Dissenting opinion of Judge Keller, in ECtHR, Case of *Al-Dulimi* v. *Switzerland* (Grand Chamber), *op. cit. supra* note 229, paras. 11 *et seq*., criticising the Grand Chamber for abandoning its reasoning based on the due diligence of UN Member States in favour of a presumption of harmonised interpretation of the UN Charter by those same States.

530. See e.g. M. Starita, *op. cit. supra* note 494.

531. On the link between the responsibility for negligence of UN Member States and the circumvention of their ECHR obligations through the transfer of their competences to the UN, see the Dissenting opinion of Judge Keller, in ECtHR, Case of *Al-Dulimi* v. *Switzerland* (Grand Chamber), *op. cit. supra* note 229, para. 11.

532. See J. Gardner and A. Honoré, "Causation in the Law", in N. Zalta (ed.), *The Stanford Encyclopedia of Philosophy*, Stanford, Metaphysics Research Lab, 2010 [online].

if it is one of the conditions of reparation pursuant to Art. 31 ARSIWA or Art. 31 ARIO). This makes the absence of a reference to causation among the conditions of responsibility less visible.

Nonetheless, causation plays an important role in the practice of international responsibility [533]. It is especially apparent in the context of "concurrent" or "plural" responsibility [534], that is, responsibilities stemming from the contribution of many States or IOs to the same injury, whether this occurs through the same wrongful act or not (referred to as "shared responsibility" in the former case) [535]. In these circumstances, a determination of causation is necessary to allocate not only responsibilities, but also reparations between the responsible States or IOs.

Legal scholarship has brought some clarity into the debate by distinguishing between four types of causation: exclusive, parallel, complementary and cumulative [536].

First, causation may be *exclusive*. In that case, a single wrongful act causes the injury. Responsibility is allocated individually to the only responsible State or IO. Second, causation may also be *parallel*. In that situation, each wrongful act could have caused the same injury independently from the others, making an individual allocation of responsibilities to each State or IO possible. Third, causation may be *complementary*: each independent wrongful act could have caused an injury, but not the full injury. The full injury is an aggregate of all the distinct injuries caused by the various wrongful acts. Responsibilities are allocated to each responsible State or IO in proportion to its share in the contribution to the injury.

Finally, causation may be *cumulative*. In that case, each of the wrongful acts had to occur in combination with the others to cause an injury that is considered indivisible; taken separately, none of the wrongful acts could have caused the injury on its

533. See I. Plakokefalos, 2015, *op. cit. supra* note 391; V. Stoyanova, 2018, *op. cit. supra* note 4.

534. See P. d'Argent, 2014, *op. cit. supra* note 68; I. Plakokefalos, 2015, *op. cit. supra* note 391.

535. On these terms, see S. Besson, "La responsabilité solidaire des organisations internationales et des États – Une institution négligée", in A. Supiot (ed.), *La responsabilité solidaire*, Paris, Publications du Collège de France, 2018, pp. 121-159; A. Nollkaemper, "Introduction", in A. Nollkaemper and I. Plakokefalos (eds.), *Principles of Shared Responsibility in International Law: An Appraisal of the State of the Art*, Cambridge, Cambridge University Press, 2014, pp. 1-24.

536. See with some variations: B. Stern, *op. cit. supra* note 476; P. d'Argent, 2014, *op. cit. supra* note 68.

own [537]. In such cases, an individual and proportional allocation of responsibilities to each responsible State or IO is impossible in terms of strict causation. Other means to allocate responsibilities include the selection of an "adequate" or reconstructed cause (the most recent one, for example) or even opting for the causes' "equivalence" and dividing responsibility by the number of responsible States or IOs [538].

Unsurprisingly, all these types of causation may come under consideration in a case of responsibility for breach of a due diligence obligation [539]. It is rare for a State or IO found responsible for negligence to be the sole responsible of the injury, which raises the question of its contribution to the injury. It will therefore be necessary to assess each type of causation linking each wrongful act to the injury. Moreover, when due diligence obligations are preventive obligations, the occurrence of the injury or of the event which should be prevented is, as mentioned earlier, a condition of the violation or breach of these obligations and as such of responsibility for negligence (see indirectly Art. 14 (3) ARSIWA; Art. 12 (3) ARIO). In such cases, establishing a causal nexus between the occurrence of the event which had to be prevented and the conduct of the responsible State or IO remains necessary.

In sum, in the context of responsibility for the breach of due diligence obligations, causation becomes an issue in at least two stages of the legal and judicial reasoning (setting aside factual causation between the different events) [540]: *(i)* causation that links the State's or IO's action or omission to the occurrence of an event constitutive of the injury, the latter being, in some cases, a condition of the breach of the due diligence obligation (condition of responsibility); and *(ii)* causation that links this wrongful act to the injury for which to make reparation (content of responsibility).

The lack of consideration for causation as well as the absence of a clear differentiation between these two types or roles of causation

537. See e.g. ICJ, The case of *Application of the Convention on the Prevention and Punishment of the Crime of Genocide*, *op. cit. supra* note 22, para. 430.

538. See P. d'Argent, 2014, *op. cit. supra* note 68. On the "equal cause", see e.g. European Group on Tort Law, *Principles of European Tort Law*, Vienna, Springer, 2005, Principle 3.105.

539. See P. Jacob, *op. cit. supra* note 466. See e.g. *Alabama Claims* Arbitration, *op. cit. supra* note 1; ICJ, The case of the *Corfu Channel*, *op. cit. supra* note 8; ICJ, The case of *Application of the Convention on the Prevention and Punishment of the Crime of Genocide*, *op. cit. supra* note 22.

540. See I. Plakokefalos, 2015, *op. cit. supra* note 391.

with regard to responsibility for negligence largely account for the weakness of the current jurisprudence on responsibility for breaches of due diligence obligations [541]. As one would expect, scholars have often called for a stronger and more rigorous jurisprudence of causation.

One of the most important and repeated critiques expressed by these authors pertains to the need for the case law to relinquish "but for" causality. According to this conception, causation would exist in a given case only if it is possible to determine that the outcome would not have happened *but for* the action or omission at issue [542]. The scholarship proposes instead a more complex and nuanced conception of causality [543]. It suggests in particular a causation based on the so-called INUS test (Insufficient but Necessary element of an Unnecessary but Sufficient set [of causes]) [544] or the test known as NESS (Necessary Element of a Sufficient Set [of causes]) [545], both of which are derived from Anglo-American tort law theory.

For example, in the *Genocide* judgment of 2007, the ICJ clearly distinguishes the causation necessary to establish the condition of the breach from the causation necessary to establish the link with the injury as a condition of reparation. There are two stages in its reasoning: the determination of whether there has been a breach and consequently responsibility and the determination of which reparation must be made for that responsibility. Yet the distinct treatment of causation at each stage of the Court's reasoning is not convincing because it rests upon different conceptions of causation. At the first stage of its reasoning, the Court aptly considers that causation can be complementary and that a State may bear responsibility for negligence even if its wrongful act was not necessarily alone in causing the injury [546]. Unfortunately, at the second stage, the Court rejects the claim for

541. See P. Jacob, *op. cit. supra* note 466.

542. See I. Plakokefalos, 2015, *op. cit. supra* note 391; P. Jacob, *op. cit. supra* note 466. This is already the case in ECtHR case law: see V. Stoyanova, 2018, *op. cit. supra* note 4.

543. See *ibid.*

544. See J. L. Mackie, *The Cement of the Universe: A Study of Causation*, Oxford, Oxford University Press, 1980.

545. See R. W. Wright, "Causation in Tort law", *California Law Review*, Vol. 73 (1985), pp. 1737-1828; R. W. Wright, "The NESS Account of Natural Causation: A Response to Criticisms", in B. Kahmen and M. S. Stepanians (eds.), *Critical Essays on "Causation and Responsibility"*, Berlin, De Gruyter, 2013, pp. 13–66.

546. See ICJ, The case of *Application of the Convention on the Prevention and Punishment of the Crime of Genocide, op. cit. supra* note 22, paras. 430-431.

compensation on the grounds that the State did not cause the injury in its entirety [547].

While allocating responsibilities and compensations is no easy task in the case of cumulative or complementary causation – as was the case in that judgment – abandoning compensation awards due to complexity is not justifiable [548]. As a matter of judicial reasoning, it even contradicts the ICJ's position on the role of causation in the determination of a violation of international law. The ICJ seems to use two different tests of causation: a complex causality test for the violation and a test of "but for" causality for the reparation.

We will examine the latter form of causality along with the content of the responsibility for negligence (including reparations) in the next section (C). We will concentrate for now on drawing a clearer picture of the first type of causation as it is the premise of the entire regime of responsibility for negligence.

As indicated earlier, notwithstanding its subsequent incoherence, the ICJ recognised in the first phase of the *Genocide* judgment that it is necessary to remove "but for" causality in order to retain responsibility for negligence [549]. Other international tribunals have since reached the same conclusion, notably in international human rights law [550].

Establishing causality in the context of breaches of due diligence obligations proves difficult already because of causation's role in the determination of these obligations' content. Due diligence requires the risk of harm to be reasonably foreseeable irrespective of whether the obligation is preventive and irrespective of whether the breach is conditioned upon the occurrence of the event to be prevented. Foreseeability, like due diligence's reasonableness test in general, is both objective in its minimum and subjective in its maximal specification. One should be able to verify not only that the risk of harm was foreseeable by the duty-bearer personally (it knew), but also that

547. See ICJ, The case of *Application of the Convention on the Prevention and Punishment of the Crime of Genocide*, *op. cit. supra* note 22, para. 462. For a critique, see P. Jacob, *op. cit. supra* note 466; P. d'Argent, 2014, *op. cit. supra* note 68.

548. See P. d'Argent, 2014, *op. cit. supra* note 68. For a recent presumption of causality and reversal of the burden of proof of the causal nexus in case of breach of due diligence in a context of territorial occupation, however, see ICJ, The case of *Armed Activities on the Territory of the Congo*, 2022, *op. cit. supra* note 123, para. 95.

549. See ICJ, The case of *Application of the Convention on the Prevention and Punishment of the Crime of Genocide*, *op. cit. supra* note 22, paras. 430-431.

550. See e.g. in international human rights law: ECtHR, Case of *O'Keeffe* v. *Ireland*, *op. cit. supra* note 301, para. 149; ECtHR, Case of *E. and others* v. *The United Kingdom*, No. 33218/96, Judgment of 26 November 2002, para. 99; CESCR, General Comment No. 24, *op. cit. supra* note 3, para. 32. See V. Stoyanova, 2018, *op. cit. supra* note 4.

it could have been reasonably expected from it (it should have known). The risk of harm's foreseeability, both objective and subjective, also implies the foreseeability, actual or constructive, of causation between a certain (active or passive) measure, that is, the conduct of the duty-bearer, and the increase or decrease of its impact on the risk of harm [551]. These various causal links, actual or constructive, are very difficult to establish in practice. And the case law [552] is not always very rigorous with regard to their elucidation [553].

C. *Due diligence and the content of international responsibility*

The second step of our inquiry into due diligence's traces in the contemporary regime of the international responsibility of States and IOs continues with the examination of the content of that responsibility and the place of due diligence in that context. The obligation to make reparation for the injury in particular needs to be outlined with greater precision. Unsurprisingly, causation will again be at the heart of the analysis, but this time in its second dimension: the one that links the wrongful act to the injury for which to make reparation.

In principle, the responsible State or IO must make full reparation for the injury which it caused. If there are several responsible States or IOs, each may have to provide full reparation (Art. 31 (1) ARSIWA; Art. 31 (1) ARIO) [554].

Scholars and the emerging case law have recently questioned that principle, especially in cases involving a plurality of responsible States or IOs [555]. For reparations more proportionate to the State's or IO's contribution to the injury and hence fairer reparations, authors suggest allocation criteria such as causation, but also the degree of fault [556].

---

551. See e.g. ECtHR, Case of *Luginbuhl* v. *Switzerland*, *op. cit. supra* note 303. See also V. Stoyanova, 2018, *op. cit. supra* note 4.

552. On the "real prospect of altering the outcome or mitigating the harm" test, see e.g. ECtHR, Case of *O'Keeffe* v. *Ireland*, *op. cit. supra* note 301, para. 149.

553. See I. Plakokefalos, 2015, *op. cit. supra* note 391; V. Stoyanova, 2018, *op. cit. supra* note 4.

554. See ARSIWA with commentaries, *op. cit. supra* note 71, pp. 97-100; ARIO with commentaries, *op. cit. supra* note 443, pp. 77-78.

555. See A. Nollkaemper, 2014, *op. cit. supra* note 535; P. d'Argent, 2014, *op. cit. supra* note 68.

556. See S. Besson, "La pluralité d'États responsables: un état des lieux", *Revue suisse de droit international et de droit européen*, Vol. 1 (2007), pp. 13-38; S. Besson, "La responsabilité solidaire", 2018, *op. cit. supra* note 535; S. Besson, 2016, *op. cit. supra* note 214; J. D. Fry, "Attribution of Responsibility", in A. Nollkaemper and I. Plakokefalos (eds.), *Principles of Shared Responsibility in International Law: An*

Both are precisely at issue when one of the States or IOs is responsible for negligence: its causation link with the injury is particular because, on the one hand, it is necessarily linked to a distinct wrongful act and, on the other, the degree of fault is lower since its act or omission is negligent and non-intentional.

Because fault is not among the conditions of international responsibility, there is a very limited body of practice that has addressed the degree of fault and therefore the lesser degree of fault of the negligent State or IO [557]. As a matter of fact, responsibility for negligence tends to be treated at the same degree as the other States directly responsible for the injury [558]. However, even if practice is not yet coherent in that respect, we are beginning to see the first signs of a jurisprudence which distances itself from the principle of full reparation and which takes into account the causal nexus between the wrongful act and the injury [559].

Yet one must consider three difficulties. The first relates to practice having become uneven and therefore unfair. Some judgments do not take into account differentiated causality. They consider that a negligent State or IO owes a full reparation just like the other responsible States or IOs [560]. By contrast, other decisions, such as the ICJ's judgment in the *Genocide* case, find that short of a full reparation (which, as discussed earlier, they eventually rejected), the negligent State or IO does not

---

Appraisal of the State of the Art, Cambridge, Cambridge University Press, 2014, pp. 98-133.

557. See J. D. Fry, *op. cit. supra* note 556; H. P. Aust, "Circumstances Precluding Wrongfulness", in A. Nollkaemper and I. Plakokefalos (eds.), *Principles of Shared Responsibility in International Law: An Appraisal of the State of the Art*, Cambridge, Cambridge University Press, 2014, pp. 169-207.

558. See e.g. *Alabama Claims* Arbitration, *op. cit. supra* note 1; ICJ, The case of the *Corfu Channel*, *op. cit. supra* note 8; ICSID, *AAPL* Arbitration, *op. cit. supra* note 8; ECtHR, Case of *Z. and others* v. *The United Kingdom*, No. 29392/95, Judgment of 10 May 2001. See also P. Jacob, *op. cit. supra* note 466.

559. See e.g. ICJ, The case of *Application of the Convention on the Prevention and Punishment of the Crime of Genocide*, *op. cit. supra* note 22, para. 462; ITLOS, *Responsibilities and Obligations of States Sponsoring Persons and Entities with Respect to Activities in the Area*, *op. cit. supra* note 41; Supreme Court of the Netherlands, *Urgenda De Staat de Nederland (Ministerie van Infrastructuur en Milieu)* v. *Stichting Urgenda*, *op. cit. supra* note 251, para. 5.7.5. See also P. Jacob, *op. cit. supra* note 466; A. Nollkaemper and L. Burgers, "A New Classic in Climate Change Litigation: The Dutch Supreme Court Decision in the Urgenda Case", *EJIL Talk!*, 6 January 2020 [online].

560. See e.g. *Alabama Claims* Arbitration, *op. cit. supra* note 1; ICJ, The case of the *Corfu Channel*, *op. cit. supra* note 8; ICSID, *AAPL* Arbitration, *op. cit. supra* note 8; ECtHR, Case of *Z. and others* v. *The United Kingdom*, *op. cit. supra* note 558. See also P. Jacob, *op. cit. supra* note 466.

have to make any reparation at all [561]. The second difficulty lies in the link that is made, especially in the second group of cases, between the principle of full reparation and "but for" causality. If the negligent State or IO does not have to make reparation in such cases, it is because the injury would have occurred even without the breach of due diligence and because negligence is not the only, or at least not the main, cause of the injury [562].

Once the degree of causation is linked to the degree of reparation and the "but for" causality test is abandoned, the third difficulty pertains to determining the precise modalities of reparation for injuries whose causation is complex or cumulative rather than merely complementary. This is often the case when one of the States or IOs involved caused the injury by negligence. By way of a reminder, unlike complementary causation, in these cases, each wrongful act taken separately could not have caused the injury on its own and had to unfold with the others to cause the indivisible injury [563]. An individual and proportional repartition of responsibilities is therefore impossible in terms of strict causality. Other means to allocate responsibilities in case of cumulative causality [564] include selecting an "adequate" or reconstructed cause (such as focusing on the most-recent-in-time cause) or even deciding for an "equivalence" [565] of causes and dividing responsibility by the number of responsible States or IOs. These options are inspired by solutions prevailing under domestic law on civil or public liability.

D. Due diligence and the implementation of international responsibility

The third and last step of our inquiry into the traces of due diligence in the contemporary regime of the international responsibility of States

561. See e.g. ICJ, The case of *Application of the Convention on the Prevention and Punishment of the Crime of Genocide*, *op. cit. supra* note 22, para. 462; ITLOS, *Responsibilities and Obligations of States Sponsoring Persons and Entities with Respect to Activities in the Area*, *op. cit. supra* note 41. See also P. Jacob, *op. cit. supra* note 466.

562. See *ibid.* For a presumption of causality and reversal of the burden of proof of the causal nexus in case of breach of due diligence in a context of territorial occupation, however, see ICJ, The case of *Armed Activities on the Territory of the Congo*, 2022, *op. cit. supra* note 123, para. 95.

563. See e.g. ICJ, The case of *Application of the Convention on the Prevention and Punishment of the Crime of Genocide*, *op. cit. supra* note 22, para. 430.

564. See P. d'Argent, 2014, *op. cit. supra* note 68.

565. On the "equal cause", see e.g. European Group on Tort Law, *op. cit. supra* note 538, Principle 3.105.

and IOs continues with the implementation of that responsibility and the place of responsibility for negligence in that context.

Two questions about the implementation of responsibility for negligence need to be addressed: (1) the invocation of responsibility in situations where a plurality of States or IOs, among which the negligent State or IO, are implicated; and (2) the countermeasures against a negligent State or IO.

1. *The invocation of responsibility for negligence in case of a plurality of responsible States and/or IOs*

The negligent State or IO is often not the only State or IO responsible for the injury. The question of the invocation of its responsibility arises therefore in relation to that of the other responsible States or IOs. One should inquire in particular whether it is possible to bring action against only one of the responsible States or IOs for the entire injury and later launch internal recourses against the other responsible States or IOs.

The principle for the invocation of international responsibility is individual and distinct responsibility: responsibilities are allocated to each responsible State or IO in proportion to its contribution to the injury (Art. 42 ARSIWA; Art. 43 ARIO) [566].

However, the ARSIWA and the ARIO also include a provision governing the special case of a plurality of responsible States or IOs (Art. 47 ARSIWA; Art. 48 ARIO) [567]. According to this principle known as joint and several responsibility, each responsible State or IO can be called to remedy the whole injury for all the others (Art. 47 (1) ARSIWA; Art. 48 (1) ARIO). The conditions for its application are very strict, however. The injury must have been caused by the same wrongful act, and there must be protection against unjust enrichment by the injured State or IO. Internal rights of recourse should also be available in order to avoid overburdening one of the responsible States or IO and favouring the others (Art. 47 (2) ARSIWA; Art. 48 (3) ARIO).

Authors have suggested several avenues to extend these conditions to other circumstances in which the application of joint and several

566. See ARSIWA with commentaries, *op. cit. supra* note 71, p. 126, paras. 6 and 8.

567. On this provision, see S. Besson, 2007, *op. cit. supra* note 556; S. Besson, 2016, *op. cit. supra* note 214; S. Besson, "La responsabilité solidaire", 2018, *op. cit. supra* note 535; S. Besson, "Shared Responsibilities", 2018, *op. cit. supra* note 214; P. d'Argent, 2014, *op. cit. supra* note 68.

responsibility could be justified [568]. These proposals could apply to all areas of international law, but, of course, especially to international human rights law. In the latter field, indeed, the victims of the injury and therefore the holders of the right to reparation are individuals, and their human right to reparation could be more efficiently protected by a mechanism of joint and several responsibility among the responsible States and/or IOs. [569]

The first proposed expansion of the scope of joint and several responsibility concerns circumstances in which causation is complex or cumulative. In such cases, although the injury was not caused by the same wrongful act, it is not possible to identify individual causation links, and the determination of proportional compensations is difficult.

This hypothesis seems particularly suited for responsibility for negligence [570]. In such cases, the responsibility to be shared between a negligent State or IO and other responsible States and IOs may derive not from the same wrongful act, but from an indivisible injury which could not have been caused by each wrongful act on its own [571]. An individual and proportional allocation of responsibilities is therefore impossible, at least on the basis of strict causality. Extending the application of joint and several responsibility to such cases would be even more appropriate when the due diligence obligation breached is an obligation of international human rights law and the injured victim an individual [572].

The second proposal of extension of the conditions of application of joint and several responsibility is the case of shared responsibility between an IO and one or several of its Member States [573].

The IO and its Member States share an institutional framework and the capacity to coordinate the allocation of internal responsibilities,

568. On these different proposals and hypotheses, see S. Besson, 2016, *op. cit. supra* note 214; S. Besson, "La responsabilité solidaire", 2018, *op. cit. supra* note 535; S. Besson, "Shared Responsibilities", 2018, *op. cit. supra* note 214; P. d'Argent, 2014, *op. cit. supra* note 68.

569. See S. Besson, 2016, *op. cit. supra* note 214; S. Besson, "La responsabilité solidaire", 2018, *op. cit. supra* note 535.

570. See M. Starita, *op. cit. supra* note 494.

571. See e.g. ICJ, The case of *Application of the Convention on the Prevention and Punishment of the Crime of Genocide*, *op. cit. supra* note 22, para. 430.

572. See S. Besson, 2016, *op. cit. supra* note 214; S. Besson, "Shared Responsibilities", 2018, *op. cit. supra* note 214.

573. See S. Besson, "La responsabilité solidaire", 2018, *op. cit. supra* note 535; S. Besson, "Individual and State Liability for an International Organization's Responsibility: The Challenge of Fairness Unveiled", in "Global Justice and International Law", special issue, *Italian Journal of Legal Philosophy*, Vol. 6, No. 1 (2017), pp. 51-78.

either before the wrongful acts or afterwards, including by way of treaties [574]. This prevents unjust enrichment concerns. Such concerns should also be obviated when the wrongful act is not the same, such as when the IO or Member State bears responsibility for the injury caused by another Member State or its IO, but for its negligence and for a distinct wrongful act. As seen in Chapter II with regard to the personal scope of due diligence, the due diligence of a Member State and an IO towards each other is grounded [575] in the institutional control exercised by a Member State over an IO or, conversely, by an IO over its Member State [576]. This control should, *a fortiori*, justify holding one or the other jointly responsible in situations where they both caused the injury, one directly and the other by negligence.

2. *The invocation of responsibility for negligence and countermeasures*

Responsibility for negligence further raises the question of the type of countermeasures suitable for the situation where a negligent State or IO is not responsible for the main wrongful act but still contributed to the same injury.

International responsibility law sets forth specific rules on countermeasures as an implementation mechanism of responsibility (Arts. 49 *et seq.* ARSIWA; Arts. 51 *et seq.* ARIO). While most of them restate and codify customary practice, some offer possibilities which have not yet been used, such as collective countermeasures (Arts. 48 and 54 ARSIWA; Arts. 49 and 57 ARIO) [577].

In principle, countermeasures may be taken in response to the breach of a due diligence obligation just like any other international wrongful act (Art. 49 (1) ARSIWA; Art. 51 (1) ARIO). They must be

574. See also L. Gasbarri, 2018, *op. cit. supra* note 214, pp. 116 *et seq.*

575. In international human rights law, see e.g. ECtHR, *Bosphorus* v. *Ireland*, *op. cit. supra* note 229, paras. 152-153; ECtHR, Case of *Michaud* v. *France*, *op. cit. supra* note 229, para. 103; ECtHR, Case of *Avotiņš* v. *Latvia*, *op. cit. supra* note 271 (for the EU); ECtHR, Case of *Al-Dulimi* v. *Switzerland*, *op. cit. supra* note 229, paras. 114 *et seq.* (for the UN); Dissenting opinion of Judge Keller, in ECtHR, Case of *Al-Dulimi* v. *Switzerland* (Grand Chamber), *op. cit. supra* note 229, paras. 11 *et seq.*

576. See J. Klabbers, *An Introduction to International Organizations Law*, 3rd ed., Cambridge, Cambridge University Press, 2015; R. Collins and N. D. White (eds.), *International Organizations and the Idea of Autonomy: Institutional Independence in the International Legal Order*, London, Routledge, 2011; L. Gasbarri, 2018, *op. cit. supra* note 214.

577. See ARSIWA with commentaries, *op. cit. supra* note 71. See also C. J. Tams, *op. cit. supra* note 185.

commensurate to the wrongful act at issue as required by the principle of proportionality (Art. 51 ARSIWA; Art. 54 ARIO). As a result, even within the limits set forth under the UN Charter, including Article 51 of the UN Charter (Art. 50 ARSIWA; Art. 51 ARIO), self-defence may not be invoked as a countermeasure against a State which did not take the necessary measures to prevent an armed aggression, including by negligence: it did not commit that aggression, nor is it an assisting State within the meaning of responsibility by attribution. If that State contributed to the injury through its negligence, it was not acting by armed aggression, and therefore self-defence cannot be exercised against it.

This issue is highly controversial in the context of cybersecurity. Some authors raise the question of whether self-defence measures may be taken against the State responsible for not having prevented hackers working from technical infrastructures located in its territory or under its territorial jurisdiction from launching a cyberattack (provided, of course, this attack had military consequences akin to a "classic" armed aggression) [578], when the State knew or should have known that the hackers would launch the attack and had the reasonable means to intervene [579].

Furthermore, and still in the context of the law of armed conflicts, some argue that the "unable or unwilling" standard corresponds to the due diligence standard [580]. By way of a reminder, according to the supporters of that minority view, this standard would justify resorting to self-defence outside of the conditions of Article 51 of the UN Charter. For example, it would apply when an armed attack is launched by a private armed group whose wrongful acts cannot be attributed to a State either by attribution of conduct or by attribution of responsibility. The interest in applying that standard is evident when trying to justify countermeasures taken against a State that is not responsible for the armed aggression itself, but merely for its negligence with regard to that aggression.

But this contention remains fallacious. This minority viewpoint does not correspond to an international custom and is based on a misguided understanding or even on an inversion of the conditions of due diligence.

578. See Ministère français des Armées, Droit international appliqué aux opérations dans le cyberespace, *op. cit. supra* note 288.

579. Contra: e.g. K. Bannelier-Christakis, 2017, *op. cit. supra* note 29. Pro: M. N. Schmitt, 2015, *op. cit. supra* note 29; *Tallinn Manual 2.0*, *op. cit. supra* note 88.

580. For a discussion, see K. Bannelier-Christakis, 2017, *op. cit. supra* note 29.

The due diligence standard requires the duty-bearer of a due diligence obligation to take reasonable measures for the protection of certain rights or interests provided that it is able to do so. In accordance with the principle of "ought implies can", if the duty-bearer does not have that reasonable capacity, it cannot incur responsibility for its lack of diligence. Yet the "unable or unwilling" standard reproaches the duty-bearer precisely for that: not having prevented what it could not have prevented.

If Article 51 of the UN Charter and Articles 49 *et seq*. ARSIWA prohibit the invocation of the right to take armed countermeasures against a State (and its people) which could have taken preventive measures against an armed aggression and did not, authorising it when the State did not have the capacity to take such measures appears even less justified.

CHAPTER IV

DUE DILIGENCE IN THE SPECIAL REGIMES OF INTERNATIONAL LAW

> "The Court recalls that it has recently had occasion to stress, in the following terms, the great significance that it attaches to respect for the environment, not only for States but also for the whole of mankind: 'the environment is not an abstraction but represents the living space, the quality of life and the very health of human beings, including generations unborn. The existence of the general obligation of States to ensure that activities within their jurisdiction and control respect the environment of other States or of areas beyond national control is now part of the corpus of international law relating to the environment' (*Legality of the Threat or Use of Nuclear Weapons*, Advisory Opinion, *ICJ Reports 1996*, pp. 241-242, para. 29.)."
>
> (ICJ, The case of *The Gabcikovo-Nagymaros Project [Hungary v. Slovakia]*, Judgment of 25 September 1997, *ICJ Reports 1997*, p. 7, para. 53)

Introduction

As indicated in the introduction and at the beginning of the second chapter, the existence of a minimal general regime of the due diligence standard in international law does not exclude variations of this standard and of the obligations that this standard qualifies in international law's special regimes. On the contrary, the general regime outlined in this course arose precisely from the variety among special regimes and from the few commonalities surfacing among them.

The object of this last chapter is to examine the variations between the special regimes that resist comparison and convergence: the specificities of these special regimes outside of the common general regime. As explained earlier, these specificities respond to the particular circumstances of the obligations of (x with due) diligence and, more generally, to the particular circumstances of the rights and interests protected by due diligence in each of those regimes.

This chapter examines due diligence in the following three special regimes: (A) international environmental law and, by way of comparison, international cybersecurity law; and (B) international human rights law.

A. Due diligence in international environmental law and international cybersecurity law

The choice of these two special regimes, that is, (1) international environmental law and (2) international cybersecurity law, for the purpose of a comparative discussion was prompted as much by their differences as by their common features [581].

First, international environmental law is, to this day, the regime of international law where due diligence's regime, especially jurisprudential, is the most developed and detailed. By contrast, international cybersecurity law is a new or, more precisely, a developing regime in which due diligence is already called to play a major role.

A second reason for the choice of these two regimes relates to some of their common features. For instance, both regimes refer to (common) "spaces" to refer to the geographic but also the personal and even the material scope of due diligence. Moreover, in both regimes, the reasonable measures which must be taken by diligent States are as much internal as external or international and require active cooperation with other States. These points of comparison make for an even more constructive analysis and discussion of due diligence's variations across regimes.

1. Due diligence in international environmental law

For a clearer understanding of due diligence's specificities in international environmental law and in order to identify the characteristics of environmental due diligence, this subsection revisits the different elements of the general regime of due diligence in international law, beginning with (a) its nature and sources; followed by (b) its content, variability and limits.

International environmental law, including the law of the sea, is a regime of modern international law which is quite recent in the history of due diligence. It has, however, left its mark upon that history in the twentieth century. Owing to the numerous conventional and jurisprudential references to environmental due diligence, indeed, international environmental law acted as a "catalyst" [582] for many elements of this standard's minimal general regime and in this way contributed to the regime's gradual consolidation.

---

581. See J. Brunnée and T. Meshel, *op. cit. supra* note 28; A. Takano, *op. cit. supra* note 194.

582. On this role of due diligence in jurisprudence in general, see also Y. Kerbrat, 2018, *op. cit. supra* note 96.

International environmental law's regime of due diligence also cross-pollinated different aspects of due diligence in other international legal regimes [583]. For example, international environmental law's duty not to harm (also called the "no harm rule") and its duty to prevent harm were exported into international telecommunications law, including the 1932 International Convention on Telecommunications [584], and later into international biotechnological law, in particular in the Nagoya Protocol and the 1992 Convention on Biological Diversity [585].

(a) The nature and sources of due diligence in international environmental law

The specificities of due diligence in international environmental law are already apparent in the interpretation of its legal nature and its sources within that regime.

First, the *nature* of due diligence in international environmental law. We will address the following two issues: the distinction between the standard and obligation of due diligence, as well as the opposition between obligations of conduct and obligations of result and between procedural and material obligations.

If there is a regime of international law in which the clarification of the nature of due diligence has been most extensive, it is surely in the international jurisprudence of international environmental law. At times, of course, this jurisprudence has also deliberately cultivated opacity, as exemplified by the ICJ's argument in the *Pulp Mills* case. By way of a reminder, the Court's reasoning in that case is built around three reversals [586]: *(i)* the due diligence standard is approached as a full-fledged obligation; *(ii)* from a general principle, it is then considered a customary obligation; and *(iii)* the principle or obligation of prevention is derived from that customary obligation rather than the other way round.

The first ambivalence to note is the one which lingers around the distinction between the due diligence standard and the obligation of (x

583. See J. Brunnée, 2010, *op. cit. supra* note 14.
584. International Telecommunication Convention of 9 December 1932, ITU Library and Archives Service.
585. Convention on Biological Diversity, *op. cit. supra* note 9; Nagoya Protocol on Access to Genetic Resources and the Fair and Equitable Sharing of Benefits Arising from their Utilization to the Convention on Biological Diversity of 29 October 2010, UNTS, Vol. 3009, p. 3.
586. See ICJ, The case of *Pulp Mills on the River Uruguay*, *op. cit. supra* note 3, paras. 101 and 204.

with) due diligence. As we saw earlier, this semantic shift led the ICJ in the *Pulp Mills* case or in the *Certain Activities* case [587], as well as other international tribunals, such as the International Tribunal for the Law of the Sea (ITLOS) [588], to identify the "standard" of due diligence with the "obligation" (of prevention, notably) which it qualifies. This allowed for a swift resolution of the issue of the source of the obligation of diligent prevention: addressing due diligence as a customary obligation led judges to recognise the customary nature of the preventive obligations which it qualifies, including the obligation to proceed with an environmental impact assessment.

The second ambiguity that is intentionally maintained is the one between due diligence and the "principles" with which it is associated in that same jurisprudence [589]. These principles are invoked both *qua* type of general norms of international law and *qua* source of international law.

While the case law has the benefit of having deepened the links tying the due diligence standard to the various principles and obligations of international environmental law that it qualifies, such as the obligation of prevention [590] and the precautionary approach [591], it has also deliberately muddled them, essentially for the purpose of generalising their sources [592]. This explains why, in the *Certain Activities* case, several ICJ judges disagreed with the majority or even among themselves on the essential question of whether the principles and obligations of prevention (and precaution) derive from due diligence or vice versa [593].

587. See e.g. ICJ, The case of *Pulp Mills on the River Uruguay*, *op. cit. supra* note 3, paras. 101 and 204; ICJ, The case of *Certain Activities carried out by Nicaragua in the Border Area*, *op. cit. supra* note 3, para. 104. Contra: Separate opinion of Judge Donoghue, in ICJ, The case of *Certain Activities carried out by Nicaragua in the Border Area*, *op. cit. supra* note 3, paras. 10-13.

588. See e.g. ITLOS, *Responsibilities and Obligations of States Sponsoring Persons and Entities with Respect to Activities in the Area*, *op. cit. supra* note 41, para. 131.

589. See e.g. Separate opinion of Judge Dugard, in ICJ, The case of *Certain Activities carried out by Nicaragua in the Border Area*, *op. cit. supra* note 3, paras. 6-7.

590. See e.g. R. Yotova, *op. cit. supra* note 14; L. A. Duvic-Paoli and J. E. Viñuales, "Principle 2: Prevention", in J. E. Viñuales (ed.), *The Rio Declaration on Environment and Development: A Commentary*, Oxford, Oxford University Press, 2015, pp. 107-138; L. A. Duvic-Paoli, *op. cit. supra* note 14.

591. See e.g. E. Hey, 1992, *op. cit. supra* note 14; M. M. Mbengue, 2009, *op. cit. supra* note 292; J. Cazala, *op. cit. supra* note 292.

592. See ICJ, The case of *Pulp Mills on the River Uruguay*, *op. cit. supra* note 3, paras. 101 and 204; ICJ, The case of *Certain Activities carried out by Nicaragua in the Border Area*, *op. cit. supra* note 3, para. 104.

593. See Separate opinion of Judge Dugard, in ICJ, The case of *Certain Activities carried out by Nicaragua in the Border Area*, *op. cit. supra* note 3, para. 7; Separate

The case law on the nature of due diligence in international environmental law also reveals – rather than clarifies – how much the distinction between obligations of conduct and obligations of result remains difficult to apprehend and implement in the international legal regimes where these obligations are qualified by a due diligence standard.

In international environmental law, some obligations of conduct, including obligations of due diligence, are so precise that they have almost become obligations of result. This is so for the many "procedural" preventive obligations, such as the obligations of notification, information or environmental impact assessment, that the case law now clearly separates from material preventive obligations or even transforms into obligations of result. Yet making the breach of these obligations dependent upon the realisation of the risk to prevent or anticipate, as for other preventive obligations with due diligence, is counterproductive: the non-occurrence of the harm would retroactively exonerate the duty-bearing States from all responsibility for breaching their obligation of environmental impact assessment [594]. Of course, it could be conceivable to entirely exempt the breach of a preventive obligation from the condition of the harm's occurrence. However, the preventive obligation would then be considered fulfilled as soon as its procedural component is respected, which is similarly counterproductive [595].

In any event, the distinction developed by the ICJ in the *Certain Activities* case between procedural and material obligations does not solve this difficulty [596]. First, the distinction itself is largely untenable: the boundaries between the two types of obligations are very difficult to establish in practice [597]. Such a distinction carries with it the understandably attractive prospect of allowing due diligence obligations to be considered as breached prior to the realisation of the harm that

---

opinion of Judge Donoghue, in ICJ, The case of *Certain Activities carried out by Nicaragua in the Border Area*, *op. cit. supra* note 3, para. 13.

594. See e.g. Separate opinion of Judge Dugard, in ICJ, The case of *Certain Activities carried out by Nicaragua in the Border Area*, *op. cit. supra* note 3, paras. 6-7; Separate opinion of Judge Donoghue, in ICJ, The case of *Certain Activities carried out by Nicaragua in the Border Area*, *op. cit. supra* note 3, para. 9.

595. See Separate opinion of Judge Dugard, in ICJ, The case of *Certain Activities carried out by Nicaragua in the Border Area*, *op. cit. supra* note 3, paras. 6-7 and 10.

596. See Separate opinion of Judge Donoghue, in ICJ, The case of *Certain Activities carried out by Nicaragua in the Border Area*, *op. cit. supra* note 3, para. 9. See also J. Brunnée, 2020, *op. cit. supra* note 14; J. Crawford, *op. cit. supra* note 24, p. 232.

597. See J. Brunnée, 2020, *op. cit. supra* note 14.

was sought to be prevented. Yet, rather than investing in this untenable distinction, it would have been better to admit (and doing so is still possible) that the breach of certain obligations of prevention with due diligence is not conditioned upon the occurrence of the harm, as is the case in other special regimes of international law, such as international human rights law. Another solution would be to envision non-preventive due diligence obligations whose violation would also not depend on that occurrence [598], but without qualifying such obligations as exclusively "procedural" or "material".

By now, however, conventional obligations in international environmental law have largely become "proceduralised". As indicated in Chapter II, this has occurred in the wake of a trend in favour of the objectivisation of the reasonableness test through the legalisation and especially the proceduralisation of due diligence's content. The reasons for this are easily comprehensible. Procedural obligations are easier to conclude between States, which is crucial at a time of crisis in the conclusion of multilateral environmental treaties [599]. Such obligations allegedly delineate the reasonable content of international obligations and make such content more universal, at least on its face.

Yet this development is questionable for the reasons outlined in Chapter II, especially the resulting exclusion of any normative evaluation by international judges and of any discretion by the duty-bearing States. Moreover, it raises valid concerns about replacing judges' evaluation with scientific expertocracy or even, depending on the cases, with external compliance audits [600]. As a matter of fact, the proceduralisation of due diligence obligations has not been sufficient to counteract the erosion of States' obligations in international environmental law [601]. Under the latest multilateral environmental treaties and the Paris Agreement in particular [602], only the procedural preventive obligations are considered binding at the detriment of material preventive obligations. Further agreements, such as the Kyoto Protocol, transformed the few residual

598. See on these other due diligence obligations, J. Crawford, *op. cit. supra* note 24, pp. 226-232. Curiously, Judge Dugard, in ICJ, The case of *Certain Activities carried out by Nicaragua in the Border Area*, *op. cit. supra* note 3, paras. 10-11, does not consider this possibility.

599. See J. Brunnée, 2020, *op. cit. supra* note 14; J. Brunnée, 2018, *op. cit. supra* note 323.

600. See M. Koskenniemi, "Peaceful Settlement of Environmental Disputes", *Nordic Journal of International Law*, Vol. 60, No. 1 (1991), pp. 73-92.

601. See J. Brunnée, 2020, *op. cit. supra* note 14, in response to M. Koskenniemi's critique, *ibid.*

602. See e.g. Paris Agreement, *op. cit. supra* note 357.

material preventive obligations into obligations of result at the price of diligent conduct obligations [603]. We will revert to this issue in the critique of the technoscientific standardisation of due diligence below since the proceduralisation of due diligence usually goes hand in hand with its technicisation.

Second, the *sources* of due diligence in international environmental law. International environmental law is the international legal regime with the most varied sources of due diligence.

To start with, international environmental law is the regime with the most conventional guarantees of due diligence [604]. As a result, it has also borne the brunt of the crisis of multilateral treaties. It is maybe precisely because of the treaty crisis in international environmental law that there has been a return to the customary standard of due diligence and to discussions about obligations related to that standard in the recent case law [605].

Moreover, and for that reason, international environment law is also the special regime in which national and international jurisprudence is most abundant even if this also results, to some extent, in fragmentation and incoherence [606]. It is mainly the case in the international law of the sea [607], where jurisprudence on due diligence is particularly rich [608]. As mentioned before, the confusion international tribunals have entertained with regard to the source (in custom or general principles) of due diligence obligations has enabled them to derive the

603. See e.g. Kyoto Protocol, *op. cit. supra* note 358.

604. See e.g. Convention on the Law of the Sea, *op. cit. supra* note 9, Arts. 58, 62, 94, 139, 192 and 194; Convention on Biological Diversity, *op. cit. supra* note 9, Art. 3; Convention on the Law of the Non-Navigational Uses of International Watercourses, *op. cit. supra* note 9, Arts. 7 (1), 21 (2) and 22. See also Stockholm Declaration, *op. cit. supra* note 116, Principles 21 and 22; Rio Declaration, *op. cit. supra* note 116, Principles 2, 14 and 15; Preamble of the United Nations Framework Convention on Climate Change, *op. cit. supra* note 116.

605. See also J. Brunnée and T. Meshel, *op. cit. supra* note 28.

606. See e.g. *Trail Smelter* Arbitration, *op. cit. supra* note 8; *Lanoux Lac* Arbitration *(Spain* v. *France)*, Final Award of 16 November 1957, RIAA Vol. XII, p. 281; ICJ, *Legality of the Threat or Use of Nuclear Weapons*, *op. cit. supra* note 8; ICJ, The case of *The Gabcikovo-Nagymaros Project*, *op. cit. supra* note 8; PCA, *Indus Waters Kishenganga* Arbitration, *op. cit. supra* note 8, paras. 449-450; ICJ, The case of *Pulp Mills on the River Uruguay*, *op. cit. supra* note 3; ICJ, The case of *Certain Activities carried out by Nicaragua in the Border Area*, *op. cit. supra* note 3.

607. See I. Caracciolo, *op. cit. supra* note 18.

608. See e.g. ITLOS, *Responsibilities and Obligations of States Sponsoring Persons and Entities with Respect to Activities in the Area*, *op. cit. supra* note 41; ITLOS, *Request for an Advisory Opinion submitted by the Sub-Regional Fisheries Commission*, *op. cit. supra* note 148; PCA, *South China Sea* Arbitration, *op. cit. supra* note 8.

customary nature of other distinct principles or obligations related to due diligence [609].

Finally, the difficulties encountered by States during the negotiation and conclusion of multilateral environmental treaties explain the growing interest and enthusiasm for soft law in this field. The flexibility of States' commitments under soft law also accounts for the prominent place of due diligence [610], which is a discretionary standard *par excellence*. Many due diligence obligations in international environmental law are actually (also) found under soft law, as confirmed in the various codifications by the ILC and the ILA [611]. This in turn explains the technoscientific specifications or standardisations of due diligence's content [612], as exemplified by the systematic inclusion of an obligation to adopt environmental impact assessment measures.

As mentioned in Chapter II, a number of multilateral environmental treaties actually entail a reference to some of these soft law standards constitutive of due diligence, thereby enabling international tribunals to apply them to those treaties' interpretation [613]. However, judicial practice has also resorted to these soft law standards for treaty interpretation without such a reference on the grounds that they are widely recognised in practice [614]. While the latter trend is rarer, it is

609. See e.g. ITLOS, *Responsibilities and Obligations of States Sponsoring Persons and Entities with Respect to Activities in the Area*, *op. cit. supra* note 41, para. 131.

610. See S. Maljean-Dubois, *op. cit. supra* note 14; J. Brunnée, 2018, *op. cit. supra* note 323; C. Brölmann, "Sustainable Development Goal 6 as a Game Changer for International Water Law", *ESIL Reflections*, Vol. 7, No. 5 (2018) [online]; J. Brunnée, 2020, *op. cit. supra* note 14.

611. See e.g. ILA, Declaration of Legal Principles Relating to Climate Change, *op. cit. supra* note 11, Arts. 7A and 7B; ILC, Draft Articles on Prevention of Transboundary Harm from Hazardous Activities, with commentaries, *op. cit. supra* note 11, Arts. 1 and 3; ILC, Draft Articles on the Protection of Persons in the Event of Disasters, *op. cit. supra* note 11, Arts. 9 and 16; ILC, Draft Principles on the Protection of the Environment in Relation to Armed Conflict, *op. cit. supra* note 11, Principle 22.

612. See e.g. the International Atomic Energy Agency's safety norms; the norms in MARPOL's Annexes, *op. cit. supra* note 349; IPCC, Climate Change 2007, *op. cit. supra* note 355.

613. See e.g. Convention on the Law of the Sea, *op. cit. supra* note 9, Art. 210 (6); Statute of the River Uruguay, *op. cit. supra* note 348, Art. 41. See ICJ, The case of *Pulp Mills on the River Uruguay*, *op. cit. supra* note 3, para. 197. See P. d'Argent and A. de Vaucleroy, *op. cit. supra* note 33, pp. 270-271.

614. See e.g. the International Atomic Energy Agency's safety norms; the norms in MARPOL's Annexes, *op. cit. supra* note 349; IPCC, Climate Change 2007, *op. cit. supra* note 355. See ICJ, The case of *Pulp Mills on the River Uruguay*, *op. cit. supra* note 3, paras. 200 and 196, which (obliquely) refers to them through the Administrative Commission of the River Uruguay. See also PCA, *South China Sea* Arbitration, *op. cit. supra* note 8, para. 956, which (squarely) refers to them through CITES (*op. cit. supra* note 349). See P. d'Argent and A. de Vaucleroy, *op. cit. supra* note 33, pp. 271 *et seq.*

nonetheless concerning [615]. Additionally, some States invoke *renvois* to soft law in their domestic law and consider them applicable to the interpretation of international treaties [616]. The latter approach carries with it all the controversies that the opposability of domestic law can raise in international law [617]. Moreover, the importance of the role ascribed to scientific experts in the judicial interpretation, both national and international, of these soft law norms or standards [618] has also been called into question.

(b) *The scope, content, variability and limits of due diligence in international environmental law*

The specificities of due diligence in international environmental law are also visible with regard to its scope, content, variability and limits within this regime.

First, the *scope* of due diligence in international environmental law. International environmental law and its jurisprudence on the international law of the sea in particular [619] has contributed significantly to the clarification of the personal scope of due diligence (including its duty-bearers, beneficiaries and third parties), as well as to the clarification of its material and geographic scope.

First, the case law on due diligence in international environmental law specifies that this standard is personally and materially applicable even outside of transboundary harms caused within the bilateral relations of good neighbourliness between States (and their respective

615. See ICJ, The case of *Whaling in the Antarctic*, *op. cit. supra* note 350.

616. See e.g. the discussion in PCA, *South China Sea* Arbitration, *op. cit. supra* note 8; ITLOS, *Responsibilities and Obligations of States Sponsoring Persons and Entities with Respect to Activities in the Area*, *op. cit. supra* note 41.

617. See Judge Donoghue's resistance to endorse a purely domestic reference to soft law in her Separate opinion, in ICJ, The case of *Certain Activities carried out by Nicaragua in the Border Area*, *op. cit. supra* note 3, para. 13 (in the absence of State practice sufficient to establish an international custom).

618. See e.g. ICJ, The case of *Whaling in the Antarctic*, *op. cit. supra* note 350; ITLOS, *Responsibilities and Obligations of States Sponsoring Persons and Entities with Respect to Activities in the Area*, *op. cit. supra* note 41; PCA, *South China Sea* Arbitration, *op. cit. supra* note 8.

619. See e.g. ITLOS, *Responsibilities and Obligations of States Sponsoring Persons and Entities with Respect to Activities in the Area*, *op. cit. supra* note 41; ITLOS, *Request for an Advisory Opinion submitted by the Sub-Regional Fisheries Commission*, *op. cit. supra* note 148; PCA, *South China Sea* Arbitration, *op. cit. supra* note 8. See I. Caracciolo, *op. cit. supra* note 18, on the three constellations of the personal scope of due diligence that are covered by these three cases: relationships between the flag State and the coastal State, between the sponsoring State and the common resources, and between the flag State and maritime environment.

peoples)[620], which had originally delineated its personal and material scope[621]. The due diligence standard may relate to individual or collective interests (interests of the State, for example)[622] that are common, that is, interests pertaining to common goods[623]. One may think of interests related to spaces and goods common to humanity and to harms caused to common spaces, such as the air, the outer space or the high sea[624]. Second, jurisprudence in international environmental law has also extended the personal scope of due diligence, including that of its beneficiaries, to future generations[625], following the principle of intergenerational equity[626].

Finally, jurisprudence in international environmental law has extended the geographic scope of due diligence beyond the strictly territorial scope that had originally been one of its distinctive features. That standard is now also applicable to harms caused in or from non-territorial "spaces", such as the deep seabed[627], and thus outside of territorial control. Jurisprudence has further extended the scope of due diligence to sources of threats to the environment other than those arising from the national territory or from a foreign territory under extraterritorial control. This extension is grounded in the control exercised through other jurisdictional links, such as personal jurisdiction, over the third parties that caused the (risk of) harm[628]. One may think of threats

620. Contra: S. Maljean-Dubois, *op. cit. supra* note 14.

621. See e.g. *Trail Smelter* Arbitration, *op. cit. supra* note 8.

622. On the notion of common interests and the false opposition between these interests and the interests of States, see S. Besson, "Community Interests in International Law", 2018, *op. cit. supra* note 246; G. Gaja, 2013, *op. cit. supra* note 246.

623. See ICJ, *Legality of the Threat or Use of Nuclear Weapons*, *op. cit. supra* note 8, paras. 241-242; ICJ, The case of *The Gabcikovo-Nagymaros Project*, *op. cit. supra* note 8, para. 53; ICJ, The case of *Pulp Mills on the River Uruguay*, *op. cit. supra* note 3, para. 101; ICJ, The case of *Certain Activities carried out by Nicaragua in the Border Area*, *op. cit. supra* note 3, para. 104.

624. See e.g. ICJ, *Legality of the Threat or Use of Nuclear Weapons*, *op. cit. supra* note 8, para. 29 ("areas beyond national control"). See also Convention on the Law of the Sea, *op. cit. supra* note 9, Art. 192; CLN, *op. cit. supra* note 116, Art. 7; Convention on Biological Diversity, *op. cit. supra* note 9, Art. 3; Preamble of the United Nations Framework Convention on Climate Change, *op. cit. supra* note 116; Stockholm Declaration, *op. cit. supra* note 116, Principles 21 and 22; Rio Declaration, *op. cit. supra* note 116, Principle 2.

625. See ICJ, The case of *The Gabcikovo-Nagymaros Project*, *op. cit. supra* note 8, paras. 53 and 141.

626. See E. B. Weiss, *op. cit. supra* note 248.

627. See ICJ, *Legality of the Threat or Use of Nuclear Weapons*, *op. cit. supra* note 8, paras. 241-242.

628. For "jurisdiction and/or control", see e.g. Convention on the Law of the Sea, *op. cit. supra* note 9, Art. 194; Convention on Biological Diversity, *op. cit. supra* note 9, Art. 3; Preamble of the United Nations Framework Convention on Climate Change, *op. cit. supra* note 116; Stockholm Declaration, *op. cit. supra* note 116,

against the environment posed by MNCs: the States of incorporation or residence of a parent company owe due diligence obligations for such threats even though they have no territorial control over the place where a given subsidiary of that MNC caused environmental harm [629]. Section B below devoted to international human rights law will address some of these questions, which are at the intersection of international environmental law and international human rights law and which arise when due diligence is grafted upon obligations relating to the human right to a healthy environment. Finally, the jurisprudence of international environmental law has also envisioned forms of "control" over the source of the (risk of) harm by means of non-jurisdictional "links" (personal, territorial or otherwise) [630].

Second, the *content* of due diligence in international environmental law. If there is an international legal regime in which the minimal content of reasonable diligence has been specified, it is surely in the international jurisprudence of international environmental law. Two examples deserve to be mentioned: institutional obligations and precautionary obligations.

First of all, international environmental law has contributed to the specification of the contours and content of certain institutional obligations of due diligence.

Originally, due diligence is the standard of the reasonable State or the standard of good government [631]: it requires the adoption of institutional measures, mostly on the internal institutional level. The good government standard includes setting up specific institutions or national procedures and enacting legislation [632]. These institutional obligations

Principles 21 and 22; Rio Declaration, *op. cit. supra* note 116, Principle 2; ILA, Declaration of Legal Principles Relating to Climate Change, *op. cit. supra* note 11, Arts. 7A and 7B; ICJ, *Legality of the Threat or Use of Nuclear Weapons*, *op. cit. supra* note 8, paras. 241-242; ICJ, The case of *The Gabcikovo-Nagymaros Project*, *op. cit. supra* note 8, para. 53. See, however, for "jurisdiction" only, ICJ, The case of *Pulp Mills on the River Uruguay*, *op. cit. supra* note 3, para. 101.

629. See e.g. J. E. Viñuales, 2016, *op. cit. supra* note 117.

630. For "jurisdiction and/or control", see e.g. Convention on the Law of the Sea, *op. cit. supra* note 9, Art. 194; Convention on Biological Diversity, *op. cit. supra* note 9, Art. 3; Preamble of the United Nations Framework Convention on Climate Change, *op. cit. supra* note 116; Stockholm Declaration, *op. cit. supra* note 116, Principles 21 and 22; Rio Declaration, *op. cit. supra* note 116, Principle 2; ILA, Declaration of Legal Principles Relating to Climate Change, *op. cit. supra* note 11, Arts. 7A and 7B; ICJ, *Legality of the Threat or Use of Nuclear Weapons*, *op. cit. supra* note 8, paras. 241-242; ICJ, The case of *The Gabcikovo-Nagymaros Project*, *op. cit. supra* note 8, para. 53.

631. See e.g. R. Kolb, 2016, *op. cit. supra* note 29; S. Heathcote, *op. cit. supra* note 26.

632. See R. Kolb, 2016, *op. cit. supra* note 29; J. Klabbers, 2017, *op. cit. supra* note 105.

progressively extended to States' international relations and have come to encompass different institutional aspects of these multilateral relations, within or outside of IOs. This is especially the case for environmental due diligence obligations which include obligations of notification, consultation, negotiation, participation and more generally cooperation with other States and their peoples [633]. These types of obligations will surely experience further development and will be more frequently invoked in the future, not only during the negotiation of multilateral environmental treaties (especially after the recent failures), but also for the development of more institutionalised forms of international cooperation in international environmental law [634].

Second, international environmental law is the regime which, above all others, contributed to the specifications of the contours and content of the principle of precaution in relation to due diligence obligations [635].

Some prefer to speak of a precautionary "approach" because the binding character and especially the customary source of that principle are not yet well-established under international law [636]. According to the few international tribunals, like the ITLOS, that treat precaution as a principle, the link with other due diligence obligations, such as the obligation of prevention, makes it possible to establish the precautionary principle's customary nature [637].

By way of a reminder, the principle of precaution requires that measures of "anticipation" [638] be taken with regard to risks of serious

633. See J. E. Viñuales, 2016, *op. cit. supra* note 117; J. Brunnée and T. Meshel, *op. cit. supra* note 28.

634. On the obligation to negotiate in the Paris Agreement, *op. cit. supra* note 357, Art. 6, see e.g. D. Desierto, "COP25 Negotiations Fail: Can Climate Change Litigation, Adjudication, and/or Arbitration Compel States to Act Faster to Implement Climate Obligations?", *EJIL Talk!*, 19 December 2019 [online].

635. See e.g. ITLOS, *Responsibilities and Obligations of States Sponsoring Persons and Entities with Respect to Activities in the Area*, *op. cit. supra* note 41, para. 131.

636. The ICJ is not clear in this regard: see ICJ, The case of *Pulp Mills on the River Uruguay*, *op. cit. supra* note 3, whereas the ITLOS is: see ITLOS, *Responsibilities and Obligations of States Sponsoring Persons and Entities with Respect to Activities in the Area*, *op. cit. supra* note 41. For an assessment, see M. Schröder, *op. cit. supra* note 292; M. M. Mbengue, 2009, *op. cit. supra* note 292.

637. See e.g. ITLOS, *Responsibilities and Obligations of States Sponsoring Persons and Entities with Respect to Activities in the Area*, *op. cit. supra* note 41, para. 131; PCA, *South China Sea* Arbitration, *op. cit. supra* note 8. On the reactions to the latter award in China, see D. Guilfoyle, "A New Twist in the South China Sea Arbitration: The Chinese Society of International Law's Critical Study", *EJIL Talk!*, 25 May 2018 [online]. For an example of such a Chinese reaction, see e.g. Chinese Society of International Law, "The South China Sea Arbitration: A Critical Study", *Chinese Journal of International Law*, Vol. 17 (2018), pp. 207-748, pp. 575 *et seq.*

638. See M. Delmas-Marty, 2013, *op. cit. supra* note 109; M. M. Mbengue, 2009, *op. cit. supra* note 292.

or irreversible harms whose existence, while probable, still remains uncertain in the current state of scientific knowledge. While we will not assess what the precautionary principle requires or its progressive relation with the principle of prevention should be [639], it is important to emphasise that when due diligence is grafted upon an obligation of precaution, its content and variability should be apprehended differently than when it is grafted upon an obligation of prevention, even though the contours of that difference still require further specification. Reasonable foreseeability and causation cannot be treated the same way, for example. And the same is true for the degree of control over the third party at the origin of the harm.

Third, the *variability* of due diligence in international environmental law. The question of the minimal content of due diligence in international law has arisen several times in this special regime. The minimal content of the reasonable measures to adopt is indeed often addressed in view of the variability of the duty-bearing States' national circumstances.

Certain international tribunals, like the ITLOS, have insisted upon the "variability" of due diligence as a standard of conduct [640]. This standard should adjust to the concrete capacities of its duty-bearer following the principle of "ought implies can". Others, however, have emphasised the minimal content of international law with regard to that issue. While certain ICJ judges understand that States must have a certain margin of appreciation with regard to the specification of the precise content of due diligence and approve on this point the jurisprudence of the ICJ [641], they nonetheless consider that a complete *renvoi* to national law, including to the technical norms upon which national law relies to define the content of environmental obligations, is not acceptable [642].

Finally, the *limits* of due diligence in international environmental law. If there is a regime in international law in which the question of

639. It is a continuum according to ILA, Declaration of Legal Principles Relating to Climate Change, *op. cit. supra* note 11, Arts. 7A and 7B. Accordingly, with the evolution of scientific knowledge and certainty, the obligation of precaution gradually becomes an obligation of prevention.

640. See e.g. ITLOS, *Responsibilities and Obligations of States Sponsoring Persons and Entities with Respect to Activities in the Area*, *op. cit. supra* note 41, para. 117; PCA, *South China Sea* Arbitration, *op. cit. supra* note 8, para. 117.

641. See e.g. ICJ, The case of *Pulp Mills on the River Uruguay*, *op. cit. supra* note 3, para. 210; ICJ, The case of *Certain Activities carried out by Nicaragua in the Border Area*, *op. cit. supra* note 3, para. 104.

642. See Separate opinion of Judge Donoghue, in ICJ, The case of *Certain Activities carried out by Nicaragua in the Border Area*, *op. cit. supra* note 3, para. 15; Separate opinion of Judge Dugard, in ICJ, The case of *Certain Activities carried out by Nicaragua in the Border Area*, *op. cit. supra* note 3, para. 18.

the relations between the limits (economic or financial, notably) and the observance of due diligence arises, it is international environmental law [643].

In the wake of the proceduralisation of obligations and of the technoscientific standardisation of their control, one also notices a tendency to apply proportionality as a way to balance contradictory interests. Yet this test is understood, without any justification, as an instrumental test in the vein of a cost-benefit analysis. Moreover, the principle of precaution or precautionary approach in which the role of scientific certainty is as deeply anchored as it is in the instrumental conception of proportionality [644] is conceived in the same way.

2. *Due diligence in international cybersecurity law by way of comparison*

International cybersecurity law is not yet a true special regime of international law, but it is developing fast. If it ever comes into its own, it will govern various aspects of human and military security in cyberspace [645]. For now, the important place occupied by the due diligence standard in international cybersecurity law matters to the present course's argument [646]. The specificities of due diligence in that field also deserve careful examination by way of comparison with due diligence in international environmental law.

Various reasons may explain the interest in due diligence in that area of international law. The first one pertains to the diffuse character of the sources of (risks of) harms in cyberspace. As indicated in this course's

643. See e.g. ICJ, The case of *The Gabcikovo-Nagymaros Project*, *op. cit. supra* note 8, para. 53; PCA, *Indus Waters Kishenganga* Arbitration, *op. cit. supra* note 8, paras. 449-450.

644. See M. Schröder, *op. cit. supra* note 292.

645. On the lack of official State practice and the difficulty in establishing the existence of customary international law in this area, see, however, D. Efrony and Y. Shany, "A Rule Book on the Shelf? Tallinn Manual 2.0 on Cyberoperations and Subsequent State Practice", *American Journal of International Law*, Vol. 112, No. 4 (2018), pp. 583-657.

646. On due diligence in cyberspace, see D. Hollis and M. Finnemore, 2016, *op. cit. supra* note 29; E. Talbot Jensen and S. Watts, *op. cit. supra* note 29; M. N. Schmitt, 2015, *op. cit. supra* note 29; M. Herdegen, *op. cit. supra* note 29; M. Ney and A. Zimmermann, *op. cit. supra* note 29; S. J. Shackelford, S. Russell and A. Kuehn, *op. cit. supra* note 29; A. Benedek, *op. cit. supra* note 29; R. Kolb, 2016, *op. cit. supra* note 29; D. Delibasis, *op. cit. supra* note 29; K. Bannelier-Christakis, 2017, *op. cit. supra* note 29; K. Bannelier-Christakis, 2018, *op. cit. supra* note 29; L. Chircop, *op. cit. supra* note 29; H.-G. Dederer and T. Singer, *op. cit. supra* note 29; E. Talbot Jensen, *op. cit. supra* note 29.

introduction, certain new threats are difficult to apprehend by means of the usual tools of international responsibility because they can be secret, such as cybersecurity threats, complex, such as climate change, or simply collective. The individualised attribution of the conduct of an organ or a private person to one institution in particular proves difficult in such cases. This is especially so, second, when considering the primarily private origin of threats to cybersecurity. It explains why responsibility for negligence has become the preferred alternative to invoking responsibility for complicity given that the latter only applies between a State (or IO) and a State (or IO) and under very strict conditions (Art. 16 ARSIWA; Arts. 14 and 58 ARIO).

According to certain scholars, responsibility for negligence would overcome all these difficulties, which explains its appeal for the States or groups of private persons concerned with cybersecurity. Yet, applying due diligence comes with its own challenges, especially proving reasonable foreseeability, control over the source of the (risk of) harm or the reasonable technical capacity to react [647]. Chapter III actually highlighted the further issue of countermeasures, including self-defence, and the difficulties of the determination of causation in relation to the allocation of multiple responsibilities and reparations.

The determination of the exact regime of due diligence in international cybersecurity law is debated. Two complementary approaches are taking shape. The first approach (as discussed in Subsection a) proposes to apply the minimal general regime of due diligence in international law presented in Chapter II with some adjustments for the specificities of cybersecurity. A second, complementary approach (as discussed in Subsection b) recommends the use of comparisons with, and possibly analogies to, the special regime of due diligence in international environmental law because of its common features with international cybersecurity law.

(a) International cybersecurity law against the background of the general regime of due diligence

One possible way to deal with the particularities of due diligence in cyberspace is to take as a guide the minimal and common general regime of due diligence in international law presented in Chapter II, and to make adjustments for the specific needs of cybersecurity. The

647. See K. Bannelier-Christakis, 2017, *op. cit. supra* note 29.

point of such a minimal general regime is indeed to answer some of the questions raised by several States and private groups about the applicability of due diligence in cyberspace.

Yet, a number of these States and private groups dispute some of the elements presented in this course as belonging to due diligence's minimal general regime. We will address four of their objections in detail. They relate to the nature, regime, source and scope of due diligence in international cybersecurity law. As we will see, all four can easily be dismissed.

First, as indicated in Chapter II, some States still question the legal character of the due diligence standard. They use its "standard" denomination as a justification for treating it as a soft law standard and for rejecting any binding consequence in its application in cyberspace [648]. Second, while a number of States rightly recognise instead that due diligence is a binding legal standard, they consider that it is not part of the general rules of international law because it is neither a general principle nor a custom. In their view, due diligence cannot apply to cybersecurity without an obligation specific to that field, especially without a specific international treaty [649].

Third, even if some other States rightly acknowledge the place of the due diligence standard in general international law and its character common to different international legal regimes, they emphasise that this standard must be grafted upon an obligation which has yet to be identified or, at least, on pre-existing rights or interests protected by international law. Strangely enough, they refute the existence of such rights or interests and the existence of due diligence obligations applicable in the context of cybersecurity. The most frequent answer to that objection points to the due diligence obligations or general obligations not to harm carelessly, which are corollaries of the principle of sovereign equality of States and invoked by reference to the *Corfu Channel* jurisprudence [650] discussed earlier in Chapter II. Still, the same States retort that sovereignty remains a general principle

648. See Russia, by reference to Cybersecurity Report, *op. cit. supra* note 88, para. 13 (c). See also M. Finnemore and D. Hollis, "Beyond Naming and Shaming: Accusations and International Law in Cybersecurity", *European Journal of International Law*, Vol. 31, No. 3 (2020), pp. 969-1003.

649. See USA, by reference to Cybersecurity Report, *op. cit. supra* note 88. For a similar albeit more nuanced position, see the position of the Government of Canada, International Law applicable in Cyberspace, 22 April 2022 [online].

650. See e.g. Cybersecurity Report, *op. cit. supra* note 88, paras. 28 (a) and (b); Ministère français des Armées, Droit international appliqué aux opérations dans le cyberespace, *op. cit. supra* note 288.

of international law whose content must be specified by international legal rules before giving rise to obligations [651]. Yet, it seems difficult to ignore the numerous specific due diligence obligations that are derived from sovereignty in the practice of States. How could the due diligence obligations protecting the territorial integrity of other States, the good functioning of their government or the protection of the rights of their nationals not be applicable in the context of cybersecurity?

Some States, however, answer with a fourth objection that as a matter of principle, sovereignty would not apply outside of States' territories, including in "cyberspace". There are two reasons to reject that objection.

To begin with, if cyberspace exists, it is closely tied to the territories of the different States where information and communication technologies are used in cyberattacks [652]. These technologies are tied to the territories where the persons whose rights and interests under threat are located. International law and the sovereignty it constitutes have legitimacy only insofar as they apply to persons. And, until further notice, these persons all live on one or the other portion of the territory. In the history of the law and institutions, whenever the existence of a new "space" has been invoked (the Church's "space" or the EU internal market's "space", for instance), the aim has always been to evade the rule of law and the obligations to which it gives rise [653].

A second answer to that objection is that under international environmental law, due diligence is also applicable to States' extraterritorial spaces, such as the sea or the air, which are considered common spaces. It is therefore difficult to extend the geographic and personal scope of due diligence, and in particular the notion of non-territorial control as a condition of due diligence in international environmental law, while refraining to take the same approach to cyberspace [654].

651. See e.g. J. Wright, the UK's Attorney General, Speech on "Cyber and International Law in the 21st Century", 23 May 2018 [online].

652. See e.g. Cybersecurity Report, *op. cit. supra* note 88, paras. 13 (c) and 28 (a) and (b); Ministère français des Armées, Droit international appliqué aux opérations dans le cyberespace, *op. cit. supra* note 288.

653. See S. Besson, "Why and What (State) Jurisdiction", 2019, *op. cit. supra* note 254; A. Supiot, "L'inscription territoriale des lois", *Esprit*, Vol. 11 (2008), pp. 151-170.

654. See J. Brunnée and T. Meshel, *op. cit. supra* note 28. See also Cybersecurity Report, *op. cit. supra* note 88, paras. 13 (c) and 28 (a) and (b).

(b) A comparative assessment of due diligence in international cybersecurity law and international environmental law

For the remainder of this subsection, and as a way to further specify what the content of due diligence in international cybersecurity law should be, it is interesting, alongside Jutta Brunnée and Tamar Meshel [655], to further examine due diligence in cybersecurity by comparison with, and then by analogy to, the regime of due diligence in international environmental law.

Two reasons explain why these two special regimes of due diligence obligations lend themselves well to comparative discussions and analogies.

First, as highlighted above, international environmental law is the area of international law in which due diligence's regime (jurisprudential, in particular) is most developed, whereas international cybersecurity law remains a new regime or, more precisely, a regime still in need of further development [656].

International environmental law already served as a source of inspiration for the application of the due diligence standard to other special regimes of international law, and it could do the same for cyberspace as well. Moreover, the crisis of environmental multilateral treaties is reminiscent of the difficulties faced by the various calls for the adoption of a multilateral treaty on cybersecurity [657] made by private actors (Microsoft [658], for instance), States [659] or the UN [660].

No wonder then that some States and private groups consider, adopt and rely on soft law for cybersecurity issues [661], just as it has been the case in international environmental law. This may actually explain the tendency of some of these States to treat their other international legal obligations in that context as soft law obligations. In so doing, however,

655. See J. Brunnée and T. Meshel, *op. cit. supra* note 28; A. Takano, *op. cit. supra* note 194.

656. See J. Brunnée and T. Meshel, *op. cit. supra* note 28.

657. See F. Delerue, "The Codification of the International Law Applicable to Cyber Operations: A Matter for the ILC?", *ESIL Reflections*, Vol. 7, No. 4 (2018) [online].

658. See B. Smith, President of Microsoft, "The Need for a Digital Geneva Convention", 14 February 2017 [online].

659. See Ministère français de l'Europe et des Affaires étrangères, Appel de Paris pour la confiance et la sécurité dans le cyberespace, 12 November 2018 [online].

660. See Cybersecurity Report, *op. cit. supra* note 88. See also G7, Declaration on Responsible States Behavior in Cyberspace, Lucca (Italy), 11 April 2017 [online].

661. See *Tallinn Manual 2.0*, *op. cit. supra* note 88. See also M. N. Schmitt, 2015, *op. cit. supra* note 29.

they contribute to the process of softening of hard law already observed in this course. As we just saw, some States even treat the due diligence standard itself as soft law. They appeal to its nature as a "standard" of conduct, which, in their opinion, means it is non-binding. They further cite, as a justification, the 2015 UN report on the international law applicable to cyberspace, which reflects the only existing consensus in that field and refers in that respect to "voluntary, non-binding norms ... of responsible behaviour" [662].

Second, the two regimes share multiple common features that lead to many parallels between the specificities of their due diligence obligations.

On the one hand, the reference to common "spaces" as the geographic but also personal and even material scope of due diligence deserves emphasis [663]. The consideration that, under international environmental law, even non-territorial "control" over the source of the risk of harm may suffice to generate a due diligence obligation is especially relevant: it makes it possible to contemplate the emergence of such an obligation in the cyberspace, that is, even in the absence of any territorial or extraterritorial control by the duty-bearer over the third party that is the source of the (risk of) harm, assuming that due diligence's other conditions are met.

On the other hand, another common feature relates to the fact that the reasonable measures which a diligent State must take in the context of cybersecurity can be internal or external and, in the latter case, rely upon cooperation with other States. On this point, the numerous obligations of notification, consultation, negotiation, participation and more generally cooperation [664] identified as part of due diligence in international environmental law could be very useful for the future of cyberspace's safe organisation. The adoption of a multilateral treaty on the topic or the creation of a common international institution [665] may be advisable and could be grounded on those obligations of diligent cooperation.

---

662. See Cybersecurity Report, *op. cit. supra* note 88, para. 13. This qualification was actually confirmed in 2021 by the Report of the Group of Governmental Experts on Advancing Responsible State Behaviour in Cyberspace in the Context of International Security, 14 July 2021, UN Doc. A/76/135 [online], Norm 13 (c). See, however, the official compendium of voluntary national contributions submitted on 13 July 2021, UN Doc. A/76/136, for more advanced national perspectives. See generally K. Bannelier-Christakis, 2017, *op. cit. supra* note 29.

663. See J. Brunnée and T. Meshel, *op. cit. supra* note 28.

664. See J. E. Viñuales, 2016, *op. cit. supra* note 117; J. Brunnée and T. Meshel, *op. cit. supra* note 28.

665. See especially M. Herdegen, *op. cit. supra* note 29.

However, two significant features of cybersecurity law diverge from international environmental law. It is important to highlight them because they may limit the comparability and the transposability of solutions across regimes with regard to due diligence.

The first feature is the secrecy prevalent in cyberspace. Secrecy makes it difficult to assess which practices are considered to comply with due diligence and consequently what constitutes a breach of that standard [666]. Identifying a custom's emergence in such a context is very difficult. Of course, as in other areas of international law, one cannot exclude that unverified or uncontested accusations or even the silence of the parties may, over time, give rise to a customary practice [667] or, at least, to some international obligations. The second feature is the absence of an international tribunal with jurisdiction and as a result the limited opportunity to develop a specialised jurisprudence to specify due diligence's content. This issue seems particularly concerning given how instrumental judicial reasoning has been to the consolidation of due diligence's regime in international environmental law.

B. Due diligence in international human rights law

Another special regime of international law with characteristics that do not fully align with the general common regime of due diligence is international human rights law. As indicated in Chapter II, its specificities respond to the specific nature of the interests protected by human rights and of the corresponding obligations (including due diligence obligations) grounded in those interests.

This explains why, even though international human rights law is a modern international legal regime which is comparatively recent in due diligence's history, it has left a mark upon that history during the second half of the twentieth century [668].

It is indeed the regime which progressively complemented States' due diligence obligations under the international law of aliens by extending that standard's protection to every person, irrespective of nationality and residence, and even in relation to their own State. So

666. See D. Efrony and Y. Shany, *op. cit. supra* note 645.
667. See e.g. Canada-US Air Quality Agreement of 13 March 1991, UNTS, Vol. 1852, p. 79, cited by M. Finnemore and D. Hollis, *op. cit. supra* note 648.
668. See e.g. R. Pisillo Mazzeschi, 2008, *op. cit. supra* note 6; M. T. Kamminga, *op. cit. supra* note 15; O. De Schutter, A. Ramasastry, M. B. Taylor and R. C. Thompson, *op. cit. supra* note 15; H. Tran, *op. cit. supra* note 15; K. Martin-Chenut, *op. cit. supra* note 15; H. Raspail, *op. cit. supra* note 15.

doing, international human rights law broke free from the scope of the rights and obligations of diplomatic protection [669]. As indicated in Chapter I, it is thanks to this regime that due diligence's scope now includes purely internal situations without transboundary dimensions. It is also thanks to international human rights law that the personal scope of due diligence has broadened: it now encompasses beneficiaries who are nationals or residents of the State, not only foreigners; it pertains to the (risk of) harm caused by third parties that are not only private, such as MNCs or NGOs, but also public, like States or IOs; and, finally, the circle of its duty-bearers is expanding incrementally to include non-State duty-bearers, such as IOs, or even perhaps, someday, MNCs or NGOs.

To this day, due diligence obligations remain central in the international human rights regime. A due diligence standard is often grafted upon this regime's specific obligations of conduct, such as obligations of prevention, protection and reparation, to the point of frequently becoming inseparable from them. It is also in relation to the protection of human rights and in case of their violation that States' responsibility for negligence developed during the second half of the twentieth century and was strengthened under both international and domestic law [670].

All this explains how international human rights law has contributed, through its numerous conventional, jurisprudential and doctrinal references to due diligence, to the consolidation of that standard's common regime. This eventually allowed international human rights law to cross-pollinate several aspects of due diligence in other international legal regimes, such as international diplomatic law. It suffices here to mention the two conditions of due diligence which were first and most extensively developed by the ECtHR: reasonable ability and reasonable foreseeability [671].

Nonetheless, it is important to understand that despite international human rights law's pivotal role in the development of due diligence, the history of due diligence should not stop there. The standard of due diligence and the general obligation not to harm carelessly the rights and interests protected by international law should be strictly respected in other regimes as well. Recent times have seen a

---

669. See C. Chinkin, *op. cit. supra* note 118; M. Hakimi, *op. cit. supra* note 13.

670. For a comparison between domestic and international law of public liability, see A. Antoine and T. Olson, *op. cit. supra* note 6, p. 17; H. Belrhali, *op. cit. supra* note 158, p. 545.

671. See ECtHR, Case of *Opuz* v. *Turkey, op. cit. supra* note 205, paras. 129-130.

constant and questionable extension of due diligence's extraterritorial obligations under international human rights law in the practice of certain international human rights bodies. That extension now threatens to distend the normative structure of those rights and to undermine the entire human rights regime. It purports, for instance, to ground States' extraterritorial due diligence obligations with regard to the extraterritorial activities of MNCs over which those States exercise control even when those States do not have jurisdiction or effective control over the alleged victims and human right-holders abroad [672]. Chapter II presented a critique of the confusion of the conditions of due diligence with those of the extraterritorial application of human rights, and we will further develop it in the present chapter.

For a clearer understanding of due diligence's specificities in international human rights law, this section revisits the different elements of the general regime of due diligence in international law, beginning with (1) its nature and sources; (2) its personal, material, geographic and temporal scope; and (3) its conditions, content, variability and limits.

1. The nature and sources of due diligence in international human rights law

This first subsection is devoted to two specific dimensions of due diligence's regime in international human rights law: the nature and the sources of due diligence.

First, the *nature* of due diligence in international human rights law. Over the years, international human rights courts have contributed greatly to the clarification of the nature of due diligence obligations.

Thus their case law specified early on how due diligence is grafted upon positive obligations of conduct, including obligations to prevent, protect or remedy. These positive obligations are typical of the jurisprudence of judicial and quasi-judicial organs in international human rights law [673]. They evolved hand in hand with the due diligence standard [674]. The latter is most often implicit as a standard qualifying

672. See S. Besson, 2020, *op. cit. supra* note 121.

673. See e.g. L. Lavrysen, *Human Rights in a Positive State*, Antwerp, Intersentia, 2016; A. Mowbray, *The Development of Positive Obligations under the European Convention on Human Rights by the European Court of Human Rights*, Oxford, Hart, 2004.

674. See e.g. IACtHR, Case of *Velasquez-Rodriguez* v. *Honduras*, *op. cit. supra* note 205, para. 172; ECtHR, Case of *Osman* v. *The United Kingdom*, *op. cit. supra* note 301, para. 116; ECtHR, Case of *Opuz* v. *Turkey*, *op. cit. supra* note 205,

the conduct expected on the basis of a positive obligation. Recently, however, human rights treaties and their judicial interpretations have included explicit references to that standard. It is the case, for instance, of Article 5 (2) of the Council of Europe Convention in Preventing and Combating Violence Against Women and Domestic Violence [675].

Importantly, the link made in the international human rights case law between positive obligations and due diligence does not mean that negative obligations may not include a due diligence standard in the abstention that they require even if this occurs more rarely. Nor does that jurisprudence exclude that certain positive obligations may not be considered due diligence obligations [676]. Indeed, while positive obligations and the different obligations deriving from them are most often obligations of conduct, it is not necessarily the case. Finally, certain obligations of result may exceptionally be considered as due diligence obligations, but this is even rarer [677].

A first difference in the normative structure of due diligence obligations in the context of human rights distinguishes them from other due diligence obligations in international law. That difference resides in the former's relational nature and in particular in the specific correlation between the rights of the right-holder and the obligations of the duty-bearer. When the due diligence obligation at stake is a human rights obligation, the beneficiary of due diligence is also related to its duty-bearer with a correlative right of which he or she is the holder. This distinguishes due diligence obligations under international human rights law from imperfect due diligence obligations which are found in most other international legal regimes, that is, obligations which are not directed and owed to a particular beneficiary.

---

paras. 129-130; ECtHR, Case of *O'Keeffe* v. *Ireland*, *op. cit. supra* note 301, paras. 144-149; ECtHR, Case of *Talpis* v. *Italy*, *op. cit. supra* note 205, paras. 29 and 98-99. See H. Tran, *op. cit. supra* note 15.

675. See Council of Europe, Explanatory Report to the Council of Europe Convention on Preventing and Combating Violence Against Women and Domestic Violence, 11 May 2011 [online], para. 58.

676. See also V. Stoyanova, "Due Diligence versus Positive Obligations: Critical Reflections on the Council of Europe Convention on Violence against Women", in J. Niemi, L. Peroni and V. Stoyanova (eds.), *International Law and Violence Against Women: Europe and the Istanbul Convention*, London, Routledge, 2020, pp. 95-129, p. 104.

677. The obligation to judge in international human rights law may thus be considered an obligation of result, while containing a conduct component qualified by the due diligence standard. See also H. Raspail, *op. cit. supra* note 15.

A second structural difference that derives from the first one concerns the link of "jurisdiction" [678] and as such the effective (personal or spatial) territorial or extraterritorial control [679] which should exist between the duty-bearer and the right-holder who is also the beneficiary of a due diligence obligation. It is only once that condition is met that the given human right and its corresponding duties will arise and that the due diligence standard can be grafted upon these obligations and qualify them. Other international legal regimes, however, do not require that the duty-bearer of due diligence exercises a particular control over the beneficiary as a prerequisite for due diligence obligations to arise.

In these other regimes, indeed, the only thing that matters for due diligence to arise is control over the source of harm, that is, control over the third party that causes this (risk of) harm, and not over the beneficiary of due diligence. As we have seen, that control does not need to be "effective" and can be rather loose as can the related degree of due diligence. These elements (subject and effectivity of the control) distinguish the conditions of the due diligence standard from those of the human right obligations upon which it is grafted.

It is useful to distinguish these general obligations of due diligence in the context of human rights (and in particular the positive due diligence obligations of prevention, protection or reparation) from two specific obligations in international human rights law which also include a due diligence dimension: the principle of *non-refoulement* and the obligations under Article 41 ARSIWA and Article 41 ARIO.

The first one is the principle of *non-refoulement* [680], which corresponds to a positive due diligence obligation of prevention specific to the human right to life and to the prohibition of torture. Although its conditions overlap with the conditions of due diligence in international human rights law, such as reasonable capacity and foreseeability and a material scope restricted to the existence of a real and immediate risk, they are slightly more specific. For *non-refoulement* to apply, indeed, the duty-bearing State needs also to have had "substantial grounds to

678. See e.g. M. Milanovic, 2011, *op. cit. supra* note 262; S. Besson, 2012, *op. cit. supra* note 259.

679. See e.g. ICJ, *Legal Consequences of the Construction of a Wall in the Occupied Palestinian Territory*, *op. cit. supra* note 263, para. 111; ECtHR, Case of *Al-Skeini and others* v. *The United Kingdom*, *op. cit. supra* note 263, paras. 133 *et seq.* and 138; ECtHR, Case of *Catan and others* v. *The Republic of Moldova and Russia*, Nos. 43370/04, 18454/06 and 8252/05, 19 October 2012, paras. 106 *et seq.*; ECtHR, Case of *Jaloud* v. *The Netherlands*, No. 47708/08, Judgment of 20 November 2014, para. 139.

680. See M. Hakimi, *op. cit. supra* note 13; V. Tzevelekos, *op. cit. supra* note 121.

believe" that a person was in a "foreseeable, present, personal and real" danger to be subjected to torture in a third State, at the hands of that State or by private persons [681].

Additionally, one must also mention the obligations of prevention, non-recognition and non-cooperation set forth under Article 41 ARSIWA and Article 41 ARIO [682]. These secondary obligations arise after the occurrence of a serious breach of a peremptory norm of international law, including primary human rights obligations, as long as they belong to *jus cogens*. They are customary and codified in the ARSIWA and can also include a due diligence component. The due diligence standard does not only qualify primary human rights obligations therefore, but also the secondary obligations of international responsibility law generated by the serious breach of the former. Distinct from primary due diligence obligations under international human rights law, these obligations may also be referred to as human rights "responsibilities" because, unlike human rights obligations *stricto sensu*, they are not directed and owed to the latter's right-holders.

As a general matter, indeed, it is important to emphasise that in international human rights law, beyond human rights obligations *stricto sensu*, due diligence can also be grafted upon and qualify what are referred to as "human rights responsibilities" [683].

In contrast to the obligations that are correlative to these rights and owed by a State exercising its jurisdiction and therefore its effective control over the alleged right-holders, these responsibilities are not correlative to rights. They are not directed and owed to these right-holders in particular, nor grounded in the exercise of jurisdiction upon them. Rather, they complement the obligations of the State of jurisdiction by requiring that all other States (collectively and at varying degrees depending on the control exercised over the third party that is the source of harm) notify or actively cooperate so that the State of jurisdiction abides by its human rights obligations (Art. 2 (1) of the International Covenant on Economic, Social and Cultural Rights, for example).

If due diligence's conditions are met, human rights responsibilities should also be implemented with due diligence. It is on that basis,

---

681. See CAT, General Comment No. 4, *op. cit. supra* note 205, paras. 30 and 38-39.
682. See M. Hakimi, *op. cit. supra* note 13.
683. See S. Besson, "The Bearers of Human Rights Duties and Responsibilities for Human Rights: A Quiet (R)Evolution", *Social Philosophy & Policy*, Vol. 32, No. 1 (2015), pp. 244-268.

for example, that States have responsibilities to prevent with all due diligence MNCs that are under their control, on their territory or under their jurisdiction from causing international human rights violations abroad and compromising the State of (human rights) jurisdiction's adherence to its human rights obligations within that territory [684]. In that example, the State of jurisdiction owes human rights "obligations" (including due diligence obligations) to the persons under its effective control, whereas other States only incur "responsibilities" (including due diligence responsibilities) for the respect of human rights in the first State.

We will address these diligent responsibilities of prevention and protection in the next subsection (2), including when they have an extraterritorial scope and pertain to threats of private origin. It is important indeed not to confuse them with extraterritorial diligent obligations of prevention and protection owed by States of jurisdiction, nor with the due diligence obligations of MNCs themselves.

Second, the *sources* of due diligence in international human rights law. International human rights law is also the regime where due diligence's sources are currently most diverse: jurisprudence, of course, but also several treaties and mostly soft law.

The central place of due diligence in the jurisprudence of international human rights bodies is no surprise. As indicated in Chapter II, due diligence is usually present in the most "judiciarised" regimes of international law, such as international human rights law [685]. This is because of the strong connection that ties general principles *qua* source of international law to judicial reasoning, but also because of the need for a normative and as such judicial evaluation which characterises the specification of the content of the due diligence standard. Human rights obligations and the due diligence standard have these two specificities in common.

---

684. See S. Besson, 2020, *op. cit. supra* note 121.

685. See e.g. ICJ, The case of *Armed Activities on the Territory of the Congo*, 2005, *op. cit. supra* note 3, paras. 247-248; ICJ, The case of *Application of the Convention on the Prevention and Punishment of the Crime of Genocide*, *op. cit. supra* note 22, para. 431; IACtHR, Case of *Velasquez-Rodriguez* v. *Honduras*, *op. cit. supra* note 205, para. 172; ECtHR, Case of *Opuz* v. *Turkey*, *op. cit. supra* note 205, paras. 129-130; ECtHR, Case of *Talpis* v. *Italy*, *op. cit. supra* note 205, paras. 29 and 98-99; IACtHR, *The Environment and Human Rights*, *op. cit. supra* note 205. The observations and findings of the UN human rights treaty bodies must also be mentioned, and especially: CESCR, General Comment No. 24, *op. cit. supra* note 3, paras. 15-16 and 30 *et seq*.; CAT, General Comment No. 4, *op. cit. supra* note 205, para. 30; CCPR, *Basem Ahmed Issa Yassin and others* v. *Canada*, *op. cit. supra* note 205, paras. 6.5. *et seq*.; CCPR, General Comment No. 36, *op. cit. supra* note 205, paras. 21-22.

Some international treaties on human rights, such as the Istanbul Convention, have recently expressly included due diligence obligations. As mentioned before, that treaty entails a provision devoted to States' positive obligations with regard to the eradication of domestic violence that refers to them specifically as due diligence obligations of the State parties (Art. 5 (2) [686]).

Article 6 of the Draft "Legally binding instrument to regulate in international human rights law, the activities of transnational corporations and other business enterprises" also mentions due diligence. However, this (possibly future) treaty does not directly set forth international due diligence obligations for States and MNCs, but only obligations for States to establish (corporate) human rights due diligence mechanisms for MNCs under domestic law [687]. As highlighted in Chapters I and II, these mechanisms originate from entrepreneurial self-regulation and have been incorporated into domestic private law in some legal orders [688] or have become international soft law standards [689]. Despite their denomination, they do not belong to the regime of the due diligence standard of international law presented in this course. Yet, as we will see, these soft law standards influence the regime of the due diligence obligations of States and other public institutions in international law [690] as they often stand alongside international law's

686. See Council of Europe, Explanatory Report, *op. cit. supra* note 675, para. 58. See e.g. M. T. Kamminga, *op. cit. supra* note 15; C. Benninger-Budel, *op. cit. supra* note 410; Z. Abdul Azizi and J. Moussa, *Due Diligence Framework: State Accountability Framework for Eliminating Violence against Women*, Malaysia, International Human Rights Initiative, 2014; J. Goldshied and D. J. Liebowitz, "Due Diligence and Gender Violence: Parsing its Power and its Perils", *Cornell International Law Journal*, Vol. 48 (2015), pp. 301-345; L. Grans, *op. cit. supra* note 375; L. D. Obreja, "Human Rights Law and Intimate Partner Violence: Towards an Intersectional Development of Due Diligence Obligations", *Nordic Journal of Human Rights*, Vol. 37, No. 1 (2019), pp. 63-80; V. Stoyanova, 2020, *op. cit. supra* note 676.

687. See De Schutter, A. Ramasastry, M. B. Taylor and R. C. Thompson, *op. cit. supra* note 15; O. De Schutter, *op. cit. supra* note 233.

688. See Swiss federal popular initiative "Entreprises responsables – pour protéger l'être humain et l'environnement" and the counter-proposals, *op. cit. supra* note 230; French law No. 2017-399 on the "vigilance duty" of parent companies, *op. cit. supra* note 230; Modern Slavery Act 2015 of the United Kingdom, *op. cit. supra* note 230. See also the recent decisions of the Supreme Court of the United Kingdom, Case of *Vedanta Resources PLC and another* v. *Lungowe and others*, [2019] UKSC 20, 10 April 2019, and the Supreme Court of Canada, Case of *Nevsun Resources Ltd.* v. *Araya*, 2020 SCC 5, 28 February 2020.

689. See e.g. HRC, Guiding Principles on Business and Human Rights, *op. cit. supra* note 88; OECD, Guidelines for Multinational Enterprises, OECD Editions, 2011.

690. On how corporate human rights due diligence standards are imposed on States by IOs through soft law, see e.g. A. O'Donoghue, *op. cit. supra* note 215.

due diligence standard and have been "hardened" though international contract law and arbitration [691].

Finally, numerous unilateral acts of IOs (the UN, for example) and multiple soft law instruments set forth due diligence "obligations" [692] relating to human rights [693] for States, but more often for IOs or MNCs. Human rights law is, with international environmental law, the field that entails the most soft law instruments referring to due diligence. It is because of the new institutional duty-bearers considered for that standard: under existing international human rights law, IOs or MNCs cannot become duty-bearers of due diligence obligations to the extent that, as things stand, international human rights only grounds obligations for States and a few IOs like the EU. This issue is addressed in the next subsection.

2. *The scope of due diligence in international human rights law*

This subsection is devoted to the third dimension of due diligence's regime: the scope of that standard in international human rights law. To do so, it examines the four dimensions of due diligence's scope: (a) its personal scope; (b) its material scope; (c) its geographic scope; and (d) its temporal scope. International human rights law has significantly contributed to the clarification of due diligence's personal scope, particularly with regard to the duty-bearers and beneficiaries, but also to the elucidation of its material, geographic and temporal scope. Nonetheless, the scope of due diligence in international human rights law displays some specific features that warrant closer examination.

---

691. See e.g. E. Vidak-Goljevic, C. Blair and M.-A. Meudic Role, "The Medium is the Message: Establishing a System of Business and Human Rights Through Contract Law and Arbitration", *Journal of International Arbitration*, Vol. 35, No. 4 (2018), pp. 379-412.

692. Strictly speaking, these are not "obligations", nor even legal norms, since these "standards" are derived from soft law. The ambivalence of the term "standard" was mentioned in Chapter II, and again in the section on due diligence in international cybersecurity law in the present chapter. It is not therefore strictly an issue of application of international human rights law, but, rather, of standards related to the respect of these rights by their duty-bearing States and which fall within the same context.

693. See e.g. HRC, Guiding Principles on Business and Human Rights, *op. cit. supra* note 88, Principles 4 and 17; Secretary-General of the United Nations, Human Rights Due Diligence Policy, *op. cit. supra* note 86, Principle 2; ILC, Draft Principles on the Protection of the Environment in Relation to Armed Conflict, *op. cit. supra* note 11, Principle 10.

(a) *The personal scope of due diligence in international human rights law*

With regard to due diligence's personal scope, it is necessary to distinguish, within the relational triangle constitutive of due diligence outlined in Chapter II, between the duty-bearers, the beneficiaries and the third parties that are sources of the (risk of) harm.

Starting, first of all, with the *duty-bearers* of human rights due diligence obligations, States are their main duty-bearers. To this day, indeed, it is only for these institutions that international human rights law generates obligations upon which due diligence can be grafted.

With respect to IOs (including the UN), the difficulties mentioned in Chapter II concerning due diligence's applicability to public institutions other than States are compounded by a second difficulty: the absence of human rights obligations owed by IOs that could be qualified by due diligence in the first place [694]. This explains why IOs, including the UN, resort to soft law to subject themselves to various due diligence "standards" in relation to human rights [695]. One should also mention specific bilateral treaties between the UN and any given State setting forth human rights due diligence obligations for the UN [696], although that avenue is less common in practice. Finally, it is arguably possible to derive obligations of diligent prevention and protection from the UN mandate to maintain peace and security (for example Arts. 1 and 24 UN Charter) [697] or from another IO's mandate, *mutatis mutandis*.

However, most of the time, what those sources give rise to are not due diligence "obligations" correlative to human rights *stricto sensu*, but IOs' "responsibilities" for human rights, including responsibilities of diligent prevention and cooperation in relation to the human rights obligations of the States of (personal or spatial) jurisdiction involved. They pertain to (risks of) harms originating as much from Member States of the IO as from private third parties, other States or IOs.

Of course, as mentioned before, there is one main exception among IOs, and that is the EU. EU fundamental rights and international human

694. On this issue in general, see e.g. G. Le Floch, "Responsibility for Human Rights Violations by International Organizations", in B. Virzo and I. Ingravallo (eds.), *Evolutions in the Law of International Organizations*, Leiden, Brill Nijhoff, 2015, pp. 381-405.

695. See Secretary-General of the United Nations, Human Rights Due Diligence Policy, *op. cit. supra* note 86, Principle 2. See H. P. Aust, 2015, *op. cit. supra* note 218; A. O'Donoghue, *op. cit. supra* note 215; E. Lagrange, *op. cit. supra* note 215; E. Campbell, E. Dominic, S. Stadnik and Y. Wu, *op. cit. supra* note 215; A. Creta, *op. cit. supra* note 218.

696. See N. D. White, 2020, *op. cit. supra* note 86.

697. See J. Klabbers, 2017, *op. cit. supra* note 105.

rights law each set forth human rights obligations for the EU that can be qualified by the due diligence standard. According to the jurisprudence of the Court of Justice of the European Union (CJEU) [698], this is the case of its positive obligations of prevention, protection and reparation. There is also some international judicial practice with regard to the due diligence obligations of the EU, but so far it has mainly been outside of human rights [699].

The lack of "obligations" owed by IOs under international human rights law *stricto sensu* and the resulting lack of due diligence obligations in that context explain why the obligations of diligent prevention and protection of the Member States of these IOs have been at the centre of attention in international human rights law.

The ECtHR's jurisprudence, for instance, developed the notion of equivalence obligations, which are due diligence obligations of the Member States of an IO requiring that the former ensure that their IO guarantees a level of human rights protection equivalent to that of the ECHR [700]. Chapter III has already examined the links between the responsibility for negligence of Member States in case of breach of these obligations and their responsibility by attribution of the responsibility of IOs for circumvention of their obligations [701].

---

698. See e.g. EGC, Case of *Front Polisario* v. *Council of the European Union*, *op. cit. supra* note 216, para. 162. See, however, CJEU, Case of *Council of the European Union* v. *Front Polisario*, C104/16, Judgment of 21 December 2016, paras. 81 *et seq.*; CJEU, Case of *Western Sahara Campaign*, *op. cit. supra* note 216, paras. 57 *et seq*. See also A. Berkes, "The Extraterritorial Human Rights Obligations of the EU", 2018, *op. cit. supra* note 216; C. M. J. Ryngaert and R. Fransen, *op. cit. supra* note 216; E. Kassoti, *op. cit. supra* note 216. It is difficult to construct this case (violation of the Sahrawi people's rights on a territory illegally occupied by Morocco caused by, in part, the application of an international trade agreement between the EU and Morocco) as an extraterritorial case of EU human rights obligations. This is mainly because of the lack of effective control (personal or territorial) of the EU over the right-holders (unless one considers that this control was exercised merely by virtue of an international agreement of the EU directly affecting these people's rights through procedural or legal control). Yet it remains possible to consider that the EU had responsibilities for the human rights of the people outside its territory because of its control over the source of the (risk of) harm caused to these people (in this case, over Morocco, by way of the trade agreement), including responsibilities of due diligence: see also S. Besson, 2020, *op. cit. supra* note 121.

699. See ITLOS, *Request for an Advisory Opinion submitted by the Sub-Regional Fisheries Commission*, *op. cit. supra* note 148, paras. 164-173.

700. See ECtHR, Case of *Waite and Kennedy* v. *Germany*, No. 26083/94, Judgment of 18 February 1999, paras. 66-67; ECtHR, *Bosphorus* v. *Ireland*, *op. cit. supra* note 229, para. 155; ECtHR, Case of *Gasparini* v. *Italy and Belgium*, No. 10750/03, Decision of 12 May 2009, pp. 6-7; ECtHR, Case of *Al-Dulimi* v. *Switzerland*, *op. cit. supra* note 229, paras. 114-121.

701. See Dissenting opinion of Judge Keller, in ECtHR, Case of *Al-Dulimi* v. *Switzerland* (Grand Chamber), *op. cit. supra* note 229, paras. 11-12.

Finally, the obligations of other institutions, particularly of private institutions, such as MNCs or NGOs, remain, for now, non-existent under international human rights law. As a result, these institutions do not owe due diligence obligations under that regime.

As previously indicated in the first two chapters of this course, however, domestic law and domestic private law [702] in particular include many homonymous standards to the due diligence standard of international law that are applicable to private institutions. It is especially the case of the due diligence standards applicable to corporations, including MNCs. Some of these standards stem from self-regulation and from so-called corporate social responsibility. They are often referred to by the term "corporate human rights due diligence". They are slowly making their way into private international law under a minimal common form [703] or, at least and in the meantime, into soft law instruments [704].

It is essential, however, to be aware of the diversity of these corporate human rights due diligence standards from one national legal regime to the next and from one soft law instrument to the next. It is also important to understand how they differ from the due diligence standard applicable to public institutions, such as States and IOs, from the perspective of both their foundation and their content [705]. As previously highlighted

---

702. See Swiss federal popular initiative "Entreprises responsables – pour protéger l'être humain et l'environnement" and the counter-proposals, *op. cit. supra* note 230; French law No. 2017-399 on the "vigilance duty" of parent companies, *op. cit. supra* note 230; UK Modern Slavery Act 2015, *op. cit. supra* note 230. For a comparison, see D. Palombo, "The Duty of Care of the Parent Company: A Comparison between French Law, UK Precedents and the Swiss Proposals", *Business and Human Rights Journal*, Vol. 4, No. 2 (2019), pp. 265-286. See also the recent decisions of the Supreme Court of the United Kingdom, Case of *Vedanta Resources PLC and another* v. *Lungowe and others*, *op. cit. supra* note 688, and the Supreme Court of Canada, Case of *Nevsun Resources Ltd.* v. *Araya*, *op. cit. supra* note 688. On French law in this area, see L. D'Ambrosio and P. Barraud De Lagerie, "La responsabilité des entreprises reformulée par la loi : un regard pluridisciplinaire", *Droit et société*, Vol. 3, No. 106 (2020), pp. 623-631.

703. See H. Van Loon, "Principles and Building Blocks for a Global Legal Framework for Transnational Civil Litigation in Environmental Matters", *Uniform Law Review*, Vol. 23, No. 2 (2018), pp. 298-318; F. Marrella, *op. cit. supra* note 30.

704. See e.g. HRC, Guiding Principles on Business and Human Rights, *op. cit. supra* note 88; OECD, Guidelines for Multinational Enterprises, *op. cit. supra* note 689. In EU law, see also European Commission, Corporate Social Responsibility, Responsible Business Conduct, and Business & Human Rights: Overview of Progress, March 2019 [online]; Regulation (EC) No. 761/2001 of the European Parliament and of the Council of 19 March 2001 Allowing Voluntary Participation by Organisations in a Community Eco-Management and Audit Scheme (EMAS); L. Smit *et al.*, *Study on Due Diligence Requirements through the Supply Chain: Final Report*, January 2020 [online].

705. On these differences, see e.g. J. G. Ruggie and J. F. Sherman, *op. cit. supra* note 30; J. Bonnitcha and R. McCorquodale, "A Rejoinder", *op. cit. supra* note 30.

in this course, it is difficult in practice to combat the progressive confusion between these homonymous due diligence standards [706] and their progressive "hardening" into hard international law, especially through international contract law and arbitration [707]. After all, the long history of the due diligence standard in international law has been the story a progressive "hybridisation" of multiple standards following their reception in various legal orders, regimes and sources.

Yet the work of comparison and uniformisation necessary to consolidate such a common minimal standard of corporate human rights due diligence has not yet been done. Judging by the state of the preparatory work for the future "Legally binding instrument to regulate in international human rights law, the activities of transnational corporations and other business enterprises" [708], we are still far from the consolidation of a precise regime of due diligence for MNCs under international law [709], let alone from the conclusion of an international treaty prescribing international due diligence obligations directly to MNCs [710].

As with IOs, the absence of human rights obligations *stricto sensu* for MNCs explains why the obligations of diligent prevention and protection of the States linked to these MNCs are at the centre of attention in international human rights law.

In principle, the States in whose "territory" these MNCs are located can be bound by positive obligations of diligent prevention, protection and reparation with regard to potential human rights violations caused by them. The same is true for the States under whose "jurisdiction" they fall (in accordance with international law; for example, personal jurisdiction over an MNC of its nationality) or even under whose "control" they are operating (there, the link is even looser). Such obligations arise irrespective of whether these corporations or their subsidiary companies contribute to the violation of the rights of persons who are on another territory, that is, under the (concurring) [711] jurisdiction of other States pursuant to international human rights law.

706. See A. O'Donoghue, *op. cit. supra* note 215.

707. See e.g. E. Vidak-Goljevic, C. Blair and M.-A. Meudic Role, *op. cit. supra* note 691.

708. See OEIGWG Draft, *op. cit. supra* note 10, Art. 6. See O. de Schutter, *op. cit. supra* note 233.

709. OEIGWG Draft, *ibid.*, Art. 6 is even more limited in this regard than Art. 9 of the previous 2018 Draft.

710. See also O. de Schutter, *op. cit. supra* note 233.

711. On jurisdiction and concurrent human rights obligations, see S. Besson, 2016, *op. cit. supra* note 214; S. Besson, "Shared Responsibilities", 2018, *op. cit. supra* note 214.

The conditions for such due diligence obligations to arise, however, are to be found both in the regime of due diligence and in the regime of human rights obligations. The latter's condition of "jurisdiction" or effective (personal or territorial) control over the human right-holders should therefore not be overlooked. The human rights obligation (which can later be qualified by due diligence if all conditions are met) will indeed only arise if that control over the right-holders exists, whether on the territory of the State owing human rights obligations (territorial jurisdiction) or abroad (extraterritorial jurisdiction).

It is important to stress this point because a recent trend in practice [712] elides this issue. Part of the international human rights case law tends indeed to confuse the conditions of human rights obligations with those of due diligence [713]. While a number of authors support these new interpretations [714], the latter dilute the jurisdiction requirement and, in doing so, also erode the normative relation which grounds human rights and their corresponding duties and ultimately human rights themselves.

In brief, and although the formulations still vary from one interpretation to the other, the gist of those new readings of the concept of "jurisdiction" in international human rights law is as follows [715]. A human rights duty-bearing State is considered to have extraterritorial jurisdiction over an alleged right-holder outside of the two types of "effective control" which usually establish a jurisdictional link in international human rights practice, that is, personal or spatial control

712. See e.g. CCPR, *Basem Ahmed Issa Yassin and others* v. *Canada*, *op. cit. supra* note 205, paras. 6.5 *et seq.*; CESCR, General Comment No. 24, *op. cit. supra* note 3, paras. 15-16 and 30-32; IACtHR, *The Environment and Human Rights*, *op. cit. supra* note 205; CCPR, General Comment No. 36, *op. cit. supra* note 205, paras. 21-22. These (mainly non-judicial) interpretations have not been emulated so far by the ECtHR and other European courts. See e.g. Supreme Court of the Netherlands, *De Staat de Nederland (Ministerie van Infrastructuur en Milieu)* v. *Stichting Urgenda*, *op. cit. supra* note 251. See on this issue, A. Nollkaemper and L. Burgers, *op. cit. supra* note 559.

713. See S. Besson, 2020, *op. cit. supra* note 121.

714. See e.g. A. Berkes, "Extraterritorial Responsibility of the Home States", 2018, *op. cit. supra* note 121; V. Tzevelekos, *op. cit. supra* note 121; J. E. Viñuales, 2016, *op. cit. supra* note 117; A. E. Boyle, 2012, *op. cit. supra* note 119; S. Grosbon, *op. cit. supra* note 265; O. de Frouville, *op. cit. supra* note 265.

715. See e.g. D. Desierto, "The ICESCR as a Legal Constraint on State Regulation of Business, Trade and Investment: Notes from CESCR General Comment No. 24", *EJIL Talk!*, 13 September 2017 [online]; A. Berkes, "A New Extraterritorial Jurisdictional Link Recognised by the IACtHR", *EJIL Talk!*, 28 March 2018 [online]; D. Møgster, "Towards Universality: Activities Impacting the Enjoyment of the Right to Life and the Extraterritorial Application of the ICCPR", *EJIL Talk!*, 27 November 2018 [online]; A. Ollino, "Human Rights in Transboundary Contexts: Some Critical Remarks over the Emergence of an 'Effects Jurisdiction' Model in International Human Rights Law", *European Journal of International Law* (2023) (forthcoming).

over that right-holder. And this, provided that the human rights duty-bearing State exercises some form of control over a potential source of harm to that right-holder. The key seems to lie in the duty-bearing State's "control" over the source of harm and in it being "causally" related to that harm or "connected" somehow to its "impact" on the right-holder.

There are at least three difficulties with these new interpretations.

The first, and the most important one, pertains to their normative confusion. They conflate the conditions for the standard of due diligence to apply (and hence for it to qualify the content of human rights duties), on the one hand, with the conditions of jurisdiction itself (and hence for those qualified human rights duties to arise in the first place), on the other [716].

Of course, these two sets of conditions both rely on some form of "control". However, as explained in Chapter II, the former requires "control" over the source or cause of harm, whereas the latter requires "control" over the right-holder. The standard of due diligence, even if it may be grounded in those cases as a standard independent from the obligation it is qualifying (in this case a human rights duty), cannot ground that obligation itself and hence cannot give rise to a human rights duty in the first place. The conditions for that duty to arise have to be met independently. The existence of a jurisdictional relationship between a duty-bearing State and a potential right-holder is one of the grounds for human rights duties to arise besides the existence of fundamental and equal interests to protect. Any other approach would turn a mere capacity to harm someone (in this case, control over the source of harm and contribution to the causation of the harm) into a duty not to harm that person and into a right of that person not to be harmed under international human rights law. "Ought implies can" seems to have been turned into a "can implies ought" in those cases.

A second objection pertains to the criteria used by those various international human rights bodies in order to assess the existence of effective control over the alleged human right-holder. Those criteria of effective control have sometimes been replaced by the two conditions of due diligence itself, that is, the reasonable foreseeability of the (risk of) harm and the reasonable capacity to intervene [717].

716. See IACtHR, *The Environment and Human Rights*, *op. cit. supra* note 205, paras. 104.e and 104.h. See also CESCR, General Comment No. 24, *op. cit. supra* note 3, paras. 30-32.

717. See Concurring opinion of de Frouville and Ben Achour, in CCPR, *Basem Ahmed Issa Yassin and others* v. *Canada*, *op. cit. supra* note 205, paras. 10-11. See also CCPR, General Comment No. 36, *op. cit. supra* note 205, paras. 21-22.

A third confusion in those interpretations is the identification of "effective control" for the purpose of attribution of the conduct of a private corporate entity to a human rights duty-bearing State with "effective control" over the alleged right-holders themselves [718]. While it may be possible in certain cases to rely on the former to establish the latter [719], the link is not straightforward. Even more so when a State's control over a corporate entity is legal or institutional rather than a more "hands-on" type, as in the command of military operations [720]. Unless a State exercises direct control over the business operations of a corporate entity, including over its subsidiary companies abroad, it is difficult to consider it to be in effective control thereof. A subsequent attribution of that actor's wrongful acts to that State on that basis is therefore unlikely, as is the consideration that the State exercises human rights jurisdiction in that manner.

A rejoinder may be that what is really at stake in those new cases is a new form of human rights "jurisdiction" which would rely on a third type of effective control. This third type, that is, "procedural" or "judicial" control, is entertained in the ECtHR's recent case law [721]. The problem, however, is that the right-holders in the cases discussed here are not legally or procedurally tied in any way to the duty-bearing State (whether in terms of rights or in terms of duties). The only legal relationship to that State lies on the involved MNCs' side, and only to the extent that they have been incorporated under its domestic law or benefit from domestic authorisations to export. Of course, if the victims of an MNC abroad decide to sue that corporation before the tribunals of its State of incorporation, that State can be considered as exercising procedural effective control over them. It could then be considered to owe them human rights that can be grounded in that kind of procedural

718. See CCPR, *Basem Ahmed Issa Yassin and others* v. *Canada*, *op. cit. supra* note 205, para. 6.5. See also Concurring opinion of de Frouville and Ben Achour, in CCPR, *Basem Ahmed Issa Yassin and others* v. *Canada*, *ibid.*, para. 8.

719. See e.g. ECtHR, Case of *Ilaşcu and others* v. *Moldova and Russia*, No. 48787/99, Judgment of 8 July 2004, paras. 314-316; ECtHR, Case of *Jaloud* v. *The Netherlands*, *op. cit. supra* note 679, para. 138.

720. See ICJ, The case of *Application of the Convention on the Prevention and Punishment of the Crime of Genocide*, *op. cit. supra* note 22, paras. 401-407.

721. See e.g. ECtHR, Case of *Romeo Castaño* v. *Belgium*, No. 8351/17, Judgment of 9 July 2019, paras. 36-43. See also ECtHR, Case of *Markovic and others* v. *Italy*, No. 1398/03, Judgment of 14 December 2006, paras. 54-56; ECtHR, Case of *Güzelyurtlu and others* v. *Cyprus and Turkey*, No. 36925/07, Judgment of 29 January 2019, paras. 187 *et seq*. For a recent and much more restrictive interpretation of this third type of effective control, see, however, ECtHR, Case of *M. N. and others* v. *Belgium*, No. 3599/18, Decision of 5 March 2020, paras. 107-109.

exercise of jurisdiction, that is, procedural rights and non-discrimination rights in particular.

Since all the conditions for the emergence of such extraterritorial obligations of diligent prevention and protection under international human rights law are not met in such cases, other possibilities can and should be explored to ground extraterritorial obligations or, at least, responsibilities of diligent protection of these individual interests protected under international law. As emphasised earlier, the history of extraterritorial due diligence obligations should not stop at international human rights law.

First, one could also approach the issue from the perspective of States' extraterritorial "responsibilities" for human rights, including of due diligence. By way of a reminder, these are the responsibilities for human rights protection that all States, and not only the State of jurisdiction, share equally under international human rights law (at varying degrees depending on the intensity of their control over the third party that is the source of harm). Unlike human rights obligations owed to the right-holders by the State of jurisdiction, however, responsibilities for human rights are not owed to those right-holders and may not be claimed by them either. They are not grounded in a jurisdictional relationship with these right-holders abroad and as such in effective control over them.

In fact, some of those responsibilities for human rights are due diligence responsibilities provided that the conditions of due diligence are fulfilled. Interestingly, they also include due diligence responsibilities of all States to regulate MNCs under their control (or on their territory or under their jurisdiction) so as to prevent them from harming the human rights of people under the (human rights) jurisdiction of other States [722]. These human rights responsibility-bearing States should assist the States of jurisdiction in abiding by their human rights duties towards those people.

There lies the potential link between States' due diligence obligations and the so-called due diligence obligations of MNCs. States' responsibilities of diligent prevention and protection also require the adoption of national or even international law to prevent MNCs from causing restrictions to the human rights of people, including people situated outside of their jurisdiction. This could imply prescribing due diligence obligations under national or international law directly to

722. See e.g. CESCR, General Comment No. 24, *op. cit. supra* note 3, paras. 30-33; CCPR, General Comment No. 36, *op. cit. supra* note 205, paras. 21-22.

MNCs themselves [723]. Ultimately, international law might even make the adoption of this kind of national regulation compulsory in order for these States to abide by their own human rights responsibilities of due diligence [724].

Second, some of States' extraterritorial obligations of due diligence may stem from other international legal regimes, while also protecting the individual interests of human right-holders, but without corresponding to extraterritorial human rights duties. For example, with regard to the protection of the interest and the right to a healthy environment, one should not underestimate the extraterritorial obligations of due diligence under international environmental law, but other international legal regimes may also prescribe due diligence obligations.

As a matter of fact, many lawyers specialised in international environmental law and interested in these questions have recently turned to international human rights law to ground their claims [725]. They endeavour to derive extraterritorial obligations for States not to harm the environment as obligations directed and owed to a human right-holder. Grounding them in international human rights law allows the right-holder to invoke them before domestic or international courts. However, as explained earlier, while this may sound like an attractive move from the perspective of international environmental law, it is not desirable from the perspective of international human rights law. By confusing the control exercised by a State over the source of a human right violation with the effective control over the alleged human right-holders, this approach risks diluting international human rights law's capacity to protect these rights.

Second, the *beneficiaries* of due diligence obligations in international human rights law. As highlighted in the previous subsection, the specificity of the beneficiaries of due diligence in that regime relates to them being also the holders of the correlative human rights corresponding to these obligations.

The link between these beneficiaries and the duty-bearers of due diligence obligations is tighter than in other regimes of international law, therefore. The obligations upon which the due diligence standard

723. See e.g. CESCR, General Comment No. 24, *op. cit. supra* note 3, paras. 16 and 30-33. See also the contrast between HRC, Guiding Principles on Business and Human Rights, *op. cit. supra* note 88, Principles 4 and 17. See N. D. White, 2012, *op. cit. supra* note 30; V. Chetail, *op. cit. supra* note 234, pp. 105-130.

724. See OEIGWG Draft, *op. cit. supra* note 10. See also O. de Schutter, *op. cit. supra* note 233.

725. See e.g. J. E. Viñuales, 2016, *op. cit. supra* note 117.

is grafted are grounded in a jurisdictional relationship, that is, effective control, between that duty-bearer and the right-holder. This is an important difference between human rights due diligence obligations and due diligence obligations in other international legal regimes which merely require control (that does not need to be effective) by the duty-bearer over the third party or any other source of (risk) of harm.

Yet the holders of rights corresponding to human rights obligations of due diligence are not the only beneficiaries one may consider. In the human rights context, indeed, due diligence obligations are obligations *erga omnes*. Duty-bearing States also owe them to other peoples and other States. While the latter are not right-holders *stricto sensu*, they can require the respect of these human rights to the benefit of their right-holders and, as seen earlier, they may even be bound by human rights responsibilities to do so [726].

Third, the *third parties*, that is, the source of the harm, of due diligence obligations in international human rights law. These can be any legal subject, public or private institution or even a natural phenomenon. One can think of private persons, but also of other States or IOs. It is especially in relation to the former that positive due diligence obligations have developed in the jurisprudence of international human rights bodies [727]. Examples include positive obligations of due diligence in the context of domestic violence [728] or human rights violations caused by MNCs.

(b) *The material scope of due diligence in international human rights law*

The material scope of due diligence obligations in international human rights law extends to all fields given that the material scope of these rights is by definition unlimited.

726. On the invocation of responsibility in those cases, see ARSIWA, *op. cit. supra* note 24, Arts. 40-41 and 42 *et seq.*; ARIO, *op. cit. supra* note 24, Arts. 41-42 and 43 *et seq.* See also G. Gaja, 2005, *op. cit. supra* note 240.

727. See e.g. IACtHR, Case of *Velasquez-Rodriguez* v. *Honduras*, *op. cit. supra* note 205, para. 172; ECtHR, Case of *Osman* v. *The United Kingdom*, *op. cit. supra* note 301, para. 116; ECtHR, Case of *Opuz* v. *Turkey*, *op. cit. supra* note 205, paras. 129-130; ECtHR, Case of *O'Keeffe* v. *Ireland*, *op. cit. supra* note 301, paras. 144-149; ECtHR, Case of *Talpis* v. *Italy*, *op. cit. supra* note 205, paras. 29 and 98-99.

728. See e.g. M. T. Kamminga, *op. cit. supra* note 15; C. Benninger-Budel, *op. cit. supra* note 410; Z. Abdul Azizi and J. Moussa, *op. cit. supra* note 686; J. Goldshied and D. J. Liebowitz, *op. cit. supra* note 686; L. Grans, *op. cit. supra* note 375; L. D. Obreja, *op. cit. supra* note 686; V. Stoyanova, 2020, *op. cit. supra* note 676.

The same is true for the risks of harm. One of international human rights law's specificities, however, is to require that the risk of harm be "real and immediate" [729]. There are exceptions in practice depending on the human right at stake (if it is absolute, for instance) or on the particular vulnerability of the human right-holder (a woman or a child, for example). In such cases, the risk does not need to be qualified for the due diligence standard to apply [730].

(c) The geographic scope of due diligence in international human rights law

The geographic scope of due diligence obligations in international human rights law extends, just as the regime itself, to multiple constellations. Some of these obligations are extraterritorial, while others are purely territorial depending on the localisation of the human right-holder and of the source of the (risk of) harm. However, as indicated previously, for a territorial or extraterritorial due diligence obligation to arise under international human rights law, some conditions must be fulfilled, including the existence of a (personal or spatial) jurisdictional link, that is, effective control, between the duty-bearing State and the holder of the corresponding rights.

In that respect, Chapter II has already outlined the distinction between "jurisdiction" in the sense of effective control over the human right-holder under international human rights law (which grounds a State's obligation) and "jurisdiction" in the meaning of a competence or right to bind under general international law (which grounds a State's right). One does not imply the other. In any event, the due diligence standard does not require either since any form of "control" over the source of harm to prevent or against which to protect is sufficient [731]. However, if due diligence qualifies an obligation arising from a regime requiring one of these forms of jurisdiction, as is the case in international human rights law, the due diligence obligation will require it too.

---

729. See e.g. ECtHR, Case of *Opuz* v. *Turkey*, *op. cit. supra* note 205, paras. 129-130. See V. Stoyanova, 2020, *op. cit. supra* note 676, pp. 117-120.

730. See ECtHR, Case of *Talpis* v. *Italy*, *op. cit. supra* note 205, paras. 29 and 98-99. See, however, the recent change in jurisprudence in ECtHR, Case of *Valiuliene* v. *Lithuania*, *op. cit. supra* note 413, which marks the return to the test developed in ECtHR, Case of *Osman* v. *The United Kingdom*, *op. cit. supra* note 301, para. 116, on this regard. See Dissenting opinion of Judge Pinto, in ECtHR, *Valiuliene* v. *Lithuania*, *ibid.*

731. See ICJ, The case of *Application of the Convention on the Prevention and Punishment of the Crime of Genocide*, *op. cit. supra* note 22, para. 430.

The second part of this course has already explained how "effective control" over a human right-holder, which is necessary for the human right and its corresponding duties to be grounded, differs from the "control" over the third party source of harm necessary for due diligence to arise, as well as how it differs from the "effective control" over a private person which underlies the direct attribution of that person's conduct and as such responsibility by attribution. To be applicable, the due diligence standard does not require that its duty-bearer exercises effective control over the beneficiary or the source of harm. As indicated in Chapter III, responsibility for negligence is not a responsibility by attribution of conduct or responsibility, but a responsibility for its own negligence. Yet, as explained previously, if the due diligence obligation at stake belongs to international human rights law, it is necessary to establish both control over the source of harm and effective control over the holder of the human right corresponding to the obligation. It is worth emphasising, however, that, under international human rights law, the degree of control over the source of harm and the degree of due diligence can be inferior when the control over the human right-holders is extraterritorial [732].

(d) *The temporal scope of due diligence in international human rights law*

The temporal scope of due diligence obligations in international human rights law corresponds to the lifespan of the holder of the corresponding human rights. Unlike in other regimes of international law, the existence of a right corresponding to the due diligence obligation is decisive, and this right cannot outlive its holder's capacity to claim it. Therefore, there can be no due diligence obligations for future generations in international human rights law [733], even if other special regimes, such as international environmental law, may allow it.

732. See e.g. ICJ, The case of *Application of the Convention on the Prevention and Punishment of the Crime of Genocide*, *op. cit. supra* note 22; ICJ, The case of *Armed Activities on the Territory of the Congo*, 2005, *op. cit. supra* note 3. See also R. Kolb, 2016, *op. cit. supra* note 29.

733. On the human right to a healthy environment, see e.g. Supreme Court of the Netherlands, *De Staat de Nederland (Ministerie van Infrastructuur en Milieu)* v. *Stichting Urgenda*, *op. cit. supra* note 251, para. 5.6.2. See more generally: J. H. Knox, *op. cit. supra* note 251.

3. *The conditions, content, variability and limits of due diligence in international human rights law*

This third subsection is devoted to the last four dimensions of the due diligence regime in international human rights law: the conditions, content, variability and limits of due diligence.

First, the *conditions* of due diligence in international human rights law. The abundant case law in that international legal regime has carefully articulated due diligence's conditions of foreseeability and reasonable ability. This is true for both international [734] and European [735] human rights law.

Second, the *content* of due diligence in international human rights law. The minimal content of the reasonable measures to adopt in light of the variability of the national circumstances of democratic States respectful of human rights has been a sustained subject of concern in the international human rights case law. Here, one may mention all the human rights standards constitutive of the good organisation of the State [736] or the standard of good government [737]. They make up part of the content of States' positive general obligations under international human rights law [738]: for instance, a minimal democratic regime, the separation of powers and judicial control.

Of course, the due diligence standard in international human rights law is not immune to the two contemporary trends identified in Chapter II, Section E.3: the proceduralisation and technicisation of due diligence's content.

The proceduralisation of due diligence obligations unfolds just as much with regard to the material content of the ECHR's positive obligations as with regard to the judicial control exercised by the ECtHR [739]. When it assesses whether positive obligations of diligent

734. See e.g. CESCR, General Comment No. 24, *op. cit. supra* note 3, para. 32.

735. See e.g. ECtHR, Case of *Osman* v. *The United Kingdom*, *op. cit. supra* note 301, para. 116; ECtHR, Case of *Opuz* v. *Turkey*, *op. cit. supra* note 205, para. 129; ECtHR, Case of *O'Keeffe* v. *Ireland*, *op. cit. supra* note 301, paras. 144-149; ECtHR, Case of *Talpis* v. *Italy*, *op. cit. supra* note 205, paras. 29 and 98-99.

736. See R. Kolb, 2016, *op. cit. supra* note 29; J. Klabbers, 2017, *op. cit. supra* note 105.

737. On the standard of good government in the history of European law, see A. A. Wijffels, *op. cit. supra* note 32.

738. See S. Besson, "International Courts", 2019, *op. cit. supra* note 107. See also L. Lavrysen, "Protection by the Law: The Positive Obligation to Develop a Legal Framework to Adequately Protect the ECHR Rights", in E. Brems and Y. Haeck (eds.), *Human Rights and Civil Liberties in the 21st Century*, Dordrecht, Springer, 2014, pp. 69-84.

739. See O. M. Arnardóttir, *op. cit. supra* note 360; E. Dubout, *op. cit. supra* note 360.

prevention or protection have been breached, the ECtHR increasingly restricts itself indeed to verifying that some procedural steps (such as organising a parliamentary debate or exercising judicial review) were taken without further examination of the national authorities' reasoning. The same is true for the determination of the material content of positive obligations of due diligence, which are frequently reduced to procedural obligations (an obligation to investigate or an obligation to enact legislation, for instance).

The technicisation of the due diligence standard is also at work in international human rights law, especially in the evaluation of whether obligations of diligent prevention or protection related the human right to a healthy environment have been breached [740]. The various human rights due diligence "standards" now included in soft law have already been mentioned. Some of them use technoscientific criteria as parameters of what can reasonably be expected in the diligent protection of human rights [741].

Third, the *variability* of due diligence in international human rights law. It is also in this regime that the different variability criteria of due diligence obligations have been specified the most.

This is the case, to start with, with variability with regard to the risk of harm: the degree of due diligence may vary depending on whether the objective degree of that risk is high, on the level of actual or constructive knowledge of that risk and on its evaluation. The same is true for the "real and immediate" character of the risk of harm required under international human rights law [742]. Furthermore, the required diligence also varies depending on the severity of the potential harm: one expects a higher degree of due diligence if the human right at issue is more fundamental than others [743]. Finally, the international human rights case law frequently resorts to the parameter of the vulnerability of the human right-holder and beneficiary of due diligence to increase the degree of diligence expected from the duty-bearer [744].

---

740. See e.g. Supreme Court of the Netherlands, *De Staat de Nederland (Ministerie van Infrastructuur en Milieu)* v. *Stichting Urgenda*, *op. cit. supra* note 251, para. 7.5.2. See more generally: J. H. Knox, *op. cit. supra* note 251.

741. For a critique, see A. Berkes, "Extraterritorial Responsibility of the Home States", 2018, *op. cit. supra* note 121. See also Separate opinion of Judge Ranjeva, in ICJ, The case of *Application of the Convention on the Prevention and Punishment of the Crime of Genocide*, *op. cit. supra* note 22.

742. See e.g. ECtHR, Case of *Opuz* v. *Turkey*, *op. cit. supra* note 205, paras. 129-130.

743. See e.g. *ibid.*, para. 130.

744. See e.g. ECtHR, Case of *O'Keeffe* v. *Ireland*, *op. cit. supra* note 301, paras. 144-149; ECtHR, Case of *Talpis* v. *Italy*, *op. cit. supra* note 205, paras. 29 and

International human rights law specifically addresses the questions of proof of these different variability parameters and of due diligence's content and, when applicable, of its breach [745]. We have already discussed the forms and burden of proof of causation [746], but other issues are even harder to prove. Each special legal regime determines whether States should have a margin of appreciation with regard to these variability parameters in the context of the control exercised by an international tribunal. International human rights law has developed its own regime of the margin of appreciation depending on the rights involved and on the existence of a transnational consensus on the matter [747].

Finally, the *limits* of due diligence in international human rights law. The question of the relationship between limits (economic or financial in particular) and respect for due diligence has been discussed in detail in international human rights law. The human rights case law insists, for instance, on taking into account the rights of other human right-holders and more generally procedural guarantees [748].

International human rights courts also resort to a well-established reasoning and in particular to the necessity test when balancing due diligence obligations with other moral considerations, such as public interest, morality, public health or security. That test of "necessity in a democratic society" was developed to justify restrictions to human rights obligations. It may be qualified as qualitative balancing for it refers to the egalitarian and relational dimension of human rights [749]. To that extent, it differs from mainstream quantitative balancing and other forms of instrumental proportionality. Other regimes of international law in which (judicial) reasoning about due diligence tends to be

---

98-99. See S. Besson, "La vulnérabilité et la structure des droits de l'homme – L'exemple de la jurisprudence de la Cour européenne des droits de l'homme", in L. Burgorgue-Larsen (ed.), *La vulnérabilité saisie par les juges*, Brussels, Bruylant, 2014, pp. 59-85.

745. See R. Pisillo Mazzeschi, 2018, *op. cit. supra* note 23.

746. See e.g. ECtHR, Case of *Luginbuhl* v. *Switzerland*, *op. cit. supra* note 303. See I. Plakokefalos, 2015, *op. cit. supra* note 391.

747. See S. Besson, "Subsidiarity in International Human Rights Law: What is Subsidiary about Human Rights?", *American Journal of Jurisprudence*, Vol. 61, No. 1 (2016), pp. 69-107.

748. See e.g. ECtHR, Case of *Opuz* v. *Turkey*, *op. cit. supra* note 205, para. 129; ECtHR, Case of *Osman* v. *The United Kingdom*, *op. cit. supra* note 301, para. 116. On this question and on the importance of not overextending the content of due diligence obligations, see Dissenting opinion of Judge Spano, in ECtHR, Case of *Talpis* v. *Italy*, *op. cit. supra* note 205, paras. 15-16. See also ICJ, The case of *Application of the Convention on the Prevention and Punishment of the Crime of Genocide*, *op. cit. supra* note 22.

749. See S. Besson, 2017b, *op. cit. supra* note 426; G. Letsas, *op. cit. supra* note 423.

reduced to a maximising and quantified application of technoscientific standards would be well-advised to borrow such a qualitative egalitarian approach to the justification and evaluation of due diligence's limits.

CONCLUSION

The time has come to offer concluding remarks in the form of a critical appraisal of the practice of due diligence in contemporary international law.

Some of the standard's strengths which prompted its return to the forefront of international law are also sometimes considered either as its weaknesses or, at least, found to be exaggerated. The previous four chapters have hopefully provided many of the required answers to those fears and critiques. These conclusions will start, first, by summarising the most important arguments advanced in the course; second, it will reply to further objections that have been made against due diligence in international law; and, finally, it will offer some recommendations for future research and practice pertaining to due diligence in international law.

To go back to Riccardo Pisillo Mazzeschi's critique that this course opened with [750], due diligence should have lost some of its "mystery" by now. Deeming it an "overrated" concept in international law, however, should clearly appear mistaken. The risk of exaggerating the importance and capacity of due diligence exists, of course. Yet, as explained in the different chapters of this course, it may be contained in different ways. One of them is the normative framework advanced here, together with the kind of reasoning guided by what this course has argued grounds due diligence in international law, that is, the sovereign equality of peoples and their international institutions. While some international lawyers' interest in due diligence, especially in international human rights law, may have at times bordered with "mania", to cite Menno Kamminga [751], it has had the merit of stimulating reflection about the distinction between obligation and responsibility in international law and clarifying human rights reasoning pertaining to positive obligations and their violation.

Reverting to due diligence's genealogy in the history of international law, it is important to remember the remarkable continuity, notwithstanding minor variations at each moment in time, of the question of the responsibility of an instituted public for the harm caused by persons or

750. R. Pisillo Mazzeschi, 2018, *op. cit. supra* note 23, p. 323.
751. M. T. Kamminga, *op. cit. supra* note 15.

entities over which it exercises institutional control, including in cases where these persons or entities do not act on its behalf.

This observation should not only humble us in our assessment of our predecessors' ingenuity, but also offer some perspective on the apparent novelty of the question of due diligence in international law. While that standard has existed under international law for a long time, it never ceased to transform itself, be it with regard to the nature of the harm, the identity of its duty-bearers, its beneficiaries or the third parties that are sources of the (risk of) harm. This dynamic dimension of the standard should be kept in mind now that the contours of a minimal general regime of due diligence in international law have been drawn: it confirms how adaptable it may be to future risks of harm. The growing hybridity of the solutions identified over time should also counsel caution with respect to the analogies one may be tempted to draw across existing special regimes of due diligence. Any transposition of the standard to a new context or a new risk necessarily demands an adaptation of its regime.

With these few lessons from the history of due diligence in international law in mind, let us revert to the reasons identified for its return to the forefront of international law's scene, both across the many special regimes of international law and its manifold sources.

As this course's introduction highlighted, the first technical reason for the "renaissance" of the due diligence standard in international law relates to the crisis of certain sources of international legal obligations (multilateral treaties, in particular), but also to the intrinsic limitations of their personal scope to States (and of the personal scope of customary obligations in particular). Against this background, it is easy to understand the eagerness of international judges or other interpreters of international law to restate that due diligence is a standard of international customary law or, at least, a general principle, implying that it is applicable across regimes of international law and also to IOs.

Due diligence's intermediary place between obligations and responsibilities, that is, between primary and secondary norms of international law, is a second technical reason accounting for the renewed interest in the standard. In practice, due diligence's simultaneous ambivalence and centrality in international legal reasoning have led to the repeated failure of all attempts to legalise that standard as a primary obligation and consequently of efforts to exclude it from the scope of the conditions, content and implementation of international responsibility law. In turn, this may explain the difficulties in delineating responsibility for negligence and responsibility for complicity, as well as those arising in the determination of causation in allocating reparations among a plurality of responsible States or IOs. It is therefore not surprising that what this course has referred to as due diligence's "double life" in international law (between a standard of conduct qualifying an obligation and a responsibility criterion) has kept specialists of both international obligations and of international responsibility on tenterhooks and has become a popular doctrinal question.

This course has identified three further and more general reasons for due diligence's renaissance. They are interrelated and pertain to different aspects of due diligence's evolution with regard to its duty-bearers, its beneficiaries and the third parties that are sources of (the risks of) harms. They have also led to the constant transformation, since antiquity, of the kind of responsibility an instituted collective or public should bear for the harms caused by its members.

The first reason for due diligence's increasing popularity relates to the important institutional changes occurring in international law and in particular to the organisation of new public institutions outside of the State: sub-State, inter-State and even non-State entities have emerged, such as cities, regions or IOs. These new institutions exercise some control over different sources of harm and should therefore bear responsibility for their potential negligence. The course has also addressed the role of the erosion of the public/private distinction and the resulting difficulty to limit the responsibility of the State or of the IO to a responsibility by attribution of private conduct as set forth under the ARSIWA and the ARIO. In those circumstances, due diligence makes it possible to hold a State or IO responsible for its negligence with respect to private action without having to dissect the public or private nature of that action and hence without having to attribute that action to the State or the IO.

The second reason for due diligence's renaissance in international law may be found in the emergence of new persons or entities among its beneficiaries, including humanity in general and/or future generations. Some of their interests may indeed be considered to be protected by contemporary international law, opening the way for a potential obligation not to harm them by negligence. This may be the case before any given international law's special regime recognises such an obligation *per se*. It is indeed one of the due diligence's standard's jusgenerative strengths to allow for the emergence of such obligations for the protection of interests recognised by international law and to hold their duty-bearers responsible for their negligence.

Finally, the third reason identified for the renewed interest in due diligence relates to the emergence of new (current or anticipated) risks and more generally to the growing security concerns of the members of the contemporary "vigilance society". At times, these risks are so secret or complex that they become difficult to prevent or anticipate in the context of the ordinary regime of primary obligations and responsibilities by attribution. In the absence of other means to hold our institutions responsible, it has become attractive to resort to the general standard of due diligence and to responsibility for negligence.

Those various reasons for the success of due diligence are mirrored by recurring critiques against resorting to due diligence in international law. Let us address three of them in turn: the risk of conservatism; the entrenchment of the public/private distinction; and, finally, the standard's indeterminacy.

The first critique admonishes due diligence for maintaining a "state-centred" international institutional order. After all, the standard is often said to be grounded in State sovereignty and the principle of territorial integrity.

As repeatedly emphasised in this course, this critique has long lost its relevance. The due diligence standard now applies to duty-bearers other than States, benefits persons and entities other than States and extends to risks beyond those arising from bilateral relations of territorial neighbourliness between sovereign States, including in common spaces. More generally, due diligence's history in international law reveals that it has been anything but a conservative force. On the contrary, thanks to the reasonableness criterion, the good government standard was adjusted to the needs of the time at different moments in history. This explains how the due diligence standard may be invoked not only to develop good government requirements adapted to IOs, as is increasingly the case in practice, but maybe also one day for MNCs and NGOs as well.

The second objection falls prey to the sirens who for several years have decried the lack of justification of the public/private distinction and called for its abandonment. As argued in Chapter II, however, this distinction, which stems from Roman law, lies at the foundation of Western modern law and by extension of contemporary international law. It underlies the distinction between the State and civil society that international law has universalised to other regions or civilisations of the world and which it progressively, sometimes forcefully, introduced across different legal cultures.

The origin of the current state of international law in this respect is admittedly questionable, and the international law standard of due diligence must urgently open itself to other forms of governmentality to achieve the universal legitimacy to which it aspires. Yet abandoning the public/private distinction on the ground that it is imperialistic rather than striving to justify it in an inclusive way, one that is respectful of the differences of what constitutes the international standard of good government, might lead to two other forms of imperialism: the "all things public" imperialism, which inspired several forms of totalitarianism and led to the Second World War, on the one hand, and the "all things private" imperialism towards which we seem to be hurtling at great speed, on the other.

Due diligence is an inheritance of the modern Western legal tradition. We should endeavour to justify this inheritance to others before dismissing it out of hand on account of imperialism. Responsibility for negligence has made it possible, in each period of its history, to hold the collectivity, group, tribe or clan (under different institutional forms: city, kingdom, empire, State, IO) responsible for the actions of its members. Remarkably, due diligence was able to achieve this by carving a third way. Due diligence does not identify the responsibility of the group (clan or tribe) with that of its individual members in a collective responsibility mode, holding the group responsible every time a member misbehaves. So doing, it avoids fostering the "all things public" inclination. At the same time, however, the international law standard of due diligence does not sever the group's responsibility entirely from that of its individual members. It does not limit that responsibility to cases where an attribution of conduct and/or responsibility may take place under contemporary international responsibility law. In doing so, it avoids favouring the "all things private" inclination. Quite the reverse, responsibility for negligence identifies the conditions under which an instituted collective or public must bear responsibility for its own negligence with regard to the conduct of its members which its institutions have not been able to control. In so doing, due diligence strikes a careful balance between the public and the private.

At a time when calls for the "commons" multiply, it is important to ensure that they do not pave the way for the return of tribalism. To that end, cultivating the balance and relation between the public and the private is essential, and due diligence amounts to one way of preserving that balance.

Finally, the third critique of due diligence's indeterminacy echoes that of the reasonableness test, which characterises a good part of the general regime of due diligence and its normative structure, from its conditions and content to its limits.

As highlighted in this course, this indeterminacy also amounts to a strength of the due diligence standard. It enables it to respect the legal and political cultures into which it is set, as well as the margin of appreciation of each State or IO under international scrutiny. Contrary to common belief, due diligence's reasonable character does not imply a complete relativity and subjectivity of its content. On the contrary, the minimal universal content of the due diligence standard has been progressively identified, by the international case law acting as a catalyst, on the grounds of the common practice of States. As it is the case of all universal norms, however, its minimal content still has to be contextualised in each specific situation to become a source of actual obligations. In turn, this normative specification in context is what our institutions should account for when they are asked to justify the reasonableness of the measures they have or have not taken on grounds of the standard of due diligence. Holding our institutions to account may not be done as well by merely asking them to provide impact assessments or other figures. It prevents them from hiding behind procedural routines imposed by the new kind of procedural obligations of due diligence developing in many special regimes of international law. The alleged universality and objectivity of the latter obligations is a mere façade: they are imposed top down without the political participation of the representatives of any of the peoples subjected to them.

Finally, the time has come to make some recommendations, particularly for those who practice due diligence in international law or approach it as an object of research.

First, several recommendations for the practitioners of due diligence. While this may seem somewhat paradoxical among lawyers, it is important to slow down the process of legalisation of the content of due diligence obligations and invest more efforts in judicial reasoning (both domestic and international) instead. This may be done by questioning the excessive proceduralisation of due diligence obligations and their technoscientific standardisation, particularly through soft law standards and their "hardening" through the reception in international jurisprudence.

With regard to the personal scope of due diligence, practitioners should pay greater attention to the due diligence obligations of international law's new institutions, whether public (like IOs) or private (like MNCs and NGOs). The international institutional order is in crisis, and the due diligence standard may provide the kind of general standard of conduct to which all international institutions should conform, be they non-State, quasi-State or inter-State. This normative international standard of good government may actually amount to a compass guiding us in the reconstruction of the international institutional order.

Second, some recommendations are also in order for researchers. For due diligence to play a role in international law in the future, it should be able to claim legitimate authority. For that purpose, serious comparative studies of domestic and international law, both private and public, have to be conducted in order to identify a common law of due diligence and learn from other good government standards in the world. This should begin with the development of a comparative history of due diligence that is not as centred on the Western law tradition as has been the case. It should also include contemporary comparative international law studies on the model of what is already being done within some legal traditions of civil and public liability in Europe. The theory of responsibility law itself should also become more comparative: it is currently largely centred on civil, rather than public, liability law and oriented chiefly after Anglo-American law and theory on that matter.

It is only with the help of comparative international law on due diligence and a more inclusive theory of international responsibility that we could hope to forge the kind of common and universal legal regime of due diligence that may claim legitimate authority: the international law of, to quote Hannah Arendt, all people who "inhabit the earth and form a world between them" [752]. What is at stake here, after all, is nothing less than the protection of the sovereign equality of States and their peoples, that collective equal autonomy that grounds the standard of due diligence in international law. Cultivating such an important standard has become urgent. It has been this course's privilege to clarify how this could be done.

752. See H. Arendt, *op. cit. supra* note 172.

BIBLIOGRAPHY

Books, chapters and articles

Abdul Azizi, Z., and J. Moussa, *Due Diligence Framework: State Accountability Framework for Eliminating Violence against Women*, Malaysia, International Human Rights Initiative, 2014.

Alemanno, A., "The Precautionary Principle", in C. Baudenbacher (ed.), *The Handbook of EEA Law*, Cham, Springer, 2016, pp. 839-852.

Antoine, A., and T. Olson (eds.), *La responsabilité de la puissance publique en droit comparé*, Paris, Société de législation comparée, 2016.

Anzilotti, D., "La responsabilité internationale des États à raison des dommages soufferts par les étrangers", *Revue générale de droit international public* (1906), pp. 285-371.

–, "Sugli effetti dell'inadempienza di obbligazioni internazionali aventi per oggetto una somma di danaro", *Rivista di Diritto Internazionale*, Vol. 7 (1913), pp. 53-67.

Arendt, H., *On Revolution*, New York, Viking Press, 1963.

Arnardóttir, O. M., "The 'Procedural Turn' under the European Convention on Human Rights and Presumptions of Convention Compliance", *International Journal of Constitutional Law*, Vol. 15, No. 1 (2017), pp. 9-35.

Aronsson-Storrier, M., "Beyond Early Warning Systems: Querying the Relationship between International Law and Disaster Risk (Reduction)", *Yearbook of International Disaster Law*, Vol. 1 (2018), pp. 51-69.

Aust, H. P., *Complicity and the Law of State Responsibility*, Cambridge, Cambridge University Press, 2011.

–, "Circumstances Precluding Wrongfulness", in A. Nollkaemper and I. Plakokefalos (eds.), *Principles of Shared Responsibility in International Law: An Appraisal of the State of the Art*, Cambridge, Cambridge University Press, 2014, pp. 169-207.

–, "The UN Human Rights Due Diligence Policy: An Effective Mechanism Against Complicity of Peacekeeping Forces", *Journal of Conflict and Security Law*, Vol. 20, No. 1 (2015), pp. 61-73.

Aust, H. P., and P. Feihle, "Due Diligence in the History of the Codification of the Law of State Responsibility", in A. Peters, H. Krieger and L. Kreuzer (eds.), *Due Diligence in International Law*, Oxford, Oxford University Press, 2020, pp. 42-58.

Bannelier-Christakis, K., "Obligations de diligence dans le cyberspace: qui a peur de la cyber-diligence ?", *Revue belge de droit international*, Vol. 50, No. 2 (2017), pp. 612-665.

–, "Le standard de due diligence et la cyber-sécurité", in SFDI (ed.), *Le standard de* due diligence *et la responsabilité internationale: Journée d'études franco-italienne du Mans*, Paris, Pedone, 2018, pp. 67-92.

Barboza, J., "International Liability for the Injurious Consequences of Acts Not Prohibited by International Law and Protection of the Environment", *Recueil des cours*, Vol. 247 (1994), pp. 293-405.

Barnidge, R. P. J., "The Due Diligence Principle under International Law", *International Community Law Review*, Vol. 8, No. 1 (2006), pp. 81-122.

–, *Non-State Actors and Terrorism: Applying the Law of State Responsibility and the Due Diligence Principle*, The Hague, T.M.C. Asser Press, 2008.

Bartolini, G., "Disaster Risk Reduction: An International Law Perspective", *Questions of International Law, Zoom-in*, Vol. 48 (2018), pp. 1-6.

–, "A Universal Treaty for Disasters? Remarks on the International Law Commission's Draft Articles on the Protection of Persons in the Event of

Disasters", *International Review of the Red Cross*, Vol. 99 (2019), pp. 1103-1137.

–, "Disaster Risk Reduction and Cultural Heritage", in K. Samuel and K. Bookmiller (eds.), *Cambridge Handbook of Disaster Risk Reduction and International Law*, Cambridge, Cambridge University Press, 2019, pp. 421-442.

–, "The Historical Roots of the Due Diligence Standard", in A. Peters, H. Krieger and L. Kreuzer (eds.), *Due Diligence in International Law*, Oxford, Oxford University Press, 2020, pp. 23-41.

Bederman, D. J., "Contributory Fault and State Responsibility", *Virginia Journal of International Law*, Vol. 30, No. 2 (1990), pp. 335-369.

Belrhali, H., "La responsabilité de la puissance publique en droit comparé. Conclusion", in A. Antoine and T. Olson (eds.), *La responsabilité de la puissance publique en droit comparé*, Paris, Société de législation comparée, 2016, pp. 541-547.

Benedek, A., "Due Diligence in Cyberspace, Guidelines for International and European Cyber Policy and Cybersecurity Policy", SWP Research Paper 7, Berlin, 2016, https://www.swp-berlin.org/fileadmin/contents/products/research_papers/2016RP07_bdk.pdf.

Benninger-Budel, C. (ed.), *Due Diligence and its Application to Protect Women from Violence*, Leiden, Martinus Nijhoff, 2008.

Berkes, A., "Extraterritorial Responsibility of the Home States for MNCs' Violations of Human Rights", in Y. Radi (ed.), *Research Handbook on Human Rights and Investment*, London, Edward Elgar, 2018, pp. 304-344.

–, "A New Extraterritorial Jurisdictional Link Recognised by the IACtHR", *EJIL Talk!*, 28 March 2018, https://www.ejiltalk.org/a-new-extraterritorial-jurisdictional-link-recognised-by-the-iacthr/.

–, "The Extraterritorial Human Rights Obligations of the EU in its External Trade and Investment Policies", *Europe and the World: A Law Review*, Vol. 2, No. 5 (2018), pp. 1-21.

Besson, S., "La pluralité d'États responsables: un état des lieux", *Revue suisse de droit international et de droit européen*, Vol. 1 (2007), pp. 13-38.

–, "General Principles in International Law: Whose Principles?", in S. Besson and P. Pichonnaz (eds.), *Les principes en droit européen / Principles in European Law* (Travaux de l'Ecole doctorale romande sur les fondements du droit européen 2010), Zurich, Schulthess, 2011, pp. 19-64.

–, "The Extra-territoriality of the European Convention on Human Rights: Why Human Rights Depend on Jurisdiction and What Jurisdiction Amounts To", *Leiden Journal of International Law*, Vol. 25, No. 4 (2012), pp. 857-884.

–, "De quelques considérations philosophiques sur la justice internationale – Ou comment dépasser l'amour impossible entre droit international et justice internationale", in S. Besson and A. R. Ziegler (eds.), *Le juge en droit international et européen / The Judge in International and European Law* (Travaux de l'Ecole doctorale romande sur les fondements du droit européen 2012), Zurich, Schulthess, 2013, pp. 15-41.

–, "La vulnérabilité et la structure des droits de l'homme – L'exemple de la jurisprudence de la Cour européenne des droits de l'homme", in L. Burgorgue-Larsen (ed.), *La vulnérabilité saisie par les juges*, Brussels, Bruylant, 2014, pp. 59-85.

–, "The Bearers of Human Rights Duties and Responsibilities for Human Rights: A Quiet (R)Evolution", *Social Philosophy & Policy*, Vol. 32, No. 1 (2015), pp. 244-268.

–, "L'extra-territorialité des droits de l'homme internationaux: juridictions concurrentes, obligations conjointes et responsabilités partagées", in P. d'Argent (ed.), *Droit des frontières internationales. Actes des Journées franco-allemandes SFDI-DGIR 2014*, Paris, Pedone, 2016, pp. 245-259.

–, "Subsidiarity in International Human Rights Law: What is Subsidiary about

Human Rights?", *American Journal of Jurisprudence*, Vol. 61, No. 1 (2016), pp. 69-107.
–, "The Sources of International Human Rights Law: How General is General International Law?", in S. Besson and J. d'Aspremont (eds.), *Oxford Handbook on the Sources of International Law*, Oxford, Oxford University Press, 2017, pp. 837-870.
–, "International Responsibility: An Introduction", in S. Besson (ed.), *International Responsibility: Essays in Law, History and Philosophy* (Travaux de l'Ecole doctorale CUS 2016), Zurich, Schulthess, 2017, pp. 3-13.
–, "Human Rights in Relation", in S. Smet (ed.), *Human Rights Conflicts*, Oxford, Oxford University Press, 2017, pp. 23-37.
–, "Individual and State Liability for an International Organization's Responsibility: The Challenge of Fairness Unveiled", in "Global Justice and International Law", special issue, *Italian Journal of Legal Philosophy*, Vol. 6, No. 1 (2017), pp. 51-78.
–, "International Legal Theory *qua* Practice of International Law", in J. d'Aspremont, A. Nollkaemper and T. Gazzini (eds.), *International Law as a Profession*, Cambridge, Cambridge University Press, 2017, pp. 268-284.
–, "Community Interests in International Law: Whose Interests Are They and How Does One Identify Them?", in E. Benvenisti and G. Nolte (eds.), *Community Interests across International Law*, Cambridge, Cambridge University Press, 2018, pp. 50-69.
–, "La responsabilité solidaire des organisations internationales et des Etats – Une institution négligée", in A. Supiot (ed.), *La responsabilité solidaire*, Paris, Publications du Collège de France, 2018, pp. 121-159.
–, "Shared Responsibilities under the ECHR: Concurrent Jurisdictions, Duties and Responsibilities", in J. Motoc and A. van Aaken (eds.), *The ECHR and General International Law*, Oxford, Oxford University Press, 2018, pp. 155-177.
–, "The Influence of the Two Covenants on States Parties across Regions: Lessons for the Role of Comparative Law and Regions in International Human Rights Law", in D. Moeckli, H. Keller and C. Heri (eds.), *The Human Rights Covenants at 50: Their Past, Present and Future*, Oxford, Oxford University Press, 2018, pp. 243-276.
–, "Comparative Law and Human Rights", in M. Reimann and R. Zimmermann (eds.), *Oxford Handbook of Comparative Law*, 2nd ed., Oxford, Oxford University Press, 2019, pp. 1222-1249.
–, "International Courts and the Jurisprudence of Statehood", *Transnational Legal Theory*, Vol. 9, Nos. 3-4 (2019), pp. 30-64.
–, "Why and What (State) Jurisdiction: Legal Plurality, Individual Equality and Territorial Legitimacy", in J. Klabbers and L. Palombella (eds.), *The Challenge of Inter-Legality*, Cambridge, Cambridge University Press, 2019, pp. 91-132.
–, "L'autorité légitime du droit international comparé: Quelques réflexions autour du *monde* et du *droit des gens* de Vico", in S. Besson and S. Jubé (eds.), *Concerter les civilisations: Mélanges en l'honneur d'Alain Supiot*, Paris, Seuil, 2020, pp. 49-60.
–, "Due Diligence and Extraterritorial Human Rights Obligations: Mind the Gap!", *ESIL Reflections*, Vol. 9, No. 1 (2020), https://esil-sedi.eu/wp-content/uploads/2020/04/ESIL-Reflection-Besson-S.-3.pdf.
–, "La *due diligence* en droit international", *Recueil des cours*, Vol. 409 (2020), pp. 153-398.
–, *Reconstruire l'ordre institutionnel international* (Leçon inaugurale), Paris, Fayard / Collège de France, 2021.
–, "Review of Francesco Lusa Bordin's *The Analogy between States and International Organizations*", *European Journal of International Law*, Vol. 31, No. 2 (2021), pp. 771-776.

– (ed.), *Theories of International Responsibility Law*, Cambridge, Cambridge University Press, 2022.

Blomeyer-Bartenstein, H., "Due Diligence", *Encyclopedia of Public International Law*, Vol. 10 (1987), pp. 138-143.

Bonafè, B. I., *The Relationship between State and Individual Responsibility for International Crimes*, Leiden, Martinus Nijhoff, 2009.

Bonnitcha, J., and R. McCorquodale, "The Concept of 'Due Diligence' in the UN Guiding Principles on Business and Human Rights", *European Journal of International Law*, Vol. 28, No. 3 (2017), pp. 899-919.

–, "The Concept of 'Due Diligence' in the UN Guiding Principles on Business and Human Rights: A Rejoinder to John Gerard Ruggie and John F. Sherman, III", *European Journal of International Law*, Vol. 28, No. 3 (2017), pp. 929-933.

Boon, K., "The United States as Good Samaritan: Immunity and Responsibility", *Chicago Journal of International Law*, Vol. 16 (2016), pp. 341-385.

Bordin, F. L., *The Analogy between States and International Organizations*, Cambridge, Cambridge University Press, 2018.

Boyle, A. E., "State Responsibility and International Liability for Injurious Consequences of Acts Not Prohibited by International Law: A Necessary Distinction?", *International and Comparative Law Quarterly*, Vol. 39 (1990), pp. 1-26.

–, "Human Rights and the Environment: Where Next?", *European Journal of International Law*, Vol. 23, No. 3 (2012), pp. 613-642.

Brölmann, C., "Sustainable Development Goal 6 as a Game Changer for International Water Law", *ESIL Reflections*, Vol. 7, No. 5 (2018), https://esil-sedi.eu/esil-reflection-sustainable-development-goal-6-as-a-game-changer-for-international-water-law/.

Brunnée, J., "Sic utere tuo ut alienum non laedas", in R. Wolfrum (ed.), *Max Planck Encyclopedia of Public International Law*, Oxford, Oxford University Press, 2010, https://opil.ouplaw.com/view/10.1093/law:epil/9780199231690/law-9780199231690-e1607?rskey=gKphMd&result=1&prd=MPIL.

–, "International Environmental Law and Community Interests: Procedural Aspects", in E. Benvenisti and G. Nolte (eds.), *Community Obligations in International Law*, Oxford, Oxford University Press, 2018, pp. 151-175.

–, "Procedure and Substance in International Environmental Law", *Recueil des cours*, Vol. 405 (2020), pp. 75-240.

Brunnée, J., and T. Meshel, "Teaching an Old Law New Tricks: International Environmental Law Lessons for Cyberspace Governance", *German Yearbook of International Law*, Vol. 58 (2015), pp. 129-168.

Campbell, E., E. Dominic, S. Stadnik and Y. Wu, "Due Diligence Obligations of International Organizations under International Law", *New York University Journal of International Law and Politics*, Vol. 50, No. 2 (2018), pp. 541-604.

Caracciolo, I., "Due diligence et droit de la mer", in SFDI (ed.), *Le standard de* due diligence *et la responsabilité internationale: Journée d'études franco-italienne du Mans*, Paris, Pedone, 2018, pp. 163-187.

Casini, L., "'Down the Rabbit-Hole': The Projection of the Public/Private Distinction Beyond the State", *International Journal of Constitutional Law*, Vol. 12, No. 2 (2014), pp. 402-428.

Cazala, J., *Le principe de précaution en droit international*, Louvain-la-Neuve, Anthemis, 2006.

Chen, L., "Realizing the Precautionary Principle in Due Diligence", *Dalhousie Journal of Legal Studies*, Vol. 25 (2016), pp. 1-24.

Chetail, V., "The Legal Personality of Multinational Corporations, State Responsibility and Due Diligence: The Way Forward", in D. Alland, V. Chetail, O. de Frouville and J. E. Viñuales (eds.), *Unité et diversité du droit international: écrits en l'honneur du Professeur Pierre-Marie Dupuy*, Leiden, Martinus Nijhoff, 2014, pp. 105-130.

Chinese Society of International Law, "The South China Sea Arbitration: A Critical Study", *Chinese Journal of International Law*, Vol. 17 (2018), pp. 207-748.
Chinkin, C., "A Critique of the Public/Private Dimension", *European Journal of International Law*, Vol. 10, No. 2 (1999), pp. 387-395.
Chircop, L., "A Due Diligence Standard of Attribution in Cyberspace", *International and Comparative Law Quarterly*, Vol. 67, No. 3 (2018), pp. 643-668.
Coco, A., and T. de Souza Dias, "Prevent, Respond, Cooperate: States' Due Diligence Duties vis-à-vis the Covid-19 Pandemic", *Journal of International Humanitarian Legal Studies*, Vol. 11, No. 2 (2020), pp. 218-236.
Cohn, M. G., "La théorie de la responsabilité internationale", *Recueil des cours*, Vol. 68 (1939), pp. 209-324.
Collins, R., and N. D. White (eds.), *International Organizations and the Idea of Autonomy: Institutional Independence in the International Legal Order*, London, Routledge, 2011.
Combacau, J., "Obligations de résultat et obligations de comportement. Quelques questions et pas de réponse", in P. Reuter (ed.), *Mélanges offerts à Paul Reuter. Le droit international: unité et diversité*, Paris, Pedone, 1981, pp. 193-198.
Contreras, J. F. L., *La noción de debida diligencia en derecho internacional público*, Barcelona, Atelier Libros Jurídicos, 2007.
Corten, O., *L'utilisation du « raisonnable » par le juge international, discours juridique, raisons et contradictions*, Brussels, Bruylant, 1997.
–, "La 'complicité' dans le droit de la responsabilité internationale: un concept inutile?", *Annuaire français de droit international*, Vol. 57 (2011), pp. 57-84.
Corten, O., and P. Klein, "The Limits of Complicity as a Ground of Responsibility: Lessons Learned from the *Corfu Channel* Case", in K. Bannelier, T. Christakis and S. Heathcote (eds.), *The ICJ and the Evolution of International Law: The Enduring Impact of the "Corfu Channel" Case*, London, Routledge, 2012, pp. 315-334.
Crawford, J., *State Responsibility: The General Part*, Cambridge, Cambridge University Press, 2013.
Crawford, J., and A. Keene, "The Structure of State Responsibility under the European Convention on Human Rights", in J. Motoc and A. van Aaken (eds.), *The ECHR and General International Law*, Oxford, Oxford University Press, 2018, pp. 178-198.
Crawford, J., and S. Olleson, "The Nature and Forms of International Responsibility", in M. Evans (ed.), *International Law*, 5th ed., Oxford, Oxford University Press, 2018, pp. 415-449.
Crawford, J., A. Pellet and S. Olleson (eds.), *The Law of International Responsibility*, Oxford, Oxford University Press, 2010.
Crawford, J., and J. Watkins, "International Responsibility", in S. Besson and J. Tasioulas (eds.), *The Philosophy of International Law*, Oxford, Oxford University Press, 2010, pp. 283-298.
Creta, A., "Implementation of the Duty of Care by the United Nations", in A. de Guttry, M. Frulli, E. Greppi and C. Macchi (eds.), *The Duty of Care of International Organizations Towards Their Civilian Personnel: Legal Obligations and Implementation Challenges*, The Hague, T.M.C. Asser Press, 2018, pp. 167-208.
D'Ambrosio, L., and P. Barraud De Lagerie, "La responsabilité des entreprises reformulée par la loi : un regard pluridisciplinaire", *Droit et société*, Vol. 3, No. 106 (2020), pp. 623-631.
D'Ambrosio, L., G. Giudicelli-Delage and S. Manacorda (eds.), *Principe de précaution et métamorphoses de la responsabilité*, Paris, Mare et Martin, 2018.
D'Argent, P., "Les principes généraux à la Cour internationale de Justice", in S. Besson and P. Pichonnaz (eds.), *Les principes en droit européen / Principles in European Law*, Zurich, Schulthess, 2011, pp. 107-120.
–, "Reparation, Cessation, Assurances and Guarantees of Non-Repetition in

Situations of Shared Responsibility", in A. Nollkaemper and I. Plakokefalos (eds.), *Principles of Shared Responsibility in International Law: An Appraisal of the State of the Art*, Cambridge, Cambridge University Press, 2014, pp. 208-250.

–, "Les obligations internationales", *Recueil des cours*, Vol. 417 (2021), pp. 27-210.

–, "Responsibility or Liability: is it that simple?", in S. Besson (ed.), *Theories of International Responsibility Law*, Cambridge, Cambridge University Press, 2022, pp. 209-228

D'Argent, P., and A. De Vaucleroy, "Le contenu de l'omission illicite: la non-utilisation de moyens raisonnables", in SFDI (ed.), *Le standard de* due diligence *et la responsabilité internationale: Journée d'études franco-italienne du Mans*, Paris, Pedone, 2018, pp. 255-279.

D'Aspremont, J., A. Nollkaemper, I. Plakokefalos and C. Ryngaert, "Sharing Responsibility Between Non-State Actors and States in International Law: Introduction", *Netherlands International Law Review*, Vol. 62 (2015), pp. 49-67.

Daugirdas, K., "Member States' Due Diligence Obligations to Supervise International Organizations", in A. Peters, H. Krieger and L. Kreuzer (eds.), *Due Diligence in International Law*, Oxford, Oxford University Press, 2020, pp. 59-74.

De Brabandère, E., "Host States' Due Diligence Obligations in International Investment Law", *Syracuse Journal of International Law and Commerce*, Vol. 42, No. 2 (2015), pp. 319-362.

Dederer, H.-G., and T. Singer, "Adverse Cyber Operations: Causality, Attribution, Evidence, and Due Diligence", *International Law Studies*, Vol. 95 (2019), pp. 431-466.

De Frouville, O., "La responsabilité des Etats pour les activités extraterritoriales des entreprises et l'interprétation de la notion de 'juridiction' par le Comité des droits de l'homme", in *Justice et Droits de l'homme. Mélanges en hommage à Christine Chanet*, Paris, Pedone, 2019, pp. 67-86.

Delerue, F., "The Codification of the International Law Applicable to Cyber Operations: A Matter for the ILC?", *ESIL Reflections*, Vol. 7, No. 4 (2018), https://esil-sedi.eu/esil-reflection-the-codification-of-the-international-law-applicable-to-cyber-operations-a-matter-for-the-ilc/.

Delibasis, D., "Cybersecurity and State Responsibility: Identifying a Due Diligence Standard for Prevention of Transboundary Threats", in J. Kulesza and R. Balleste (eds.), *Cybersecurity and Human Rights in the Age of Cybersurveillance*, Lanham, MD, Rowman & Littlefield, 2016, pp. 17-38.

Delmas-Marty, M., *Pour un droit commun*, Paris, Editions du Seuil, 1994.

–, *Résister, responsabiliser, anticiper*, Paris, Editions du Seuil, 2013.

–, *Sortir du pot au noir: l'humanisme juridique comme boussole*, Paris, Buchet-Chastel, 2019.

De Nanteuil, A., "Due diligence et investissements étrangers", in SFDI (ed.), *Le standard de* due diligence *et la responsabilité internationale: Journée d'études franco-italienne du Mans*, Paris, Pedone, 2018, pp. 93-106.

Dennerley, J. A., "State Liability for Space Object Collisions: The Proper Interpretation of 'Fault' for the Purposes of International Space Law", *European Journal of International Law*, Vol. 29, No. 1 (2018), pp. 281-301.

De Schutter, O., "Towards a New Treaty on Business and Human Rights", *Business and Human Rights Journal*, Vol. 1, No. 1 (2015), pp. 41-67.

De Schutter, O., A. Ramasastry, M. B. Taylor, and R. C. Thompson, *Human Rights Due Diligence: The Role of States*, December 2012, http://humanrightsinbusiness.eu/wp-content/uploads/2015/05/De-Schutter-et-al.-Human-Rights-Due-Diligence-The-Role-of-States.pdf.

De Vaucleroy, A., *Le droit de la responsabilité internationale à l'épreuve des obligations de comportement*, 2023 (forthcoming).

Desierto, D., "The ICESCR as a Legal Constraint on State Regulation of Business, Trade and Investment: Notes from CESCR General Comment No. 24", *EJIL Talk!*, 13 September 2017, https://www.ejiltalk.org/the-icescr-as-a-legal-constraint-on-state-regulation-of-business-trade-and-investment-notes-from-cescr-general-comment-no-24-august-2017/.

–, "COP25 Negotiations Fail: Can Climate Change Litigation, Adjudication, and/or Arbitration Compel States to Act Faster to Implement Climate Obligations?", *EJIL Talk!*, 19 December 2019, https://www.ejiltalk.org/cop25-negotiations-fail-can-climate-change-litigation-adjudication-and-or-arbitration-compel-states-to-act-faster-to-implement-climate-obligations/.

De Vattel, E., *The Law of Nations*, trans. J. Chitty (1834), Cambridge, Cambridge University Press, 2011. Originally published as *Le droit des gens* in 1758.

Dinstein, Y., "Command Responsibility", in R. Wolfrum (ed.), *Max Planck Encyclopedia of Public International Law*, Oxford, Oxford University Press, 2015, https://opil.ouplaw.com/view/10.1093/law:epil/9780199231690/law-9780199231690-e273?rskey=sSEQIG&result=1&prd=MPIL.

Dubout, E., "Procéduralisation et subsidiarité du contrôle de la Cour européenne des droits de l'homme", in F. Sudre (ed.), *Le principe de subsidiarité au sens de la Convention européenne des droits de l'homme*, Brussels, Nemesis, 2014, pp. 265-300.

Dubuisson, F., "Vers un renforcement des obligations de diligence en matière de lutte contre le terrorisme ?", in K. Bannelier, T. Christakis, O. Corten and B. Delcourt (eds.), *Le droit international face au terrorisme*, Paris, Pedone, 2002, pp. 141-157.

Dunoff, J. L., "Is Sovereign Equality Obsolete? Understanding Twenty-First Century International Organizations", *Netherlands Yearbook of International Law*, Vol. 43 (2012), pp. 99-127.

Dupuy, P.-M., "Due Diligence in the International Law of Liability", in OECD (ed.), *Legal Aspects of Transfrontier Pollution*, Paris, OECD, 1977, pp. 369-379.

–, "Reviewing the Difficulties of Codification: On Ago's Classification of Obligations of Means and Obligations of Result in Relation to State Responsibility", *European Journal of International Law*, Vol. 10 (1999), pp. 371-385.

Duvic-Paoli, L. A., *The Prevention Principle in International Environmental Law*, Cambridge, Cambridge University Press, 2018.

Duvic-Paoli, L. A., and J. E. Viñuales, "Principle 2: Prevention", in J. E. Viñuales (ed.), *The Rio Declaration on Environment and Development: A Commentary*, Oxford, Oxford University Press, 2015, pp. 107-138.

Economides, C., "Content of the Obligation: Obligation of Means and Obligations of Result", in J. Crawford, A. Pellet and S. Olleson (eds.), *The Law of International Responsibility*, Oxford, Oxford University Press, 2010, pp. 371-382.

Efrony, D., and Y. Shany, "A Rule Book on the Shelf? Tallinn Manual 2.0 on Cyberoperations and Subsequent State Practice", *American Journal of International Law*, Vol. 112, No. 4 (2018), pp. 583-657.

European Group on Tort Law, *Principles of European Tort Law*, Vienna, Springer, 2005.

Fairgrieve, D., *State Liability in Tort: A Comparative Law Study*, Oxford, Oxford University Press, 2003.

Fairgrieve, D., M. Andenas and J. Bell (eds.), *Tort Liability of Public Authorities in Comparative Perspective*, London, British Institute of International and Comparative Law, 2002.

Favre, A.-C., "La responsabilité des autorités lors de la prévention des dangers naturels", *ASPAN, Territoire et environnement*, Vol. 6 (2007), pp. 1-19.

–, "Le droit de la responsabilité de l'État: les enjeux", in A.-C. Favre, V. Martenet and E. Poltier (eds.), *La responsabilité de l'État*, Geneva, Schulthess, 2012, pp. 9-21.

Finkelstein, C., "Is Risk a Harm?", *University of Pennsylvania Law Review*, Vol. 151 (2003), pp. 963-1001.

Finnemore, M., and D. Hollis, "Beyond Naming and Shaming: Accusations and International Law in Cybersecurity", *European Journal of International Law*, Vol. 31, No. 3 (2020), pp. 969-1003.

Fitzmaurice, M. A., "Due Diligence in the Use of International Watercourses", in A. Peters, H. Krieger and L. Kreuzer (eds.), *Due Diligence in International Law*, Oxford, Oxford University Press, 2020, pp. 129-146.

Fleming, S., "Moral Agents and Legal Persons: The Ethics and the Law of State Responsibility", *International Theory*, Vol. 9, No. 3 (2017), pp. 466-489.

Forteau, M., "The Legal Nature and Content of 'Due Regard' Obligations in Recent International Case Law", *International Journal of Marine and Coastal Law*, Vol. 34, No. 1 (2019), pp. 25-42.

Foster, C., *Global Regulatory Standards in Environmental and Health Disputes: Regulatory Coherence, Due Regard and Due Diligence*, Oxford, Oxford University Press, 2021.

Fry, J. D., "Attribution of Responsibility", in A. Nollkaemper and I. Plakokefalos (eds.), *Principles of Shared Responsibility in International Law: An Appraisal of the State of the Art*, Cambridge, Cambridge University Press, 2014, pp. 98-133.

Gaja, G., "Do States Have a Duty to Ensure Compliance with Obligations *Erga Omnes* by Other States?", in M. Ragazzi (ed.), *International Responsibility Today: Essays in Memory of Oscar Schachter*, Leiden, Martinus Nijhoff, 2005, pp. 31-36.

–, "The Protection of General Interests in the International Community", *Recueil des cours*, Vol. 364 (2013), pp. 9-185.

Gardner, J., "Relations of Responsibility", in R. Cruft, M. H. Kramer and M. R. Reiff (eds.), *Crime, Punishment, and Responsibility: The Jurisprudence of Antony Duff*, Oxford, Oxford University Press, 2011, pp. 87-102.

–, "What is Tort Law For? Part 1: The Place of Corrective Justice", *Law and Philosophy*, Vol. 30 (2011), pp. 1-50.

–, "The Many Faces of the Reasonable Person", *Law Quarterly Review*, Vol. 131 (2015), pp. 563-584.

–, "The Negligence Standard: Political, Not Metaphysical", *Modern Law Review*, Vol. 80 (2017), pp. 1-21.

–, "Reasonable Person Standard", in H. LaFolette (ed.), *The International Encyclopedia of Ethics*, 2nd ed., Chichester, Wiley-Blackwell, 2019, https://onlinelibrary.wiley.com/doi/abs/10.1002/9781444367072.wbiee920#:~:text=The%20reasonable%20person%2C%20once%20known,the%20defense%20of%20provocation%20in.

–, "Tort Law and its Theory", Oxford Legal Studies Research Paper No. 2/2018. Also in J. Tasioulas (ed.), *The Cambridge Companion to the Philosophy of Law*, Cambridge, Cambridge University Press, 2020, pp. 352-370.

Gardner, J., and A. Honoré, "Causation in the Law", in N. Zalta (ed.), *The Stanford Encyclopedia of Philosophy*, Stanford, Metaphysics Research Lab, 2010, https://plato.stanford.edu/entries/causation-law/.

Gasbarri, L., "Responsabilità di un'organizzane internazionale in materie di competenza esclusiva: imputazione e obbligo di risultato secondo il Tribunale internazionale per il diritto del mare", *Rivista di diritto internazionale*, Vol. 98, No. 3 (2015), pp. 911-917.

–, "Overlapping Responsibility: The Legal Relationship between the International Organization and the Host State", in A. de Guttry, M. Frulli, E. Greppi and C. Macchi (eds.), *The Duty of Care of International Organizations Towards their Civilian Personnel: Legal Obligations and Implementation Challenges*, The Hague, T.M.C. Asser Press, 2018, pp. 103-125.

Gattini, A., "La notion de faute à la lumière du projet de convention de la Commission du Droit International sur la responsabilité internationale", *European Journal of International Law*, Vol. 3, No. 2 (1992), pp. 253-284.

–, "Smoking/No Smoking: Some Remarks on the Current Place of Fault in the ILC Draft Articles on State Responsibility", *European Journal of International Law*, Vol. 10, No. 2 (1999), pp. 397-404.
Gentili, A., *Three Books on the Law of War*, trans. J. C Rolfe, Oxford, Clarendon Press, 1933. Originally published as *De Iure [Jure] Belli Libri Tres* in 1598.
Goldshied, J., and D. J. Liebowitz, "Due Diligence and Gender Violence: Parsing its Power and its Perils", *Cornell International Law Journal*, Vol. 48 (2015), pp. 301-345.
Grans, L., "The Concept of Due Diligence and the Positive Obligation to Prevent Honour-Related Violence: Beyond Deterrence", *International Journal of Human Rights*, Vol. 22, No. 5 (2018), pp. 733-755.
Grosbon, S., "L'Observation générale n°24 du Comité des droits économiques, sociaux et culturels sur les obligations des États dans le contexte des activités des entreprises: vigilance raisonnable et extraterritorialité", *Journal européen des droits de l'homme*, Vol. 19, No. 4 (2018), pp. 355-371.
Grotius, H., *On the Laws of War and Peace*, trans. F. W. Kelsey, New York, W. S. Hein & Co., 1995. Originally published as *De jure belli ac pacis* in 1646.
Guilfoyle, D., "A New Twist in the South China Sea Arbitration: The Chinese Society of International Law's Critical Study", *EJIL Talk!*, 25 May 2018, https://www.ejiltalk.org/a-new-twist-in-the-south-china-sea-arbitration-the-chinese-society-of-international-laws-critical-study/.
Hafner, G., and I. Buffard, "Obligations of Prevention and the Precautionary Principle", in J. Crawford, A. Pellet and S. Olleson (eds.), *The Law of International Responsibility*, Oxford, Oxford University Press, 2010, pp. 521-534.
Hakimi, M., "State Bystander Responsibility", *European Journal of International Law*, Vol. 21, No. 2 (2010), pp. 341-385.
Hall, W. E., *A Treatise on International Law*, Oxford, Clarendon Press, 1880.
Heathcote, S., "State Omissions and Due Diligence: Aspects of Fault, Damage and Contribution to Injury in the Law of State Responsibility", in K. Bannelier, T. Christakis and S. Heathcote (eds.), *The ICJ and the Evolution of International Law: The Enduring Impact of the "Corfu Channel" Case*, London, Routledge, 2012, pp. 295-314.
Heieck, J., *A Duty to Prevent Genocide: Due Diligence Obligations Among the P5*, Cheltenham, Edward Elgar, 2018.
Herdegen, M., "Possible Legal Framework and Regulatory Models for Cyberspace: Due Diligence Obligations and Institutional Models for Enhanced Inter-State Cooperation", *German Yearbook of International Law*, Vol. 58 (2015), pp. 169-188.
Hessbruegge, J. A., "The Historical Development of the Doctrines of Attribution and Due Diligence in International Law", *New York University Journal of International Law and Politics*, Vol. 26, No. 2 (2004), pp. 265-306.
Hey, E., "The Precautionary Concept in Environmental Policy and Law: Institutionalizing Caution", *Georgetown International Environmental Law Review*, Vol. 4 (1992), pp. 303-318.
–, "Common but Differentiated Responsibilities", in R. Wolfrum (ed.), *Max Planck Encyclopedia of Public International Law*, Oxford, Oxford University Press, 2010, https://opil.ouplaw.com/view/10.1093/law:epil/9780199231690/law-9780199231690-e1568?rskey=swcQaQ&result=1&prd=MPIL.
Hollis, D., and M. Finnemore, "Constructing Norms for Global Cybersecurity", *American Journal of International Law*, Vol. 110 (2016), pp. 425-479.
Hovell, D., "Due Process in the United Nations", *American Journal of International Law*, Vol. 110, No. 1 (2016), pp. 1-48.
Hurd, H., "Finding No Fault with Negligence", in J. Oberdiek (ed.), *Philosophical Foundations of the Law of Torts*, Oxford, Oxford University Press, 2013, pp. 387-405.
Jackson, M., *Complicity in International Law*, Oxford, Oxford University Press, 2015.

Jacob, P., "Le contenu de la responsabilité de l'État négligent", in SFDI (ed.), *Le standard de* due diligence *et la responsabilité internationale: Journée d'études franco-italienne du Mans*, Paris, Pedone, 2018, pp. 281-296.

Jacquet, C., "Le recours à la notion de 'due diligence' par le juge international en droit de l'environnement", *L'Observateur des Nations Unies*, Vol. 34, No. 1 (2013), pp. 167-190.

Johns, F., "Theorizing the Corporation in International Law", in A. Orford and F. Hoffmann (eds.), *The Oxford Handbook of the Theory of International Law*, Oxford, Oxford University Press, 2016, pp. 635-654.

Kamminga, M. T., "Due Diligence Mania: The Misguided Introduction of an Extraneous Concept into Human Rights Discourse", in I. Westendorp (ed.), *The Women's Convention Turned 30*, Cambridge, Intersentia, 2012, pp. 407-413.

Kassoti, E., "The *Front Polisario v Council* Case: The General Court, *Völkerrechtsfreundlichkeit* and the External Aspect of European Integration", *Insight: European Papers*, Vol. 2, No. 1 (2017), pp. 339-356.

Keller, H., and R. Walther, "Evasion of the International Law of State Responsibility? The ECtHR's Jurisprudence on Positive and Preventive Obligations under Article 3", *International Journal of Human Rights*, Vol. 24, No. 7 (2019), pp. 957-978.

Kelly, E., "The Precautionary Approach in the Advisory Opinion Concerning the Responsibilities and Obligations of States Sponsoring Persons and Entities with Respect to Activities in the Area", in ITLOS (ed.), *The Contribution of the International Tribunal for the Law of the Sea to the Rule of Law: 1996-2016*, Leiden, Brill Nijhoff, 2018, pp. 45-57.

Kerbrat, Y., "Obligations procédurales et obligations de fond en droit international des dommages transfrontières", in I. Prezas (ed.), *Substance et procédure en droit international public: dialectique et influences croisées*, Paris, Pedone, 2016, pp. 7-18.

–, "Le standard de due diligence, catalyseur d'obligations conventionnelles et coutumières pour les États", in SFDI (ed.), *Le standard de* due diligence *et la responsabilité internationale: Journée d'études franco-italienne du Mans*, Paris, Pedone, 2018, pp. 27-38.

Kerbrat, Y., S. Maljean-Dubois and R. Mehdi (eds.), *Le droit international face aux enjeux environnementaux*, Paris, Pedone, 2010.

Klabbers, J., "The EJIL Foreword: The Transformation of International Organizations Law", *European Journal of International Law*, Vol. 26, No. 1 (2015), pp. 9-82.

–, *An Introduction to International Organizations Law*, 3rd ed., Cambridge, Cambridge University Press, 2015.

–, "Reflections on Role Responsibility: The Responsibility of International Organizations for Failing to Act", *European Journal of International Law*, Vol. 28, No. 4 (2017), pp. 1133-1161.

Knox, J. H., "Constructing the Human Right to a Healthy Environment", *Annual Review of Law and Social Science*, Vol. 16 (2020), pp. 79-95.

Koivurova, T., "What is the Principle of Due Diligence", in J. Petman and J. Klabbers (eds.), *Nordic Cosmopolitanism: Essays in International Law for Martti Koskenniemi*, Leiden, Martinus Nijhoff, 2003, pp. 341-349.

–, "Due Diligence", in R. Wolfrum (ed.), *Max Planck Encyclopedia of Public International Law*, Oxford, Oxford University Press, 2010, http://opil.ouplaw.com/view/10.1093/law:epil/9780199231690/law-9780199231690-e1034?rskey=7g1OSB&result=1&prd=EPIL.

Kolb, R., *La bonne foi en droit international*, Paris, Presses universitaires de France, 2001.

–, "Reflections on Due Diligence Duties and Cyberspace", *German Yearbook of International Law*, Vol. 58 (2016), pp. 113-128.

König, D., "The Elaboration of Due Diligence Obligations as a Mechanism to

Ensure Compliance with International Legal Obligations by Private Actors", in ITLOS (ed.), *The Contribution of the International Tribunal for the Law of the Sea to the Rule of Law: 1996-2016*, Leiden, Brill Nijhoff, 2018, pp. 83-95.

Kortmann, J., *Altruism in Private Law: Liability for Nonfeasance and Negotiorum Gestio*, Oxford, Oxford University Press, 2005.

Koskenniemi, M., "Peaceful Settlement of Environmental Disputes", *Nordic Journal of International Law*, Vol. 60, No. 1 (1991), pp. 73-92.

–, *The Gentle Civilizer of Nations*, Cambridge, Cambridge University Press, 2001.

–, "International Law's Futures: Yesterday, Today, Tomorrow", in R. Hoffmann and S. Kadelbach (eds.), *Law Beyond the State: Pasts and Futures*, Frankfurt, Campus Verlag, 2016, pp. 71-92.

Krajewski, M., "Due Diligence in International Trade Law", in A. Peters, H. Krieger and L. Kreuzer (eds.), *Due Diligence in International Law*, Oxford, Oxford University Press, 2020, pp. 312-328.

Kuijper, P. J., "Attribution — Responsibility — Remedy: Some Comments on the EU in Different International Regimes", *Revue belge de droit international*, Vol. 47, No. 1 (2013), pp. 57-77.

Kulesza, J., *Due Diligence in International Law*, Leiden, Brill Nijhoff, 2016.

Lagrange, E., "La responsabilité des organisations internationales pour violation d'une obligation de diligence", in SFDI (ed.), *Le standard de* due diligence *et la responsabilité internationale: Journée d'études franco-italienne du Mans*, Paris, Pedone, 2018, pp. 189-230.

Lanovoy, V., "Complicity in an Internationally Wrongful Act", in A. Nollkaemper and I. Plakokefalos (eds.), *Principles of Shared Responsibility in International Law: An Appraisal of the State of the Art*, Cambridge, Cambridge University Press, 2014, pp. 134-168.

–, *Complicity and its Limits in the Law of International Responsibility*, Oxford, Hart, 2016.

–, "The Use of Force by Non-State Actors and the Limits of Attribution of Conduct", *European Journal of International Law*, Vol. 28, No. 2 (2017), pp. 563-585.

–, "The Use of Force by Non-State Actors and the Limits of Attribution of Conduct: A Rejoinder to Ilias Plakokefalos", *European Journal of International Law*, Vol. 28, No. 2 (2017), pp. 595-599.

Lauterpacht, H., *Private Law Sources and Analogies of International Law*, reprint, Clark, NJ, The Lawbook Exchange, 2013. Originally published in 1927.

Lavrysen, L., "Protection by the Law: The Positive Obligation to Develop a Legal Framework to Adequately Protect the ECHR Rights", in E. Brems and Y. Haeck (eds.), *Human Rights and Civil Liberties in the 21st Century*, Dordrecht, Springer, 2014, pp. 69-84.

–, *Human Rights in a Positive State*, Antwerp, Intersentia, 2016.

–, "Causation and Positive Obligations under the European Convention on Human Rights: A Reply to Vladislava Stoyanova", *Human Rights Law Review*, Vol. 18 (2018), pp. 705-718.

Le Floch, G., "Responsibility for Human Rights Violations by International Organizations", in B. Virzo and I. Ingravallo (eds.), *Evolutions in the Law of International Organizations*, Leiden, Brill Nijhoff, 2015, p. 381-405.

Leme, R., "Individual Criminal Liability and State Responsibility for Genocide: Boundaries and Intersections", *American University International Law Review*, Vol. 34, No. 1 (2018), pp. 89-142.

Letsas, G., "Rescuing Proportionality", in R. Cruft, S. M. Liao and M. Renzo (eds.), *Philosophical Foundations of Human Rights*, Oxford, Oxford University Press, pp. 316-340.

Longobardo, M., "The Relevance of the Concept of Due Diligence for International Humanitarian Law", *Wisconsin International Law Journal*, Vol. 37, No. 1 (2019), pp. 44-87.

–, "Due Diligence in International Humanitarian Law", in A. Peters, H. Krieger and L. Kreuzer (eds.), *Due Diligence in International Law*, Oxford, Oxford University Press, 2020, pp. 183-199.

Lévy, D., "La responsabilité pour omission et la responsabilité pour risque en droit international public", *Revue générale de droit international public*, Vol. 65 (1961), pp. 744-764.

Mackie, J. L., *The Cement of the Universe: A Study of Causation*, Oxford, Oxford University Press, 1980.

Maljean-Dubois, S., "Les obligations de diligence dans la pratique: la protection de l'environnement", in SFDI (ed.), *Le standard de* due diligence *et la responsabilité internationale: Journée d'études franco-italienne du Mans*, Paris, Pedone, 2018, pp. 145-162.

Marrella, F., "Protection internationale des droits de l'homme et activités des sociétés transnationales", *Recueil des cours*, Vol. 385 (2017), pp. 33-435.

Martin-Chenut, K., "Les mécanismes conventionnels de prévention des violations des droits de l'homme au niveau universel", in E. Decaux and S. Touzé (eds.), *La prévention des violations des droits de l'homme*, Paris, Pedone, 2015, pp. 61-89.

Mayer, B., "The Relevance of the No-Harm Principle to Climate Change Law and Politics", *Asia-Pacific Journal of Environmental Law*, Vol. 19 (2016), pp. 79-104.

Mbengue, M. M., *Essai sur une théorie du risque en droit international public: L'anticipation du risque environnemental et sanitaire*, Paris, Pedone, 2009.

–, "The South China Sea Arbitration: Innovations in Marine Environmental Fact-Finding and Due Diligence Obligations", *American Journal of International Law*, Vol. 110 (2016), pp. 285-289.

McDonald, N., "The Role of Due Diligence in International Law", *International and Comparative Law Quarterly*, Vol. 68, No. 4 (2019), pp. 1041-1054.

Mettraux, G., *The Law of Command Responsibility*, Oxford, Oxford University Press, 2009.

Michalowski, S., "Due Diligence and Complicity: A Relationship in Need of Clarification", in S. Deva and D. Bilchitz (eds.), *Human Rights Obligations of Business: Beyond the Corporate Responsibility to Respect?*, Cambridge, Cambridge University Press, 2013, pp. 218-242.

Milanovic, M., *Extraterritorial Application of Human Rights Treaties: Law, Principles, and Policy*, Oxford, Oxford University Press, 2011.

–, "State Acquiescence or Connivance in the Wrongful Conduct of Third Parties in the Jurisprudence of the European Court of Human Rights (September 15, 2019)", 2019, https://papers.ssrn.com/sol3/papers.cfm?abstract_id=3454007.

Møgster, D., "Towards Universality: Activities Impacting the Enjoyment of the Right to Life and the Extraterritorial Application of the ICCPR", *EJIL Talk!*, 27 November 2018, https://www.ejiltalk.org/towards-universality-activities-impacting-the-enjoyment-of-the-right-to-life-and-the-extraterritorial-application-of-the-iccpr/.

Monnheimer, M., *Due Diligence Obligations in International Human Rights Law*, Cambridge, Cambridge University Press, 2021.

Mowbray, A., *The Development of Positive Obligations under the European Convention on Human Rights by the European Court of Human Rights*, Oxford, Hart, 2004.

Moynihan, H., "Aiding and Assisting: The Mental Element under Article 16 of the International Law Commission's Articles on State Responsibility", *International and Comparative Law Quarterly*, Vol. 67 (2018), pp. 455-471.

Ney, M., and A. Zimmermann, "Cyber-Security beyond the Military Perspective: International Law, Cyberspace, and the Concept of Due Diligence", *German Yearbook of International Law*, Vol. 58 (2015), pp. 51-66.

Nolan, D., "Deconstructing the Duty of Care", *Law Quarterly Review*, Vol. 129 (2013), pp. 559-588.

–, “Negligence and Human Rights Law: The Case for Separate Development”, *Modern Law Review*, Vol. 76, No. 2 (2013), pp. 286-318.

Nollkaemper, A., “The ECtHR Finds Macedonia Responsible in Connection with Torture by the CIA, but on What Basis?”, *EJIL Talk!*, 24 December 2012, https://www.ejiltalk.org/the-ecthr-finds-macedonia-responsible-in-connection-with-torture-by-the-cia-but-on-what-basis/.

–, “Introduction”, in A. Nollkaemper and I. Plakokefalos (eds.), *Principles of Shared Responsibility in International Law: An Appraisal of the State of the Art*, Cambridge, Cambridge University Press, 2014, pp. 1-24.

–, “Responsibility”, in J. d’Aspremont and S. Singh (eds.), *Concepts for International Law: Contributions to Disciplinary Thought*, Cheltenham, Edward Elgar, 2019, pp. 760-772.

Nollkaemper, A., and L. Burgers, “A New Classic in Climate Change Litigation: The Dutch Supreme Court Decision in the Urgenda Case”, *EJIL Talk!*, 6 January 2020, https://www.ejiltalk.org/a-new-classic-in-climate-change-litigation-the-dutch-supreme-court-decision-in-the-urgenda-case/.

Nollkaemper, A., J. d’Aspremont, C. Ahlborn, B. Boutin, N. Nedeski and I. Plakokefalos, “Guiding Principles on Shared Responsibility in International Law”, *European Journal of International Law*, Vol. 31, No. 1 (2020), pp. 15-72.

Oberdiek, J., “The Moral Significance of Risking”, *Legal Theory*, Vol. 18 (2012), pp. 339–356.

Obreja, L.-D., “Human Rights Law and Intimate Partner Violence: Towards an Intersectional Development of Due Diligence Obligations”, *Nordic Journal of Human Rights*, Vol. 37, No. 1 (2019), pp. 63-80.

O’Donoghue, A., “The Exercise of Governance Authority by International Organisations: The Role of Due Diligence Obligations after Conflict”, in M. Saul and J. A. Sweeney (eds.), *International Law and Post-Conflict Reconstruction Policy*, London, Routledge, 2015, pp. 45-65.

Oliphant, K., “The Liability of Public Authorities in Comparative Perspective”, in K. Oliphant (ed.), *The Liability of Public Authorities in Comparative Perspective*, Cambridge, Intersentia, 2016, pp. 847-887.

Ollino, A., *Due Diligence Obligations under International Law*, Cambridge, Cambridge University Press, 2022.

–, “Human Rights in Transboundary Contexts: Some Critical Remarks over the Emergence of an ‘Effects Jurisdiction’ Model in International Human Rights Law”, *European Journal of International Law* (2023) (forthcoming).

Oppenheim, L., *International Law: A Treatise*, 1st ed., London, Longmans, 1905, Vol. I.

Ouedraogo, A., “La neutralité et l’émergence du concept de *due diligence* en droit international: l’affaire de l’Alabama revisitée”, *Journal of the History of International Law*, Vol. 13, No. 2 (2011), pp. 307-346.

–, “La *due diligence* en droit international: de la règle de la neutralité au principe général”, *Revue générale de droit*, Vol. 42, No. 2 (2012), pp. 641-683.

Pacholska, M., *Complicity and the Law of International Organizations*, London, Edward Elgar, 2020.

Palchetti, P., “La violation par l’Union européenne d’une obligation de due diligence”, in SFDI (ed.), *Le standard de* due diligence *et la responsabilité internationale: Journée d’études franco-italienne du Mans*, Paris, Pedone, 2018, pp. 231-242.

Palmisano, G., “Fault”, in R. Wolfrum (ed.), *Max Planck Encyclopedia of Public International Law*, Oxford, Oxford University Press, 2007, https://opil.ouplaw.com/view/10.1093/law:epil/9780199231690/law-9780199231690-e1955?rskey=LC6GTF&result=2&prd=EPIL.

Palombo, D., “The Duty of Care of the Parent Company: A Comparison between French Law, UK Precedents and the Swiss Proposals”, *Business and Human Rights Journal*, Vol. 4, No. 2 (2019), pp. 265-286.

Papanicolopulu, I., "Due Diligence in the Law of the Sea", in A. Peters, H. Krieger and L. Kreuzer (eds.), *Due Diligence in International Law*, Oxford, Oxford University Press, 2020, pp. 147-162.

Pellet, A., "The Definition of Responsibility in International Law", in J. Crawford, A. Pellet and S. Olleson (eds.), *The Law of International Responsibility*, Oxford, Oxford University Press, 2010, pp. 3-16.

–, "The ILC's Articles on State Responsibility for Internationally Wrongful Acts and Related Texts", in J. Crawford, A. Pellet and S. Olleson (eds.), *The Law of International Responsibility*, Oxford, Oxford University Press, 2010, pp. 75-94.

Perry, S., "The Impossibility of General Strict Liability", *Canadian Journal of Law & Jurisprudence*, Vol. 1, No. 2 (1988), pp. 147-171.

–, "The Role of the Duty of Care in a Rights-Based Theory of Tort Law", in A. Robertson and T. Hang Wu (eds.), *The Goals of Private Law*, Oxford, Hart, 2009, pp. 79-112.

–, "Torts, Rights, and Risk", in J. Oberdiek (ed.), *Philosophical Foundations of the Law of Torts*, Oxford, Oxford University Press, 2014, pp. 38-64.

Peters, A., H. Krieger and L. Kreuzer (eds.), *Due Diligence in International Law*, Oxford, Oxford University Press, 2020.

Pisillo Mazzeschi, R., *Due Diligence e responsabilità internazionale degli Stati*, Milan, Giuffrè, 1989.

–, "The Due Diligence Rule and the Nature of the International Responsibility of States", *German Yearbook of International Law*, Vol. 35 (1992), pp. 9-51.

–, "Responsabilité de l'État pour violation des obligations positives relatives aux droits de l'homme", *Recueil des cours*, Vol. 333 (2008), pp. 175-506.

–, "Le chemin étrange de la due diligence: d'un concept mystérieux à un concept surévalué", in SFDI (ed.), *Le standard de* due diligence *et la responsabilité internationale: Journée d'études franco-italienne du Mans*, Paris, Pedone, 2018, pp. 323-338.

Plakokefalos, I., "Prevention Obligations in International Environmental Law", *Yearbook of International Environmental Law*, Vol. 23, No. 1 (2012), pp. 3-43.

–, "Causation in the Law of State Responsibility and the Problem of Overdetermination: In Search of Clarity", *European Journal of International Law*, Vol. 26, No. 2 (2015), pp. 471-492.

–, "The Use of Force by Non-State Actors and the Limits of Attribution of Conduct: A Reply to Vladyslav Lanovoy", *European Journal of International Law*, Vol. 28, No. 2 (2017), pp. 587-593.

Popovski, V., "State Negligence before and after Natural Disasters as Human Rights Violations", in C. Hobson, P. Bacon and R. Cameron (eds.), *Human Security and Natural Disasters*, London, Routledge, 2014, pp. 94-110.

Pyhälä, M., A. C. Brusendorff and H. Paulomäki, "The Precautionary Principle", in M. Fitzmaurice, D. M. Ong and P. Merkouris (eds.), *Research Handbook on International Environmental Law*, Cheltenham, Edward Elgar, 2010, pp. 203-226.

Radi, Y., *La standardisation internationale. Contours d'une théorie dialectique de la formation du droit*, Brussels, Larcier, 2013.

Rajamani, L., "Due Diligence in International Climate Change Law", in A. Peters, H. Krieger and L. Kreuzer (eds.), *Due Diligence in International Law*, Oxford, Oxford University Press, 2020, pp. 163-182.

Rajput, A., "Due Diligence in International Investment Law: From the Law of Aliens to Responsible Investment", in A. Peters, H. Krieger and L. Kreuzer (eds.), *Due Diligence in International Law*, Oxford, Oxford University Press, 2020, pp. 273-287.

Raspail, H., "Due diligence et droits de l'homme", in SFDI (ed.), *Le standard de* due diligence *et la responsabilité internationale: Journée d'études franco-italienne du Mans*, Paris, Pedone, 2018, pp. 107-134.

Raz, J., *The Practice of Value*, Oxford, Clarendon Press, 2003.

–, "Responsibility and the Negligence Standard", *Oxford Journal of Legal Studies*, Vol. 30 (2010), pp. 1-18.
–, *From Normativity to Responsibility*, Oxford, Oxford University Press, 2011.
Regan, D., "International Adjudication: A Response to Paulus – Courts, Custom, Treaties, Regimes, and the WTO", in S. Besson and J. Tasioulas (eds.), *The Philosophy of International Law*, Oxford, Oxford University Press, 2010, pp. 225-244.
Renold, M.-A., "The International Scope of Application of the Swiss Rules on the Due Diligence of Dealers in Cultural Property", in K. Boele-Woelki, T. Einhorn, D. Girsberger and S. Symeonides (eds.), *Convergence and Divergence in Private International Law: Liber Amicorum Kurt Siehr*, Zurich, Schulthess, 2010, pp. 847-856.
Reuter, P., *Institution internationales*, 4th ed., Paris, Presses universitaires de France, 1963.
Ruggie, J. G., "Multinationals as Global Institution: Power, Authority and Relative Autonomy", *Regulation & Governance*, Vol. 12 (2018), pp. 317-333.
Ruggie, J. G., and J. F. Sherman, "The Concept of 'Due Diligence' in the UN Guiding Principles on Business and Human Rights: A Reply to Jonathan Bonnitcha and Robert McCorquodale", *European Journal of International Law*, Vol. 28, No. 3 (2017), pp. 921-928.
Ryngaert, C. M. J., *Jurisdiction in International Law*, 2nd ed., Oxford, Oxford University Press, 2015.
Ryngaert, C. M. J., and R. Fransen, "EU Extraterritorial Obligations with Respect to Trade with Occupied Territories: Reflections after the Case of Front Polisario before EU Courts", *Europe in the World: A Law Review*, Vol. 2, No. 1 (2018), pp. 1-20.
Salmon, J., *Dictionnaire de droit international public*, Brussels, Bruylant, 2001.
Samuel, K. L. H., M. Aronsson-Storrier and K. Nakjavani Bookmiller (eds.), *The Cambridge Handbook of Disaster Risk Reduction and International Law*, Cambridge, Cambridge University Press, 2019.
Schmitt, M. N., "In Defense of Due Diligence in Cyberspace", *Yale Law Journal Forum*, Vol. 125 (2015), pp. 6881.
Schmitt, M. N., and L. Vihul (eds.), *Tallinn Manual 2.0 on the International Law Applicable to Cyber Operations, Prepared by the International Groups of Experts at the Invitation of the NATO Cooperative Cyber Defence Centre of Excellence*, 2nd ed., Cambridge, Cambridge University Press, 2017.
Schröder, M., "Precautionary Approach/Principle", in R. Wolfrum (ed.), *Max Planck Encyclopedia of Public International Law*, Oxford, Oxford University Press, 2014, https://opil.ouplaw.com/view/10.1093/law:epil/9780199231690/law-9780199231690-e1603?rskey=f1F1XO&result=1&prd=MPIL.
Seibert-Fohr, A., "From Complicity to Due Diligence: When Do States Incur Responsibility for their Involvement in Serious International Wrongdoing?", *German Yearbook of International Law*, Vol. 60 (2018), pp. 667-707.
Seršić, M., "Due Diligence: Fault-Based Responsibility or Autonomous Standard?", in R. Wolfrum, M. Seršić and T. M. Šošić (eds.), *Contemporary Developments in International Law: Essays in Honour of Budislav Vukas*, Leiden, Brill Nijhoff, 2016, pp. 151-172.
SFDI (ed.), *Les collectivités territoriales non étatiques dans le système juridique international*, Paris, Pedone, 1997.
– (ed.), *Le standard de* due diligence *et la responsabilité internationale: Journée d'études franco-italienne du Mans*, Paris, Pedone, 2018.
Shackelford, S. J., S. Russell and A. Kuehn, "Unpacking the International Law on Cybersecurity Due Diligence: Lessons from the Public and Private Sectors", *Chicago Journal of International Law*, Vol. 17, No. 1 (2016), pp. 1-50.
Shiffrin, S., "Enhancing Moral Relationships Through Strict Liability", *University of Toronto Law Journal*, Vol. 66, No. 3 (2016), pp. 353-379.
–, "The Moral Neglect of Negligence", in D. Sobel, P. Vallentyne and

S. Wall (eds.), *Oxford Studies in Political Philosophy*, Vol. 3, Oxford, Oxford University Press, 2017, pp. 197-228.

Sinclair, G. F., *To Reform the World: The Legal Powers of International Organizations and the Making of Modern States*, Oxford, Oxford University Press, 2017.

Smit, L. *et al.*, *Study on Due Diligence Requirements through the Supply Chain: Final Report*, January 2020, https://op.europa.eu/en/publication-detail/-/publication/8ba0a8fd-4c83-11ea-b8b7-01aa75ed71a1/language-en.

Smits, J. M., *The Good Samaritan in European Private Law: On the Perils of Principles Without a Programme and a Programme for the Future*, Deventer, Kluwer, 2000.

Starita, M., "Négligence illicite et responsabilités multiples: partage ou cumul de responsabilités ?", in SFDI (ed.), *Le standard de* due diligence *et la responsabilité internationale: Journée d'études franco-italienne du Mans*, Paris, Pedone, 2018, pp. 297-321.

Stern, B., "The Obligation to Make Reparation", in J. Crawford, S. Olleson and A. Pellet (eds.), *The Law of International Responsibility*, Oxford, Oxford University Press, 2010, pp. 563-571.

Stoyanova, V., "Causation between State Omission and Harm within the Framework of Positive Obligations under the ECHR", *Human Rights Law Review*, Vol. 18 (2018), pp. 309-346.

–, "Common Law Tort of Negligence as a Tool for Deconstructing Positive Obligations under the European Convention on Human Rights", *International Journal of Human Rights*, Vol. 24, No. 5 (2020), pp. 632-655.

–, "Due Diligence versus Positive Obligations: Critical Reflections on the Council of Europe Convention on Violence against Women", in J. Niemi, L. Peroni and V. Stoyanova (eds.), *International Law and Violence Against Women: Europe and the Istanbul Convention*, London, Routledge, 2020, pp. 95-129.

Strydom, H., "The Due Diligence Principle in International Law and its Relevance for Climate Change Law", in V. Sancin (ed.), *International Environmental Law: Contemporary Concerns and Challenges*, Ljubljana, Založba, 2012, pp. 279-300.

Supiot, A., "L'inscription territoriale des lois", *Esprit*, Vol. 11 (2008), pp. 151-170.

–, "The Public-Private Relation in the Context of Today's Refeudalization", *International Journal of Constitutional Law*, Vol. 11, No. 1 (2013), pp. 129-145.

–, "Etat, Entreprise et Démocratie", in P. Musso (ed.), *L'entreprise contre l'Etat?*, Paris, Manucius / IEA de Nantes, 2017, pp. 13-31.

–, *La gouvernance par les nombres, cours au Collège du France (2012-2014)*, Paris, Fayard, 2018.

Takano, A., "Due Diligence Obligations and Transboundary Environmental Harm: Cybersecurity Applications", *Laws*, Vol. 7, No. 4 (2018), pp. 1-12.

Talbot Jensen, E., "Due Diligence in Cyber Activities", in A. Peters, H. Krieger and L. Kreuzer (eds.), *Due Diligence in International Law*, Oxford, Oxford University Press, 2020, pp. 252-272.

Talbot Jensen, E., and S. Watts, "A Cyber Duty of Due Diligence: Gentle Civilizer or Crude Destabilizer?", *Texas Law Review*, Vol. 95 (2017), pp. 1555-1577.

Tams, C. J., "The Development of International Law by the International Court of Justice", in *Decisions of the ICJ as Sources of International Law?*, Rome, International and European Papers, 2018, pp. 63-106, http://crde.unitelmasapienza.it/sites/default/files/GMLS_2_2018_3_CTams.pdf.

Tran, H., *Les obligations de vigilance des États parties à la Convention européenne des droits de l'homme: Essai sur la transposition en droit européen des droits de l'homme d'un concept de droit international général*, Brussels, Bruylant, 2013.

Triepel, H., "Les rapports entre le droit interne et le droit international", *Recueil des cours*, Vol. 1 (1923), pp. 73-121.

Trouwborst, A., "Prevention, Precaution, Logic and Law: The Relationship between the Precautionary Principle and the Preventive Principle in International Law and Associated Questions", *Erasmus Law Review*, Vol. 2, No. 2 (2009), pp. 105-127.

Tzevelekos, V., "Reconstructing the Effective Control Criterion in Extraterritorial Human Rights Breaches: Direct Attribution of Wrongfulness, Due Diligence, and Concurrent Responsibility", *Michigan Journal of International Law*, Vol. 36, No. 1 (2014), pp. 129-178.

Urueña, R., "Law-Making Through Comparative International Law?", in R. Livoja and J. Petman (eds.), *International Law-Making: Essays in Honour of Jan Klabbers*, London, Routledge, 2014, pp. 149-68.

Van Dam, C., *European Tort Law*, 2nd ed., Oxford, Oxford University Press, 2013.

Van den Herik, L., and E. Irving, "Due Diligence and the Obligation to Prevent Genocide and Crimes Against Humanity", in A. Peters, H. Krieger and L. Kreuzer (eds.), *Due Diligence in International Law*, Oxford, Oxford University Press, 2020, pp. 200-216.

Van Loon, H., "Principles and Building Blocks for a Global Legal Framework for Transnational Civil Litigation in Environmental Matters", *Uniform Law Review*, Vol. 23, No. 2 (2018), p. 298-318.

Venturini, G., "Les obligations de diligence dans le droit international humanitaire", in SFDI (ed.), *Le standard de* due diligence *et la responsabilité internationale: Journée d'études franco-italienne du Mans*, Paris, Pedone, 2018, pp. 135-144.

Verdross, A., "Règles internationales concernant le traitement des étrangers", *Recueil des cours*, Vol. 37 (1931), pp. 323-412.

Vidak-Goljevic, E., C. Blair and M.-A. Meudic Role, "The Medium is the Message: Establishing a System of Business and Human Rights Through Contract Law and Arbitration", *Journal of International Arbitration*, Vol. 35, No. 4 (2018), pp. 379-412.

Viñuales, J. E., "A Human Rights Approach to Extraterritorial Environmental Protection: An Assessment", in N. Bhuta (ed.), *The Frontiers of Human Rights*, Oxford, Oxford University Press, 2016, pp. 177-222.

–, "Due Diligence in International Environmental Law: A Fine-Grained Cartography", in A. Peters, H. Krieger and L. Kreuzer (eds.), *Due Diligence in International Law*, Oxford, Oxford University Press, 2020, pp. 111-128.

Violi, F., "The Function of the Triad 'Territory', 'Jurisdiction' and 'Control', in Due Diligence Obligations", in A. Peters, H. Krieger and L. Kreuzer (eds.), *Due Diligence in International Law*, Oxford, Oxford University Press, 2020, pp. 75-91.

Von Bar, C., *The Common European Law of Torts*, Vol. 2, Oxford, Oxford University Press, 2000.

Von Bar, C., E. Clive and H. Schulte-Nölke (eds.), *Draft Common Frame of Reference, Prepared by the Study Group on a European Civil Code and the European Research Group on Existing EC Private Law (Acquis Group) Based in part on a revised version of the Principles of European Contract Law*, Munich, Sellier, 2009, https://www.law.kuleuven.be/personal/mstorme/2009_02_DCFR_OutlineEdition.pdf.

Waldron, J., *"Partly Laws Common to All Mankind": Foreign Law in American Courts*, New Haven, CT, Yale University Press, 2012.

Webb, P., "Binocular Vision: State Responsibility and Individual Criminal Responsibility for Genocide", in L. van den Herik and C. Stahn (eds.), *The Diversification and Fragmentation of International Criminal Law*, Leiden, Martinus Nijhoff, 2012, pp. 117-148.

Weiss, E. B., "Intergenerational Equity", in R. Wolfrum (ed.), *Max Planck Encyclopedia of Public International Law*, Oxford, Oxford University Press, 2013, https://opil.ouplaw.com/view/10.1093/law:epil/9780199231690/law-9780199231690-e1421?rskey=oFJpbJ&result=1&prd=MPIL.

White, N. D., "Due Diligence Obligations of Conduct: Developing a Responsibility Regime for PMSCs", *Criminal Justice Ethics*, Vol. 31, No. 3 (2012), pp. 233-261.

–, "Due Diligence, the UN and Peacekeeping", in A. Peters, H. Krieger and L. Kreuzer (eds.), *Due Diligence in International Law*, Oxford, Oxford University Press, 2020, pp. 217-233.

Wijffels, A. A., *Le droit européen a-t-il une histoire ? En a-t-il besoin ?* (Leçon inaugurale), Paris, Fayard/Collège de France, 2017.

Wolff, C., *Principes du droit de la nature et des gens*, trans. J.-H.-S. Formey (1758), Caen, Presses Universitaires de Caen, 2012. Originally published *Jus naturae* in 1740-1748.

Wright, R. W., "Causation in Tort Law", *California Law Review*, Vol. 73 (1985), pp. 1737-1828.

–, "The NESS Account of Natural Causation: A Response to Criticisms", in B. Kahmen and M. S. Stepanians (eds.), *Critical Essays on "Causation and Responsibility"*, Berlin, De Gruyter, 2013, pp. 13-66.

Wyler, E., "From State Crime to Responsibility for Serious Breaches of Obligations under Peremptory Norms of General International Law", *European Journal of International Law*, Vol. 13, No. 5 (2002), pp. 1147-1160.

Yotova, R., "The Principles of Due Diligence and Prevention in International Environmental Law", *Cambridge Law Journal*, Vol. 75, No. 3 (2016), pp. 445-448.

Zannas, P. A., *La responsabilité internationale des États pour des actes de négligence*, Montreux, Ganguin & Laubscher, 1952.

Zimmermann, R., *The Law of Obligations: Roman Foundations of the Civilian Tradition*, Oxford, Clarendon Press, 1996.

Zorzi Giustiniani, F., "Something Old, Something New: Disaster Risk Reduction in International Law", *Questions of International Law, Zoom-in*, Vol. 49 (2018), pp. 7-27.

Official documents

International Law Commission

ILC, Draft Declaration on Rights and Duties of States, *Yearbook of the International Law Commission*, Vol. 1 (1949), pp. 286-290.

ILC, Second Report on State Responsibility, by Mr James Crawford, Special Rapporteur, 17 March 1999, UN Doc. A/CN.4/498.

ILC, Draft Articles on Prevention of Transboundary Harm from Hazardous Activities, with commentaries, *Yearbook of the International Law Commission*, Vol. II, Part 2 (2001), pp. 157-183.

ILC, Draft Articles on the Responsibility of States for Internationally Wrongful Acts, 12 December 2001, as it appears in the General Assembly Resolution A/RES/56/83.

ILC, Draft Articles on the Responsibility of States for Internationally Wrongful Acts, with commentaries, *Yearbook of the International Law Commission*, Vol. II, Part 2 (2001), pp. 26-154.

ILC, Draft Principles on the Allocation of Loss in the Case of Transboundary Harm out of Hazardous Activities, *Yearbook of the International Law Commission*, Vol. II, Part 2 (2006), pp. 59-95.

ILC, Draft Articles on the Responsibility of International Organizations, 9 November 2011, adopted and submitted to the General Assembly.

ILC, Draft Articles on the Responsibility of International Organizations, with commentaries, *Yearbook of the International Law Commission*, Vol. II, Part 2 (2011), pp. 46-105.

ILC, Draft Articles on the Protection of Persons in the Event of Disasters, *Yearbook of the International Law Commission*, Vol. II, Part 2 (2016), pp. 12-16.

ILC, Draft Principles on the Protection of the Environment in Relation to Armed

Conflict, *Yearbook of the International Law Commission*, Vol. II, Part. 2 (2019), pp. 221-316.

International Law Association

ILA, Committee on the Accountability of International Organisations, Final Report, Berlin Conference (2004), https://ila.vettoreweb.com/Storage/Download.aspx?DbStorageId=1058&StorageFileGuid=04c9caf1-2834-4490-9125-7d9ba3683246.

ILA, Study Group on Due Diligence in International Law, First Rapport, Duncan French (Chair) and Tim Stephens (Rapporteur), 7 March 2014, https://olympereseauinternational.files.wordpress.com/2015/07/due_diligence_-_first_report_2014.pdf.

ILA, Committee on the Legal Principles relating to Climate Change, Declaration of Legal Principles Relating to Climate Change (Resolution 2/2014), 7-11 April 2014, https://ila.vettoreweb.com/Storage/Download.aspx?DbStorageId=1253&StorageFileGuid=f93d2f56-5629-40aa-a940-34c7da6e8545.

ILA, Study Group on Due Diligence in International Law, Second Rapport, Duncan French (Chair) and Tim Stephens (Rapporteur), July 2016, https://ila.vettoreweb.com/Storage/Download.aspx?DbStorageId=1427&StorageFileGuid=ed229726-4796-47f2-b891-8cafa221685f.

Institute of International Law

IIL, Resolution "International Responsibility of States for Injuries on their Territory to the Person or Property of Foreigners", Leo Strisower (Rapporteur), 1 September 1927.

United Nations General Assembly

Group of Governmental Experts on Developments in the Field of Information and Telecommunications in the Context of International Security, 22 July 2015, UN Doc. A/70/173, https://undocs.org/fr/a/70/174.

Group of Governmental Experts on Advancing Responsible State Behaviour in Cyberspace in the Context of International Security, 14 July 2021, UN Doc. A/76/135, https://documents-dds-ny.un.org/doc/UNDOC/GEN/N21/075/86/PDF/N2107586.pdf?OpenElement.

Secretary-General of the United Nations

Secretary-General of the United Nations, Human Rights Due Diligence Policy on United Nations Support to non-United Nations Security Forces, Annex to the identical letters dated 25 February 2013 addressed to the President of the General Assembly and to the President of the Security Council, 5 March 2013, UN Doc. A/67/775-S/2013/110, https://undocs.org/fr/A/67/775.

Human Rights Council

HRC, Guiding Principles on Business and Human Rights: Implementing the United Nations "Protect, Respect and Remedy" Framework, 16 June 2011, UN Doc. HR/PUB/11/04, https://www.ohchr.org/documents/publications/guidingprinciplesbusinesshr_en.pdf.

OEIGWG, Revised Draft Legally Binding Instrument to Regulate, in International Human Rights Law, the Activities of Transnational Corporations and others Business Enterprises, 17 August 2021, https://www.ohchr.org/sites/default/files/LBI3rdDRAFT.pdf.

Human Rights Committee

CCPR, General Comment No. 36 on Article 6 of the International Covenant on Civil and Political Rights, on the right to life, 3 September 2019, UN Doc. CCPR/C/GC/36.

Committee on Economic, Social and Cultural Rights

CESCR, General Comment No. 24 on State obligations under the International Covenant on Economic, Social and Cultural Rights in the context of business activities, 10 August 2017, UN Doc. E/C.12/GC/24.

Committee Against Torture

CAT, General Comment No. 4 on the implementation of Article 3 of the Convention in the context of Article 22, 4 September 2018, UN Doc. CAT/C/GC/4.

Organization for Economic Co-operation and Development

OECD, Guidelines for Multinational Enterprises, 2011 Edition, https://www.oecd-ilibrary.org/governance/oecd-guidelines-for-multinational-enterprises_9789264115415-en.

Miscellaneous

Council of Europe, Explanatory Report to the Council of Europe Convention in Preventing and Combating Violence Against Women and Domestic Violence, 11 May 2011, https://rm.coe.int/16800d383a, https://rm.coe.int/16800d38c9.

European Commission, Corporate Social Responsibility, Responsible Business Conduct, and Business & Human Rights. – Overview of Progress, March 2019, https://ec.europa.eu/docsroom/documents/34963.

French Commercial Code (Ccom/FR), introduced by the French law No. 2017-399 on the "vigilance duty" of parent companies of 27 March 2017, https://www.legifrance.gouv.fr/affichTexte.do?cidTexte=JORFTEXT000034290626.

Government of Canada, International Law applicable in cyberspace, 22 April 2022, https://www.international.gc.ca/world-monde/issues_development-enjeux_developpement/peace_security-paix_securite/cyberspace_law-cyberespace_droit.aspx?lang=eng#a5.

G7, Declaration on Responsible States Behavior in Cyberspace, Lucca (Italy), 11 April 2017, https://www.mofa.go.jp/files/000246367.pdf.

IPCC, B. Metz, O. R. Davidson, P. R. Bosch, R. Dave and L. A. Meyer (eds.), Cimate Change 2007: Mitigation. Contribution of Working Group III to the ourth Assessment Report of the Inter-governmental Panel on Climate Change, Cambridge / New York, Cambridge University Press, 2007, https://www.ipcc.ch/site/assets/uploads/2018/03/ar4_wg3_full_report-1.pdf.

Ministère français de l'Europe et des Affaires étrangères, Appel de Paris pour la confiance et la sécurité dans le cyberespace, 12 November 2018, https://pariscall.international/assets/files/appel-de-paris.pdf.

Ministère français des Armées, Droit international appliqué aux opérations dans le cyberespace, 2019, https://www.defense.gouv.fr/content/download/565895/9750877/file/Droit+internat+appliqu%C3%A9+aux+op%C3%A9rations+Cyberespace.pdf.

Modern Slavery Act 2015 of the United Kingdom of 26 March 2015, http://www.legislation.gov.uk/ukpga/2015/30/contents/enacted/data.htm.

Smith, B., President of Microsoft, "The Need for a Digital Geneva Convention", 14 February 2017, https://blogs.microsoft.com/on-the-issues/2017/02/14/need-digital-geneva-convention/#sm.00018k1n01i3tfomwyo20tis4co2l.

Swiss federal popular initiative "Entreprises responsables – pour protéger l'être humain et l'environnement", Feuille fédérale 2017 6043-6044, https://www.bk.admin.ch/ch/f/pore/vi/vis462t.html, and the counter-proposals to this Swiss federal popular initiative "Entreprises responsables – pour protéger l'être humain et l'environnement", https://www.bj.admin.ch/bj/fr/home/wirtschaft/gesetzgebung/konzernverantwortungsinitiative.html and https://www.bj.admin.ch/dam/data/bj/wirtschaft/gesetzgebung/konzernverantwortungsinitiative/gegenueberstellung-kvi-gegenvorschlag-f.pdf.

Wright, J., UK's Attorney General, Speech on "Cyber and International Law in the 21st Century", 23 May 2018, https://www.gov.uk/government/speeches/cyber-and-international-law-in-the-21st-century.

Case law

Permanent Court of International Justice and International Court of Justice

PCIJ, The case of the *S.S. Wimbledon (United Kingdom* v. *Japan)*, Judgment of 17 August 1923, *PCIJ Reports 1923*, Series A No. 1.

PCIJ, The case of the *S.S. Lotus (France* v. *Turkey)*, Judgment of 7 September 1927, *PCIJ Reports 1927*, Series A No. 10.

PCIJ, The case of the *Factory at Chorzów (Germany* v. *Poland)*, Judgment of 13 September 1928, *PCIJ Reports 1928*, Series A No. 17.

ICJ, *Reparation for Injuries Suffered in the Service of the United Nations*, Advisory Opinion of 1 April 1949, *ICJ Reports 1949*, p. 174.

ICJ, The case of the *Corfu Channel*, Judgment of 9 April 1949, *ICJ Reports 1949*, p. 4.

ICJ, *Legal Consequences for States of the Continued Presence of South Africa in Namibia (South West Africa) notwithstanding Security Council Resolution 276 (1970) du Conseil de sécurité*, Advisory Opinion of 21 June 1971, *ICJ Reports 1971*, p. 16.

ICJ, The case of the *United States Diplomatic and Consular Staff in Tehran (United States of America* v. *Iran)*, Judgment of 24 May 1980, *ICJ Reports 1980*, p. 3.

ICJ, *Interpretation of the Agreement of the 25 March 1951 between the WHO and Egypt,* Advisory Opinion of 20 December 1980, *ICJ Reports 1980*, p. 73.

ICJ, The case of *Military and Paramilitary Activities in and against Nicaragua (Nicaragua* v. *United States of America)*, Judgment of 27 June 1986, *ICJ Reports 1986*, p. 14.

ICJ, *Legality of the Threat or Use of Nuclear Weapons*, Advisory Opinion of 8 July 1996, *ICJ Reports 1996*, p. 226.

ICJ, The case of *The Gabcikovo-Nagymaros Project (Hungary* v. *Slovakia)*, Judgment of 25 September 1997, *ICJ Reports 1997*, p. 7.

ICJ, The case of *LaGrand (Germany* v. *United States of America)*, Judgment of 27 June 2001, *ICJ Reports 2001*, p. 466.

ICJ, *Legal Consequences of the Construction of a Wall in the Occupied Palestinian Territory*, Advisory Opinion of 9 July 2004, *ICJ Reports 2004*, p. 136.

ICJ, The case of *Armed Activities on the Territory of the Congo (Democratic Republic of the Congo* v. *Uganda)*, Judgment of 19 December 2005, *ICJ Reports 2005*, p. 168.

ICJ, The case of *Application of the Convention on the Prevention and Punishment of the Crime of Genocide (Bosnia and Herzegovina* v. *Serbia and Montenegro)*, Judgment of 26 February 2007, *ICJ Reports 2007*, p. 43.

ICJ, The case of *Pulp Mills on the River Uruguay (Argentina* v. *Uruguay)*, Judgment of 20 April 2010, *ICJ Reports 2010*, p. 14.

ICJ, The case of *Whaling in the Antarctic (Australia* v. *Japan: New Zealand intervening)*, Judgment of 31 March 2014, *ICJ Reports 2014*, p. 226.

ICJ, The case of *Certain Activities carried out by Nicaragua in the Border Area (Costa Rica* v. *Nicaragua)* and *Construction of a Road in Costa Rica along the San Juan River (Nicaragua* v. *Costa Rica)*, Judgment of 16 December 2015, *ICJ Reports 2015*, p. 665.

ICJ, The case of *Armed Activities on the Territory of the Congo (Democratic Republic of the Congo* v. *Uganda)*, Judgment of 9 February 2022, *ICJ Reports 2022*, not yet published.

Arbitral awards

Alabama Claims Arbitration *(United States of America* v. *United Kingdom)*, Final Award of 15 September 1872, RAI Vol. II p. 713.

Frederick Wipperman Arbitration *(United States of America* v. *Venezuela)*, Final Award of 2 September 1890, RAI Vol. III p. 3041.
British Property in Spanish Morocco Arbitration *(Spain* v. *United Kingdom)*, Final Award of 1 May 1925, RIAA Vol. II p. 615.
Island of Palmas Arbitration *(The Netherlands* v. *United States of America)*, Final Award of 4 April 1928, RIAA Vol. II p. 829.
William E. Chapman Arbitration *(United States of America* v. *United Mexican States)*, Final Award of 24 October 1930, RIAA Vol. IV p. 632.
Trail Smelter Arbitration *(United States of America* v. *Canada)*, Final Award of 11 March 1941, RIAA Vol. III p. 1938.
Lanoux Lac Arbitration *(Spain* v. *France)*, Final Award of 16 November 1957, RIAA Vol. XII, p. 281.
ICSID, *Asian Agricultural Products Ltd. (AAPL)* v. *Republic of Sri Lanka*, Case No. ARB/87/3, Final Award of 27 June 1990.
ICSID, *Pantechniki S.A.* v. *Albania*, Case No. ARB/07/21, Final Award of 30 July 2009.
PCA, *Indus Waters Kishenganga* Arbitration *(Pakistan* v. *India)*, Partial Award of 18 February 2013, PCA 2011-01.
PCA, *South China Sea* Arbitration (*Philippines* v. *China*), Final Award of 12 July 2016, PCA 2013-19, p. 296.

International Tribunal for the Law of the Sea

ITLOS, *Responsibilities and Obligations of States Sponsoring Persons and Entities with Respect to Activities in the Area*, Advisory Opinion of 1 February 2011, *ITLOS Reports 2011*, p. 10.
ITLOS, *Request for an Advisory Opinion submitted by the Sub-Regional Fisheries Commission*, Advisory Opinion of 2 April 2015, *ITLOS Reports 2015*, p. 4.

European Court of Human Rights

ECtHR, Case of *Osman* v. *The United Kingdom*, No. 23452/94, Judgment of 28 October 1998, ECLI:CE:ECHR:1998:1028JUD002345294.
ECtHR, Case of *Waite and Kennedy* v. *Germany*, No. 26083/94, Judgment of 18 February 1999, ECLI:CE:ECHR:1999:0218JUD002608394.
ECtHR, Case of *Z. and others* v. *The United Kingdom*, No. 29392/95, Judgment of 10 May 2001, ECLI:CE:ECHR:2001:0510JUD002939295.
ECtHR, Case of *E. and others* v. *The United Kingdom*, No. 33218/96, Judgment of 26 November 2002, ECLI:CE:ECHR:2002:1126JUD003321896.
ECtHR, Case of *Ilaşcu and others* v. *Moldova and Russia*, No. 48787/99, Judgment of 8 July 2004, ECLI:CE:ECHR:2004:0708JUD004878799.
ECtHR, Case of *Bosphorus Hava Yolları Turizm ve Ticaret Anonim Şirketi* v. *Ireland*, No. 45036/98, Judgment of 30 June 2005, ECLI:CE:ECHR:2005:0630JUD004503698.
ECtHR, Case of *Luginbuhl* v. *Switzerland*, No. 42756/02, Judgment of 17 January 2006, ECLI:CE:ECHR:2006:0117DEC004275602.
ECtHR, Case of *Markovic and others* v. *Italy*, No. 1398/03, Judgment of 14 December 2006, ECLI:CE:ECHR:2006:1214JUD000139803.
ECtHR, Case of *Gasparini* v. *Italy and Belgium*, No. 10750/03, Decision of 12 May 2009, ECLI:CE:ECHR:2009:0512DEC001075003.
ECtHR, Case of *Opuz* v. *Turkey*, No. 33401/02, Judgment of 9 June 2009, ECLI:CE:ECHR:2009:0609JUD003340102.
ECtHR, Case of *Al-Skeini and others* v. *The United Kingdom*, No. 55721/07, Judgment of 7 July 2011, ECLI:CE:ECHR:2011:0707JUD005572107.
ECtHR, Case of *Djokaba Lambi Longa* v. *The Netherlands*, No. 33917/12, Judgment of 9 October 2012, ECLI:CE:ECHR:2012:1009DEC003391712.
ECtHR, Case of *Catan and others* v. *The Republic of Moldova and Russia*, Nos. 43370/04, 18454/06 and 8252/05, 19 October 2012, ECLI:CE:ECHR:2012:1019JUD004337004.

ECtHR, Case of *Michaud* v. *France*, No. 12323/11, Judgment of 6 December 2012, ECLI:CE:ECHR:2012:1206JUD001232311.
ECtHR, Case of *El-Masri* v. *The Former Yugoslav Republic of Macedonia*, No. 39630/09, Judgment of 13 December 2012, ECLI:CE:ECHR:2012:1213 JUD003963009.
ECtHR, Case of *Valiuliene* v. *Lithuania*, No. 33234/07, Judgment of 26 March 2013, ECLI:CE:ECHR:2013:0326JUD003323407.
ECtHR, Case of *Al-Dulimi* v. *Switzerland*, No. 5809/08, Judgment of 26 November 2013 (Chamber of the Second Section) and of 21 June 2016 (Grand Chamber), ECLI:CE:ECHR:2013:1126JUD000580908.
ECtHR, Case of *O'Keeffe* v. *Ireland*, No. 35810/09, Judgment of 28 January 2014, ECLI:CE:ECHR:2014:0128JUD003581009.
ECtHR, Case of *Jaloud* v. *The Netherlands*, No. 47708/08, Judgment of 20 November 2014, ECLI:CE:ECHR:2014:1120JUD004770808.
ECtHR, Case of *Avotiņš* v. *Latvia*, No. 17502/07, Judgment of 23 May 2016, ECLI:CE:ECHR:2016:0523JUD001750207.
ECtHR, Case of *Talpis* v. *Italy*, No. 41237/14, Judgment of 2 March 2017, ECLI:CE:ECHR:2017:0302JUD004123714.
ECtHR, Case of *Al Nashiri* v. *Romania*, No. 33234/12, Judgment of 31 May 2018, ECLI:CE:ECHR:2018:0531JUD003323412.
ECtHR, Case of *Abu Zubaydah* v. *Lithuania*, No. 46454/11, Judgment of 31 May 2018, ECLI:CE:ECHR:2018:0531JUD004645411.
ECtHR, Case of *Güzelyurtlu and others* v. *Cyprus and Turkey*, No. 36925/07, Judgment of 29 January 2019, ECLI:CE:ECHR:2019:0129JUD003692507.
ECtHR, Case of *Romeo Castaño* v. *Belgium*, No. 8351/17, Judgment of 9 July 2019, ECLI:CE:ECHR:2019:0709JUD000835117.
ECtHR, Case of *M. N. and others* v. *Belgium*, No. 3599/18, Decision of 5 March 2020, ECLI:CE:ECHR:2020:0505DEC000359918.

Inter-American Court of Human Rights

IACtHR, Case of *Velasquez-Rodriguez* v. *Honduras*, Judgment of 29 July 1988, Series C No. 4.
IACtHR, *The Environment and Human Rights*, Advisory Opinion OC-23/17 of 15 November 2017, Series C No. 23.

Human Rights Committee

CCPR, *Basem Ahmed Issa Yassin and others* v. *Canada*, Communication No. 2285/2013, 7 December 2017, UN Doc. CCPR/C/120/D/2285/2013.

Court of Justice of the European Union

EGC, Case of *Front Polisario* v. *Council of the European Union*, T-512/12, Judgment of 10 December 2015, ECLI:EU:T:2015:953.
CJEU, Case of *Council of the European Union* v. *Front Polisario*, C104/16, Judgment of 21 December 2016, ECLI:EU:C:2016:973.
CJEU, Opinion of Advocate General M. Melchior Wathelet, in the case *Western Sahara Campaign UK, The Queen* v. *Commissioners for Her Majesty's Revenue and Customs, Secretary of State for Environment, Food and Rural Affairs*, C266/16, Conclusions of 10 January 2018, ECLI:EU:C:2018:1.
CJEU, Case of *Western Sahara Campaign UK, The Queen* v. *Commissioners for Her Majesty's Revenue and Customs, Secretary of State for Environment, Food and Rural Affairs*, C266/16, Judgment of 27 February 2018, ECLI:EU:C:2018:1.

Domestic supreme courts

Supreme Court of Canada, Case of *Nevsun Resources Ltd.* v. *Araya*, 28 February 2020, 2020 SCC 5.
Supreme Court of the United Kingdom, Case of *Vedanta Resources PLC and another* v. *Lungowe and others*, 10 April 2019, [2019] UKSC 20.

Supreme Court of the Netherlands, Case of *De Staat de Nederland (Ministerie van Infrastructuur en Milieu)* v. *Stichting Urgenda*, 19/00135, 20 December 2019, ECLI:NL:HR:2019:2006.

PUBLICATIONS DE L'ACADÉMIE
DE DROIT INTERNATIONAL
DE LA HAYE

PUBLICATIONS OF THE
HAGUE ACADEMY OF INTERNATIONAL
LAW

RECUEIL DES COURS

Depuis 1923, les plus grands noms du droit international ont professé à l'Académie de droit international de La Haye. Tous les tomes du *Recueil* qui ont été publiés depuis cette date sont disponibles, chaque tome étant, depuis les tout premiers, régulièrement réimprimé sous sa forme originale.

Depuis 2008, certains cours font l'objet d'une édition en livres de poche.

En outre, toute la collection existe en version électronique. Tous les ouvrages parus à ce jour ont été mis en ligne et peuvent être consultés moyennant un des abonnements proposés, qui offrent un éventail de tarifs et de possibilités.

INDEX

A ce jour, il a paru sept index généraux. Ils couvrent les tomes suivants:

1 à 101	(1923-1960)	379 pages	ISBN 978-90-218-9948-0
102 à 125	(1961-1968)	204 pages	ISBN 978-90-286-0643-2
126 à 151	(1969-1976)	280 pages	ISBN 978-90-286-0630-2
152 à 178	(1976-1982)	416 pages	ISBN 978-0-7923-2955-8
179 à 200	(1983-1986)	260 pages	ISBN 978-90-411-0110-5
201 à 250	(1987-1994)	448 pages	ISBN 978-90-04-13700-4
251 à 300	(1995-2002)	580 pages	ISBN 978-90-04-15387-7

A partir du tome 210 il a été décidé de publier un index complet qui couvrira chaque fois dix tomes du *Recueil des cours*. Le dernier index paru couvre les tomes suivants:

311 à 320 (2004-2006) 392 pages Tome 320A ISBN 978-90-04-19695-7

COLLOQUES

L'Académie organise également des colloques dont les débats sont publiés. Les derniers volumes parus de ces colloques portent les titres suivants: *Le règlement pacifique des différends internationaux en Europe: perspectives d'avenir* (1990); *Le développement du rôle du Conseil de sécurité* (1992); *La Convention sur l'interdiction et l'élimination des armes chimiques: une percée dans l'entreprise multilatérale du désarmement* (1994); *Actualité de la Conférence de La Haye de 1907, Deuxième Conférence de la Paix* (2007).

CENTRE D'ÉTUDE ET DE RECHERCHE

Les travaux scientifiques du Centre d'étude et de recherche de droit international et de relations internationales de l'Académie de droit international de La Haye, dont les sujets sont choisis par le Curatorium de l'Académie, faisaient l'objet, depuis la session de 1985, d'une publication dans laquelle les directeurs d'études dressaient le bilan des recherches du Centre qu'ils avaient dirigé. Cette série a été arrêtée et la dernière brochure parue porte le titre suivant: *Les règles et les institutions du droit international humanitaire à l'épreuve des conflits armés récents*. Néanmoins, lorsque les travaux du Centre se révèlent particulièrement intéressants et originaux, les rapports des directeurs et les articles rédigés par les chercheurs font l'objet d'un ouvrage collectif.

COLLECTED COURSES

Since 1923 the top names in international law have taught at The Hague Academy of International Law. All the volumes of the *Collected Courses* which have been published since 1923 are available, as, since the very first volume, they are reprinted regularly in their original format.

Since 2008, certain courses have been the subject of a pocketbook edition.

In addition, the total collection now exists in electronic form. All works already published have been put "on line" and can be consulted under one of the proposed subscription methods, which offer a range of tariffs and possibilities.

INDEXES

Up till now seven General Indexes have been published. They cover the following volumes:

1 to 101	(1923-1960)	379 pages	ISBN 978-90-218-9948-0
102 to 125	(1961-1968)	204 pages	ISBN 978-90-286-0643-2
126 to 151	(1969-1976)	280 pages	ISBN 978-90-286-0630-2
152 to 178	(1976-1982)	416 pages	ISBN 978-0-7923-2955-8
179 to 200	(1983-1986)	260 pages	ISBN 978-90-411-0110-5
201 to 250	(1987-1994)	448 pages	ISBN 978-90-04-13700-4
251 to 300	(1995-2002)	580 pages	ISBN 978-90-04-15387-7

From Volume 210 onwards it has been decided to publish a full index covering, each time, ten volumes of the *Collected Courses*. The latest Index published covers the following volumes:

311 to 320 (2004-2006) 392 pages Volume 320A ISBN 978-90-04-19695-7

WORKSHOPS

The Academy publishes the discussions from the Workshops which it organises. The latest titles of the Workshops already published are as follows: *The Peaceful Settlement of International Disputes in Europe: Future Prospects* (1990) ; *The Development of the Role of the Security Council* (1992); *The Convention on the Prohibition and Elimination of Chemical Weapons: A Breakthrough in Multilateral Disarmament* (1994); *Topicality of the 1907 Hague Conference, the Second Peace Conference* (2007).

CENTRE FOR STUDIES AND RESEARCH

The scientific works of the Centre for Studies and Research in International Law and International Relations of The Hague Academy of International Law, the subjects of which are chosen by the Curatorium of the Academy, have been published, since the Centre's 1985 session, in a publication in which the Directors of Studies reported on the state of research of the Centre under their direction. This series has been discontinued and the title of the latest booklet published is as follows: *Rules and Institutions of International Humanitarian Law Put to the Test of Recent Armed Conflicts.* Nevertheless, when the work of the Centre has been of particular interest and originality, the reports of the Directors of Studies together with the articles by the researchers form the subject of a collection published by the Academy.

Requests for information, catalogues and orders for publications must be addressed to

MARTINUS NIJHOFF PUBLISHERS

P.O. Box 9000, 2300 PA Leiden The Netherlands **http://www.brill.nl**

TABLE PAR TOME DES COURS PUBLIÉS CES DERNIÈRES ANNÉES

INDEX BY VOLUME OF THE COURSES PUBLISHED THESE LAST YEARS

Tome/Volume 356 (2011)

Talpis, J.: Succession Substitutes, 9-238.

Lagrange, E.: L'efficacité des normes internationales concernant la situation des personnes privées dans les ordres juridiques internes, 239-552.

(ISBN 978-90-04-22730-9)

Tome/Volume 357 (2011)

Dugard, J.: The Secession of States and Their Recognition in the Wake of Kosovo, 9-222.

Gannagé, L.: Les méthodes du droit international privé à l'épreuve des conflits de cultures, 223-490.

(ISBN 978-90-04-22731-6)

Tome/Volume 358 (2011)

Brand, R. A.: Transaction Planning Using Rules on Jurisdiction and the Recognition and Enforcement of Judgments, 9-262.

Hafner, G.: The Emancipation of the Individual from the State under International Law, 263-454.

(ISBN 978-90-04-22732-3)

Tome/Volume 359 (2012)

Opertti Badán, D.: Conflit de lois et droit uniforme dans le droit international privé contemporain: dilemme ou convergence? (conférence inaugurale), 9-86.

Chen Weizuo: La nouvelle codification du droit international privé chinois, 87-234.

Kohler, Ch.: L'autonomie de la volonté en droit international privé: un principe universel entre libéralisme et étatisme, 285-478.

(ISBN 978-90-04-25541-8)

Tome/Volume 360 (2012)

Basedow, J.: The Law of Open Societies — Private Ordering and Public Regulation of International Relations. General Course on Private International Law, 9-516.

(ISBN 978-90-04-25550-0)

Tome/Volume 361 (2012)

Pinto, M. C. W.: The Common Heritage of Mankind: Then and Now, 9-130.

Kreindler, R.: Competence-Competence in the Face of Illegality in Contracts and Arbitration Agreements, 131-482.

(ISBN 978-90-04-25552-4)

Tome/Volume 362 (2012)

Arsanjani, M. H.: The United Nations and International Law-Making (Opening Lecture), 9-40.

Alland, D.: L'interprétation du droit international public, 41-394.

(ISBN 978-90-04-25554-8)

Tome/Volume 363 (2012)

Sur, S.: La créativité du droit international. Cours général de droit international public, 9-332.

Turp, D.: La contribution du droit international au maintien de la diversité culturelle, 333-454.

(ISBN 978-90-04-25556-2)

Tome/Volume 364 (2012)

Gaja, G.: The Protection of General Interests in the International Community. General Course on Public International Law (2011), 9-186.
Glenn, H. P.: La conciliation des lois. Cours général de droit international privé (2011), 187-470. (ISBN 978-90-04-25557-9)

Tome/Volume 365 (2013)

Crawford, J.: Chance, Order, Change: The Course of International Law. General Course on Public International Law, 9-390. (ISBN 978-90-04-25560-9)

Tome/Volume 366 (2013)

Hayton, D.: "Trusts" in Private International Law, 9-98.
Hobér, K.: Res Judicata and Lis Pendens in International Arbitration, 99-406.
(ISBN 978-90-04-26395-6)

Tome/Volume 367 (2013)

Kolb, R.: L'article 103 de la Charte des Nations Unies, 9-252.
Nascimbene, B.: Le droit de la nationalité et le droit des organisations d'intégration régionales. Vers de nouveaux statuts de résidents?, 253-454.
(ISBN 978-90-04-26793-0)

Tome/Volume 368 (2013)

Caflisch, L: Frontières nationales, limites et délimitations. — Quelle importance aujourd'hui? (conférence inaugurale), 9-46.
Benvenisti, E.: The International Law of Global Governance, 47-280.
Park, K. G.: La protection des personnes en cas de catastrophes, 281-456.
(ISBN 978-90-04-26795-4)

Tome/Volume 369 (2013)

Kronke, H.: Transnational Commercial Law and Conflict of Laws: Institutional Co-operation and Substantive Complementarity (Opening Lecture), 9-42.
Ortiz Ahlf, L.: The Human Rights of Undocumented Migrants, 43-160.
Kono, T.: Efficiency in Private International Law, 161-360.
Yusuf, A. A.: Pan-Africanism and International Law, 361-512.
(ISBN 978-90-04-26797-8)

Tome/Volume 370 (2013)

Dominicé, Ch.: La société internationale à la recherche de son équilibre. Cours général de droit international public, 9-392. (ISBN 978-90-04-26799-2)

Tome/Volume 371 (2014)

Lagarde, P.: La méthode de la reconnaissance est-elle l'avenir du droit international privé?, 9-42.
Charlesworth, H.: Democracy and International Law, 43-152.
de Vareilles-Sommières, P.: L'exception d'ordre public et la régularité substantielle internationale de la loi étrangère, 153-272.
Yanagihara, M.: Significance of the History of the Law of Nations in Europe and East Asia, 273-435. (ISBN 978-90-04-28936-9)

Tome/Volume 372 (2014)

Bucher, A.: La compétence universelle civile, 9-128.
Cordero-Moss, G.: Limitations on Party Autonomy in International Commercial Arbitration, 129-326.
Sinjela, M.: Intellectual Property: Cross-Border Recognition of Rights and National Development, 327-394.
Dolzer, R.: International Co-operation in Energy Affairs, 395-504.
(ISBN 978-90-04-28937-6)

Tome/Volume 373 (2014)

Cachard, O.: Le transport international aérien de passagers, 9-216.
Audit, M.: Bioéthique et droit international privé, 217-447.
(ISBN 978-90-04-28938-3)

Tome/Volume 374 (2014)

Struycken, A. V. M.: Arbitration and State Contract, 9-52.
Corten, O., La rébellion et le droit international: le principe de neutralité en tension, 53-312.
Parra, A.: The Convention and Centre for Settlement of Investment Disputes, 313-410. (ISBN 978-90-04-29764-7)

Tome/Volume 375 (2014)

Jayme, E.: Narrative Norms in Private International Law – The Example of Art Law, 9-52.
De Boer, Th. M.: Choice of Law in Arbitration Proceedings, 53-88.
Frigo, M.: Circulation des biens culturels, détermination de la loi applicable et méthodes de règlement des litiges, 89-474.
(ISBN 978-90-04-29766-1)

Tome/Volume 376 (2014)

Cançado Trindade, A. A.: The Contribution of Latin American Legal Doctrine to the Progressive Development of International Law, 9-92.
Gray, C.: The Limits of Force, 93-198.
Najurieta, M. S.: L'adoption internationale des mineurs et les droits de l'enfant, 199-494. (ISBN 978-90-04-29768-5)

Tome/Volume 377 (2015)

Kassir, W. J.: Le renvoi en droit international privé – technique de dialogue entre les cultures juridiques, 9-120.
Noodt Taquela, M. B.: Applying the Most Favourable Treaty or Domestic Rules to Facilitate Private International Law Co-operation, 121-318.
Tuzmukhamedov, B.: Legal Dimensions of Arms Control Agreements, An Introductory Overview, 319-468.
(ISBN 978-90-04-29770-8)

Tome/Volume 378 (2015)

Iwasawa, Y.: Domestic Application of International Law, 9-262.
Carrascosa Gonzalez, J.: The Internet – Privacy and Rights relating to Personality, 263-486. (ISBN 978-90-04-32125-0)

Tome/Volume 379 (2015)

Lowe, V.: The Limits of the Law.
Boele-Woelki, K.: Party Autonomy in Litigation and Arbitration in View of The Hague Principles on Choice of Law in International Commercial Contracts.
Fresnedo de Aguirre, C.: Public Policy: Common Principles in the American States.
Ben Achour, R.: Changements anticonstitutionnels de gouvernement et droit international.
(ISBN 978-90-04-32127-4)

Tome/Volume 380 (2015)

Van Loon, J. H. A.: The Global Horizon of Private International Law.
Pougoué, P.-G.: L'arbitrage dans l'espace OHADA.
Kruger, T.: The Quest for Legal Certainty in International Civil Cases.
(ISBN 978-90-04-32131-1)

Tome/Volume 381 (2015)

Jayme, E.: Les langues et le droit international privé, 11-39.
Bermann, G.: Arbitrage and Private International Law. General Course on Private International Law (2015), 41-484.
(ISBN 978-90-04-33828-9)

Tome/Volume 382 (2015)

Cooper, D., and C. Kuner: Data Protection Law and International Dispute Resolution, 9-174.
Jia, B. B.: International Case Law in the Development of International Law, 175-397.
(ISBN 978-90-04-33830-2)

Tome/Volume 383 (2016)

Bennouna, M.: Le droit international entre la lettre et l'esprit, 9-231.
Iovane, M.: L'influence de la multiplication des juridictions internationales sur l'application du droit international, 233-446. (ISBN 978-90-04-34648-2)

Tome/Volume 384 (2016)

Symeonides, S. C.: Private International Law Idealism, Pragmatism, Eclecticism, 9-385.
(ISBN 978-90-04-35131-8)

Tome/Volume 385 (2016)

Berman, Sir F.: Why Do we Need a Law of Treaties?, 9-31.
Marrella, F.: Protection internationale des droits de l'homme et activités des sociétés transnationales, 33-435.(ISBN 978-90-04-35132-5)

Tome/Volume 386 (2016)

Murphy, S. D.: International Law relating to Islands, 9-266.
Cataldi, G.: La mise en œuvre des décisions des tribunaux internationaux dans l'ordre interne, 267-428.
(ISBN 978-90-04-35133-2)

Tome/Volume 387 (2016)

Lequette, Y. : Les mutations du droit international privé : vers un changement de paradigme ?, 9-644. (ISBN 978-90-04-36118-8)

Tome/Volume 388 (2016)

Bonell, M. J. : The Law Governing International Commercial Contracts : Hard Law versus Soft Law, 9-48.

Hess, B. : The Private-Public Divide in International Dispute Resolution, 49-266. (ISBN 978-90-04-36120-1)

Tome/Volume 389 (2017)

Muir Watt, H. : Discours sur les méthodes du droit international privé (des formes juridiques de l'inter-altérité). Cours général de droit international privé, 9-410.

(ISBN 978-90-04-36122-5)

Tome/Volume 390 (2017)

Rau, A. S. : The Allocation of Power between Arbitral Tribunals and State Courts, 9-396. (ISBN 978-90-04-36475-2)

Tome/Volume 391 (2017)

Cançado Trindade, A. A. : Les tribunaux internationaux et leur mission commune de réalisation de la justice : développements, état actuel et perspectives, Conférence spéciale (2017), 9-101.

Mariño Menéndez, F. M. : The Prohibition of Torture in Public International Law, 103-185.

Swinarski, C. : Effets pour l'individu des régimes de protection de droit international, 187-369.

Cot, J.-P. : L'éthique du procès international (leçon inaugurale), 371-384. (ISBN 978-90-04-37781-3)

Tome/Volume 392 (2017)

Novak, F. : The System of Reparations in the Jurisprudence of the Inter-American Court of Human Rights, 9-203.

Nolte, G. : Treaties and their Practice – Symptoms of their Rise or Decline, 205-397. (ISBN 978-90-04-39273-1)

Tome/Volume 393 (2017)

Tiburcio, C. : The Current Practice of International Co-Operation in Civil Matters, 9-310.

Ruiz De Santiago, J. : Aspects juridiques des mouvements forcés de personnes, 311-468. (ISBN 978-90-04-39274-8)

Tome/Volume 394 (2017)

Kostin, A. A. : International Commercial Arbitration, with Special Focus on Russia, 9-86.

Cuniberti, G. : Le fondement de l'effet des jugements étrangers, 87-283. (ISBN 978-90-04-39275-5)

Tome/Volume 395 (2018)

Salerno, F.: The Identity and Continuity of Personal Status in Contemporary Private International Law, 9-198.
Chinkin, C. M.: United Nations Accountability for Violations of International Human Rights Law, 199-320. (ISBN 978-90-04-40710-7)

Tome/Volume 396 (2018)

Jacquet, J.-M.: Droit international privé et arbitrage commercial international, 9-36.
Brown Weiss, E.: Establishing Norms in a Kaleidoscopic World. General Course on Public International Law, 37-415. (ISBN 978-90-04-41002-2)

Tome/Volume 397 (2018)

D'Avout, L.: L'entreprise et les conflits internationaux de lois, 9-612.
(ISBN 978-90-04-41221-7)

Tome/Volume 398 (2018)

Treves, T.: The Expansion of International Law, General Course on Public International Law (2015), 9-398. (ISBN 978-90-04-41224-8)

Tome/Volume 399 (2018)

Kanehara, A.: Reassessment of the Acts of the State in the Law of State Responsibility, 9-266.
Buxbaum, H. L.: Public Regulation and Private Enforcement in a Global Economy: Strategies for Managing Conflict, 267-442. (ISBN 978-90-04-41670-3)

Tome/Volume 400 (2018)

Chedly, L.: L'efficacité de l'arbitrage commercial international, 9-624.
(ISBN 978-90-04-42388-6)

Tome/Volume 401 (2019)

Wood, P.: Extraterritorial Enforcement of Regulatory Laws, 9-126.
Nishitani, Yuko: Identité culturelle en droit international privé de la famille, 127-450. (ISBN 978-90-04-42389-3)

Tome/Volume 402 (2019)

Kinsch, P.: Le rôle du politique en droit international privé. Cours général de droit international privé, 9-384.
Dasser, F.: "Soft Law" in International Commercial Arbitration, 385-596.
(ISBN 978-90-04-42392-3)

Tome/Volume 403 (2019)

Daudet, Y.: 1919-2019, le flux du multilatéralisme, 9-48.
Kessedjian, C.: Le tiers impartial et indépendant en droit international, juge, arbitre, médiateur, conciliateur, 49-643.
(ISBN 978-90-04-42468-5)

Tome/Volume 404 (2019)

Rajamani, L.: Innovation and Experimentation in the International Climate Change Regime, 9-234.
Sorel, J.-M.: Quelle normativité pour le droit des relations monétaires et financières internationales ?, 235-403. (ISBN 978-90-04-43142-3)

Tome/Volume 405 (2019)

Paulsson, J.: Issues arising from Findings of Denial of Justice, 9-74.
Brunée, J.: Procedure and Substance in International Environmental Law, 75-240. (ISBN 978-90-04-43300-7)

Tome/Volume 406 (2019)

Bundy, R.: The Practice of International Law, Inaugural Lecture, 9-26.
Gama, L.: Les principes d'UNIDROIT et la loi régissant les contrats de commerce, 27-343. (ISBN 978-90-04-43611-4)

Tome/Volume 407 (2020)

Wouters, J.: Le statut juridique des standards publics et privés dans les relations économiques internationales, 9-122.
Maljean-Dubois, S.: Le droit international de la biodiversité, 123-538.
(ISBN 978-90-04-43643-5)

Tome/Volume 408 (2020)

Cançado Trindade, A. A.: Reflections on the Realization of Justice in the Era of Contemporary International Tribunals, 9-88.
González, C.: Party Autonomy in International Family Law, 89-361.
(ISBN 978-90-04-44504-8)

Tome/Volume 409 (2020)

Shany, Y: The Extraterritorial Application of International Human Rights Law, 9-152.
Besson, S.: La *due diligence* en droit international, 153-398.
(ISBN 978-90-04-44505-5)

Tome/Volume 410 (2020)

Koh, H. H.: American Schools of International Law, 9-93.
Peters, A.: Animals in International Law, 95-544. (ISBN 978-90-04-44897-1)

Tome/Volume 411 (2020)

Cahin, G: Reconstrution et construction de l'Etat en droit international, 9-573.
(ISBN 978-90-04-44898-8)

Tome/Volume 412 (2020)

Momtaz, D: La hiérarchisation de l'ordre juridique international, cours général de droit international public, 9-252.
Grammaticaki-Alexiou, A.: Best Interests of the Child in Private International Law, 253-434. (ISBN 978-90-04-44899-5)

Tome/Volume 413 (2021)

Ferrari, F.: Forum Shopping Despite Unification of Law, 9-290.
(ISBN 978-90-04-46100-0)

Tome/Volume 414 (2021)

Pellet, A.: Le droit international à la lumière de la pratique: l'introuvable théorie de la réalité. Cours général de droit international public, 9-547.
(ISBN 978-90-04-46547-3)

Tome/Volume 415 (2021)

Trooboff, P. D.: Globalization, Personal Jurisdiction and the Internet. Responding to the Challenge of adapting settled Principles and Precedents. General Course of Private International Law, 9-321. (ISBN 978-90-04-46730-9)

Tome/Volume 416 (2021)

Wolfrum, R: Solidarity and Community Interests: Driving Forces for the Interpretation and Development of International Law. General Course on Public International Law, 9-479. (ISBN 978-90-04-46827-6)

Tome/Volume 417 (2021)

d'Argent, P.: Les obligations internationales, 9-210.
Schabas, W. A.: Relationships Between International Criminal Law and Other Branches of International Law, 211-392. (ISBN 978-90-04-47239-6)

Tome/Volume 418 (2021)

Bollée, S.: Les pouvoirs inhérents des arbitres internationaux, 9-224.
Tladi, D.: The Extraterritorial Use of Force against Non-State Actors, 225-360.
(ISBN 978-90-04-50380-9)

Tome/Volume 419 (2021)

Kolb, R.: Le droit international comme corps de «droit privé» et de «droit public». Cours général de droit international public, 9-668.
(ISBN 978-90-04-50381-6)

Tome/Volume 420 (2021)

Perrakis, S.: La protection internationale au profit des personnes vulnérables en droit international des droits de l'homme, 9-497.
(ISBN 978-90-04-50382-3)

Tome/Volume 421 (2021)

Estrella Faria, J. A.: La protection des biens culturels d'intérêt religieux en droit international public et en droit international privé, 9-333.
(ISBN 978-90-04-50829-3)

Tome/Volume 422 (2021)

Karayanni, M.: The Private International Law of Class Actions: A Functional approach, 9-248.
Mahmoudi, S.: Self-Defence and "Unwilling or Unable" States, 249-399.
(ISBN 978-90-04-50830-9)

Tome/Volume 423 (2022)

Kinnear, M.: The Growth, Challenges and Future Prospects for Investment Dispute Settlement, 9-36.

Weller, M.: "Mutual Trust": A Suitable Foundation for Private International Law in Regional Integration Communities and Beyond?, 37-378.

(ISBN 978-90-04-51411-9)

Tome/Volume 424 (2022)

Asada, M.: International Law of Nuclear Non-proliferation and Disarmament, 9-726.

(ISBN 978-90-04-51769-1)

Tome/Volume 425 (2022)

Metou, B. M.: Le contrôle international des dérogations aux droits de l'homme, 9-294.

Silva Romero, E.: Legal Fictions in the Language of International Arbitration, 295-423.

(ISBN 978-90-04-51770-7)

Tome/Volume 426 (2022)

Kuijper, P. J.: Delegation and International Organizations, 9-240.

McCaffrey, S. C.: The Evolution of the Law of International Watercourses, 241-384.

(ISBN 978-90-04-51771-4)

Tome/Volume 427 (2022)

Kaufmann-Kohler, G.: Indépendance et impartialité du juge et de l'arbitre dans le règlement des différends entre investisseurs et Etats (leçon inaugurale), 9-50.

Boyle, A.: International Lawmaking in an Environmental Context, 51-108.

Weller, M.-P.: La méthode tripartite du droit international privé: désignation, reconnaissance, considération, 109-210.

Mourre, A.: La légitimité de l'arbitrage, 211-288.

(ISBN 978-90-04-52770-6)

Printed in November 2022
by Triangle Bleu,
59600 Maubeuge (France)

Setting : R. Mirland,
59870 Warlaing (France)